American Rivals
of James Bond

American Rivals of James Bond

GRAHAM ANDREWS

McFarland & Company, Inc., Publishers

Jefferson, North Carolina

Library of Congress Cataloguing-in-Publication Data

Names: Andrews, Graham, author.
Title: American rivals of James Bond / Graham Andrews.
Description: Jefferson, North Carolina : McFarland & Company, Inc., Publishers, 2023 |
Includes bibliographical references and index.
Identifiers: LCCN 2022057917 | ISBN 9781476673684 (paperback : acid free paper) ∞
ISBN 9781476647630 (ebook)
Subjects: LCSH: Spy stories, American—History and criticism. | Espionage in literature. | Spy films—
United States—History and criticism. | Espionage in motion pictures. | Spy television programs—
United States—History and criticism. | James Bond films—Influence.
Classification: LCC PS374.S764 A63 2023 | DDC 813/.087209—dc23/eng/20221206
LC record available at https://lccn.loc.gov/2022057917

British Library cataloguing data are available

ISBN (print) 978-1-4766-7368-4
ISBN (ebook) 978-1-4766-4763-0

Front cover: Robert Vaughn as the American spy Napoleon Solo from
the 1960s TV series *The Man from U.N.C.L.E.* (NBC/Photofest)

Printed in the United States of America

*McFarland & Company, Inc., Publishers
Box 611, Jefferson, North Carolina 28640
www.mcfarlandpub.com*

Contents

Preface

Be it known that I was born in Belfast, Northern Ireland, and raised there from 1948 through the early 1960s, an uneasy time, before the full-scale Troubles erupted later that decade. But I won't add to the exponential pile of misery memoirs. In happier fact, it was the well-stocked public libraries in the Belfast of those days that fired my love for books. *Every* kind of book, both fiction and nonfiction. I was, however, irresistibly drawn to popular genres like westerns, science fiction, historical novels, and—of particular interest here—spy fiction.

Because of the protected British empire and Commonwealth market, only the most Anglocentric pulp fiction was readily available in the United Kingdom. Extreme example: *Superman* comic books came to the UK via Australian versions, in which Metropolis was cunningly changed to Sydney and dollars were turned into pounds. There was what could be called "booklegging" between the Irish Republic and Northern Ireland, but the spotty supply always fell far short of the demand. British hardcover and paperback editions of American spy novels were few and far between, and most reputable paperback companies—notably the paternalistic Penguin Books—pulled their cover-art punches. Pan helped to break that mold, publishing "poplit" titles with full-color pictorial covers that some puritanical people thought to be dangerously modern and in questionable taste. They would bring James Bond to a wider reading public (see the Introduction, "Enter Ian Fleming"). Also, the Frederick Muller editions of Gold Medal (q.v.) books used the original racy American cover artwork; only a price change, from 35¢ to 2/6d, marked the transatlantic difference. All that changed for the better circa 1960, when those import restrictions were either relaxed or removed altogether.

Round about the same time, I read the *Classics Illustrated* rendition of *The Spy*, by James Fenimore Cooper (see Chapter One, "The Brave and the Bold"). That eventually led to my writing a two-part article titled "The American Rivals of James Bond," for the British magazine *Book and Magazine Collector* (June and July 2008)—and thence to the present book-length study.

The more immediate upshot was my introduction to the seminal place of American writers in the early development of what became contemporary spy fiction. I also realized that spy fiction does not exist in separate boxes on either side of the Atlantic Ocean and never the twain shall meet. It takes the form of a synergic reaction, i.e., an "acting together of processes or influences" (*A Dictionary of Psychology*: Penguin Books), whose ebb and flow has matched the geopolitical fortunes of each country. American isolationism—both geographical and political—meant that the spy fiction written there tended to be partially eclipsed by the British imperial and cultural reach. An oversimplification, granted, considering the formation of what Gore Vidal (1925–2012) has called the informal "American Empire": *vide* "The Paradoxical Patriot," my article for *Book and Magazine Collector* (January 2010). British writers claimed a substantial share of the U.S. spy-fiction market from (roughly) 1910 until 1935, and their influence must be considered in some little detail. After that, however, the main analytical focus will be upon American practitioners of the genre.

Ian Fleming and James Bond played a comparatively small part in the 1950s "revival" of American-published spy fiction. They had been cast adrift in the storm of "paperback original" novels that was then sweeping across the country. But things soon looked up, following a timely presidential endorsement and the spate of successful feature films based upon the most famous fictional secret agent in the world. Everybody wanted to get in on the act, and everybody who could manage it did, with "rival" Bonds breaking out all over the media marketplace. Less than fifteen years after Fleming's death, however, his literary influence was on the wane, with even the films beginning to falter at the box office. By the mid–1980s, a new generation of particularly American spy-fiction writers had sprung up who either reacted against the Fleming "school" or ignored it altogether. Credit will be given where credit is due, including for the new generation that is coming along now, although a full study would require a book half as long again.

I have, for the most part, concentrated upon individual spy heroes and heroines. They are—after all the hurly-burly's done—what fires the imagination of the reading and video public, not the "alphabet soup" official agencies that employ them.

Introduction: Enter Ian Fleming

"My name is Bond... James Bond."

As all the cine-literate world should know, those were the first words spoken by Sean Connery[1] playing 007 in the 1962 film version of Ian Fleming's 1958 novel *Dr. No*. James Bond soon became the best-known fictional adventurer of the late twentieth century. His fame has persisted to the present day—in celluloid or digital form, if not primarily on the printed page. The character has inspired a host of imitators, not always flattering, and his American rivals are especially legion.

Bond's actual debut, in *Casino Royale*,[2] was, however, more long-drawn-out and less pithily memorable. Extract from page 1, chapter 1, "The Secret Agent":

> James Bond suddenly knew that he was tired. He always knew when his body or his mind had had enough and he always acted on the knowledge. This helped him to avoid staleness and the sensual bluntness that breeds mistakes.
>
> He shifted himself unobtrusively away from the roulette he had been playing and went to stand for a moment at the brass rail which surrounded breast-high the top table in the *sale privée*.

Casino Royale was first published on April 23, 1953, with a print run of 4,728 copies (many of which went to public libraries). It sold out almost immediately, as did a similar print run that very same month. A third sellout print run, of more than 8,000 copies, came in May 1954. Jonathan Cape duly offered Fleming a three-book deal. In April 1955, Pan issued their two-shilling/25 cents paperback edition (#334) on April 18, 1955, which sold 41,000 copies within the year. The back cover featured both an uncommonly detailed plot summary and a potted biography of Ian Fleming: "The setting is a French resort somewhere near Le Touquet, where the British agent is engaged in a battle of wits with the senior Communist agent who uses the name of Le Chiffre and works for a Russian organization known as 'Smersh.' Ian Fleming [now Foreign Manager of the *Sunday Times*] entered journalism ... and served throughout the [Second World War] as Personal Assistant to the Director of Naval Intelligence. Since the war he has built a small house in Jamaica."

A more detailed life history: Ian Lancaster Fleming was born in London on May 28, 1908. He was educated at Durnford School (in county Dorset), Eton College, and the Royal Military Academy, Sandhurst. He also studied languages at the universities of Munich and Geneva. After narrowly failing an examination for the

Diplomatic Service, he joined Reuters News Agency as a foreign correspondent. He was in Moscow in 1933 to cover the trial of six British engineers of the Metropolitan Vickers Armaments Company, who had been charged with spying by the OGPU (*Obediennoe Gossudarstvennoe Politicheskoe Upravleniye*), the Soviet secret police organization. From 1935 until 1939, he was gainfully employed as a merchant banker and stockbroker in the City of London.

During World War II, Fleming served as a lieutenant and then commander in the Royal Naval Volunteer Reserve, mainly as a personal assistant to Admiral John Henry Godfrey (1888–1970), the Director of Naval Intelligence. He organized the No. 30 Assault Unit. Nicknamed "Fleming's Private Navy," it enjoyed great success in reconnaissance and information gathering.[3] Fleming befriended William Joseph "Wild Bill" Donovan (1883–1959), an officer in the American OSS (Office of Strategic Services) who is regarded as the founding father of the CIA (Central Intelligence Agency). After demobilization in late 1945, he became the Foreign Manager of Kemsley (later Thomson) Newspapers and held that post until 1959.

Although Fleming had often toyed with the idea of becoming a fiction writer, it was not until just before his marriage to Anne Geraldine Mary Charteris (1913–1981) in 1952 that he began serious work on a novel. He had already written a concise guide for the foreign correspondents on his staff, which is now a rare collector's item. *Casino Royale*, like most future Bond books, was written at Goldeneye, Fleming's house in Jamaica, which he had owned since 1946. It was named after Operation Goldeneye, one of his wartime plans to counter a possible alliance between Fascist Spain and the Axis powers by mounting sabotage missions from British-held Gibraltar. He would work there during January and February of every year, up until his death on August 12, 1964, at the age of 56.

By a happy accident, Fleming named his "trademark" character after the American ornithologist James Bond (January 4, 1900, to February 14, 1989), who had written *Birds of the West Indies: An Account of All the Birds Known to Have Occurred in the West Indian Islands* (1936). As Fleming wrote in a letter to Mrs. Bond: "It struck me that this brief, unromantic, Anglo-Saxon and yet very masculine name was just what I needed, and so a second James Bond was born."

Fleming took his time about developing 007 into more than just a human cipher. As he told Jack Fishman: "At first, I didn't even give Bond a complete personality. In my earlier books, you will find few of his later mannerisms, no real in-depth characterization of him. I didn't even provide him with a detailed personal appearance. I kept him virtually blank.... The paradox is that I made him rather anonymous, quite deliberately, and that, I am sure, enabled people to identify themselves with him."[4]

The backstory goes that James Bond was born on November 11, 1924, to a Scottish father, Andrew, who worked for the Vickers Armament Company, and a Swiss mother, Monique Delacroix. Andrew's job involved a lot of European travel, so James learned to speak fluent French and German. Both his parents were killed in a climbing accident in 1935, and he was raised by a spinster aunt called Charmian Bond. After being "asked" to leave Eton over some unspecified dalliance with a maid in his second year, James transferred to Fettes College, Edinburgh. He left school at 17, then lied about his age to take up a position with the Special Branch of the Royal Naval Volunteer Reserve. After World War II, Commander Bond was invited to join the British Secret Service. Two assassinations later, he was awarded the seventh Double-0 number (out of nine), which gave him a legal license to kill in the line of duty.

Ian Fleming himself designed the dust jacket art for the first edition of *Casino Royale*. It featured nine red bleeding hearts on a gunmetal-gray background, with the enigmatic words "a whisper of love, a whisper of hate" inscribed around the central heart. Kenneth Lewis, the in-house artist for the Kemsley Newspapers Group, did the work itself, a memorable example of minimalist illustration. But James Bond was conspicuous by his absence.

It was the British artist Roger Hall (1914–2014), who produced the first book-cover representation of James Bond, for the 1955 Pan paperback edition. His image of a smooth card-playing 007 was, according to the official Ian Fleming website (www.ianfleming.com), based upon the American actor Richard Conte (1910–1975). There is a strong facial resemblance, though Hall's Bond is blond haired and Conte was darkly Italian.

Fleming's first detailed physical description of Bond was in *From Russia with Love* (1957), by courtesy of a personnel file held by SMERSH (a contraction of "Smiert Spionen"—Russian for "death to spies"). SMERSH was then the most secret department of the Soviet government and Bond's most dangerous and implacable foe. The file is read out by General G (short for Grubozaboyschikov), who actually did head the organization at that time: "Height: 183 centimetres [six feet], weight: 76 kilograms [167 pounds]; slim build; eyes: blue; hair: black; scar down right cheek and on left shoulder; signs of plastic surgery on back of right hand...; all-round athlete; expert pistol shot, boxer, knife-thrower; does not use disguises ... invariably armed with a .25 Beretta automatic carried in a shoulder holster under his arm. In general, fights with tenacity and has a high tolerance of pain...."[5]

The above-mentioned biographical and lifestyle details reveal that James Bond was an idealized self-portrait of Ian Fleming, writing himself to be an impossibly valiant hero in both hot war and lukewarm peace. He also stirred his elder brother, Peter Fleming,[6] the distinguished traveler and author, into the creative mix. Peter's war record included service with the Grenadier Guards, helping Ian establish the Auxiliary Units, and heading D Division, which—based in India—organized military deception operations in Southeast Asia. Ian also hero-worshipped his father, Valentine Fleming (1882–1917), who was killed in action during the First World War and posthumously awarded the DSO (Distinguished Service Order).

Although Pan became Fleming's regular paperback publisher, with seven editions of *Casino Royale* alone over the next ten years, he was consistently outsold by other authors on their "thriller" list. For example, Agatha Christie, Erle Stanley Gardner, Leslie Charteris, and even that old warhorse Edgar Wallace. And the hardcovers remained midlist material. Fleming is little more than mentioned in *Bestsellers: Popular Fiction Since 1900*.[7] The same goes for *American Best Sellers*.[8]

The American hardcover from Macmillan had sold well enough to attract a paperback edition from Popular Library (#660), dated April 1955. There were also several positive reviews, one of which was quoted on the back cover: "A superlative thriller! Replete with elegant, enigmatic women ... explosions, torture, and a sudden death!" (*Boston Globe*). Popular Library was founded by Noah Lewis "Ned" Pines (1905–1990) in 1942. Pines had been a successful pulp-magazine publisher, especially with the Thrilling Group (*Thrilling Wonder Stories, Detective Stories, Western Stories*, and so forth). The first 100 titles on the Popular Library list were routine mysteries, thrillers, romances, and westerns. Recommended background reading: *UnderCover [sic]: An Illustrated History of the American Mass Market Paperbacks*.[9]

Popular Library changed the title to *You Asked for It* (with *Casino Royale* small-printed in brackets), perhaps fearing that American readers might find an unfamiliar foreign word like "royale" hard to pronounce. Fleming's own alternative titles, *The Double-O Agent* and *The Deadly Gamble*, were not considered suitable. The cover illustration, by Ray Johnson, owed a lot more to Mickey Spillane and Mike Hammer than it did to Fleming and Bond, as did the front-cover blurb: "She Played a Man's Game with a Woman's Weapons." On the back cover, 007 was called "Jimmy Bond"—and not for the first time (see below).

As a matter of bibliographical interest, *Live and Let Die* (1954) was given its first paperback edition by Perma Books (#M-3048, New York, June 1956). James Meese's cover artwork faithfully depicted a key scene from the novel. And the front-cover blurb was just as accurate: "The world's toughest secret agent tangles with America's most ruthless crook" [Mr. Big/alias Kananga]. Perma, founded in 1949 by Doubleday & Co., was a more prestigious firm than Popular Library, publishing low-priced hardcover editions until Pocket Books took them over in 1954.

Fleming, however, fell out with Perma after they published *Moonraker* (1955) as *Too Hot to Handle* (#M-3070, New York, December 1956). The cover artist this time was Lou Marchetti. N.B. The evocative word "moonraker" refers to the missile built to destroy London by ex–Nazi rocket scientist Sir Hugo Drax, but it was obviously deemed too esoteric for American readers. According to the *Concise Oxford Dictionary*, it means a native of the county of Wiltshire (with reference to the Wiltshire story of "men caught raking a pond for kegs of smuggled brandy, who feigned madness to fool the revenue men, by saying they were raking out the moon").

Diamonds Are Forever (1956) was also published by Perma (#M-3084, New York, September 1957), with a damsel-in-distress cover illustration by William Rose. After that, Fleming had the U.S. paperback rights transferred to Signet Books, published by New American Library (founded in 1948). It proved to be a long and lucrative relationship for both parties. *From Russia with Love* was the first Bond novel published by Signet (#S-1563, New York, September 1958). The cover artist, Barye Phillips, was more at home with private-eye fiction, and it showed.

All of the above data goes to show that Ian Fleming's work had reached a high level of acceptance on both sides of the Atlantic before 1960. But it was America where James Bond started his on-screen career, in the third episode of *Climax! Mystery Theater*, a live television anthology series produced by the CBS network. This 50-minute "reduced" version of *Casino Royale* was broadcast on October 21, 1954, directed by William H. Martin, Jr. The script was written by Anthony Ellis and Charles Bennett.[10] The host, William Lundigan (1914–1975), explained the basic rules of baccarat for the uninitiated viewer. This episode was believed lost until the film historian Jim Schoenberger found a 16mm kinescope (made by filming a TV monitor screen) in 1981. Fleming was paid $1,000 for the TV rights only.

For all its fidelity to the story line, this first video rendition of *Casino Royale* might well have been subtitled *The Americanization of James Bond*. Barry Nelson (1917–2007) played 007—by which code name he is never called—more like a brash, fast-talking private eye than a steel-cold secret agent. He works for some organization called Combined Intelligence—shades of Universal Export/s (and later Transworld Consortium), which is a cover for the "real" James Bond's British Secret Service. His character is referred to as "Card Sense Jimmy Bond" by Clarence—not Felix—Leiter—an English counterspy played by the Australian actor Michael Pate (1920–2008). The blurb writer at Popular Library must have taken careful note (see above). Pate also delivered another mini-lecture on How to Play Baccarat. M—Bond's immediate superior—is never even mentioned.

The teleplay begins with Bond coming under a burst of gunfire as he enters the titular casino (actually a set built at Television City, Hollywood), which prompted his first words spoken beyond the printed page. The doorman asks: "Are you hurt?" Bond replies: "I'm still in one piece, but I don't know how." Linda Christian (1923–2011) was the first actress to play a Bond girl. But the novel's Vesper Lynd became Valerie Mathis, an agent of the French Deuxiéme Bureau, replacing the original and very masculine René Mathis. However, the Hungarian-born Peter Lorre[11] stole every scene in which he appeared, making the Communist agent Le Chiffre a sinister but strangely sympathetic character. The violence is toned down, for obvious reasons, with the threatened emasculation of Bond changed to equally effective toenail torture—in a bathtub!

Casino Royale made no more impact than any other episode of *Climax!* But four years later, CBS approached Fleming with the proposal of making a James Bond TV series and he wrote treatments for thirteen episodes. When this deal eventually fell through, three of the treatments were turned into short stories and published with two new stories in his collection entitled *For Your Eyes Only: Five Secret Occasions in the Life of James Bond* (1960). In 1955, Gregory Ratoff (1897–1960) paid Fleming $6,000 for all film rights to *Casino Royale*, though nothing came of it until the 1967 "spoof" version—which co-starred Woody Allen as young Jimmy Bond.

Also, in 1957, producer Harry Morgenthau III commissioned Fleming to write the pilot episode for a TV series to be called either *Commander Jamaica* or *James Gunn, Secret Agent*. The failed pilot episode concerned a super villain working to destroy an Anglo-American rocket test site in the Caribbean who went by the name of Dr. No.

More television offers would follow, but the biggest boost to Fleming and Bond came from a quite unexpected source. John F. Kennedy (1917–63) nominated *From Russia with Love* as his ninth favorite book in an article, "The President's Voracious Reading Habits," written by Hugh Sidey for the March 17, 1961, issue of *Life* magazine. It came above the only other novel on the list, Stendhal's *The Red and the Black* (1839). All the other listed books were on the highbrow side, with Lord David Cecil's biography of Lord Melbourne (1779–1848) in first place. Fleming and JFK had met before, on friendly terms, but it has been suggested that the midlist spy thriller had only been included to prove that the "playboy" president was both well- and widely read. Be that as it may, this White House endorsement lit the blue touch paper where American sales of the Bond books were concerned—especially in paperback.

Colin Wilson (1931–2013) revealed a significant Ian Fleming American connection in *Dreaming to Some Purpose*,[12] his book of autobiographical sketches: "Marion [Leiter] was a famous Washington hostess who had been a friend of President Kennedy. Her husband [Chicago millionaire John Leiter] had worked for the CIA and was a friend of Ian Fleming, who had put him into the James Bond novels as Bond's American counterpart, Felix Leiter. It was Leiter who had introduced Kennedy to the Bond novels, and Kennedy had said something complimentary about them that had helped turn them into bestsellers in America." Wilson added that Fleming had returned the compliment by making Bond read Kennedy's *Profiles in Courage*.[13] The passage is in chapter 7 of Fleming's last novel, *The Man with the Golden Gun*.

Combined sales of the British Pan paperback editions had been accumulating: 41,000 in 1955; 58,000 in 1956; 72,000 in 1957; 105,000 in 1958; 237,000 in 1959; 323,000 in 1960; 670,000 in 1961. After the UK release of *Dr. No* on October 5, 1962 (May 27, 1963, in the USA), combined sales hit the million mark—and kept on rising throughout the decade, as reported in *Bond and Beyond: The Political Career of a Popular Hero*.[14] There were a spate of foreign-language editions, many "pirated" behind the Iron Curtain. "The KGB evidently took James Bond so seriously that they commissioned the Bulgarian novelist Andrei Gulyashi to create a Communist hero who could liquidate Bond. And so *Avakum versus 07* [sic] was published in 1966."[15] I will provide no further biographical details about Ian Fleming, only making brief forays into those areas where his life and work coincide. My primary source has been *The Life of Ian Fleming*,[16] by John Pearson, who later wrote a "factional" companion piece entitled *James Bond: The Authorized Biography of 007*.[17]

Richard Gant's *Ian Fleming: The Man with the Golden Pen*[18] skims much more lightly over the same ground. O.F. Snelling's *007 James Bond: A Report*[19] was the first extended critical study of the Bond books. Kingsley Amis (April 16, 1922, to October 22, 1995) then followed wittily on with *The James Bond Dossier*.[20] Bondian studies have since become a veritable cottage industry.

According to Amis, spy is an inaccurate job description for James Bond, "in the strict sense of one who steals or buys or smuggles the secrets of foreign Powers. The term does occur in the SMERSH file on him, but the Russian word *sphion* is often used very loosely [applicable to any person considered to be undesirable who is not actually in an enemy uniform]. Bond's only proper secret-stealing exploit, the acquiring of a Soviet cipher-machine in *From Russia, With Love*, is forced upon him as a Soviet plot. Neither he nor his superiors think of it as a normal assignment. Vivienne Michel, narrator of *The Spy Who Loved Me* [Jonathan Cape, 1962], gave Bond a wrong label out of desire for euphony and simplicity, or perhaps minor paradox. *The Medium-Grade Civil Servant Who Loved Me* would have been more accurate as well as more acceptable to M."[21]

The claim that Bond is a *counterspy*—someone who works against the evil doings of enemy agents (Le Chiffre, Mr. Big, Scaramanga, *et al.*)—is considered by Amis to be much more substantial. On the other hand, a villain such as Sir Hugo Drax is initially under secret-departmental scrutiny for reasons that have got nothing to do with espionage in any way, shape or form. SPECTRE ("Special Executive for Counter-Intelligence, Terrorism, Revenge and Extortion") is a purely private-enterprise organization with no ideological axes to grind. Its erstwhile chairman, Ernst Stavro Blofeld, is hunted past reason by 007 in *You Only Live Twice* (1964) as an act of personal revenge for matters arising from *On Her Majesty's Secret Service* (1963)—not national security.

Amis finally settles on the phrase *secret agent* to define James Bond's occupation. "He sees himself in these terms, rather self-consciously at a climactic point in *Moonraker*. Bearers of this designation, which no doubt belongs more to fiction and imagination than to life, have flourished at least since the turn of the century."[22] *Secret Agent* was, in fact, the American title of the British TV series *Danger Man*, which ran on the CBS network in the mid–1960s. It starred Patrick McGoohan[23] as John Drake, a much more confident and self-controlled version of 007. *Danger Man* had started video life as a half-hour program in 1960 and was also shown in the USA under that title. This influential series will be considered in greater detail further along.

The media profile of James Bond had risen steadily during the 1950s. Apart from TV (see above), there had been a radio adaptation of *Moonraker*, produced by Springbok Radio in Durban, South Africa. The Licensed to Kill website cites 1956 as the most likely year for the probably unrecorded broadcast. Bond was played by Bob Holness (1928–2012). *Casino Royale* was published as a comic strip in the London *Daily Express*, running from July 7 to December 13, 1958. *You Only Live Twice* rounded off the initial series (May 17, 1965, to January 8, 1966).[24] But the best was yet to come.

Fleming's fortunes—both literary and financial—rose synergistically with the release of each new James Bond film. The Pan paperback edition of *Dr. No* alone went through ten substantial printings during 1962 and 1964. Ironically, Albert R. (Romolo) Broccoli[25] and Harry Saltzman,[26] who founded Eon Productions, found great difficulty in persuading a film studio to fund the making of *Dr. No*. United Artists finally invested $1,000,000 in the project, which realized a total profit of $59,367,035 on its initial release.

The James Bond "brand" is a worldwide phenomenon that has inspired a multitude of rival fictional super spies, both in print and on the screen. But it was not long after Fleming's untimely death that the gulf between book–Bond and film–Bond widened until they have now become two separate characters who just happen to share the same code name. By a similar process, Hollywood scriptwriters have—for the most part—turned the aristocratic Tarzan created by Edgar Rice Burroughs into an inarticulate oaf. It is beyond doubt that the films have done more to influence the public perception of 007 than the original novels, and they also had a synergistic effect on the mushroom-growth literary imitations. Of the many book-length studies, I can particularly recommend *The James Bond Films: A Behind the Scenes History*,[27] by Stephen Jay Rubin, and *Licence to Thrill: A Cultural History of the James Bond Films*,[28] by James Chapman.

But neither the 1950s Bond novels nor the early 1960s films existed in a social vacuum. They both represented, and even helped to bring about, the "cultural revolution" that marked the middle decades of the twentieth century. On July 15, 1960, the then presidential candidate John F. Kennedy had said, at the Democratic National Convention in Los Angeles: "We stand today on the edge of a New Frontier—the frontier of unknown opportunities and perils, the frontier of unfilled hopes and unfilled threats.... Beyond that frontier are uncharted areas of science and space, unsolved problems of peace and war, unconquered problems of ignorance and prejudice, unanswered questions of poverty and surplus." Those sentiments were echoed by the British prime minister, Harold Wilson (1916–1995), at a Labour Party Conference on October 1, 1963: "The Britain that is going to be forged in the white heat of this [scientific] revolution will be no place for restrictive practices or outdated methods on either side of industry."

This cultural revolution—in the Westernized world, at any rate—also saw the rise of "permissiveness," especially where sex was concerned. Arthur Marwick (1936–2006), the British social historian, summed up these radically changing times in *The Sixties: Cultural Revolution in Britain, France, Italy, and the United States c. 1958–1974* as a "general sexual liberation, entailing striking changes in public and private morals and ... a new frankness, openness, and indeed honesty in personal relationships and modes of expression."[29] But as James Chapman has pointed out, there is no full nudity in the Bond films, because, as Albert Broccoli once observed: "His image must be clean cut. We can't risk offending his massive family audience in any way."[30] Be that as it may, it was the release of *Goldfinger* in London, on September

17, 1964, that led to the eruption of "Bondmania" proper. The novel itself (1959) went on to sell like wildfire in its Pan and Signet paperback editions.

*   *   *

Real-life spying began in the dim morning of humankind. It is not unreasonable to imagine prehistoric hominids keeping a sharp eye on rival tribes who might muscle into their living space or hunting grounds. Espionage has, in fact, been called the second oldest profession, and it may be an even more honorable—or dishonorable—one than the first (prostitution). Philip Knightley's seminal work, *The Second Oldest Profession: Spies and Spying in the Twentieth Century,*[31] can be read either way. There are oblique references to spying, or at least surveillance of enemy activities, in the fragmentary records from those ancient civilizations that emerged in Mesopotamia over 5,000 years ago. *The Enemy Within: A History of Espionage,*[32] by Terry Crowdy, does what it says in the title. Likewise *Spy Fiction: A Connoisseur's Guide,*[33] by Donald McCormick and Katy Fletcher.

CHAPTER ONE

The Brave and the Bold

Fast forward to the Seven Years' War (1756–1764), which split Europe up into two rival factions, one led by France and the other by Great Britain. It has been called the first truly worldwide war, affecting not just Europe but India, North and Central America, West Africa, and the Philippines. The North American component of the Seven Years' War became known as the French and Indian Wars (1680–1763). It had been preceded by King William's War (1688–1687), which consisted chiefly of French attacks on British frontier settlements. Both sides made ruthless use of their Native American allies. But the ins and outs of this convoluted conflict need not concern us here. The Treaty of Paris, signed on February 10, 1763, ended French hegemony in Canada and the northeastern sector of North America, though not the still-smoldering cause of French-Canadian nationalism.

James Fenimore Cooper[1] based his most famous novel, *The Last of the Mohicans: A Narrative of 1757,*[2] on the capture of Fort William Henry, at the southern end of Lake George, in the then–Province of New York. Cooper knew the area well, having been born in Burlington, New Jersey, and brought up in Cooperstown, New York, founded by his father, Judge William Cooper. The first notable British novel about the French and Indian Wars, *With Wolfe in Canada,*[3] was produced by G.A. [George Alfred] Henty (1832–1902).

Less than two years after winning the French and Indian Wars, however, the British government provoked North American colonists into open rebellion by trying to regulate transatlantic commerce to the imperial advantage. The Stamp Act passed by Parliament in 1765 caused such a violent reaction as an act of taxation without representation that it had to be withdrawn. And the Tea Act of 1773 led to the Boston Tea Party (December 16, 1773), when angry colonists disguised as Native Americans boarded three ships and threw their tea cargo into Boston Harbor. For a full blow-by-blow account, read *The Glorious Cause: The American Revolution, 1763–1789,*[4] by Robert Middlekauff. The standard work on American and British espionage during the War of Independence bids fair to be *Turncoats, Traitors and Heroes,*[5] by John J. Bakeless.

The Battle of Lexington, which took place on April 19, 1775, in Middlesex County, Province of Massachusetts Bay, sparked off open hostilities between Great Britain and her thirteen American colonies. *April Morning,*[6] by Howard Fast, paints a vivid novelistic picture of those initial fateful engagements. Both sides knew full well that war might come at any time and had made their preparations for it. The British army was, of course, already in place, but the Americans had to build up their military forces almost from scratch (starting with the Minutemen militia, named because they were ready to fight at a minute's notice). It was the British who scored the first win in the spying stakes. The redcoats arrived at Lexington that morning because a British secret agent had sent a message to General Thomas Gage (1718 [or 1719]–1787) in Boston. But they came with no artillery support, just infantry, having taken the advice of the spy who had told them that the colonists would not fight without the chance of capturing enemy field cannons. It was a mistake that the British would never make again.

Gage's closest opposite number on the American side was General George Washington (1732–1799). As a matter of fact, during the French and Indian Wars, the then–Colonel Washington (commanding the Virginia militia) had been accused of being a French spy. The charges were soon dropped, however, so that the future Father of His Country probably didn't know that they had ever been brought in the first place. Just after that conflict, Gage had suspected Gershom Hicks, a trader from Pennsylvania, of espionage and called for him to be court-martialed. But Hicks, whose guilt was by no means certain, never went on trial—and he would later spy for the Americans, against Gage.

The Americans might have been slow off the espionage mark, but they soon made up for lost time. There had, in fact, been an "amateur" spy ring based in Boston ever since the autumn of 1774. This thirty-strong committee, established by Paul Revere (1734 to some date in or after 1778), met at the Green Dragon Tavern on Union Street. As unprofessional secret agents, their first mistake was the very act of holding regular meetings in such a public place. And, to make matters worse, they failed to conceal their identities. The fundamental rule in secret-service work is that—apart from messengers and necessary associates—the agents must never meet or know each other by name.

The first official United States Army intelligence service came in 1776, when George Washington asked Lieutenant-Colonel Thomas Knowlton (1753–1814) to head a prototype "special forces unit" of undercover agents. Knowlton himself would soon be killed at the Battle of Harlem Heights. Among these 150 officers and men was Captain Nathan Hale (1716–1785), from Coventry in the Connecticut Colony. Hale's first spying mission into New York City was also his last. He was arrested on September 21, found guilty of espionage (after his own admission), and hanged the next day on the orders of General William Howe (1754–1835). His last words are purported to be "I only regret that I have but one life to give for my country." Although Hale was a singularly unsuccessful spy, he has gone down in history as the first martyr of the Revolutionary War. In 1985, he was honored as the state hero of Connecticut.

American espionage improved considerably with the creation of what became known as the Culper Ring, which operated for almost six years, under the direction of Washington, and—from 1778—his deputy intelligence chief, Major Benjamin Tallmadge (1734–1818). Tallmadge recruited Abraham Woodhull (1741–1801) to be his main field agent. Woodhull then signed up his own man in New York City, Robert Townsend (1750–1780), who operated under the alias of Samuel Culper, Junior. Their activities were concentrated in Westchester County, New York, the so-called Neutral Ground between the British forces based in and around New York City and the Continental Army, which held most of the Hudson River Valley and upstate New York. In 1780, the Culper Ring helped to expose General Benedict Arnold (1741–1801) as a traitor.

One of the most effective, but comparatively unsung American secret agents during the Revolutionary War was Enoch Crosby (1750–1815). Crosby—who had been working as a shoemaker in Danbury, Connecticut, when the rebellion began—fell into espionage by accident. For more than six years, Crosby served as a spy in the Neutral Ground and further north to Lake Champlain. He worked his vagabond way as a cobbler, hog butcher, and woodcutter, while following the same routine of infiltration, capture, and escape. Every man's hand was against every stranger in this dangerous area, filled with regular British and American troops, forcing him to hide out in caves and travel mostly by night. After the cessation of hostilities, Crosby and his brother, Benjamin, settled down on a farm they had bought near Brewster, New York. He expressed his feelings in a letter to the *Journal of Commerce*: "having been spared to enjoy these blessings—independence and prosperity—for half a century and see them all still continued, I can lay down my weary and worn out limbs in peace and happiness."

Fourteen years before the death of Enoch Crosby, James Fenimore Cooper published his second novel, *The Spy*.[7] It was the first major work of fiction to have a spy as the central—and, more to the point, a sympathetic—character. Secret agents were not considered to be fit fictional company for "gentleman rogues" such as merry outlaw bands or highwaymen, A necessary evil, at best; deep-dyed villains, at worst. *The Spy* followed the literary trail blazed by the popular "Waverley" historical novels of Sir Walter Scott (1771–1832), which were named after the first volume in the series: *Waverley or 'Tis Sixty Years Hence.* (1814). Cooper would beat Scott at the master's own game, particularly in his six-part saga about Natty Bumppo, the wide-ranging hunter known variously as Deerslayer, Hawkeye, Pathfinder, *La Longue Carabine* (or Long Rifle), Leatherstocking, and Trapper. At the same time, Cooper created the first truly sympathetic fictional Native American in Natty's Mohican companion, Chingachgook, father of the doomed Uncas.[8]

Cooper himself lived in Westchester County, so he gathered firsthand accounts of the conflict from veterans who had fought there. He knew the area just as well—or better—than Sir Walter Scott knew the border country between England and Scotland. But Cooper's most important source of information was John Jay, who told him the tale of Enoch Crosby, although neither man was named in his author's introduction to *The Spy*. In fact, Cooper never once met Crosby. Relevant extract: "It will readily be conceived that a service like this was attended with great personal hazard. In addition to the daily risk of falling into the hands of the Americans themselves, who invariably visited sins of this nature more severely on the natives of the country than on the Europeans who fell into their hands…. In this manner he continued to serve his country in secret during the early years of the struggle, hourly environed by danger, and the constant subject of unmerited opprobrium."

The similarities between this unnamed spy and Cooper's protagonist—Harvey Birch—are more striking than the differences. Birch, using for a cover his prewar occupation as an itinerant peddler, moves like a gaunt wraith through the Neutral Ground. George Washington, dressed in civilian clothes and using the pseudonym of "Mr. Harper," is—at the same time—spying out the land for himself. There follows a suitably convoluted plot, which need not concern us here, apart from the fact that Birch's fate is linked with that of the Wharton and Dunwoodie families. Toward the end of 1781, the grateful General Washington summons the now worn-out Birch to his quarters and offers him a reward of 100 doubloons for his services to the fledgling American Republic:

> "Now, indeed, I know you; and although the same reasons which have hitherto compelled me to expose your valuable life will still exist, and prevent my openly asserting your character, in private I can always be your friend—fail not to apply to me when in want or suffering, and so long as God giveth to me, so long will I freely share with a man who feels so nobly, and acts so well. If sickness or want should ever assail you, and peace smiles upon our efforts, seek the gate of him whom you have often met as Harper, and he will not blush to acknowledge you in his true character."[9]

Thirty-three years later, on 25 July 1814, the young Captain Wharton Dunwoodie and his friend, Lieutenant Tom Mason, Jr., take advantage of in some quiet moments in the Battle of Niagara Falls to reminiscence about their respective families. They are being attentively overheard by an old man, who bears a light unmilitary pack, but he also seems to be lost in his own thoughts. When Captain Dunwoodie mentions his mother, the stranger exclaims "An angel!" Before he can say anything further, however, a British artillery barrage sweeps across the field, along with a volley of small-arms fire. Mason is wounded and the old man killed outright. Dunwoodie removes a small tin box from the hands of the softly smiling corpse. Inside the box is a note which reads:

> Circumstances of political importance, which involve the lives and fortunes of many, have hitherto kept secret what this paper now reveals. Harvey Birch has for years been a faithful and unrequited servant of his country. Though man does not, may God reward him for his conduct!
> Geo. Washington[10]

John Jay did not divulge Crosby's name to Cooper because he feared that the ex-secret agent would be the victim of reprisals for real or fancied wrongs. But the obituary of Crosby printed in the *Cabinet Newspaper* (Schenectady, New York) for July 8, 1835, explicitly stated that he was the inspiration for Harvey Birch. The cat was well and truly out of the bag. Then, in 1886, came a book that was lengthily entitled *The Spy Unmasked; or, Memoirs of Enoch Crosby, alias Harvey Birch, the hero of Mr. Cooper's tale of the neutral ground; being an authentic account of the secret services which he rendered his country during the revolutionary war. (Taken from his own lips, in shorthand.) Comprising many interesting facts and anecdotes never before published. Embellished with a correct likeness of the hero.*[11]

A stage version of *The Spy*, written in double-quick time by novice playwright Charles P. Clinch (1797–1880), was performed at the Park Theatre, New York, on March 1, 1822. It was the first public dramatization of an American novel. In April 2009, a new adaptation, by Jeffrey Hatcher, was staged at George Mason University, Fairfax, Virginia. The surprisingly only (to date) film version was made by Universal Studios in 1914, directed by Otis Turner, with Herbert Rawlinson as Harvey Birch and William Worthington as Harper/Washington. But the original novel, apart from its seminal use of the spy-as-hero motif, also prefigures the downbeat realism that typifies modern secret-agent fiction.

Armed conflict between Great Britain and its former American colonies erupted again during the War of 1812, partly brought about by British impressment of foreign sailors into the Royal Navy and the confiscation of American ships. The conflict lasted from June 18, 1812, until it was brought to an indecisive close by the Treaty of Ghent (December 24, 1814). But the Americans did win the Battle of New Orleans, January 14, 1815, which took place before the treaty took effect. Recommended reading: *The Dawn's Early Light,*[12] by Walter Lord.

At roughly the same time, Europe was convulsed by the French Revolution (1789), the French Revolutionary Wars (1798–1802), and the Napoleonic Wars (1802–1815). Espionage played its part, of course, though the mixture remained much as before. The British Depot of Military Intelligence, formed by the Secretary of War in 1803 to help counter the threat of a French invasion, was hampered by a lack of available personnel. Sir Arthur Wellesley, later created the first Duke of Wellington (1769–1852), perforce became his own chief of intelligence. He maintained that "all the business of war, and indeed all the business of life, is to endeavour to find out what you don't know by what you do: that's what I called 'guessing what was on the other side of the hill.'" This kind of "inspired guesswork" would be a key factor in making him one of the few generals who never lost a battle.

Wellington's archenemy, the Emperor Napoleon Bonaparte (1769–1821), made extensive use of the French secret police and a well-run network of spies. His opinion of them both, however, was very low. From *The Mind of Napoleon: A Selection from His Written and Spoken Words,*[13] edited and translated by J. Christopher Herold: "So you think the [Paris] police foresees and knows everything. The police invents more than it discovers" (conversation with an officer, Elba, 1814 or 1815). "Whatever the spies and secret agents say, unless it is something they have seen with their own eyes, is nothing; and often, even if they have seen it, it is not much" (conversation, St. Helena, 1817, reported in English).

There were simultaneous developments on the literary espionage front. Edgar Allan Poe[14] has been called the Father of Detective Fiction, Horror Fiction, and the Modern Short Story itself. But he was also at least the Godfather of Spy Fiction as we know it today. Peter Ackroyd's *Poe: A Life Cut Short*[15] provides all the salient bio-bibliographical facts in just 170 pages. Poe's idiosyncratic hero, C. Auguste Dupin, made his first bow in "The Murders in the Rue Morgue,"[16] the original locked-room murder mystery. Dupin, however, was in many ways more of an unofficial spy than a consulting detective. In "The Purloined Letter,"[17] he is engaged by "Monsieur G" to retrieve the all-important missing epistle, after the secret policemen have failed. Apart from Dupin, "The Gold Bug"[18] involves cryptography, with the protagonist solving a substitution code using letter frequency. It was largely based upon his seminal article, "A Few Words on Secret Writing."[19] Real life would follow fiction. From 1850 onward, all military intelligence organizations formally included codebreaking in their training courses.

Of the making of books on the American Civil War (April 12, 1861, until April 1, 1865) there is no end in sight. A blow-by-blow account would take up too much unnecessary space here. Fletcher Pratt's *Ordeal by Fire: An Informal History of the Civil War*[20] was one of the first, and still one of the best, overviews for the general reader. A more recent single-volume study is *The War for a Nation*,[21] by Susan-Mary Grant. As Pratt stated in his introduction to *Ordeal by Fire*, the Civil War is worthy of study "not so much because … such modern devices as automatic firearms, armoured warships, submarines and fields of fire first appeared, as because the tactics and even the strategies developed in those campaigns in America controlled all subsequent wars down to the beginning of the atomic age. Nobody has improved very much on Lee's methods of deception, Sherman's treatment of logistics or Sheridan's handling of combined arms."[22]

The same thing could be said for how the work of secret agents, on both sides, during the Civil War affected the future conduct of espionage—not just in North America, but all over the world. *Spies for the Blue and Gray*,[23] by Harnett T. Kane, describes the "engaging collection of gamblers who insistently played for mortal stakes" (from a book review in *The New York* Times). Kane sets the scene in his introduction: It was a spy-conscious war, and sometimes it seemed that everybody was spying on everybody else and talking volubly on the subject, in newspapers, parlours, bars, and at street corners. Nevertheless, few officials did anything to stop the enemy's espionage. The present-day reader may be astonished at the ease with which agents made their way across the lines and through opposition territory. Repeatedly they presented themselves to civilian and military officials, pumped them of information, and rode off with a bright good-by…. The American spies improvised, experimented, and what they lacked in finesse they made up in energy and determination. They broke rules usually because they had never heard of them."[24]

The complete story of espionage during the Civil War can never be told at this late date. Even the official records were riddled with gaps, the individual agents could not see the big picture, and a lot of them died obscure deaths before getting the chance to report back. Ex-president Jefferson Davis (1815–1864) always discouraged any research into the history of Confederate spying. On the Union side, General Grenville Dodge (1831–1916) also held out against efforts to reveal names and operational activities—mainly because too many people could still be in danger of reprisals. But much significant information is available from other sources (court records, official correspondence, private letters, etc.), primarily about civilian spies, though with some reference to military scouts.

The Blues were quicker off the mark than the Grays when it came to espionage, thanks in no small part to an immigrant Scotsman.

Allan Pinkerton was born in Glasgow, on either July or August 21, 1819, to William Pinkerton and his wife Isobel, *née* McQueen. He left Scotland for the United States in 1842, soon establishing his own cooperage business in Dundee, Illinois. Pinkerton became a deputy Sheriff and then full-time investigator for Cook County, based in Chicago, where he set up a detective force to counter theft from railway companies. This North-Western Police Agency developed into Pinkerton's National Detective Agency, with a wide-open eye emblem and the motto "We Never Sleep" (which the firm has used ever since). Pinkerton died on July 1, 1884. The whole story can be found in *Allan Pinkerton: The First Private Eye*,[25] by James Mackay. Successful sleuthing for the Illinois Central Railroad brought him to the attention of George B. McClellan, then its chief engineer and vice president, and the company lawyer, Abraham Lincoln.[26]

The world's first private detective began his secret-agent career—unofficially—a few months before the declaration of war. In February 1861, he got wind of a plan by Maryland secessionists to assassinate president-elect Lincoln when he arrived in Baltimore, by train, on the way to Washington, D.C., for his inauguration ceremony. He went straight to Lincoln with this information and advised him to change trains at Philadelphia. A female Pinkerton agent had reserved three sections of the sleeping car on the Washington night express, for her "ailing brother" and friends. The ruse succeeded, and thus ended the Baltimore Plot of 1861, the details of which Civil War historians have been arguing about ever since. For just one example, a New York police detective named John Alexander Kennedy (1803–1873) played a significant, though now rather overlooked, role in foiling the attempt on Lincoln's life.[27] However, it would soon lead to the newly appointed General McClellan, commander of the Department of the Ohio, asking Pinkerton to form a military intelligence network throughout the Southern states.

Pinkerton made full use of the investigative techniques he had developed during his prewar career as a detective. For example, "shadowing" (close but discreet surveillance of suspects) and "assuming a role" (undercover work, as it is known today). Using the alias Major E.J. Allen, he often insinuated himself behind enemy lines, posing as a soldier or civilian sympathizer. But his most important contribution to intelligence work lay in setting up a counter-espionage service in Washington, D.C., which was a hotbed of Confederate spies and double agents. He suffered a stroke in 1869, which left him partially paralyzed, and the actual management of the agency was passed to his sons, William Allan (1826–1868) and Robert Allan (1814–1869).

Dime novels—known as "penny dreadfuls" in Britain—were usually little more than 20,000-word novelettes, but the New York firm of Beadle and Adams made a fortune with these cost-effective publications during the Civil War. They made popular-culture heroes out of such real-life westerners as Kit Carson, Davy Crockett, and Buffalo Bill, along with truly fictitious characters like Frank Reade, Jr., created by Luis Senarens (1863–1939). Edward S. Ellis (1840–1916) wrote *The Forest Spy: A Tale of the War of 1812*,[28] an above-average example of its kind. *The Dime Novel Companion*,[29] by J. Randolph Cox, is the ideal sourcebook on this relatively underresearched subject. Entire libraries could be filled with more substantial novels about the Civil War period, including *The Red Badge of Courage*, by Stephen Crane; *Gone with the Wind*, by Margaret Mitchell; *The Horse Soldiers*, by Harold Sinclair; the *North and South* trilogy, by John Jakes; and *Lincoln*, by Gore Vidal.[30]

There would be little consequential work for the U.S. Secret Service until the Spanish-American War of 1898. Meanwhile, in Europe, Otto von Bismarck (1815–1898), president of Prussia from 1862 until 1890, had set about unifying the independent German states into a single political entity. Wilhelm Steiber (1818–1882) was Bismarck's master spy, both at home and abroad. Bismarck ordered Steiber to undertake a reconnaissance of Austrian military readiness, and he duly supplied the Prussian generals with such accurate intelligence that the Austro-Prussian War turned out to be one of the shortest on record (June 15 to August 23, 1866). Steiber played an equally important role in helping Prussia to win the Franco-Prussian War of 1870–71, after which Bismarck became the "Iron Chancellor" of Germany.

"The Great Game" was the strategic rivalry between the British Empire and the Russian Empire for supremacy in Central Asia, which ran roughly from the Russo-Persian Treaty of 1813 to the Anglo-Russian Convention of 1907. Captain Arthur Connolly (1807–1842), an intelligence officer serving with the 6th Bengal Light Cavalry, is generally regarded to have coined the term. It was introduced to mainstream awareness by Rudyard Kipling (1865–1936) in his novel *Kim* (1901). Recommended reading: *The Great Game: On Secret Service in High Asia*,[31] by Peter Hopkirk.

American spy fiction was then mostly confined to "pulp magazines" (so-called from the cheap wood-pulp paper that was used to print popular fiction periodicals), which had largely replaced dime novels by the end of the nineteenth century. *Golden Argosy: Freighted with Treasures for Boys and Girls* (December 2, 1882) has been recognized as the very first pulp magazine. It was published by Frank A. Munsey (1854–1925), a former telegraph operator from Augusta, Maine. He soon reduced the title to *Argosy*, aiming for a more adult readership, and then continued with *Munsey's Weekly*, later *Monthly* (1889), *All-Story* (1899), and *Cavalier* (1908) magazines. Street & Smith followed suit in 1903 with *Popular Magazine* and several other titles.

Ron Goulart's *Cheap Thrills: An Informal History of the Pulp Magazine*[32] is an ideal primer volume for the pulp-fiction historian and general reader alike.

Argosy, *Popular Magazine*, and all the other pulp magazines presented their readers with "a mixed bag of heroics each issue. One cowboy, one legionnaire, one pirate and two or three musketeers."[33] Specialized "genre" magazines also entered this lucrative market, e.g., *Love Story* (1922) and *Frontier* (1924). The oft-reprinted casebooks of Allan Pinkerton led to the creation of many private detective and/or secret-agent heroes, the most successful of whom was "Master Detective" Nick Carter, who made his entrance in "The Old Detective's Pupil; or, The Mysterious Crime of Madison Square,"[34] by John Russell Coryell (1848–1924). This durable fictional character headlined *Nick Carter Detective Magazine* (1933 to 1936), appeared in several films, and was even brought back to life as a James Bond clone. Sexton Blake is the nearest, and equally long-lasting, British equivalent. Blake began his career in "The Missing Millionaire,"[35] by Hal Meredeth, a pseudonym of Harry Blyth, who died in 1898.

CHAPTER TWO

The War That Did Not End War

At the outset of what would soon be called the Great War, H.G. Wells[1] published a collection of eleven polemical articles that viewed the conflict in an optimistic light: *The War That Will End War*.[2] His bestselling novel *Mr. Britling Sees It Through*,[3] though not uncritical, also took a hope-for-the-best attitude. However, his subsequent tours of the Western Front convinced him that the only hope for enduring world peace lay in the establishment of a League of Nations. The younger Wells had also written several future-war fantasias, most famously *The War of the Worlds*.[4] *H.G.: The History of Mr. Wells*,[5] by Michael Foot, covers his life and works economically well.

But even Wells was only the latest in a long line of literary future warriors, as can be seen in *Voices Prophesying War 1763-1984*,[6] by I. (Ignatius) F. (Frederick) Clarke (1918–2009): "In the early summer of 1871 an anonymous story about a successful German invasion of the United Kingdom alarmed the nation and astounded many readers throughout Europe. This story was *The Battle of Dorking*, which came out in the May issue of *Blackwood's Magazine*; and its tale of disaster and defeat had such an effect that the Prime Minister [William Ewart Gladstone] felt it necessary to speak out against what he called the alarmism of a clever magazine article. [By the April of 1872] the fortunate author, Lieutenant-Colonel Sir George Tomkyns Chesney [1830–1895], had received a handsome sum from *Blackwood's* in final settlement of the large profit made from the many reprints."[7]

The Battle of Dorking (which is a 20,000-word novelette), may be found in Michael Moorcock's *Before Armageddon: An Anthology of Victorian and Edwardian Imaginative Fiction Published before 1914*, of which *England Invaded* is a companion piece.[8] *Before Armageddon* includes the last eight episodes from *The Great War in England in 1897*,[9] by William Le Queux.[10] This shock-horror novel deals with a Franco-Russian invasion of Great Britain, which is thwarted by plucky patriots— and the intervention of Germany, on the British side. Before long, the British have annexed both Algeria and Russian Central Asia, thus winning the Great Game once and for all, while the Germans reduce France to a mere vassal state.

There was no immediate American equivalent of this subgenre, because "the United States lacked the strong and permanent sense of a foreign menace required to touch off tales of future wars."[11] Likewise, Russia "lacked the free Press and the free play of opinion that alone could produce private solutions for public perils." But this complacent situation changed after Japan won the Russo-Japanese War of 1904–1905. In "The Dam,"[12] by Hugh S. Johnson (1881–1942), an American-Japanese War has been waged for some time and the problematical end is not yet in sight. Johnson later rose to the rank of brigadier general during the Great War. "The Dam" was reprinted in *Science Fiction by Gaslight: A History and Anthology of Science Fiction in the Popular Magazines, 1891–1911*, edited by Sam Moskowitz.[13]

Meanwhile, the strains between the major European powers were approaching critical mass. As Field-Marshal Viscount Montgomery of Alamein explained in *A Concise History of Warfare*: "Britain was acutely conscious of the challenge by Germany to her commercial and industrial power, and had been actively engaged in building up her naval and merchant fleets. In France there was resentment ... at Germany's possession of Alsace and Lorraine. Germany and Russia were rivals for influence in the Balkans. The Ottoman Empire in its ramshackle state had nothing conceivable to gain from being hostile to anybody; but the Germans had been wooing the Turks—who had a score to pay off against Britain and Russia, the two powers which had patronized or bullied them through the nineteenth century. While these antagonisms were by no means enough to make war inevitable, they did mean that there was a highly charged atmosphere in which war might break out."[14]

The First Anglo-Boer War (1880–81)—or the Transvaal Rebellion—and the Second Anglo-Boer War (1899–1902)—or the South African War—caused further friction between Britain and Germany, with the Germans taking the side of the Boers (Dutch-speaking settlers) against the British colonists. (Sir) Arthur Conan Doyle[15] wrote *The War in South Africa*.[16] Conan Doyle had his most famous creation, Sherlock Holmes, enter the espionage lists, most notably in "The Bruce-Partington Plans" (*The Strand Magazine* and *Collier's Weekly Magazine*, both December 1908), which was later reprinted in *His Last Bow*.[17] Set in November 1895, the story concerns the theft of blueprints for a new submarine. The submarine menace was highlighted by Doyle in his short story "Danger!" (*The Strand Magazine*, July 1914).

A wake-up call for the sleepy British Secret Service was sounded with the publication of a novel entitled *The Riddle of the Sands: A Record of Secret Service Recently Achieved*.[18] Its author, Erskine Childers,[19] had led something of a James Bond–type life himself. Childers was executed by the Irish Free State Government for being a suspected British double agent. The full story is told in *Damned Englishman: A Study of Erskine Childers*,[20] by Tom Cox. *Riddle*, Childers's only novel, was actually propaganda covered in a sugar-coating of popular fiction. The story concerns two clean-cut young Englishmen, Davies and Carruthers, who—during a yachting journey to the Frisian Islands, near the northwest coasts of Germany and the Netherlands—discover German preparations for an imminent naval invasion of England, using barges and torpedo boats. Apart from writing the most literate spy novel since James Fenimore Cooper's *The Spy*, Childers had set the cat among the Whitehall pigeons. *Aprés* Childers, *le déluge*. A cogent account of these late–Victorian and

Edwardian-era cautionary tall tales may be found in *The British Spy Novel: Styles in Treachery*,[21] by John Atkins.

Two years after *The Riddle of the Sands*, Edgar Wallace[22] self-published *The Four Just Men*,[23] in which the titular antiheroes defend European "anarchists" who had taken their "liberation" struggle to London. They threaten to execute the British Secretary of State for Foreign Affairs if he does not abandon his draconian Aliens Extradition (Political Offences) Bill. Sir Philip Ramon won't—so they do, in the name of Justice.

Joseph Conrad's *The Secret Agent*[24] was a much more serious—even somber—state-of-disunion novel. Conrad[25] used his boyhood experiences in Russia to get inside the skull of the terrorist Verloc. Alfred Hitchcock (1899–1980) directed a film version, *Sabotage*, in 1936, starring Oskar Homolka as Verloc. Conrad's other "spy" novel, *Under Western Eyes*,[26] took a long, hard look at the lonely life of a double agent. The most "anarchic" spy novel ever written is, however, *The Man Who Was Thursday*,[27] by G.K. Chesterton (1874–1936), which more than lives up to its subtitle—*A Nightmare*. A young poet called Syme joins the Underground Movement, a secret society of revolutionaries sworn to destroy the world. But no one is what he pretends to be, and the novel ends in a paradoxical fantasia that sends up the whole double-triple-multiple-agent syndrome—in fact, as it has since turned out, as well as fiction.

E. Phillips Oppenheim[28] would become a leading exponent of the foul-foreigners-bent-on-bringing-England-to-her-knees brand of middlebrow fiction. *Mysterious Mr. Sabin*[29] made Oppenheim's reputation as a thriller writer. This blurb concisely sets the scene: "War with Germany is imminent, and London is holding its breath for news from the Continent. Seeming insignificant in the atmosphere of growing tension, an attempt is made on the life of a certain Mr. Sabin outside a fashionable London restaurant. Lord Wolfenden, who witnessed the incident with no little interest, suddenly finds himself caught up in a web of espionage and high treason from which there is no escape" (Digit paperback edition, London, 1963). Mr. (no first name) Sabin is a cut-rate combination of Professor Moriarty and Ernst Stavro Blofeld. His return appearance in *The Yellow Crayon*[30] also turned out to be his last. "Oppy" (affectionate nickname) served as a propagandist in the 1914–18 war. See *The Prince of Storytellers*,[31] by Robert Standish.

The first explicitly anti–German novel, by William Le Queux (pronounced "Q"), was *The Invasion of 1910–14*[32]—yet another scare-tactics diatribe. In *The Mystery of a Motor-Car*,[33] a country doctor who treats the victim of an automobile accident finds himself involved with a deep-dyed plot hatched in Berlin. *Spies of the Kaiser*[34] warned that "thousands of German agents" had long been infiltrating every level of British society. After the war began, Le Queux lost no time in producing such "nonfictional" titles as *German Atrocities: A Record of Shameless Deeds* and *Britain's Deadly Peril: Are We Told the Truth?*[35] War novels flowed from his dreadfully fluent pen, including *The Zeppelin Destroyer* (1916) and the above-average *Cipher Six* (1919).

Further reading: *William Le Queux: Master of Mystery*,[36] by Chris Patrick and Stephen Baister.

Captain Vernon Kell (1873–1942) and Captain Mansfield Smith-Cumming (1859–1923) were selected by Colonel James Edward Edmonds (Directorate of Military Operations) to head His majesty's Secret Service Bureau. Kell and Smith-Cumming did not work well together as a team. In 1910, they decided to split the Bureau into two distinct sections, Home and Foreign. With bureaucratic exactitude, the Home Section, or Security Service (MI5), initially run by Kell (code-named "K"), was responsible for counter-espionage operations inside the United Kingdom and the British Empire. The Foreign section—MI-1c, later MI6, and eventually the Secret Intelligence Service—worked abroad, in non–British territories. It was commanded by Smith-Cumming—code-named "C"—as the head of SIS is known to this very day. Hence "M," in the James Bond fictional franchise. As a general rule, MI5 works closely with the Special Branch of Scotland Yard, but the SIS has generally set itself beyond—if not above—the laws of the land.

Germany declared war on Russia on August 1, 1914, then France on August 3, and Britain declared war on Germany the next day. There have been countless books written about the Great War, of varying complexity, and more will follow *ad infinitum*. A good starting point for the general reader is, however, *The First World War: An Illustrated History*,[37] by A.J.P. Taylor (1906–1990).

Mati Hari, the most famous convicted spy of the Great War, is also the most overhyped and least operationally effective. Margaretha Geertruida Zelle (1876–1917) was born in Leeuwarden, the Netherlands. She moved to Paris in 1903, performing as a circus horse rider (perhaps inspiring Octopussy's circus troupe, in the 1983 James Bond film of that title). But she soon became a successful exotic dancer under the stage name of Mata Hari (Malayan for "The Eye of the Morning"), passing herself off as a Javanese princess who had studied the art of sacred Indian dancing since childhood. Mati Hari did not dance naked in her public performances, as legend has it, but wore a flesh-colored body stocking. No firm evidence was produced to prove that Mata Hari had passed any kind of military information to the Germans, which the French finally admitted, in 1932. As a matter of fact, even the German Secret Service has never been able to clarify her official relationship with them—if any. But the court found her guilty of espionage and sentenced her to death. She was executed by firing squad at Vincennes, an eastern suburb of Paris, on October 15, 1917. It could be argued that Mata Hari was a "soft target" for prosecution and an easy propaganda victory.

The main drawback to spy fiction gaining long-term popularity was the lack of a series character with whom readers could build up a close personal relationship. Harvey Birch and Carruthers were one-offs, and the tract-like "novels" of Chesney and Le Queux had nothing resembling real people in them, let alone identifiable heroes. Nick Carter and his ilk merely dabbled in espionage. All that changed, however, with the publication of *The Thirty-Nine Steps*,[38] by John Buchan,[39] which introduced Richard Hannay to the thriller-reading world. It sold 25,000 copies between October and December of 1915—an extraordinary total for those days. The Scottish-born was attached to the HQ Staff of the British Army in France from 1916 to 1917, with the temporary rank of lieutenant-colonel, then finished his Great War service as Director of Information—also, briefly, Intelligence. His autobiography, *Memory Hold-the-Door*,[40] appeared in 1940. Further reading: *Beyond the Thirty-Nine Steps: A Life of John Buchan*,[41] by Ursula Buchan (granddaughter).

It was in *The Power-House*,[42] written in the smooth days before the war (*Blackwood's* magazine, December 1913), that Buchan worked out the "shocker" formula that was to serve him so well for twenty years. He did not just emulate the likes of Oppenheim, but easily surpassed them, with a man-on-the-run-from-evil-masterminds narrative that never lets up from start to finish. *The Power-House* marked the novel-length début of Sir Edward Leithen, who had started his heroic career in "Space" (*Blackwood's Magazine*, May 1911). Although total sales of *The Thirty-Nine Steps* have long since passed the million mark, its high reputation mainly rests upon the film version directed by Alfred Hitchcock in 1935. Robert Donat played Hannay, with Madeleine Carroll as the non-canonical leading lady, Pamela. Buchan's novel was so freely adapted by Hitchcock (and screenplay writers Charles Bennett and Alma Reville) that not much of the original plot remained. From *The Films of Alfred Hitchcock*,[43] by Robert A. Harris and Michael S. Lasky: "[Buchan] was, at first, naturally upset that his book was used only as a foundation but later, after viewing the film, admitted that it was actually much better than the novel."[44]

Greenmantle[45] represented a quantum leap forward for Buchan as a fiction writer. Major Hannay commands an infantry battalion on the Western Front. He is urgently recalled to London for a meeting with Sir Walter Bullivant, Permanent Secretary of the Foreign Office, who sends him on a secret mission to the Middle East. From the blurb to the 1947 Pan paperback edition: "To the British Foreign Office come warnings and reports from many sources—pedlars in South Russia, Afghan horse-dealers, Turcoman merchants, pilgrims on the road to Mecca, sailors on Black Sea coasters, as well as from respectable Consuls who use ciphers—telling that the East is waiting: waiting for a promised revelation, for some man, some star, some prophecy that will come from the West. The enemies of Britain are aware of this; presumably they have arranged it. So Richard Hannay and his two dauntless friends [Sandy Arbuthnot and John S. Blenkiron] set out on the desperate mission of finding the 'prophet'—the mysterious 'Greenmantle' who plans to rouse the East and prepare Britain's downfall."

Richard Hannay ended the Great War in *Mr. Standfast* (1919). He is pitted against the evil Graf von Schwabing, a member of the Black Stone group, who—disguised as "Moxon Ivery"—now heads a network of usefully idiotic pacifist spies in Britain. Von Schwabing could have inspired Fleming's Ernst Stavro Blofeld, along with Dominick Medina, from *The Three Hostages* (1924). As a British officer and a gentleman, Hannay was never referred to as a "spy"—that pejorative epithet was only applied to dastardly foreigners who knew not how to fairly Play the Game. Further reading: *Clubland Heroes: A Nostalgic Study of Some Recurrent Characters in the Romantic Fiction of Dornford Yates, John Buchan and Sapper,*[46] by Richard Usborne.

Greenmantle channeled Western imperial anxieties about threats from the Middle East. It also has a prescient echo in our present-day world of jihads and worldwide Islamic terrorism. However, even more deep-seated fears concerning "native" revolts against European rule in the Far East—especially China—are dealt with in *The Yellow Peril: Dr. Fu Manchu and the Rise of Chinaphobia,*[47] by Christopher Frayling. Dr. Fu Manchu, the archetypal Oriental villain created by Sax Rohmer,[48] employed an international spy network to forward his plans for world domination. Fu's main adversary, Sir Denis Nayland Smith, unfeasibly headed both the British Secret Service and the Criminal Investigation Department of Scotland Yard. The saga ran through fourteen books, from *The Mysterious Dr. Fu-Manchu* (1913) to *The Wrath of Fu Manchu and Other Stories* (1973). Ian Fleming always freely admitted his debt to Buchan for inspiring both his heroic and villainous characters. The same expression of gratitude applied to Sax Rohmer. James Bond and Nayland Smith have zero points of similarity, but compare the following descriptions of (a) Dr. Fu Manchu and (b) Dr. No:

> Imagine a person, tall, lean, and feline; with a brow like Shakespeare and a face like Satan: a close-shaven skull and long magnetic eyes of the true cat green (a generic pen portrait).
>   Doctor No was at least six inches taller than Bond, but the straight immobile poise of his body made him seem still taller. The head also was elongated and tapered from a round, completely bald head to a sharp chin....[49]

When war came to Europe in 1914, President Woodrow Wilson (1856–1924) felt obliged to uphold the basic principle of American neutrality. Wilson did, however, warn Germany to curtail, if not stop, its submarine attacks on merchant vessels, especially after the sinking of the *Lusitania*, a British liner, off the Irish coast on May 7, 1915. Of the 1,195 lives lost, 128 were U.S. citizens, and American sentiment was moved in favor of entering the war against Germany. But the German High Command took the calculated risk that the continuance of unrestricted U-boat warfare would defeat the Allies before the United States could intervene, either directly or indirectly. The gamble might very well have succeeded, had it not been for the Zimmermann Telegram (or Zimmermann Note) incident. For a full account, read *The Zimmermann Telegram,*[50] by Barbara Tuchman. Congress declared war against Germany on April 6, 1917, and on the Austro-Hungarian Empire eight months later. The success of U.S. signals intelligence during 1917–18 led to the establishment of a unit called the Government Code and Cipher School.

As the United States entered the Great War, Russia was well on its way to leaving it. The Russian Revolution was actually a long and violent process, foreshadowed by Bloody Sunday (January 22, 1905), when Czarist troops opened fire on dissident workers who were marching to protest at the Winter Palace in St. Petersburg. Czar

Nicholas II (1868–1918) made some half-hearted reforms, including an "advisory" legislature called the Duma. The two Revolutions of 1917 (April and October) were sparked off by major military defeats on the Eastern Front. They were led by Vladimir Ilyich Lenin (1870–1924), from political exile in Switzerland. On March 3, 1918, the new Bolshevik government, simultaneously faced with the unstoppable German advance and internal unrest, signed the peace treaty of Brest-Litovsk. A bloody civil war followed. *The Russian Revolution*,[51] by Alan Moorehead, remains a straightforward overview of the subject, though inevitably overtaken by subsequent findings.

After a smaller-scale revolution broke out in Germany, Emperor Wilhelm II (1859–1941) abdicated, and an armistice came into effect on November 11, 1918. The Treaty of Versailles (signed on June 28, 1919), which brought a formal end to the hostilities, radically changed the map of Europe and the Middle East. Four great empires—Germany, Austria-Hungary, Czarist Russia, and the Turkish Ottoman Empire—had gone. They were replaced by several new states, such as Czechoslovakia and Yugoslavia, with governments ranging from liberal democracies and constitutional monarchies to the Bolshevik dictatorship in the USSR (Union of Soviet Socialist Republics). When the military and geopolitical dust settled, normal spying service was resumed, between friends and foes alike. The Russian Revolution would be a Great Game Changer where espionage was concerned, in both fact and fiction, through what remained of the twentieth century—and beyond.

*   *   *

H.G. Wells (again): "The end of the most horrible and destructive war that the world had ever known was naturally enough the signal for a wave of happiness, optimism, and relief; there was a post-war euphoria which was deceptive and pathetic enough, but was not wholly baseless."[52] But this "post-war euphoria" turned out to be only the cruel breaking of a false dawn. Twilight fell even before the ink had dried on the Treaty of Versailles, signed at the Paris Peace Conference (June 28, 1919). According to Marshal Ferdinand Foch (1851–1920): "This is not peace; it is an armistice for 20 years."

One of the first and most significant postwar spy novels to run out of the blocks was *The Adventures of Heine*,[53] by Edgar Wallace, which concerns a remarkably sympathetic German spy who operates during the early years of the conflict. Background reading: *Stranger Than Fiction: The Life of Edgar Wallace, the Man Who Created KING KONG*,[54] by Neil Clark.

E. Phillips Oppenheim's *Up the Ladder of Gold*[55] takes the "willing suspension of disbelief" and hangs it out in the wind to dry. Warren Rand—"the human riddle of two hemispheres"—is an American billionaire media mogul who plays the financial and political world markets like a game of three-dimensional chess. His particularly cunning plan is to corner the world's market in gold: "In a week, the question the political economists are never tired of asking will be answered—how can a nation deal with its exchange without gold? How can it continue to buy and sell now that the days of primitive barter have passed?"[56] Unlike Auric Goldfinger, then, Warren Rand wants to buy Fort Knox, not burgle the place and make off with its bullion deposits. Ian Fleming admitted to being an Oppenheim fan during his formative years. It beggars belief that he never read *Ladder.*

"Sapper"—the inverted commas were later dropped—was the pseudonym of Lt. Col. Herman Cyril McNeile, M.C.,[57] a Regular Army Officer in the Royal Engineers (nicknamed the "Sappers" because they dug tunnels in order to plant mines under enemy positions). Serving officers were not then permitted to use their real names, hence the *nom de plume.* After his demobilization, Captain McNeile set about establishing himself as a full-time writer, with quick-march military precision. *Bull-dog Drummond: The Adventures of a Demobilized Officer Who Found Peace Dull*[58] made his pen name famous and earned him a not-inconsiderable fortune. Captain Hugh "Bulldog" (the hyphen eventually fell into disuse) Drummond, D.S.O., M.C. was a more muscular (six feet tall, broad, weighing fourteen stone, with attractively ugly facial features) and somewhat less cerebral Richard Hannay. Ian Fleming once said that James Bond was "Sapper from the waist up and Mickey Spillane from the waist down."[59] Enter Carl Peterson, the most dangerous man in England, if not the whole of Europe. One violent thing leads to another, over a tetralogy of books, which have been reprinted in an omnibus volume entitled *Bulldog Drummond: His Four Rounds with Carl Peterson. Described by Sapper.*[60] Peterson is Professor Moriarty, Mysterious Mr. Sabin, Dominic Medina, and—yes—Ernst Stavro Blofeld—all rolled into one sinister package.

Dornford Yates (real name Cecil William Mercer)[61] is the third seminal scribbler in Richard Usborne's *Clubland Heroes.* Yates was born in Upper Walmer, Kent, and—after active service in both world wars—ended his long life in Southern Rhodesia (Zimbabwe since 1980). For full details read *Dornford Yates: A Biography,*[62] by A.J. Smithers. He is best remembered today for his ten books concerning the comical misadventures of Major Bertram ("Berry") Pleydell, his idle-rich family, and their fearfully feckless friends. Yates, however, put aside such lighthearted shilly-shallying when he took to writing thrillers, of which *Blind Corner*[63] is the prime exemplar. It features Jonathan—"Jonah"—Mansel, the most active member of the Berry *menage*, whose crime-fighting and counterspy exploits were recorded by Richard Chandos, his younger and even more energetic assistant.

But it was Sapper's thud-and-blunder style that would inspire a new wave of British—and American—thriller writers, with Drummond clones rampaging all over the printed-page place. Sydney Horler[64] was the most immediately apparent of these damn-and-blast disciples. During the First World War, he was commissioned as a second lieutenant, but weak eyesight led to an assignment in the Propaganda Section of Air Force Intelligence. Horler took up full-time freelance authorship soon after he was demobbed. *The Curse of Doone*[65] featured a secret agent named Ian Heath, who works for the Foreign Branch of the British Secret Service—then spymastered by Sir Harker Bellamy. In due course, Bellamy became the head of Q.1

(later Y.1) British Intelligence. He also played M to Horler's best-known series character, the Honourable Timothy Overbury "Tiger" Standish ("the second son of the
Earl of Quorn"). *Tiger Standish*[66] was followed by eight other novels and two collections. Gerald Frost, alias Nighthawk, came to fictional life in *They Called Him
Nighthawk*.[67] Five other novels followed. Frost is a former safecracker who acts as an
authorized vigilante, solving cases that had left both Scotland Yard and the British
Secret Service stymied.

Although Sydney Horler had got off to a fast start in the Replacement Stakes
for Sapper and Edgar Wallace Stakes, he was overtaken and quickly outdistanced
by a young writer, Leslie Charteris,[68] whose birth names were Leslie Charles Bowyer Yin. An Anglo-Chinese, he was the son of Dr. Suat Chwan Yin (1877–1958), a
noted Singapore physician/surgeon, and his English wife, Lydia Florence Bowyer
(1876–1956). He "went up" to King's College, Cambridge, on October 10, 1925—but
"dropped out" the following year, to pursue his long-held literary ambitions. For
what-happened-next in a long and active life see *A Saint I Ain't*,[69] by Ian Dickerson.
After five stand-alone novels from Ward Lock—*X Esquire* (1927), *The White Rider*
(1928), *Meet the Tiger* (1928), *Daredevil* (1929), and *The Bandit* (1929)—it struck him
that the hero of *Meet the Tiger* (later retitled *The Saint Meets the Tiger*) seemed the
best of the bunch. He was Simon Templar—nicknamed the Saint, a gentleman crook
who took justice into his own hands. This durable desperado would undergo several
"regenerations" over the next sixty-odd years, from gentleman outlaw to freelance
spy to international troubleshooter. Further reading: *The Saint: A Complete History
in Print, Film and Television* [...] *1928–1992*,[70] by Burl Barer.

The London-born Dennis (Yeats) Wheatley[71] was yet another writer to be influenced by Sapper, and who would have a similar effect upon the young Ian Fleming. After being mustard-gassed and medically discharged from the army in 1918,
Wheatley entered the family business as a wine merchant. More details may be
found in his three-volume autobiography, collectively entitled *The Time Has Come*.[72]
The Devil Is a Gentleman: The Life and Times of Dennis Wheatley,[73] by Phil Baker, is
a brisk one-volume overview. Gregory Sallust was Wheatley's first "official" secret-
agent character, but *two* characters could lay claim to that name. Sallust A is the
hero—if such he can be called—of *Black August* (1934). This novel is set thirty years
in the then future, circa 1966, when the world is faced with total economic and
political collapse—the British General Strike of 1926 writ larger than life. Sallust
B appeared two years later, in *Contraband* (1936), as a thirty-something journalist
with good naval cadet and Great War military experience who does a spot of Secret
Service work on the side. Ian Fleming must have read chapter 1—"Midnight at the
Casino"—and filed it away for future *Casino Royale* reference. The non–Sallust novel
Such Power Is Dangerous (1933) concerns an attempt to take over the entire Holly-
wood film history—by hook and by crook.

Horler, Charteris, and Wheatley would inspire their own imitators, the most
successful of whom—both in book sales and career longevity—was their fellow

Englishman John Creasey.[74] It is sufficient merely to hint at his fantastic pop-lit career: 500+ novels under 20+ pseudonyms, and more than 60 million copies of his books have been sold worldwide. He created several long-running crime-fiction series, notably the Toff (58 titles), Inspector West (43 titles), the Baron (49 titles: as Anthony Morton), and Gideon (21 titles: as J.J. Marric). Authoritative reference book: *John Creasey—Fact or Fiction? A Candid Commentary in Third Person, With a Bibliography by John Creasey and Robert E. Briney.*[75] Although all these characters became embroiled with espionage from time to time—especially the Baron (real name: John Mannering, an ex–jewel thief turned antiques dealer and erstwhile secret agent)—Creasey's main forays into spy fiction concerned Bruce Murdoch (6 titles), Department Z (28 titles), Dr. [Stanislaus Alexander] Palfrey (31 titles), and Patrick Dawlish (53 titles: as by Gordon Ashe). The Department Z novels are Creasey's most sustained and substantial contribution to spy fiction. They really got going with *The Death Miser.*[76] Its man-about-town hero, the Honourable James Quinion, is effortlessly eclipsed by his lantern-jawed Scottish boss, Gordon Craigie—the first of many operatives to suffer this indignity.

All these idiosyncratic British spymasters—along with Buchan's Sir Walter Bullivant—can be traced back to the aforementioned Captain Mansfield Smith-Cumming, alias C, the original head of what would become MI6. He was first given the full literary treatment in *Ashenden: or, The British Agent,*[77] by W. Somerset Maugham[78]: "The Colonel, who was known in the Intelligence Department, as Ashenden later discovered, by the letter R., rose when he came in and shook hands with him…. He asked Ashenden a good many questions and then, without further to-do, suggested that he had particular qualifications for the secret service. Ashenden was acquainted with several European languages and his profession was excellent cover; on the pretext that he was writing a book he could without attracting attention visit any neutral country."[79]

William Somerset Maugham was a preeminent British dramatist (*The Letter*: 1927), novelist (*Of Human Bondage*: 1915), and short-story writer (*The Trembling of a Leaf*: 1921 collection). Recommended biography: Robert Calder's *Willie: The Life of Somerset Maugham.*[80] During the Great War, Maugham volunteered to become a medic, ambulance driver, and interpreter for a Red Cross unit in France. But he was quickly transferred to the Intelligence Department. His first assignment as a secret agent entailed the investigation of an Englishman living in Lucerne, Switzerland, with a German wife. This would be fictionalized into the is-he-or-isn't-he-a-traitor episode of *Ashenden*, which is a collection of loosely linked short stories. Maugham's literary avatar takes charge of an Allied spy network, with his headquarters in neutral Geneva. Anthony Masters called Maugham the Workaday Spy, in *Literary Agents.*[81] *Ashenden* was filmed by Alfred Hitchcock in 1936, as *The Secret Agent*, which led to his 1937 version of Conrad's novel being retitled *Sabotage* (American title: *A Woman Alone*).

Most "Golden Age" thriller writers followed the *Greenmantle* lead—or that of

Talbot Mundy's (1879–1940) companion piece, *King—of the Khyber Rifles* (the dash is optional), which came out the very same year (1916). The titular Captain Athelstan King is a secret agent of the British Raj in India at the beginning of the Great War. His mission is to stop a Turkish-instigated holy war on the North West Frontier, with the help of the mystical Princess Yasmini and a Turkish mullah called Muhammed Anim. Mundy, an Englishmen whose birth names were William Lancaster Gribbin, was something of an unlovable nomadic rogue before settling in the USA. He also created Jimgrim (James Schuyler Grim), an American Secret Service agent who spent most of his time working for the British Empire in, e.g., *The Nine Unknown* (1924). The prolific Mundy was far more popular in the United States, his adopted country, than in his native United Kingdom. But he played a significant part in how British writers laid the groundwork for what became "modern" spy fiction, during the early twentieth century. At the same time, American spy-fiction writers were evolving along different—although eventually convergent—lines.

CHAPTER THREE

Pulps and Serials

Dime novels—or their lineal descendants—continued to be published, right through the Great War and for some years beyond. For example: *A Woman's Hand; or The Hardest Kind of a Case*, by Nicholas Carter, Street & Smith's New Magnet Library No. 968 (1890; reprinted 1919). More Nick Carter adventures were scheduled for the near future, including *A Broken Bond* (July 1919). Sexton Blake was still strongly righting wrongs in the UK. See *The Casebook of Sexton Blake*,[1] edited by David Stuart Davies. However, dime-novel (and penny-dreadful) publishers would soon go the way of buggy-whip manufacturers, except for those who switched to the Next Big Thing—pulp magazines—during the Depression era.

The term "pulp magazine" derives from the wood-pulp paper used for printing cheap popular-fiction magazines. Acidic residue and abrasive wood particles ensured that all these periodicals were doomed to short-term destruction, unless kept sealed within airtight bags. "Pulp" can also describe the fiction itself, in which characters habitually beat other characters to a pulp. Following Frank A. Munsey (see Chapter One), entrepreneurs like George T. Delacorte (Dell), Aaron A. Wyn (Ace), and Ned L. Pines (Popular Publications) hopped aboard the lucrative pulp bandwagon. Pulp magazines evolved into a standardized format. They measured 10×7 inches (with rare exceptions), contained 128–144 pages (ditto), and the vivid covers were printed on expensive, photographic stock. Frank Gruber (1904–1969), the bestselling mystery and western writer, described what it was like to inhabit "the pulp jungle," in his autobiographical book of the same title.[2]

The best-known—if not always the actual best—of all pulp magazines was *The Black Mask* (April 1920 to July 1951: the definite article was dropped in 1927). In the beginning, *Black Mask* was billed as a "Detective, Mystery, Adventure, Romance and Spiritualism" magazine. All that changed, however, with the successive editorships of George W. Sutton, Philip C. Cody, and—most famously—Joseph Thompson "Cap" Shaw (1874–1952). Ever-more radical stories came from Erle Stanley Gardner (1889–1970), Horace McCoy (1897–1955), Raoul Whitfield (1898–1945), Dashiell Hammett (1895–1961), and Raymond Chandler (1888–1959). Recommended reading: *The Black Mask Boys*,[3] by William F. Nolan. *Black Mask* had mostly kept its distance from spies and spying. Until, as Nolan pointed out: "In the early 1940s [Kenneth S. White, its then editor] ran 'timely' stories of government agents, Nazi villains, and espionage—but these efforts did little to increase circulation."[4]

Chapter 7 of Ron Goulart's *Cheap Thrills*—entitled "Special Agents"—opens with this pithy and punchy paragraph: "All the Federal Bureau of Investigations and the other government undercover agencies had to contend with in the '30s were John Dillinger, Machine Gun Kelly; Ma Barker, Baby Face Nelson and the spies Hitler sent over. In real life, anyway. In the pulps it was a much harder life and the occupational hazards were monumental. Next to the masked mystery men, nobody in the Depression years pulp magazines had more troubles than the spies and secret agents."[5] The "spies and secret agents" in pulp magazines were, much more often than not, star-billed heroes rather than one-off protagonists. It was—to use advertising terminology—a simple matter of brand recognition. *Spy Novels Magazine*, which published only stand-alone stories, lasted for only three issues in 1935, cover-dated February, April, and June. The first issue featured "Dealers of Doom," by William E. Barrett (1900–1986), who would later write two bestselling novels, *The Left Hand of God* (1951) and *The Lilies of the Field* (1962).

An editor/publisher's eye-view of the pulp magazine in its mid–20th-century heyday is to be seen in *Leo Margulies. Giant of the Pulps. His Thrilling, Exciting, and Popular Journey,*[6] by Philip Sherman (nephew of the biographical subject). Leo Margulies (1900–1975) rose to become editorial director of the whole Standard Magazines group. He edited the short-lived *Thrilling Spy Stories* (Fall 1939 to Summer 1940: four quarterly issues). It featured the exploits of a counterspy known simply as the Eagle. For example: "Storm over the Americas" (lengthily subtitled "When Nazi Intrigue Menaces the Panama Canal, the Eagle Swoops Down on a Spy Ring Guarding Hidden Weapons of War!"), by Capt. Kerry McRoberts, in the Fall 1939 issue. Goulart, however, began his survey of pulp-fiction special agents with the more famous and longer-lasting Operator 5: Operator 5 began his career in the middle of the Depression in one of the several [pulps] which were extravagantly alert to the possibility of foreign invasion. The complete title of his magazine was *Secret Service Operator #5*, with the subtitle *America's Undercover Ace*. Signed with the forceful penname Curtis Steele, the Operator 5 novels were initially by Frederick C. Davis."[7]

Frederick Clyde Davis (1902–1977)—or the editorial staff at Popular Publications—did not let physical descriptions of Jimmy Christopher, alias Operator 5, get in the way of the whirlwind action. But here is a thumbnail sketch, from *Legions of Starvation* (December 1934): "He was in his early twenties, yet there was an unshakable confidence in his bearing that added dignity to his years. On the back of his right hand a scar shone. It was a mark of black and white and gray which resembled to an astonishing degree a spread-winged American eagle. There was a tiny charm affixed to his watch-chain fashioned delicately of gold, a skull and crossbones with eyes of ruby-red." Also a skull ring, containing enough high explosive to blow up entire buildings. And just to be on the safe side, he kept a rapier curled up inside his belt. Jimmy (Operator 5) Christopher had a host of helpers, including his topping girlfriend and sometime-in-the-future wife, Diane Elliott. But he spends a lot more time with Tim Donovan, his youthful freckle-faced assistant, who bears an uncanny resemblance to Sexton Blake's Tinker. Just as Jimmy Christopher is a father figure to Tim Donovan, so Operator 5 is himself in patriarchal thrall to his M-type boss, who is "so secretive that few knew that this man was the Commander-in-Chief of the United States Intelligence Service. To even his most trusted agents he was known only by the cryptic designation of Z-7."

The Invisible Empire (May 1934) is a synonym for the "Yellow" Empire, i.e., Japan, which—at the point of bankruptcy—has initiated an undeclared war against the USA (eight years before the actual Japanese attack on Pearl Harbor). Their plan is to force America into handing over its gold reserves, by raining down bombs and poison gas from the *Atlantis*, a camouflaged and unassailable high-altitude airborne fortress. Attack planes are ripped from the sky, pilots hurled frozen to the ground. Even the President's son is taken hostage. Furthermore, Kwo Taska, Chief of the Yellow Empire's Espionage Office, has issued this Most Urgent general order: "*Operator 5 … Dispose of him at all costs and at soonest possible moment … *"

Jimmy Christopher was decommissioned because cold fact had become uncomfortably close to extravagant fiction. The Japanese were still annexing large areas of mainland China as part of their imperial ambitions in the Pacific region. On October 21, 1938, they occupied Canton (now Guangzhou) and surrounded the then British Crown colony of Hong Kong. Recommended reading: Nick Carr's *America's Secret Service Ace: The Operator 5 Story*.[8]

Operator 5's closest competitor in the Pulp Magazine Super-Spy Stakes was the even more cryptically code-named Secret Agent X. Ron Goulart presented a succinct overview of this Man of Mystery character in *Cheap Thrills*:

> Over at Ace [pulp-publishing company] they had Secret Agent X, many of whose problems were alliterative. Every other month he had to worry about such things as "Satan's Syndicate," [August 1937] "Slaves of the Scorpion," [June 1937], "Corpse Contraband" [December 1938], and "The Curse of the Crimson Horde." [September 1938]. X was not exactly a G-man and "his name, if he had one, was unknown. That was exactly as he preferred it. And while he was closely allied with the men of the F.B.I., and sponsored by a powerful Washington official, his unorthodox methods of crime detection had so frequently carried him into lawless shadows that he had been branded a desperate criminal. [His] ability as an impersonator is a combination of superlative voice mimicry, character acting that great Thespians might well envy, and a sculptor-like skill in moulding plastic material over his own features so that they resemble those of another man."[9]

Everything anyone would like to ask about "X" has been answered in *Secret Agent X: A History*,[10] by Tom Johnson and Will Murray. But even they confess themselves baffled on a few basic points. For example: "The exact source of Secret Agent X's unlimited powers as an investigator of crime has never been revealed; however, he does hold a document of commendation from someone high in the nation's trust, a man known only as 'K9' [X ultimately goes to work of a U.S. Government Agency called the K-R group]. The Agent is alert always to defeat the possibility of capture and imprisonment. In his warfare on criminals the law is a constant threat, for they misunderstand his motives [*à la* the early and latter-day Batman], thus he must always be prepared for any eventuality. Rarely in his strange and adventurous career has the Agent ever slain an adversary. The ingenious defensive weapons he employs [e.g., a gas pistol] are not lethal. He prefers, with few exceptions, to work by wit and courage and his masterly disguises."[11] The first issue of *Secret Agent "X"* was cover-dated February 1934, leading with *The Torture Trust*, by Brant House—the most transparent "house name" in all pulp-magazine or paperback history. Paul Chadwick (c. 1902–c. 1972) was the first—but not the last—scribe for *Secret Agent X* (the quotation marks were dropped from the November 1935 issue onward). He wrote 14 of the 38 novellas.

X could have taught 007 a thing or three about the brains-over-brawn kind of unarmed combat. Muscular without being muscle-bound, he was a past master at jui-jitsu (the Japanese for "gentle art"). Jui-jitsu—like judo or kung fu—involves using an attacker's superior physical strength, energy, and weight against him. He can also strike with stiffened fingers against the nerve centers in the human body—but only to stun, never to maim or kill. There was a period of study at a Korean school of martial arts. His main teacher, however, was Tatsuo Shima, chief instructor to the bodyguards of his Imperial Highness, as told in *The Spectral Strangers* (March 1934).

And now for something not-so-completely different. The most exotic—and bestselling—"air pulps" were those that featured a regular series hero with whom readers could identify and build up a strong loyalty factor. And the most durable of these high-flying hero magazines was *G-8 and His Battle Aces*, which lasted from late 1933 until early 1941. All the 110 novellas had been written by Robert J. (Jasper) Hogan (1897–1963), a rare one-author thing in pulp-fiction circles. Hogan's otherwise anonymous air-captain hero was named after his own G-8 ranch—and it also referenced the G for Government Man craze that was then sweeping the country. From *The Flying Spy: A History of G-8*,[12] by Nick Carr: "Chief of Intelligence was an individual known only as A-1. There were times when his participation became very important. Behind a façade of someone who just never looked [very special] rested a brilliant mind. Usually calm, this gentle-voiced American was of medium build, hair greying at the temples. Perhaps the outstanding feature of this mild-mannered person was his eyes. They caught and held attention immediately. It was almost as if A-, like G-8, possessed an identical type of 'mesmerism,' although we never saw any evidence of hypnotic technique as far as he was concerned."[13] America's Master Spy first took to the skies in *The Bat Staffel*, which led the October 1933 issue of *G-8 and His Battle Aces*. It was reprinted in paperback form by Berkley Medallion (1969), the first of an eight-book series.

Two notable superspy aviators came from the typewriter of Donald E. Keyhoe (1897–1988): Captain Philip Strange and Richard Wright, both appearing in *Flying Aces* magazine. Major Donald Edward Keyhoe knew well of what he wrote, having been a U.S. Marine Corps pilot (1919–23) and an aide to Charles Lindbergh after his transatlantic flight. But he would become most famous/notorious for his part in kick-starting the UFO (Unidentified Flying Objects) craze with *The Flying Saucers Are Real*.[14] Strange is strange by name, and stranger by nature. He had a 64-novella run in *Flying Aces*. From *The Great Pulp Heroes*,[15] by Don Hutchinson: "Known as 'the Brain Devil' [and 'the Phantom Ace of G-2'] because of his ESP and other near-occult mental powers, Strange was an ex–child prodigy who had performed feats of magic, ventriloquism and hypnotism in showbiz. Like G-8 [he] was also an ace flier and Intelligence agent who used the art of disguise to confound the machinations of the Kaiser's evil scientists."[16] The first six exploits are available in *Captain Philip Strange: Strange War*.[17] "Keyhoe developed a more contemporary barnstormer in Richard Knight, who was blind as a bat by day but eagle-eyed after dark. Not tied to the Western Front, Knight clocked considerably more miles than [Philip Strange], including flights to the Far East."[18] *Flying Aces* published 35 Knight stories, from 1936 until 1942.

Even more excessive than any of the aforementioned super airmen was Dusty Ayres, who appeared in twelve issues of *Dusty Ayres and His Battle Birds* from July 1934 (*Black Lightning*) to July 1935 (*The White Death*). These dust-up adventures were penned by Robert Sydney Bowen (1900–1977)—though his middle name was bylined as Sidney. Goulart has given us a capsule description of the "Dusty Ayres" series:

> Dusty, often called the Top Eagle of Uncle Sam's Brood, began in 1933 to fight the Next Great War. The recurring problem faced by Dusty Ayres and His Battle Birds was the Blacks. "In Central Asia had arisen a man of mystery [called] Fire-Eyes, Emperor of the World. Without warning, his fierce and cruel armies, who became known as the Black Invaders, had started sweeping across the world, crushing everything that civilized man had built up since the beginning of time. In three years all Europe and Asia was ground beneath the iron hell of Fire-Eyes. And next—the greatest nation of all, the United States of America."[19]

All things considered, Operator #5, Secret Agent X, G8, Dusty Ayres, *et al.*, were—like James Bond to come—more in the nature of loose-cannon counterspies than work-to-rule secret agents. They might have had government spymasters giving out orders, from time to time, but the operational details were left largely up to them. At least these characters had some kind of connection with legally constituted authority, which is more than can be said for snappily named vigilantes like The Phantom Detective, The Spider, The Shadow, and The Avenger. Their rough-justice activities lie far outside the scope of this inquiry. But The Shadow is worthy of an honorable mention, especially since his name will crop up again in later chapters. Goulart devotes a whole chapter ("A.K.A. The Shadow") to him in *Cheap Thrills*, as does Hutchinson, in *The Great Pulp Heroes* ("The Shadow's Shadow"). Hutchinson's dramatic description:

> A generation of radio buffs would intone, "The Shadow is, in reality, Lamont Cranston, wealthy young man about town who, years ago in the Orient, learned the hypnotic power to cloud men's minds so they could not see him." And another generation of pulp story enthusiasts would reply, "Not so." It seems that pulp readers were privy to more confidential disclosures. In the magazine stories Lamont Cranston was but one of the disguises of

the real Shadow who was Kent Allard, an explorer-aviator-adventurer whose identity as the Master of Darkness is known only to two Xinca Indians sworn to eternal secrecy.[20]

In his erudite overview, *The Great Radio Heroes*,[21] Jim Harmon explained: "On radio The Shadow was the name given to a mysterious voice that introduced *Street and Smith's Detective Magazine Hour* by inquiring 'Who knows what evil lurks in the hearts of men?' and then proceeded to answer the question by simply reading a story from the current issue of the crime magazine published by the sponsor. The Shadow character became an instant hit and the whole show was devoted to his own exploits instead of merely introducing other stories. The program became a full-scale drama with actors [including a young Orson Welles], music, and sound effects. Street and Smith also issued a new magazine, *The Shadow Mystery Magazine*."[22] The first issue (cover-dated Winter 1931), led with a novella entitled *The Living Shadow*. It was by Maxwell Grant, a previously unknown writer.

"Maxwell Grant" was, in all truth, Walter B. (Brown) Gibson,[23] who had previously worked on the *Philadelphia Ledger*. As a reporter, young Walter Brown had made the acquaintance of Harry Houdini and Howard Thurston, two famous magicians, for whom he ghost-wrote many books and articles. He wrote 283 Shadow novels, a total of over a million words, over the next sixteen years. The last one, *Return of the Shadow*,[24] appeared in 1963—under his own name, at last. Gibson published several nonfiction books, e.g., *The Complete Illustrated Book of Psychic Sciences*,[25] in collaboration with his wife, Litzka R. Gibson. Biography: *Walter B. Gibson and the Shadow*,[26] by Thomas J. Shimeld.

The most James Bond mastermind–like of all The Shadow's archenemies was Shiwan Khan, who involved the Man of Mystery with cataclysmic capers that would have taxed 007 himself. Frank Eisberger, Jr., summarized the mini-saga as follows, in his *Gangland's Doom: The Shadow of the Pulps*[27]: "Shiwan Khan, descendent of Genghis Khan, would-be ruler of the world, fought The Shadow four times. Unlike other [Sax] Rohmer influenced villains, Khan was no mad racist wishing to annihilate the white race. His goal was power, the same as Napoleon and Stalin and a hundred others wanted it. Khan had great mental abilities—he could mentally communicate and rule men's minds. The Shadow has to use his entire crime fighting force in each battle with Shiwan Khan and he even had to unite forces with a Tibetan high priest before destroying Khan."[28] Running order: *The Golden Master* (September 15, 1939); *Shiwan Khan Returns* (December 1, 1939); *The Invincible Shiwan Khan* (March 1, 1940); *Masters of Death* (May 15, 1940).

Another noteworthy Street and Smith hero who had his very own magazine was Doc Savage. It lasted from cover dates March 1933 (*The Man of Bronze*) until Summer 1949 (*Up from Earth's Center*): 181 entries, all of them told by Kenneth Robeson. Don Hutchinson wrote, in his "Doc!" chapter of *The Great Pulp Heroes*: "A man of superhuman strength and protean genius, whose life is dedicated to the destruction of evildoers, Doc Savage was the original inspiration for literally hundreds of superhuman freaks who, in 1933, were yet to be imagined. There is much to indicate, for instance, that when teenagers Jerry Siegel and Joe Shuster created the comic book adventures of Superman, their model was Doc Savage, The Man of Bronze, who antedated The Man of Steel and *his* host of imitators by several years."[29] Clark (named after Clark Gable) Savage, Jr. = Clark Kent, and Doc owned a *Fortress of Solitude* (October 1938) long before his Kryptonian successor.

Doc Savage was dreamed up by Henry W. Ralston (1897–1955), business manager of Street and Smith, and John L. Nanovic (1905–2001), then editor of *The Shadow* magazine. The character spent a year in development, finally acquiring a team of highly talented sidekicks: William Harper Littlejohn (archaeologist); Colonel John "Renny" Renwick (engineer); Lieutenant Colonel Andrew "Monk" Blodgett Mayfair (chemist); Major Thomas J. "Long Tom" Roberts (an electrical wizard); Brigadier General Theodore Marley "Ham" Brooks. Nanovic drafted a pilot novella—*Doc Savage, Supreme Adventurer*—which remained unpublished for nigh on sixty years.[30]

Ralston and Nanovic chose the 28-year-old Lester Dent[31] to script the new series, as by Kenneth Robeson. *The Man of Bronze* got things off to a good, rousing start. Born in La Plata, Missouri, Dent had worked as a telegrapher and teletype operator at the Tulsa office of Associated Press before landing a house-writer job with Dell in 1930. Among many other successes, Dent would sell two oft-anthologized stories to *Black Mask*, featuring the Floridian treasure-hunting detective Oscar Sail: "Angel" (November 1936) and "Angelfish" (December 1936). But a change of editor—and editorial policy—cost him the chance of furthering his career with that influential magazine. In later years, he published several novels, including *Lady in Peril*,[32] and the posthumously published *Honey in His Mouth*.[33] N.B. Several of the Doc Savage stories were ghostwritten for Dent by William Bogart, Norman Danberg, Alan Hathaway, and Ryerson Johnson.

Doc Savage and his "Amazing Crew" were the freest of free agents, only interacting with government security agencies on their own idiosyncratic terms. But they did fight the good fights against umpteen super-villains bent upon world domination, such as "Khan Nadir Shar, Son of Divinity, Destined Master of Ten Thousand Lances, Khan of Tanar, Ruler of Outer Mongolia"—otherwise known as *The Mystic Mullah* (January 1935).[34] Critical studies of Lester Dent/Kenneth Robeson abound: *Doc Savage: His Apocalyptic Life*,[35] by Philip José Farmer; *The Man Behind Doc Savage*,[36] edited by Robert Weinberg; *Doc Savage* and *Secrets of Doc Savage*,[37] both by Will Murray. A one-off feature film, *Doc Savage: The Man of Bronze* (release date: June 1975), starred Ron Ely (1938–).

Meanwhile, the film serial—or "chapter play"—had been a popular form of escapist cinema since just before the Great War. *Fantomas* (France: 1913–14) encouraged the Selig Polyscope Company to make *The Adventures of Kathryn* (15 episodes: 1913). The Pathé Film Company then premiered the most famous of all silent-film serials—*The Perils of Pauline*—at Loew's Theatre, New York City, on March 23, 1914. The heroine was eponymously played by Pearl (Fay) White (1889–1938). From the mid–1920s until the early 1950s, a thousand and more movie serials did the picture-palace rounds. Recommended reading: *The Great Movie Serials: Their Sound and Fury*,[38] by Jim Harmon and Donald F. Glut.

Fictional detective and/or secret agents appeared in silent movies, with Sherlock Holmes and Sexton supreme among them. The same thing happened after *The Jazz Singer* (1927), starring Al Jolson (1886–1950), heralded the era of "talking" pictures. Most of these pop-lit-character-based series were "B" movies, i.e., short films—seldom more than sixty or seventy minutes long—distributed as the bottom half of a "double bill" with the main feature "A" film. Recommended reading: *The Big Book of B Movies: Or, How Low Was My Budget*,[39] by Robin Cross.

Nick Carter had been translated into several pre–Great War French motion pictures. In 1908, Pierre Bressol played Carter in a six-episode serial, *Nick Carter, le roi des détectives*, made by the Éclair Production Company. Four sequels, starring André Liabel, followed between 1909 and 1912. Back in the USA, Thomas "Tom" Corrigan (1886–1941) essayed the role in 14 films made in 1921, from *The Great Opium Case* to *The Mysterious Bond Case*. The following year, Edmund Lowe (1890–1971) took over the role: *Unseen Foes*; *The Spirit of Evil*; *The Last Call*; *A Game of Graft*. This resilient super-sleuth/spy came to "talkie" cinema in three unusually lavish B movies, made by MGM, which starred Walter Pidgeon (1897–1984), the Canadian-born A-list actor: (1) *Nick Carter, Master Detective* (1939). Director: Jacques Tourneur (1904–1977). "Pidgeon is good, tracking down industrial spy in slickly done detective film. Starts out very snappy, then slows to a crawl and loses its way. Memorable for some striking aerial shots" (Maltin). (2) *Phantom Raiders* (1940); Tourneur, again: "Slick, fast-paced Nick Carter detective story has our hero investigating sabotage in the Panama Canal after Allied ships are sunk" (Maltin). And (3) *Sky Murder* (1940); director: George Seitz (1888–1944). "Pidgeon as detective Nick Carter decides to help refugee Verne [uncover a fifth-columnist spy ring] in above-average private-eye yarn" (Maltin).

"The quality of these endless B's varied from company to company," wrote William K. Everson, in *The Detective in Film*.[40] But Everson gives credit to a now-footnote-fodder series that straddled the line between domestic crime and foreign intrigue: "systematically working its way through alien smuggling, counterfeiting, and other crimes, to be stopped only when star Ronald Reagan (1911–2004), playing daredevil pilot Lt. 'Brass' Bancroft, was promoted to better things [film roles—not yet the Presidency!]. Nevertheless, in 1939–40, *Secret Service of the Air*, *Code of the Secret Service*, *Smashing the Money Ring*, and *Murder in the Air* [1940] managed to cover a lot of territory in the usual high-powered Warner Brothers manner, with stories (and fights and chases) that moved along too fast and too professionally for anyone to notice any holes in logic. Ronald Reagan was a breezy detective, Eddie Foy, Jr., his more sensible-than-usual comedy relief [Gabby Watters], and John Litel [Saxby] their Washington superior."[41]

Serials were aimed squarely at the juvenile audience, especially for midweek and/or Saturday matinees, although many adults enjoyed them as well. The abysmal budgets precluded the participation of top-flight actors, directors, writers, and technicians, so there wasn't much in the way of quality control. And the more far-fetched fantasy, the better. From *An Introduction to American Movies*:[42] "Aside from the excursions of Flash Gordon and Buck Rogers, the serials seldom extended themselves beyond the thriller. In the 1940's, they relied more and more on the comics for material, as in *Batman* (1943), *The Spider Returns* (1941), *The Purple Monster Strikes* (1945), and *King of the Rocket Men* (1949). This childhood world of passwords, elaborate costumes, and dark secrets (although only a juvenile auxiliary of the science fiction medium) exerted a profound influence on two generations of filmgoers."[43]

The comic-book superheroes didn't really get going until during the Second World War, mainly because they hadn't existed before Superman erupted into *Action Comics* #1, June 1938. Batman joined him almost a year later (*Detective Comics* #26, April 1939). Ron Goulart's *Great History of Comic Books*[44] is a good scholarly overview. Newspaper comic strips have been around—in one form or another—since the closing years of the nineteenth century. Background reading: *American Newspaper Comics: An Encyclopedic Reference Guide*,[45] by Allan Holtz, and *The History of the British Newspaper Comic Strip*,[46] by Denis Gifford. Of the detective and counterspy heroes, two stand out for special attention: *Dick Tracy*, and *Secret Agent X-9*.

Dick Tracy was the brainchild of Oklahoma-born commercial artist Chester Gould (1900–1985), who found a home for it with the *Chicago Tribune-New York News Syndicate*. The original character bore the moniker "Plainclothes" Tracy. But Gould's editor, Captain Joseph Medill Patterson (1879–1946), suggested the name change to "Dick"—a colloquial term for any civilian-dressed detective (who also spends a lot of his time "tracing" people). *Dick Tracy* first saw print in the October 4, 1931, edition of the *Detroit Monitor*. Tracy lived and had his roughnecked being in a thinly disguised Chicago that was even more violent than the real thing. Chris Steinbrunner and Otto Penzler gave a succinct description of the "Tracy-verse" in their *Encyclopedia of Mystery and Detection*[47]:

> [Tracy] vows to catch the killers of his sweetheart's father. His square-jawed face, with its hawk nose and lean lines, is an idealized conception of the visage of Sherlock Holmes. A rugged, two-fisted, hard-boiled detective, he is tough enough to handle even the most vicious criminals. The villains with whom he must deal are colourful gangsters whose physical or facial deformities have earned them their names: Pruneface, Flattop (his head resembles an aircraft carrier), the Brow, the Mole (who lives underground), Little Face, B.B. Eyes, the Blank (a faceless killer), Mumbles, and Pear Shape.

Tracy and 007 shared a passion for state-of-the-future-art gadgetry—the movie Bond, at any rate. But Tracy most certainly did not take Bond's permissive attitude to casual love-them-and-leave-them sex. Ultra-violence in the line of duty was a strong common factor, though, with both native criminals and foreign spies getting a hard punch-bag time of it. Ian Fleming must have at least been aware of the comic strip, even if he wasn't a regular reader.

Hollywood soon came knocking on Dick Tracy's door, in the shape of Republic

Pictures (1935–1967), a studio then best-known for B-movie westerns and all-action serials. A 15-episode *Dick Tracy* serial hit cinema screens in 1937 (directed by Ray Taylor and Alan James). Tracy was transformed from a regular, if unorthodox, big-city cop into a government-issue special agent. Finding the right actor to play an oddball character like Dick Tracy was no easy task. From *The Great Movie Serials*: "Naturally no one really had an angular face like the one drawn in the comic strip. [In a *Dick Tracy* TV pilot film made in the late 1960s, an actor was made up to look exactly like the comic-strip Tracy—to unpleasant effect.] Republic's casting office was, however, able to find a handsome young actor who managed to 'suggest' the comic strip features of Dick Tracy, in the line of the jaw, especially, although his nose was not at all angular. He was Ralph Byrd [1909–1952], recently out of a Universal feature, *Chinatown Squad* (1935). Byrd accepted the role and as a result was to be associated with the character of Dick Tracy even after his death of a heart attack when only forty-three years of age."[48] Follow-ups: *Dick Tracy Returns* (1938); *Dick Tracy's G-Men* (1939), *Dick Tracy vs. Crime, Inc.* (1941). The latter serial proved to be so popular that it was re-released in 1952, under the title *Dick Tracy vs. Phantom Empire.*

Republic then passed the Dick Tracy franchise to RKO (= Radio-Keith-Orpheum: 1928 until 1959), a more-upmarket studio that produced classic films like *King Kong* (1933) and *Citizen Kane* (1941). RKO made four feature films based upon the character: *Dick Tracy* (1945); *Dick Tracy vs. Cueball* (1946); *Dick Tracy's Dilemma* (1947); *Dick Tracy Meets Gruesome* (1947). From *The Detective in Film*: "Morgan Conway (1903–1981) was a rather dour Tracy in the first two films and then, fortunately, Ralph Byrd took over again. These were quite elaborate 'B' films, well mounted and making a serious attempt to capture the larger-than-life action and characters of the comic strip."[49]

Steinbrunner and Penzler documented Dick Tracy's career in radio and television: "The program *Dick Tracy* began on Mutual [Broadcasting System] in 1935 and spanned more than a decade, both as a Monday-to-Friday serial and as a weekly series … actor Ned Wever (1902–1984) was Tracy's most familiar voice. Ralph Byrd played Tracy again in an early half-hour television series, *The Adventures of Dick Tracy* (1950–52). In 1960 a group of five-minute color cartoons called *The Dick Tracy Show* were produced in which Tracy (the voice was that of Everett Sloane: 1909–1965) battled humorous juvenile versions of the comic strip's more famous villains … although he left most of the legwork to such newly created cartoon underlings as Hemlock Holmes, Go-Go Gomez, Joe Jitsu and a police squad called the 'Retouchables.'" The 1990 film *Dick Tracy* (produced, directed, and written by Warren Beatty: 1937–) received mixed reviews, but it became a box-office hit regardless. Max Allan Collins (1948–) wrote an above-average novelization.[50] Collins has scripted *Dick Tracy* ever since Chester Gould's death in 1977.

Like most other pulp-magazine and comic-strip/-book heroes, Dick Tracy holds only an entertaining but peripheral place in the spy-fiction pantheon. As the title implies, *Secret Agent-X-9* was a much more realistic—if much less financially successful—detective/spy comic strip than *Dick Tracy*. It ran nationwide from January 22, 1934, until February 10, 1996, under the aegis of King Features Syndicate. X-9 was the joint creation of author (Samuel) Dashiell Hammett[51] and artist Alex (Gillespie) Raymond,[52] who both led illustrious professional lives with other fictional characters.

Dashiell Hammett was born in St. Mary's County, Maryland, and studied at the Baltimore Polytechnic Institute until he was thirteen. He then had a number of jobs, working as a clerk, a stevedore, and—off and on between 1908 and 1922—as a private detective with the Pinkerton Agency. Hammett began writing in 1922, but all his best work was done by 1934. This includes five outstanding novels (see below) and a few dozen short stories, which mostly feature "The Continental Op," an otherwise unnamed self-described fat and middle-aged operative for the Continental Detective Agency. Recommended reading: *The Big Knockover: Selected Stories and Short Novels*.[53] But Hammett's enduring fame rests upon his novels: *Red Harvest* (1929); *The Dain Curse* (1929); *The Maltese Falcon* (1930); *The Glass Key* (1931); *The Thin Man* (1934).

Alex Raymond, who initiated the "look" of *Secret Agent X-9*, was to newspaper comic strips what Dashiell Hammett was to the more literate form of mystery fiction. He was born in New Rochelle, New York. Following the Great Crash of 1929, Raymond enrolled part-time at the Grand Central School of Art in New York City, while employed as a mortgage-broker solicitor. Russ Westover (1886–1966), a former neighbor and now creator of the *Tillie the Toiler* (1921–59) strip for the King Features Syndicate, offered him a job as his assistant. Raymond soon became a regular staff artist, contributing to *Blondie* and *Tim Tyler's Luck*.

The runaway success of *Dick Tracy* led King Features to produce its own hardboiled newspaper strip. But they decided to go one better by making their hero a secret agent—*and* a private eye (his mundane "cover" identity). William Randolph Hearst (1863–1951), the publisher-power behind King Features, issued an action-this-day edict. "I want 'Dash' Hammett to write it, in his own way. And money is no object" (or words to that dictatorial effect). Hammett—who had never evinced much enthusiasm for writing cloak-and-dagger fiction—duly signed a $500-per-week contract stipulating that he produce dialogue and continuity on four stories over the next twelve months. From *Dashiell Hammett. A Life at the Edge*[54]: "It was not uncommon for a writer of Hammett's stature to associate himself with a newspaper comic page. Authors Ring Lardner, Anita Loos, and Gene Fowler had all signed to write original scripts. The money was good, and the artist did most of the work. It was not hard for Hammett to come up with a character and concept; he simply borrowed heavily from his own novels."[55]

It isn't quite true to say that Secret Agent X-9 was a Spy with No Name. He called himself Dexter in Hammett's first story, "The Top" (running from January 22, 1934): "It's not my name, but it'll do." This anemic alias cropped up every now and then. X-9 did briefly serve as an FBI operative, but the "agency" he primarily worked for started off nameless and it would end up that way. "You're The Top" got things off with a bang—several bangs, in fact. Hammett kept the pot boiling away with car crashes, piracy, cryptic messages, and a slew of horrible homicides. But creative differences between Hammett and King Features led to a parting of the ways before the first full year was out.

Bill Blackbeard, in his introduction to *Dashiell Hammett's Secret Agent X-9*,[56] which collected the Hammett/Raymond continuities, intimated that most of the "irregularities" and "gaffes" were caused by what he called "jerry-scripting" of Hammett's original script. "Between the delivery of the first Hammett scenario to the syndicate and the transference to Alex Raymond, a considerable admixture of cuts and alterations seems to have occurred. The notion of X-9 as a government agent using a private detective role as a front was thrown out. The King concept of a completely mysterious agent was clumsily substituted. [As a dire result] X-9's occupation veered back and forth between secret agent and private eye. We had the [supposedly nameless] X-9 ... called upon [via the telephone directory?] to help a rich man out of a jam." The underworld knows and fears him, it seems, but law enforcement officers know him not. All the same, he takes unchallenged control of a murder investigation. Even Edgar Wallace might have balked at this incredible idea.

The Hollywood-bound Hammett cut himself loose from *Secret Agent X-9* immediately after the expiration of his contract. King Features replaced him with Don Moore (1904–1986), a well-established magazine writer/editor, and (in September of 1935) Leslie Charteris, who had recently migrated to the United States, co-scripted with Seton I. Miller (1902–1974). He would eventually write *The Saint* radio series (1945 through 1951), based upon his own Simon Templar character. Charteris wrote three more *Secret Agent X-9* continuities before calling it a day, beginning with *The Phantom Plane* (November 18, 1935, until January 11, 1936). Alex Raymond illustrated two scripts by Moore and one by Charteris.[57] Then he also bade farewell to *Secret Agent X*—but not to King Features Syndicate. He had been commissioned to script (with Don Moore as ghostwriter) and draw *Flash Gordon*, a science fiction newspaper comic strip meant to rival the successful *Buck Rogers in the 25th Century*.

After his World War II military service (1943–46), Major Alex Raymond abandoned *Flash Gordon* (and *Jungle Jim*) for a brand-new syndicated strip entitled *Rip Kirby*, which ran from March 4, 1946, until June 26, 1999. Ex–U.S. Marine (à la Raymond) Remington "Rip" Kirby takes up work as a very different kind of freelance detective (and erstwhile counterspy), more given to "cogitating than fisticuffing" (comic-book chronicler Don Markstein)—and he even wore glasses! Recommended reading: *Alex Raymond: His Life and Art*, by Tom Roberts.[58]

Meanwhile, the *Secret Agent X-9* strip had become a bibliographical cat's cradle that researcher Mark Carlson-Ghost did well to unravel in "Secret Agent X-9: Spies, Strong Women and One Hip Mohawk."[59] (Which leads to the aside that, in *Cat's Cradle* [1963], by Kurt Vonnegut, the character Franklin Hoenikker was nicknamed

Secret Agent X-9 during his high school years.) It's a complex business that cannot quickly be explained in detail. Enough to point out that Mel Graff (1907–1975), the artist/writer from 1940 until 1960, not only married off X-9 but gave him a fixed identity—that of Phil Corrigan (the strip duly changed its title to *Secret Agent Corrigan*). Graff had a character named Phil Cardigan in his own long-running newspaper strip, *The Adventures of Patsy* (1935–75).

Universal—the Hollywood studio most closely associated with King Features Syndicate, e.g., *Tom Tyler's Luck* and *Flash Gordon*—made two serials based upon *Secret Agent X-9*, both of which were imaginatively entitled *Secret Agent X-9*. The 1937 serial starred Scott Kolk (1905–1993) as X-9/Agent Dexter, who has been ordered by Chief FBI agent Wheeler (Larry J. Blake: 1916–1991) to prevent the Belgravian crown jewels from being stolen by a notorious female thief known only as "Brenda." In 1945, the young Lloyd Bridges (1913–1998) took a more charismatic stab at playing X-9—or Phil Corrigan, to give him his new, and possibly even real, name. The action takes place on the inexplicably "neutral" Shadow Island, located somewhere between Formosa and mainland China, which provides the source material for a synthetic aviation fuel code-named Element 722. Chinese agent Ah Fong (Keye Luke: 1904–1991), and lovely Australian spy Lynn Moore (Jan Wiley: 1916–1993) are pitted against a Japanese dragon lady called Nabura (Victoria Horne: 1911–2003). This would be the last comic-strip serial adaptation to be produced by Universal. N.B. Benson Fong: (1916–1987) played Dr. Hakahima.

If there had ever been any talk about producing a *Secret Agent X-9* radio program, it must have remained just that—talk. Wikipedia reports, however: "*Secret Agent X-9* was adapted as a radio drama broadcast on BBC Radio 7 in January 2009, starring Stuart Milligan as X-9 and Connie [*Fawlty Towers*] Booth as Grace Powers. There were four episodes, adapted by Mark Brissenden and directed by Chris Wallis." Also: "An Australian comic book, *Phil Corrigan: Secret Agent X-9*, was published by Atlas Publications between 1948 and 1956. It featured reprints of the newspaper strips."

The Whitman Publishing Company of Racine, Wisconsin, issued two *Secret Agent X-9* volumes under their "Big Little Books" imprint (which ran from 1932 through 1989). Whitman, a subdivision of the Western Printing and Lithographing Company, had been in the children's bookselling business since 1918. Their then-president, Sam Lowe, conceived the notion of a unique book that would be substantial but light enough to be held and perused by young readers. Early examples were palm-of-the-hand sized and averaged 300 pages in length, with sturdy hardboard covers. In next to no time, increasing sales at five-and-dime outlets led to the production of original titles and comic strip/radio/film tie-in editions.

Whitman's first *Secret Agent X-9* (so titled)[60] book was both written and illustrated by Charles Flanders (1907–1973). Dimensions: 4.5" × 3"; 424 pages; 11 chapters. As per usual, the text (12 lines, including numeration and "SECRET AGENT X-9" strapline) is printed on the verso pages, black-and-white illustrations on the recto (apart from the frontispiece). X-9 goes about his own thud-and-blunder merry way, with no backup team whatsoever. Whitman published just one more X-9 book: *Secret Agent X-9 and the Mad Assassin*[61]—published as by "Robert Storm" (the house name used on the newspaper strip from 1936 until 1944). That *ne plus ultra* of pulp-fiction heroes—the Shadow—was also published in the Big Little Book series. For example: *The Shadow and the Ghost Makers*,[62] which had been loosely based upon a same-titled novella in *The Shadow* magazine (October 15, 1932). "Lamont Cranston" also took center soundstage in one movie serial and seven feature films.

Matinée idol Rod La Roque (1898–1969) played the debonair criminologist Lamont Granston [*sic*]?? and Lynn Anders (1913–2008) Marcia Delthern in *The Shadow Strikes* (Grand National, 1937) B movie. Director: Lynn Shores (1893–1949). It was "based on the Street & Smith story, *The Ghost of the Manor*" (June 15, 1933). Maltin: "[Here] the character out of cloak seems more like Philo Vance than he did on the radio or in the pulps." La Roque played Lamont Cranston in *International Crime* (Grand National, 1938). Director: Charles Lamont (1896–1993). Cranston is a crime reporter who hosts a daily radio program and who also tracks down secret agents of pre–World War II foreign powers. He often identifies himself as the Shadow—but only on the air, never in real life. No cloak, no slouch hat, no brace of automatic pistols. Astrid Allwyn (1905–1978) portrayed Phoebe—not Margo—Lane, his ditzy secretary and would-be radio star. The film was ostensibly followed by *Foxhound* (June 15, 1937), a Shadow novella written by Theodore L. Tinsley (1894–1979). Maltin: "Breezy, entertaining quickie [61 minutes] is graced with snappy dialogue and the presence of witty, urbane La Roque, who at one point wryly admits, 'The Shadow doesn't know.' Far better than his first *Shadow* outing...."

The Shadow returned in *The Shadow Returns*, the first of three budget-challenged B movies released by Monogram Pictures in 1946. Directors: Phil Rosen (1888–1951) and the uncredited William ("One Shot") Beaudine (1892–1970). Kane Richmond (1906–1973) essayed the role of Lamont Cranston, while Barbara Read (1917–1963) played Margo Lane—as they did throughout the trilogy. Tough taxi driver Moe Shrevnitz (Tom Dugan 1889–1955) was transplanted from the radio and magazine stories to be the comic-relief "Shrevvie" character. Steinbrunner and Penzler: "The eerie opening scene takes place in a cemetery, and the action occurs mainly within the familiar walls of a murder mansion. [The Shadow] discovers gems that contain secret formulas and also uncovers a 'murder method' that causes the victims to fall from balconies." Same-year sequels, both directed by Phil Karlson (1908–1982): *Behind the Mask* and *The Missing Lady*. Background reading: *The Monogram Checklist: The Films of Monogram Pictures*,[63] by Ted Okuda.

Invisible Agent was cobbled together by Republic in 1958, from the two pilot episodes for an unsold *Shadow* TV series, one of which had been directed by eminent cinematographer James Wong Howe (1899–1976). (The other directors being Ben Parker and John Sledge.) Screenplay credit went to George Bellak (1917–1955) and Ruth Jeffries (1917–1995)—with some unsung help from Shadow creator Walter B.

Gibson. Richard Derr (1919–2002) played Lamont Cranston. Helen Westcott (1918–1992) provided the love interest (Tara O'Neill, not Margo Lane). It was rereleased in 1962, as *Bourbon Street Shadows*, by the Louisiana-based MPA Films, who added some "adult" scenes. Steinbrunner and Penzler: "In this film Cranston has the power to become invisible, having learned how to cloud men's minds from an Oriental mystic named Jogendra (Mark Daniels 1916–1990) who has accompanied him to New Orleans."

It would take forty-six years for the next film to appear. *The Shadow* was a big-budget Hollywood blockbuster starring Alec Baldwin (Lamont Cranston), Penelope Ann Miller (Margo Lane), and Peter Boyle (Moses "Moe" Shrevnitz). John Lone made an effective Shiwan Khan, the most villainous of all the *Shadow* magazine villains. Director: Russell Mulcahy. Writer: David Koepp. Critical reception was mixed. Maltin: "…comes frustratingly close to working, but fails. Cranston is both inscrutable and uninteresting. Great production design and wonderful effects get lost in a movie which keeps the viewer at arm's length throughout."[64] James Luceno wrote the better-received novelization,[65] which went with the idea that the Shadow's real secret identity was Kent Allard. See *The Shadow's Shadow* (February 1, 1933) and *The Shadow Unmasks* (August 1, 1937).

Perhaps the perfect actor to play the Shadow did so in the most imperfect cinematic adaptation. Victor Jory (1902–1982) not only *looked* the part in the 1940 Columbia Pictures serial, but he also *acted* the part, whenever the hackneyed script (by Joseph O'Donnell, Ned Dandy, and Joseph Poland) gave him the chance. The naturally hawk-named Jory—who could play both heroes and villains with equal facility—also had the spine-chilling laugh down to a sonic T. Cranston employed a backup secret identity, as the Oriental Lin Chang. Veda Ann Borg (1915–1973) made an equally impressive, if somewhat sarcastic, Margo Lane. Harry Vincent, the Shadow's regular sidekick, was played by Roger Moore (1901–1982)—*not* the future 007 actor of that name, who'd have just entered his teenage years at the time. Director James W. Horne (1881–1942) kept the 15 chapters going at a headlong and even headcase pace. N.B. Philip Ahn (1901–1999) had a small part as Wu Yung. Ahn achieved his greatest fame playing Master Kan in the TV series *Kung Fu* (1972–75). He was also the first Korean-American actor to be awarded a star on the Hollywood Walk of Fame. He was the Spider, well-described by Don Hutchinson:

> For a solid decade, from [*The Spider Strikes*, October 1933] to [*Recruit for the Spider Legion*, March 1943], the Spider—cryptically billed as "the Master of Men"—entranced loyal readers who may have found the Shadow too tame for jaded tastes. Even compared to his chief rival in the phantom hero game, the Spider was one creepy character. Beneath the fright rags and vampire make-up lurked Richard Wentworth, millionaire philanthropist. He gave thousands of dollars to the poor, and relaxed by playing his Stradivarius like a virtuoso; but as the Spider he killed without mercy and used his cigarette lighter to brand the foreheads of murdered thugs and their gloating masters with a vermilion seal of tensed hairy legs and poison fangs—his weird symbol of swift and ruthless justice.[66]

The first two Spider novels, *The Spider Strikes* (see above) and *The Wheel of Death* (November 1933) were written by R.T.M. (Reginald Thomas Maitland) Scott (1882–1966). All the other Spider novellas bore the "Grant Stockbridge" house name—mostly used by the infinitely more flamboyant Norwell W. Page (1906–1961)—from *Wings of the Black Death* (December 1933) onward.

Although *The Spider* pulp magazine sold in respectable quantities, it never matched the high circulation figures of its newsstand archenemy. The Shadow, to be sure, had the advantage of a nationwide radio series, and a more clean-cut brand image. All that sadomasochistic violence might have turned off more readers than it turned on. And yet, as Harmon and Glut point out, *The Spider's Web* in 1938 managed to "suggest the frantic pace of the novels" and the Columbia Pictures movie serial (directed by old hands James W. Horne and Ray Taylor) "accurately retained many minor characters and details" from the source material. They go on to write: "Warren Hull (1903–1974) was a reasonable choice for the Spider's alter-ego, Richard Wentworth. His costume as the Spider was too flamboyant, with a huge cape embroidered with webbing, but Hollywood had to be granted some licence, one supposes. Iris Meredith (1903–1972) was an attractive and unusually efficient (for a serial heroine) Nita Van Sloan."[67]

The Spider Returns (1941) was the most popular film serial of its year, according to a straw poll published in *The Motion Picture Herald*.[68] Warren Hull and Kenne Duncan reprised their roles as the Spider and Ram Singh, but Nita Van Sloan was played by Mary Ainslee (1919–1991). Richard Wentworth is called out of his wedded-bliss retirement to thwart the villainous Gargoyle (played by—*spoiler alert*—Corbet Harris), whose gang is employing industrial sabotage and mass murder in a bid to disrupt the American national defense system. The voice of the villainous Gargoyle was provided by Forrest Taylor (1885–1965). Wentworth acts more like a G-man counterspy than a masked vigilante in this outing. N.B. *The Spider Returns* was not given a British release until 1943, in an edited 80-minute feature-film version.

For whatever reasons there might be, the Spider has never taken the same hold on the collective national/international imagination as the Shadow. There was, however, a two-book flurry from Berkley Books in 1969: *Wings of the Black Death* (see above) and *City of Flaming Shadows* (January 1934). Critical study: *Spider*, by Robert Sampson.[69] Philip José Farmer provides a delightfully demented form of literary genealogy in *Tarzan Alive: A Definitive Biography of Lord Greystoke*.[70] He proves—to his own satisfaction, at any rate—that Kent Allard/Lamont Cranston, Richard Wentworth, and G-8 are, in fact, one and the same person.

The Great Movie Serials were, indeed, full of "sound and fury"—signifying not all that much, especially where "serious" espionage fiction was concerned. But the same criticism could just as well be leveled at the James Bond novels or many another "literary" spy-thriller series. "Sense of wonder" was the main leave-your-brains-outside-the-cinema thing. At the same mid–1930s time, however, two well-respected American mainstream authors were taking a shot at writing spy fiction—F. Van Wyck Mason and John P. Marquand.

CHAPTER FOUR

Hugh North Sees It Through

Pulp magazines were at the extreme opposite end of the publishing spectrum from the respectable slick magazines. The term "slick" derived from the high-quality, photographic paper on which mass-market weeklies like *Collier's*, *Esquire*, and *The Saturday Evening Post*—the lineal descendants of *Harper's New Monthly* (founded in June 1850)—were printed. Unlike pulps, however, these prestigious periodicals relied heavily upon regular "glossy" advertising to offset their expensive production costs and the top-dollar fees necessarily paid to attract such Big-Name writers as F. Scott Fitzgerald and C.S. ("Hornblower") Forester. P.G. Wodehouse once remarked that he might earn $50 per story from a pulp magazine but could made upwards of $300 from a slick magazine for a story of the same length.

But the slicks finally gave way to the competition generated by cheap paperbacks and the new mass-market "girlie" magazines like *Playboy* (first issue: December 1953), which attracted more advertisers and could afford to outbid them for bestselling contributors. By the late 1970s, most of them had either folded or become shadows of their former selves. While the slicks lasted, however, they provided an "escape route" for ambitious pulp-fiction writers and a "found money" source of serialization income for mainstream novelists. Among the latter was F. Van Wyck Mason[1]—who created the American James Bond, long before 007 was even a gleam in Ian Fleming's brain.

Francis Van Wyck (pronounced "wike") Mason was born in Boston, Massachusetts, the son of Ermengarde "Emma" Arville (*née* Coffin) and Francis Payne Mason, who were both descended from 17th century British and Dutch immigrants to North America. Mason spent his first eight years in Europe, where his paternal grandfather served as the American Consul in Berlin and Paris. "I didn't learn English until I was nearly ten," Mason told interviewer Robert Van Gelder. "I spoke French."[2] Mason's Illinois high school education was cut short in 1917, when he volunteered to be an ambulance driver with the French Army, based in the Verdun sector. Mason then transferred to the United States Army, as an artillery officer. After celebrating Armistice Day (and his 17th birthday) on November 11, 1918, Second Lieutenant Mason soldiered on with the Allied Expeditionary Forces until the summer of 1919.

Mason attended Berkshire School, Sheffield, Massachusetts (1919–20). He then took a Bachelor of Science degree course at Harvard University (graduating in 1924).

His college days were not completely without incident. From the dust jacket blurb to *The Branded Spy Murders*:[3] "Mr. Mason claims the distinction of being one author who has actually been arrested for murder. He was returning from a party in a borrowed dinner coat during his Harvard days. The police were looking for a waiter who had committed a gruesome murder. They spied Mr. Mason in what they mistook for a waiter's coat and took him to jail. When they discovered that every garment the culprit wore was marked with initials other than his own, they locked him up. And there he cooled his heels until friends answered his S.O.S. the next morning."

The untimely death of his father meant that Mason had to forget about joining the U.S. Diplomatic Corps and focus upon running a Universal Imports–type business. For the next few years, he roamed the world buying antique furniture, rugs, old maps, and antiquarian books. Based in New York, Mason did not neglect his military duties: second lieutenant, New York National Guard (1924–29); sergeant, Maryland National Guard Field Artillery (1930–33). Time was also found for polo and hunting expeditions. On November 26, 1927, Mason married Dorothy Louise Macready. They would have two children: Francis Van Wyck II and Robert Ashton.

Then, in 1927, a conversation between Mason and Canadian-born John Gallishaw, one of his old college professors, led him to consider freelance fiction writing as a full-time career. He joined Gallishaw's creative-writing course, with the proviso that the course fees would be paid for out of future short-story sales.[4] With true military precision, Mason devised a plan of action and put it into practice. As by F.V.W. Mason, he had eleven stories published in various pulp magazines during 1928: from "The Fetish of Sergeant M'Gourra" (*The Danger Trail*, May) to "The Sword of Vengeance" (*Argosy All-Story Weekly*, December 22 and 29, January 5, 1929). Fifteen stories followed in 1929. Random sampling: from "The Doubting Legionnaire Terris" (*Adventure Trails,* January: with the Kipling-esque "Yank & 'Ector") to "Spoils of the Sargasso" (*Flyers,* December). He was, moreover, preoccupied with writing his first full-length novel, the historical epic *Captain Nemesis* (*Argosy All-Story Weekly*, May 30, April 6, 13, 20, and 27). It wasn't long before Mason not only paid off the course fees but also had a large house built in Riderwood (on the outskirts of Baltimore, Maryland). Over the next several years, Mason made his main mark with serialized historical novels for *Argosy All-Story Weekly*, four of which had the word "captain" in their titles: *Captain Judas* (April 4, 11, 18, 25 & May 9, 1931); *Captain Renegade* (April 4, 11, 18, 25, and May 9, 1931); *Captain Redspurs* (September 30, October 7, 14, 21, 29 & November 1933); *Captain Long Knife* (December 29, 1934, January 5, 12, 19, 26, and February 2, 1935).[5] *Lysander of Chios* (June 15, 22, 29 & July 6, 15, 20, 27, 1935) was later rewritten as simply *Lysander*.[6] *The Barbarian* (May 19, 26 & June 2, 16, 23, 1934)—later *The Barbarians*[7]—will repay special attention.

Mason had set his novel during the Second Punic War (218 to 201 BC), one of three distinct conflicts between Carthage (a Phoenician colony located in modern-day Tunisia) and the fast-rising Roman Republic. Rome declared war when the Carthaginians, commanded by Hannibal Barca (247 to 183 BC), captured the Iberian

(Spanish) city of Saguntum (now Sagunto). Hannibal then crossed the Alps with a small army, strengthened with 37 combat-trained elephants. Harold Lamb (1892–1962), one of Mason's pulp magazine-to-hardcover contemporaries, wrote the biographical *Hannibal: One Man Against Rome*.[8] Mason alludes to the relevant historical background, but he doesn't let the Devil bog him down in too much detail. A pseudo-scholarly foreword sets the scene: "*Waxen writing tablet discovered in the excavation of the ruins of the ancient citadel of The Byrsa in Carthage, found by Dr. Raoul Gearrabrandt of the Brussels Archaeological Society and Dr. Philip Piecky of Amsterdam on September 28, 1952.*"

The Barbarians/Lysander formed part of the 1950s historical-fiction boom, both in hardcover and paperback original novels. A whole generation of authors rode high on this bestseller tide, including the two famous Franks: Frank G. Slaughter (1908–2001), e.g., *The Song of Ruth* (1954), and Frank Yerby (1916–1991), e.g., *The Saracen Blade* (1952). From 1949 (*Samson and Delilah*) to 1964 (*The Fall of the Roman Empire*), historical epics dominated Hollywood. It is no coincidence that epics flourished during the years when the upstart television industry was eating into studio profits. *The Robe* (1953), based upon the bestselling novel by Lloyd C. Douglas (1877–1951), was the first film to be shot in the widescreen process known as Cinemascope. Movies became bigger and bigger—if not always better and better. Recommended reading: *The Hollywood History of the World*,[9] by George MacDonald Fraser.

The Barbarians would become the only one of Mason's oft-optioned historical novels to make it on-screen—in a roundabout way, and under several different titles. It was originally the pilot episode for a projected 90-minute TV mini-series, covering the entire novel, but the project fell through. Production values were unusually high, being filmed on location in Italy at a then-record cost of $750,000. The director was Rudolph Maté (1898–1964)—the eminent Polish-Hungarian cinematographer—and it had a literate script by John Lee Mahon and Martin Rackin. Main cast list: Jack Palance (1919–2006: Revak); Milly Vitale (1932–2006: Princess Cherata); Guy Rolfe (1911–2003: Kainus, Governor of Carthage).

Apart from *Return of the Eagles*,[10] Mason's other 24 historical novels were published in hardcover, often after serialization in upmarket slick magazines. *Eagle in the Sky*[11] is an exception, actually having "*This novel has not been serialized before publication*" emblazoned on its dust jacket. Dedication: "To my uncle ROCKWELL A. COFFIN, M.D. A very gifted physician." N.B. The author's middle name is spelled with the lowercase initial "v," which morphed into the higher-case "V" over the years. *Eagle in the Sky* was the latest in a long line of bestselling Mason historical novels that had helped him get off the pulp-magazine treadmill. The breakthrough novel had been *Three Harbours*,[12] which dealt with the founding of the American Navy during the pre–Revolutionary years.

Mason's research was impeccable, though always geared to the needs of the story. He once wrote: "The main facts, dates and figures are as nearly correct as a painstaking and selective research can make them. The same also applies to such details as uniforms, military movements, legal proceedings, customs, currency and documents. The writer of a novel which employs a historical setting is, I believe, to the careful historian somewhat as a landscape painter to an architect.... Therefore, in the selection of incidents used in this tale, I have necessarily omitted or glossed over some historical events of great importance which unfortunately did not bear on the story."[13]

Mason was appointed Chief Historian for SHAPE (Supreme Headquarters, Allied Expeditionary Force) from 1942 until 1945. Among his official duties was the editing of an ultra-patriotic volume entitled *The Fighting American*.[14] As "Frank W. Mason" he also wrote three juvenile (or Young Adult) novels: *Q-Boats* (1943); *Pilots, Man Your Planes!* (1944); *Flight into Danger* (1946). His post–Second World War historical novels include *Cutlass Empire*[15] (about Sir Henry Morgan) and *The Brimstone Club*[16] (a thinly veiled version of the notorious 18th-century Hellfire Club: founded by Sir Francis Dashwood).

Along the way, Mason was establishing his parallel literary career as a writer of mystery fiction, initially with pulp magazines. For example: "The Shadow of the Leopard" *Detective Action Stories* (December 1930) and "The Vanishing Millionairess" (ditto, January 1931). "Charles Kane" featured in two other yarns for *Detective Action Stories*: "The Mystery of the Strange Explosions" (October 1930); "The Murders at Fort Sangre" (June 1931). There was more than a touch of E. Phillips Oppenheim about these stories. The same observation can be applied to Mason's early mystery novels, of which *Spider House*[17] and *Murder in the Senate*[18] can bear silent witness. The "locked-room mystery" of *Spider House* is unraveled by Captain Catlin, who works out that the real murder weapon was a horn-tipped arrow—not a gun, as formerly thought. Mason would avoid this kind of subgenre stuff in future plotlines. Inspector Scott Stuart starred in the latter novel, co-written by one Helen Brawner and published as by Geoffrey Coffin.

Mason, however, had come up against the same problem that then (c. 1928–29) faced his British contemporary, Leslie Charteris: i.e., choosing a viable series character who could be taken "off the shelf" for every new story or novel. The detective/spy characters already "in stock"—Major Stalker (e.g., "Death Is Trumps": *Three Star Stories*, February 1929), Charles Kane, and Scott Stuart—were good enough in the short run, but they lacked the necessary charisma and/or staying power. As it happened, the right man for the job made his presence felt at just the right time— Captain Hugh North, who was vaguely attached to an even vaguer Intelligence organization.

North first appeared in "Anti-Tank" (*Three Star Short Stories*, April 1, 1929) and "Kamerad" (ditto, April 2, 1929). He would feature in several more short stories over the next ten years, from "Murder on Swan Island" (*Detective Fiction Weekly*, May 26, 1934) to "An Enemy at the Dinner Table" (*Short Stories*, June 25, 1937: aka 'The Plum Coloured Corpse,' in *The Saint Detective Magazine*, September 1956). But Mason quickly saw Hugh North's potential as a moneymaking hero of novel-length mystery fiction, à la Charteris and the Saint. As Richard Dalby has pointed out (in his *Book and Magazine Collector* article: No. 313, November 2009), *Seeds of Murder*[19] coincided with the death of Sir Arthur Conan Doyle. Captain North happens to be at a dinner party thrown by an affluent stockbroker. The host's partner is found hanged—a suspected suicide. Then the host himself is stabbed to death. And what of the three seeds found at each death scene … ?

The Vesper Service Murders[20] followed a year later. North investigates the murder of a fellow officer, deciphering tricky codes and puzzles. "Vesper" is an unidentified traitor from the Great War. Early North novels are traditional whodunits, quite "pulpy" in style, in which the sleuth's connection with army Intelligence is only of accidental significance (in *Vesper*, he investigates the death of a fellow officer, deciphering tricky codes and puzzles). His first two exploits are, indeed, narrated by the very Watsonian Dr. Walter Allan. The Good Doctor Allan—who mostly just got in everybody's way—was given the old heave-ho after *The Fort Terror Murders* (set in the Philippines).[21]

Hugh North followed much the same military career path as Mason himself (see below). Dust jacket blurbs also likened North's physical appearance to that of his creator. A composite description: Tall, sun-bronzed, with high cheekbones, suggesting Native American ancestry; a neatly trimmed mustache; and distinctive patches of gray at the temples. Imagine, if you will, the British-born actor Stewart Granger (1913–1993) playing white hunter Allan Quatermain in the 1950 film *King Solomon's Mines* (loosely based upon the 1885 novel by H. Rider Haggard). The mustache could be on loan from the invariably debonair David Niven (1910–1983), who personified Phileas Fogg in *Around the World in 80 Days* (1956).

It seems that Mason couldn't make up his mind whether Captain Hugh North was an army intelligence officer who did some amateur-detective work on the side or the other way round. But things were about to improve, if not quite beyond all recognition. J. Randolph Cox (in *Twentieth-Century Crime & Mystery Writers*):

> These early novels may be called unsophisticated melodrama. They are delightfully dated by a few over-written passages of suspense, a heritage of Mason's pulp training. By the fourth novel, *The Yellow Arrow Murders*,[22] with North assigned by G-2 to get the secret of the Doelger torpedo and solve the murder of a Navy Intelligence agent, the series becomes *sophisticated* melodrama.
>
> Stripped to their essential detective structure, the novels involve a problem for North to solve which includes a series of murders and a puzzle to unravel. This may be a message to be deciphered, the true meaning of a word or phrase, or the location of a treasure, all of which become keys to the larger mystery.

N.B. "G-2 refers to the military intelligence staff of a unit in the United States Army. It is contrasted with G-1 (personnel), G-3 (operations), G-4 (logistics) and G-5 (civil-military operations)" (from the United States Intelligence Official Website, courtesy of Wikipedia).

The "Hugh North" novels might not have outsold Mason's historical novels, but they kept their author in a lot more than just beer money. Over the next few years, a winning formula was developed, with Captain North as more of an intrepid man of action than introspective armchair detective. Slow to anger, but best avoided whenever his blood was up. Checklist (Doubleday, unless otherwise stated):

The Branded Spy Murders (see above). North is in Honolulu, chasing a suspected Russian spy. Then he finds himself investigating the—possibly related—murder of a young woman.

The Shanghai Bund Murders (1933). North finds evidence of powerful new Chinese secret weapons, hidden in a coin. Revised as *The China Sea Murders* (Pocket Books, New York, 1957).

The Sulu Sea Murders (1933). Takes place in the Sulu Archipelago, a group of about 870 islands off southwest Mindanao in the Philippines. Later revised (Pocket Books, New York, 1957).

The Budapest Parade Murders (1935) "Make it a point to read this book, if you like speed, action and thrilling situations" (*The New York Times*: cited on front cover of bestselling Mystery paperback edition, 1945).

The Washington Legation Murders (1936). North tracks down spies who are trying to steal plans of the latest American military technology, finding murder and a green-glowing skeleton along the way!

The Seven Seas Murders: Four Cases in the Career of Captain North (1936). Contents: ("Shanghai Sanctuary"; "The Repeater"; "The Port of Intrigue"); "The Munitions Ship Murders."

The Hong Kong Airbase Murders (1937). North is in the British crown colony of Hong Kong. He has been sent to protect the formula for a new fuel that can vastly increase an aircraft's range. It is, of course, stolen immediately upon his arrival.

The Cairo Garter Murders (1938). North is enjoying a rest-and-recreation leave in the South of France. But he must cut it short to help his agent friend, Sam Kilgour, smash a gang of gunrunners.

By the time Mason wrote *The Singapore Exile Murders* (1939), Captain Hugh North had matured to match his creator's increasingly more matter-of-fact literary style.

Mason managed to get across the geopolitical temper of those uncertain times—without hitting his readers over the head with heavy encyclopedic facts, à la Dennis Wheatley. As the above titles indicate, Hugh North's roving commission took him from the continental United States to the Far East and any number of points between. *The Singapore Exile Murders* is particularly good at explaining the complex relationship between the European colonial powers in the Orient and—it must be said—the no-less imperialistic Americans, who then held the Philippines within their benign sphere of influence. There is, for example, a revealing dialogue—in more ways than one—between North and Curtis Taylor, the U.S. Consul General in Singapore:

> North held a light to his pipe, raised an eyebrow and asked, "What seems to be the attitude of our British cousins?"

"Friendly."

"Thank God! If there's one outfit I don't like to buck against it's the Johnny Bulls. Ever think of it, Mr. Taylor? They're a lot like the baby-doll type of chorus girl who looks up so trustingly at you with wide, innocent blue eyes and gets a mink wrap out of you before she's done."[23]

On a more personal level:

[Taylor removed] from his safe a long cardboard cylinder and a fat envelope bright with official seals. Both were addressed to "Major Hugh North, U.S.A."

It was odd to think of himself as a major—he'd been a captain so long. Some of the frail sex fell harder for a major's maple leaves than for a captain's bars.[24]

North was 38 years of age at this point in his career. Captain—no, Major—Hugh North eventually wins the day, along with the heart of his latest fair lady *de jour*:

For the first time in years, Madé [Sayu] felt her eyes fill. And she believed that, long ago, her capacity for grief had been stamped out. "Ah, Hugh, *mon brave* Hugh. You must not leave me. I—I could not bear that!"

"Welldon is coming to the fishing village," [Hugh] announced, catching her in his arms. "But first he must talk by radio to a ship, a warship of the United States. He will not meet me till midnight and now it is ten o'clock."

"Two hours, then, is all we shall have?" Madé sighed as her arms slipped up about his neck.

"Two hours—tonight."

"Ah, my own, my love," she whispered.

The glowing Buddha seemed to smile more radiantly than ever.[25]

As well it might.

Hugh North generally prefers to use his "little grey cells" (à la Hercule Poirot) than flex his "mighty thews" (ditto Tarzan). But he is very well-versed in the manly arts of self-defense—especially good old-fashioned roughhousing. For example:

The Japanese stepped closer, bronze-coloured features heavy with menace. "You give."

Slowly North got up. He raised the supper tray a trifle in search of the fold of letter paper he knew lay beneath. He drew it out and offered it so quickly that the gunman's eyes flickered downward. In that instant North's other hand flung the contents of the pepper dish into the fellow's face.

Before the Japanese was able to give even a startled gasp, North had belted the pistol free and, hurdling the table, landed on the gunman with the full impact of a hundred and seventy pounds. Hissing like a furious serpent, the Japanese rolled blindly about trying to claw the spice from his eyes. A carefully calculated right to the gunman's jaw stretched him inert.

Panting slightly, North retrieved his towel then methodically searched the intruder. There was nothing of interest on him.[26]

North, in reply to Joan Buckley asking him if he knew Singapore: "Only by hearsay. 'Drinks, stinks, Chinks' is the way some people describe it. It's got the reputation of being the hardest-drinking city in the East—and *that's* something."[27] The British writer James Hadley Chase (1906–1985) was even more offhandedly racist less than a year later, with his titular *Twelve Chinks and a Woman*.[28]

A long scholarly monograph might be penned about "The Journeys of Hugh

North," much like the travelogue chapter in Hugh Chancellor's *James Bond: The Man and His World*. His final approach to Singapore aboard an Imperial Airways (which operated between 1924 and 1939) seaplane would be one of the scenic highlights:

> Under a smoke smudge of a peculiar bronze green, Singapore lay sprawled in a gigantic semicircle within a cordon of rubber plantations, golf courses and oil tanks. The smoke, North soon saw, was rising from a series of smelters situated on an island not far offshore. Rising vertically, the fumes climbed until they reached a cool air current where they flattened out, creating the effect of a titanic shade tree for the city.
> The smallness of the island upon which Singapore was built soon became apparent. North caught a view of two magnificent harbours crowded with shipping. Keenly curious, he picked out in succession the great new naval base, a military airport and Number IX, the famous floating dry dock. He wondered how many people over yonder were aware that a Japanese cruiser, with scouting plane aloft, idled not fifty miles away.[29]

Nor did Mason ever stint on the description of exotic culinary delights, enjoyed in equally exotic and delightful settings:

> After a clear soup made of native vegetables, baked turtle eggs were served. On the terrace, a native *gamélin* orchestra commenced to play; softly the musicians struck bells of varying pitch. Miss Van Vleck, at North's elbow, identified the *gangsas* or treble bells. She spoke of Bali and the beauty of life there. She made him see furious cock fights, gay dance festivals which continued for weeks at a time. She described sweet-toned wooden bells worn by the fat white cattle and sketched for his mind's eye the infinitely intricate friezes along temple walls.... At last the *rijst-taffel* was brought in; platters, heaped with rice and chicken, or mutton, or beef, or pork, followed in rapid succession. All were swimming in a fiery curry sauce.[30]

The Spirit—almost the Letter—of James Bond to Come. It beggars belief that an eclectic bibliophile like Ian Fleming (he had co-founded *The Book Collector* magazine in 1952) would not have known about the Hugh North novels, which were published in the UK by Eldon Press, Jarrolds, Arthur Barker, and Robert Hale. And he must have caught sight, at least, of the American hardcover and paperback editions during his many wartime liaison missions. Not to mention the slick-magazine serializations.

The shadow of what would soon come to be called the Second World War hangs over *The Singapore Exile Murders*: "On his way to detective headquarters on Robinson Road [Hugh North] sensed an official activity which, with each passing hour, was gathering momentum. Everywhere he encountered scenes reminiscent of late July 1914. Army, naval, and volunteer-force lorries and official cars sped about on errands. A great rash of Union Jacks was breaking out all over the city. In front of newspaper offices, amazed polyglot crowds stood reading bulletins posted from time to time, in English, Chinese and Malay. 'Russian Divisions Mass on Polish Border,' read a notice pasted to the hoardings of the Straits Settlements *Gazette*. Below it was another: 'Soviets Will Fight if Poland Joins Hitler.' 'Chamberlain Flies to Conference.' 'Czechs in Defiant Mood.'"[31]

Singapore Exile can be seen as a thematic template for just about every Hugh North novel. Reduced to the bare essentials, North is assigned—or falls into—a mission that involves at least one gruesome murder and some Gordian Knotty problems to unravel. These usually entail a cryptic message that must be decoded (a radiogram, in this case), a seemingly innocent word or phrase "seeded" here and there, the location of (say) buried treasure, and the recovery of a stolen scientific formula or international treaty. A brace of beautiful women is *de rigueur*—one bad in a good way and one bad all the way through (who might temporarily break Hugh's heart). A dastardly villain—of foreign and preferably mixed nationality. There must be an occasional outbreak of violence, to liven things up and show Our Hero in perilous physical action. All of this "shaken and stirred" with hard-drinking gastronomical interludes, well-researched think pieces, and local-color articles worthy of publication in *National Geographic* magazine. Nobody ever actually says "We were expecting you, Mr. North," but….

Fate then directs Major Hugh North to a splendid villa in Romania, where he must solve *The Bucharest Ballerina Murders* (1940). North also joins yet another hunt for yet another vital formula and romances the exotic Contessa di Bruno—who is actually Connie Fletcher, all the way from Kansas. Brazil comes next, in *The Rio Casino Murders* (1941). North has been tasked to find a ship—name and destination unhelpfully not known—which carries gold bullion meant to finance a revolution. Mason "stood down" North for the duration of World War II, being preoccupied with his own reactivated military career (see above). Three "omnibus" volumes were published: *Military Intelligence-8* (1941: Frederick A. Stokes), *Oriental Division G-2* (1942: Reynal & Hitchcock), and *The Man from G-2* (1943: Reynal & Hitchcock), which at least kept the character in public view. *Captain North's Three Biggest Cases* had appeared some years before (1936: Putnam). Normal fictional secret service was resumed after the last all-clear had been sounded.

This "natural break" provides an opportunity to consider Mason's most unusual—and downright quirky—mystery novel. *The Castle Island Case*[32] had "candid camera clues" taken by the noted photographer, Henry Clay Gipson (1887–1956), scattered throughout the text. It does rather invite comparison with the first "Crime File Dossier"—*Murder off Miami*/aka *File on Bolitha Blane*—published by Dennis Wheatley in the UK and USA during the previous year. The no fewer than 22 characters in this Bermuda-set whodunit are led by Mason himself, as Inspector Boyd, aided by "ace private investigator" Roger Allenby (played by Reginald Carrington). Crime writer, psychologist, and Bermuda resident Charles Daly King (1895–1963) essayed the role of millionaire Barnard Grafton. Marjorie Saunders played Grafton's beautiful young wife, Barbara, who is found strangled to death—and naked (explicit photo supplied)—on a Bermuda beach. *The Castle Island Case* was later extensively rewritten as a Hugh North novel, which will be dealt with in its proper chronological place.

Saigon Singer (1946), Hugh North's first post–World War II assignment, took him to what was then French Indochina and which has been the Socialist Republic of Vietnam since 1976. European powers—the British, French, Dutch, and

Portuguese—tried to "repossess" their colonies in the Far East, but the imperialist clock could not be turned back. French attempts to establish a puppet Indochinese government ended with ignominious defeat at Dien Bien Phu on May 7, 1954. And it wasn't just a freedom-fighter backlash against European hegemony. The Philippines (occupied by the Japanese from 1942 until 1945) gained its full independence from the United States in 1946. If Mason foresaw much of this political hugger-mugger, he chose not to let it clutter up his already complicated plot. As for the eponymous warbler:

MAJOR NORTH AND THE BLACK CHRYSANTHEMUM

Xenia Morel was the most perfectly beautiful woman Hugh North had ever seen. From her jewel-laced blonde crown to the perfect white feet below the hem of her moulded evening gown, every plane of her face, every curve of her body was breathtaking. Her voice, when she sang in the opera house in Saigon, or in Ira [Tecumseh] Benton's mansion, was almost as devastating.[33]

Hugh North makes short shrift of his war service record to Natalie Converse ("a girl with good sense to match her looks"):

"Did you serve in the Pacific theatre, Major?" he heard her asking.

North might have explained that before Pearl harbour he had served nearly two-thirds of his career in the Far East, but he didn't feel called to.

"No, worse luck," and he smiled. "Spent the beginning of the war among the chairborne troops in the Pentagon." The recollection was not pleasing. "Unfortunately, I seemed to know a bit more about the Boches [Germans] than some of the bright boys in G-2 and OSS [Office of Strategic Services: forerunner of the CIA.]. So I got stuck there in Washington until, thank God, I was detailed to missions in some so-called neutral countries."[34]

This present mission wasn't the sort North relished. "[In fact] it was utterly distasteful. Ever since the tale of Benedict Arnold had horrified his boyhood imagination, traitors, in his opinion, existed at the nadir of human vileness, especially traitors for profit—the Judas Iscariots, the Alcibiadeses, the Quislings." Moreover: "Though admitting the fact, Hugh North found it difficult to believe an American capable of delivering his fellows to the cruelties of the Imperial Intelligence for the sake of Japanese yen. Yet there had been not one, but several, of these creatures. Of course, the English, the French, and the Dutch also had their troubles along that line."[35]

Hugh North maintained a becomingly modest silence about his secret-service stint during the Second Great War. But we can rest secure in the knowledge that he didn't spend the whole time behind a desk, shuffling paperwork from G-2 HQ. Mason might have spilled the beans, of course, but then North would have been forced to kill him. The above briefing session also demonstrates the respect in which North is held by his many M-like superior officers. He is invariably treated as a semi-equal rather than some interchangeable "00" agent to be told what to do and what to do when he gets there. *Saigon Singer* presents North as a more mature human being, seasoned by hard-won experience; though he would never lose his innate sense of decency and "schoolboy" sense of humor. Fleming followed psychological suit with James Bond, but the stronger-minded North never plunged anywhere near so far into the Slough of Despond (see *You Only Live Twice* and *The Man with the Golden Gun*). It was also 20,000 words longer than *Singapore Exile*'s 60,000, allowing a lot more space for character development and background details, while still moving at the same headlong speed.

Dardanelles Derelict (1949) takes the Hugh North saga even more firmly into the post–World War Two superpower world. Blurb to the 1951 Pocket Books edition:

> *GERM WARFARE* was Russia's threat to the world. More deadly than any atom or hydrogen bomb, it was to be delivered by jet propulsion.
>
> But somewhere in Communist territory was an American agent with the plans for that jet hidden in a hollow key. Major Hugh North, ace of G-2, was sent to contact the man. North was up against Russia's best agents: Ben Gramont—American renegade. Velvalee Petrie—her body bought the secrets Russia wanted, and Esmé Murfee—hate was her only passion.
>
> In a race against time, Hugh North braved the torture racks of the Communist inquisition chambers to bring out the key to peace.

For Your Information. The Dardanelles, known as the Hellespont in ancient times, is a Turkish strait (measuring 75 km long and 5–6 km wide) that links the Sea of Marmara with the Mediterranean Sea. The eponymous "derelict" is Major Hugh North himself, who is working undercover—particularly *deep* undercover: "Jingles [Lawson] gasped—and a small sound not unlike a moan escaped her. Obviously North's crisp, brown-black hair had not experienced the pressure of a brush for days on end, nor had he shaved any more recently. The tall and muscular figure's shirt was deplorable; it suggested that also it had served its owner as napkin, towel and handkerchief and had been slept in not one, but many, nights. Of the derelict's coat or vest there was no visible trace and, in place of a belt, a piece of dirty twine was knotted about North's abdomen. Dully, the drunkard's deep-set eyes swung towards that oddly assorted group crowding the doorway. No longer of their usual clear blue-grey, North's eyes more suggested pink than any other colour and their lids were granulated, red and bloated."[36]

Hugh North spruced himself up in plenty of time for his *Himalayan Assignment* (1952). This entails a journey through Nepal to Jonkhar, a fictitious "buffer protectorate" kingdom (not unlike Bhutan). His initial mission is to investigate the murder of an American Intelligence officer, who had been operating with a nonpolitical scientific expedition. More importantly, however, he must ensure that the country's leader does not go over to the Chinese Communist dark side. The Americans have taken over the anti–Red Menace role in this part of the world from the British, who had left the Indian subcontinent in 1947. James Bond isn't even asked along for the ride. Snipers, a landslide, the requisite two lovely ladies, and violent encounters with an old enemy called Sam Steele keep the plot-pot nicely boiling over.

N.B. North becomes Colonel Hugh North in this pivotal novel—so much for a voluntary demotion to captain!

Two Tickets for Tangier (1955) is more conventional fare. "Lady Angela For-ester—fair, vivacious, voluptuous—and Colonel Hugh North—rugged agent from G-2—made a handsome couple as they sipped their drinks in a plush London restau-rant," ran the hardcover blurb. "The one-time lovers had met accidentally and were now renewing the glorious days of old. But something was different, Hugh kept tell-ing himself. Angela had changed…. It was only after Hugh North set out on his dan-gerous and delicate mission to Tangier [a port city in North Morocco; also known as Tangiers or Tanger]—with Angela at his side—that he learned his lovely girlfriend was now an important MI-2 agent!" (blurb). The *Chicago Sunday Tribune* enthused: "Quite exciting."

Mason must have felt a lot more at home with *The Gracious Lily Affair* (1957), which he half-set on his adopted home island of Bermuda (now a fully self-governing British colony in the north-west Atlantic). The blurb writer for the 1965 British Mayflower-Dell paperback edition has given us the gist of the plot: "Colonel North's mission in this exciting new case is first to determine the authenticity of documents found in a courier case shackled to the wrist of a victim of a plane accident, and then to decipher them. Step by step it is ascertained that a syndicate of gold smugglers operating from Portugal and their colony in Macao near Hong Kong are preparing to make a huge delivery. North's job is to determine whether the plan is genuine or a plot to embroil America with China; and if genuine, to prevent the gold shipment from reaching Macao."

Gracious Lily was possibly inspired by *The Man Who Never Was*.[37] Ewen Mon-tagu (1901–1985) told his insider story of how Operation Mincemeat tricked the Germans into changing their Mediterranean defense plans so that the Allies could successfully invade Sicily (Operation Husky: July 10, 1943). "METHOD: Take one anonymous corpse. Outfit him as a major of the Royal Marines, plant secret mes-sages on him, and cast him from a submarine into the sea where he will float to the shores of neutralist Spain. Hope and pray that the Spaniards will find the body with the false messages and turn them over to the Nazis" (from blurb to the 1964 Corgi paperback edition). In Mason's variation, the courier-case corpse information found off Trident Rocks (on the southern shores of Bermuda) is all too horribly real.

BOOK ONE: CROWN COLONY EAST segues into BOOK TWO: CROWN WEST. After a fact-finding stopover in Hong Kong, North moves for the endgame to the "sleepy, age-old colony of Macao, fulsomely described by local travel brochures as the 'Gem of the Orient Earth' [but which] sweltered malodorously under the noon-day sun. The stench of decomposing sewage, fish, offal, squid drying on long rows of rocks and tidal mud-flats hung heavily in the hot and lifeless air and drifted far out over muddy brown water."[38] Macao, with its neighboring British enclave, was the last remnant of what had once been several Treaty Ports held by the European Great Powers.

The title of *Secret Mission to Bangkok* (1960) is short and to the point. "When Tao Muong, the beautiful child-wife of the famed U.S. space scientist, Hans Bracht, suddenly disappears, the country's security is put in drastic danger. Bracht leaves on a frantic world search for his beloved, insisting that he travel alone, and unthinkingly placing himself in the reach of Communist hands. Colonel North's assignment is to guard Bracht's safety—without Bracht's knowledge. When the scientist turns out to be as unpredictable and temperamental as he is brilliant, with a past as secret as his vital equations, and a host of unseemly acquaintances around the world, North's mission becomes more and more difficult—and more and more deadly" (blurb to 1963 Popular Library paperback edition). "Superior" (*The New York Times*).

As a change of pace, Mason went over the carbons of *The Castle Island Case* (see above) to produce *The Multi-million-dollar Murders*.[39]

It was "based in part" upon the earlier novel, with the same basic plot structure, but—of course—minus the evidentiary photographs taken by Henry Clay Gipson. *Murders* is, essentially, an old-fashioned "country house" mystery with espionage elements tacked on—rather like many of the early Hugh North books, in fact. Mason could have made a considerable name for himself in "straight" crime fiction, had he decided to go down that road.

Trouble in Burma (1962) means just that. "Colonel North, intrepid U.S. agent, has come to Burma [independence achieved from UK in 1948; known as Myanmar since 1989] on the most dangerous assignment of his career: to secretly locate and destroy a rocket capsule which had disappeared deep in the steaming jungle—before the enemy does. Searching for the forsaken area, he finds himself aboard a riverboat with a regiment of Burmese soldiers, their over-inquisitive General, a Red Chinese officer and three beautiful women" (blurb to 1963 Popular Library paperback edition). "In the Mason tradition and all good … from start to finish" (*Pittsburgh Press*). It was the same dirty business as usual in *Zanzibar Intrigue* (1963): "Who had murdered the hotel proprietor who was North's contact in Zanzibar … ?" and *Maracaibo Mission* (1965): "…set in the dark and stormy lakes of central Venezuela."

The twenty-sixth—and last—non-omnibus Hugh North book was *The Deadly Orbit Mission* (1968). Mason pulled out all the stops on what would be his last spy-fiction hurrah, with a bang-up to the middle of next week plot that anticipated many techno-thriller novels and films to come. An artificial satellite armed with a nuclear warhead powerful enough to destroy New York City was passing over the United States every 88 minutes. But its now-erratic orbit is beyond the control of those Soviet rocket scientists who had launched this weapons-grade "sputnik" into space. Moscow and Washington are locked in frantic hot-line discussions (à la *Fail-Safe* and *Dr. Strangelove*). Meanwhile, Hugh North is on a secret mission to Tangier— one of his old stomping grounds (see above). Somewhere in the Medina section of that crowded city lurks a Chinese Communist spy named Lu Tse-pu, Director of the Peking School of Sabotage. Lu has been ordered to activate a top-secret ultraviolet device that would detonate the Russian bomb-satellite as it orbits across the USA, thus initiating a world war between the two inimical superpowers. Red China will then step in to rule what's left of the planet. North can almost hear the atomic clock going tick-tick-tick.

Colonel Hugh North's final signing-off:

> Before leaving the Sûreté's Headquarters North made two phone calls. The first was to the Voice of America office where he was assured that the message from Moscow had been relayed.
>
> His second call was to Liz Warburton whose sleepy voice brightened instantly. "Too late for a message? Not at all, my dear. Specially since you have an early plane to catch—to Washington perhaps?"
>
> "Thanks, my dear, I'm on my way and, Lord God, do I need relaxation. It's been one hell of a day and night—"
>
> "Only so far—darling," murmured Liz Warburton and hung up.

In some metafictional parallel universe, Mason had chosen Scott Stuart as his main-man series character. This ex–army colonel and now-unconventional police Inspector made only one chronicled appearance, in *The Forgotten Fleet Mystery*[40] (as by Geoffrey Coffin, co-written with Helen Brawner). Description: "Immeasurably startled and relieved, Geneva Connolly found herself surveying a squarely solid individual built on the general proportions of a good middleweight, but what chiefly attracted her attention were his grey eyes, slightly twisted nose and the deep blue stain disfiguring the left cheek of his deeply tanned face. His clothes were no less unique—for a coat he wore a grey officer's tunic, boasting red piped shoulder-straps, but no insignia of rank—only the threads which had secured them. On his head the stranger wore a jaunty military cap of unfamiliar design."

Scott Stuart is a juvenile-lead version of Bulldog Drummond who also warbles like the early Simon Templar at his inconsequential worst. We are vouchsafed the traditional getting-the-agent-up-to-speed dialogue (between Stuart and Major-General Fox-Conroy):

> "Back in the spring of 1914 both the Army and the Navy departments were approached by a certain Dr. Anton Cusack, who was a chemist and a naturalized citizen. I was present when the first test was made. He had to offer, he said, a most amazing discovery [salt or fresh water turned into a substitute for gasoline.]."
>
> "Why—it's—it's—" overwhelming—revolutionary! Hell! Such a substance would make it possible for "planes to alight and refuel themselves from the sea! A sub-chaser could cross the Pacific, while a submarine could—"[41]

The *Birmingham* [England] *Sunday Mercury* raved: "Throbbing with excitement." N.B. The "Forgotten Fleet" is a dramatic-backdrop collection of mothballed Great War liners kept as reserve transports off the coast of Maryland. Good journeyman stuff. All things considered, however, it's just as well that Mason dropped Scott Stuart in favor of the more two-dimensional Hugh North.

It is an unsolved mystery in itself why the Hugh North novels were never adapted for motion pictures and/or television, despite being optioned by producers on a regular basis. James Bond—beaten to the Hollywood punch. Apart from *The Barbarians* (see above), the only other Mason work to be filmed was "The Enemy's

Goal" (*Argosy*, May 8, 1935). Retitled *The Spy Ring* (Universal Pictures, 1938), it was directed by Joseph H. Lewis (1907–2000) and written by George Waggoner (1894–1984), from a story by Frank Van Wyck Mason. It starred William Hall (1905–1986: Captain Todd Hayden) and Jane Wyman (1917–2007: Elaine Burdette). The plot concerns two American army officers who have developed a more efficient anti-aircraft machine gun. When one of them is murdered, his partner goes after the spy ring that is out to steal the new weapon.

By way of compensation, Hugh North did push through a transfer to the airwaves—but not quite as we know him from the books. *The Man from G-2* (aka *Major North, Army Intelligence*) had a choppy run on the ABC radio network. Broadcasting history: April 12–May 24, 1945 (Thursday: 7:30 p.m.); June 29–August 24, 1945 (Friday: 10:00 p.m.); September 1, 1945–February 2, 1946 (Saturday: 8:30 p.m.). Each episode lasted 30 minutes. Hugh North was played by Staats Cotsworth (1908–1979). Joan Alexander (1902–1994) provided the voice of "the Girl" (no other name), North's previously unheard-of female assistant. Recommended reading: *Radio Crime Fighters: More Than 300 Programs from the Golden Age.*[42] *G-2* dealt with counter-espionage cases during the Second World War—just when the real-life hostilities were drawing to an end. So it was that Hugh North had increasingly little to occupy his professional time, and—after the final Axis capitulation—the program faded away into thin ethereal air. Unfortunately, no episodes of the "Hugh North" radio series are known to exist at this time.

Mason had settled permanently on the semi-tropical island of Bermuda—about 650 miles off the coast of North Carolina—during 1956. When the chronically ill Dorothy Louise Van Wyck died, less than two years later, he married his longtime secretary, Jean-Louise Hand.[43] He himself drowned at sea (in 1978) while taking a regular daily swim near his Bermudan home—probably due to a massive heart attack.[44]

After *Deadly Orbit*, Hugh North became the Spy Sent Out in the Cold. Mason went back to writing historical novels, the last one published before his death being *Roads to Liberty*.[45] He spent years researching *Armoured Giants*.[46] which told of the epic first combat between two ironclad warships, the USS *Monitor* and the CSS *Merrimack* (March 8–9, 1862). We may never know if Mason contemplated a comeback for the counterspy colonel, perhaps giving him a more developed private life and backstory. However, the extant North novels operate on a basic competence level that most popular-fiction writers can only hope to emulate. The texture is invariably even; any random page displays the same well-toned tension, the same economy of expression, and the same firm structure. They provided a template for most of the spy thrillers that would pepper the next forty-odd years—not excluding Ian Fleming and James Bond.

CHAPTER FIVE

Thank You, Mr. Marquand

One of the most popular fictional spies created by an American author during the 1930s wasn't American and he only made fleeting appearances in his own novels. The shy spy was "Mr. Moto"; the author was John P. Marquand.[1]

John Phillips Marquand was born in Wilmington, Delaware, the son of Margaret (née Fuller) and Philip Marquand. They were connected to an old Newburyport, Massachusetts, family, but now lived in the suburbs of New York City. He was a great-nephew of the 19th-century writer Margaret Fuller (1810–1850) and a cousin of Buckminster Fuller (1895–1983), the architect and author who invented the geodesic dome. He was elected to the editorial board of the *Harvard Lampoon*. After graduation, Marquand worked as a reporter on *The Boston Evening Transcript* (also its biweekly Sunday magazine section) and *The New York Tribune*—with a short stint in advertising. While a Harvard undergraduate, Marquand had joined Battery A of the Massachusetts National Guard, which was posted to the Mexican border in 1916. Basic training at Camp Plattsburgh army base, New York State, led to a Commission as lieutenant in the Field Artillery. He served with the 4th Brigade in France (1917–18). Further biographical information can be found in *John P. Marquand*,[2] by John J. Gross.

Marquand worked as an advertising copywriter from 1920 until 1921, quitting soon after his first novel—*The Unspeakable Gentleman*[3]—had been accepted for book publication. It was written in the style of a great Victorian melodrama. Captain Sheldon suddenly returns home years after fleeing America under a cloud. Secret agents from revolutionary France are pursuing him, for some long-undisclosed reason, and that would seem to be the least of his worries. There followed, in slow succession, *The Black Cargo* (1925) and *Do Tell Me, Dr. Johnson* (1928). But it was *Warning Hill*[4] that would begin his close and profitable association with Little, Brown, the prestigious Bostonian publishing house. Over the next few years, Marquand contributed to major slick magazines like *Collier's, Cosmopolitan, Good Housekeeping*, and *The Saturday Evening* Post, bypassing the pulps altogether. Many of these stories appeared in *Four of a Kind* (1923), *Sun, Sea and Sand* (1950), and *Life at Happy Knoll* (1957).

Marquand upped his authorial game in 1938 when he won the Pulitzer Prize for *The Late George Apley*.[5] It was a pseudo-biographical novel about the titular Bostonian gentleman who "lived" from 1866 until 1933. This "memoir" has purportedly been written by an anonymous friend of the Apley family, with free access to all personal papers and correspondence. The wry result commemorates a now vanished way of New England life. *Apley* met with immediate success on both sides of the Atlantic. Howard Spring (1889–1965), the bestselling British novelist, reviewed it as follows: "Mr. Marquand has created a real character here, and the age in which Apley lived is as finely conveyed as Apley himself. This book can be read with no sense of strangeness, for Apley is just another Victorian living on the other side of the water" (*Evening Standard*).

Reality was the hallmark of almost every Marquand story or novel, even *Ming Yellow*[6]—the exotic thriller that became his first national bestseller. The plot concerns a dangerous search through warlord-infested China for a rare type of earthenware porcelain called Ming Yellow, from the Ming dynasty (1368–1644 CE). Adapted from blurb to the 1950 Pocket Books (UK) paperback edition:

> Edwin Newall, wealthy American collector, wants to buy Ming Yellow, the Imperial yellow porcelain of the reign of Suen-te [1426–1436 A.D.] With his daughter Mel he is prepared to go into the interior for it. Rodney Jones [green but game young American] journalist, knows it is dangerous and warns him not to risk it. Philip Liu, Western-educated Chinese, pretends it is perfectly safe and promises to take Mr. Newall to faraway Ho Hsien, where, he says, the porcelain is to be had. Newall is obstinate and goes—but why does he want Jones to lead the party? And what has Mel to do with Jones's going? Why does Jones distrust Liu? How does General Wu happen to possess the porcelain? Is it genuine? Is it true that the ["mud-faced"] bandit Hei Ch'I is in the neighborhood of Ho Hsien? And who is the soldier called the Golden-Haired Rat?

All these questions—and a good few more—are answered during the sure-footed course of *Ming Yellow*. Marquand takes an unusually sympathetic attitude toward Chinese culture, knocking the Yellow Peril novels of Sax Rohmer and his imitators into a cocked coolie hat. The description of Philip Lui is particularly significant, taking his own imminent career-path change into account:

> A young Chinese was speaking [to Rodney Jones] who might have been any one of the Europeanized Chinese who drank their tea and cocktails at the hotel of an afternoon. The stamp of the West was on him. He must have been turned out by an English tailor, judging by the white suit he wore. The suit and the Panama which he carried in his right hand, both were good and unobtrusive. Yet neither of them belonged with his face and hands. Once you saw his face, you might have thought of one of those formal portraits done on yellowing silk in meticulous hairline strokes, besides which the work of Holbein would seem impressionistic. His face was long and oval and tinted yellow-brown, like old ivory. His lips were mobile and serene. His dark eyes were slightly protruding, half courteous, half inquisitive.[7]

Ming Yellow marked a significant turning point in both Marquand's relationship with *The Saturday Evening Post* and the forward momentum of his career. Earl Derr Biggers[8] had written five "Charlie Chan" novels—all of them serialized in the *SEP*—that were the inspiration for a popular movie series made by Twentieth Century–Fox studios. When Biggers passed away in 1933, *SEP* editor George Horace Lorimer (1867–1937) asked Marquand to create a new character to replace the Chinese master detective (about whom more follows). He sweetened the deal by sending Marquand on two all-expenses-paid trips to the Far East, with the object of gathering background material and local color. The first trip, during March 1934, took him to Korea, Japan, Manchuria (this northern Chinese province was then called Manchukuo, a Japanese possession since its conquest in 1931), and "free" China. Hence *Ming Yellow*.

But it was Marquand's second Oriental-jaunts inspired novel that really set the seal on his perennial mystery-writer fame. *No Hero*[9] followed hard on the heels of *Ming Yellow*'s book publication, following mandatory serialization in *The Saturday Evening Post* (March 30 to May 4, 1935). Five years later, the British publisher made a wise and commercially sound title-change to *Mr. Moto Takes a Hand*.[10] Mr. Moto is the name of its pivotal protagonist—a Japanese secret agent who works in mysterious ways, his wonders to perform.

Marquand: "I was sent to China in 1934 by *The Saturday Evening Post* with instructions to do a series of stories with authentic Oriental background. Naturally, I did a great deal of poking around in Chinese cities and finally wandered to Japan. There I was constantly shadowed by a polite little Japanese detective. Suddenly, it dawned on me that he was just the protagonist I was looking for—and while my shadow did his duty very conscientiously, 'Mr. Moto,' the shrewd, the polite, the efficient sleuth was born" (cited in David Zinman's *Saturday Night at the Bijou*[11]).

If Marquand and Lorimer wanted to avoid creating a mere Chinese copycat of Charlie Chan—which they undoubtedly did—then Japan was the only viable Oriental way for them to go. Almost every other country in the Far East was dominated by European colonialist powers, in one way or another, with no meaningful autonomy and/or foreign policies whatsoever. Japan, meanwhile, had become an expanding military and economic power to be reckoned with in the area. However, most Americans turned a blind eye to these seemingly irrelevant-to-them developments. As for espionage, Terry Crowdy has summed up the Japanese secret-service situation as follows:

[Modern] Japan built up separate army and naval intelligence services, each with an accompanying branch of secret military police (Kempetai for the army and Toketai for the navy). ... However, where the Japanese were unique was in the use of spies belonging to unofficial secret societies working alongside or independently of the official intelligence agencies. These shadowy institutions were ultra-nationalist by nature, drawing their membership from a cross-section of Japanese society, including the military, politics, industry and Yakusa. Under ruthless leadership, their henchmen would spy on, subvert and corrupt Japan's Far East neighbours.[12]

Strictly speaking, Charlie Chan was a Chinese-Hawaiian-American Detective Sergeant (later Inspector) of the Honolulu Police Department, and as patriotic as they come. Hawaii had been "annexed" by the United States in 1898, became a U.S. territory two years later, and was finally granted statehood in 1959. Biggers endowed his super-intelligent sleuth with a sizable biography. Chan is a married man, has eleven children, and lives in a necessarily large house on Punchbowl Hill. He wears Western-style clothing, speaks broken though not overly ungrammatical English, is fond of quoting *faux*–Confucian aphorisms, and has a reputation for always getting his criminal man or woman. But his first appearance—well into *The House without a Key*[13]—is an unprepossessing minor-character one. He speaks a form of Pidgin English: "No knife are present in the neighbourhood of crime."[14] A veteran court reporter named Chester A. Doyle did complain that no Chinese detective would ever use the language attributed to Chan. However, most readers considered that Biggers had succeeded in his avowed intention to create a Chinese hero who was trustworthy, benevolent, and philosophical.

Chan continued: *The Chinese Parrot* (1927); *Behind That Curtain* (1928); *The Black Camel* (1929); *Charlie Chan Carries On* (1930); *The Keeper of the Keys* (1932). The *SEP* paid Biggers $25,000 for the serialization rights to *Behind That Curtain* alone, a substantial sum in those days. Book publication, royalties, and movie rights would have added significantly to his income over a less than 10-year period. Biggers, however, never reaped the full benefits from this mystery-writing windfall. He died of heart disease, just turned 70 years old, at his home in Pasadena.

A lengthy scholarly monograph could be penned on the Life and Times of Charlie Chan. It already has been done, in a sense, with *Charlie Chan: The Untold Story of the Honourable Detective and His Rendezvous with American History*,[15] by Yunte Huang. This book is actually two scholarly monographs bound together, one about the fictional Charlie Chan and the other a biography of his real-life counterpart, Chang Apana (1871–1933). Any such "bio-fictional" inquiry into the real-life antecedents of Mr. Moto might—just about—make it to the double-digit page mark. *Ming Yellow*'s Philip Liu could be represented as a proto–Moto—but that way desperation lies. Moto appears early in chapter 1 of *No Deal*. The following (abridged) passage comes from the hardcover reprint of a later paperback edition, retitled *Your Turn, Mr. Moto*[16]:

> "May I help you to bed, perhaps?"
> "No. What's your name?"
> "Moto. That is my name, please, and I should be glad to assist you. I was once a valet to several American gentlemen in New York. America is a magnificent country."
> "Well, you're not a valet here in Japan."
> "No, but Americans always interest me. I saw that you were not well and that your friends had left you."
> "Listen, Mr. Moto, when they can't get anything more out of you, Americans always go away."
> "It was not kind of them. I am sorry."[17]

There will be little need for any more extended pen portraits of Mr. Moto, except for the occasional pertinent detail that crops up from time to time. The narrator's first—but far from last—encounter with the high-ranking Japanese secret agent finishes with these enigmatic and perhaps hallucinatory words: "America is very proud of you, Casey Lee." Kenneth F.C. Lee is (in his own words) "the 'Casey' Lee who flew the Atlantic at a time when previous flyers had rather taken the first bloom off that feat. My reputation and my personality used to be as carefully built up in those days as a pugilist's or a motion-picture star's, for my personality meant money."[18] But this sub–Hemingway casualty of the Depression finds himself "pushed more and more into the background with others of my kind. Thus, it was not strange that when money was running very short and a large tobacco company offered me the chance of making a flight from Japan to the United States, I should have welcomed the opportunity."[19]

Marquand makes it abundantly clear from the opening paragraphs that Casey Lee is the *No Hero* of his original title:

> Commander James Driscoll, attached to the Intelligence branch of the United States Navy, has asked me to write this, in order that my version may be placed in the files with his own account.
> "Honest to goodness—no one in his right mind, Driscoll, if he isn't in the scenario department of some movie outfit, writes this sort of stuff."
> "Don't let that worry you. Any sort of narrative has to have a hero in it to get over with the public, and, believe me, you weren't any hero.[20]"

Marquand's no-hero narrator, Casey Lee, plays a more active role throughout the novel than its ostensible hero, James Driscoll, who fulfills the role of stage manager for most of the running time. Driscoll and Lee fall to blows at one point, but it turns out to have been a minor misunderstanding. Least said, soonest mended.

The *de facto* hero of *No Hero* is Mr. I.A. Moto, even if he doesn't have American—or European—interests at heart. It has been pointed out that Moto—not being a proper Japanese surname—must be an alias. Casey Lee actually says as much. Mr. Moto is the very model of an inscrutable and enigmatic Oriental, saying a lot but telling little, until the last possible moment. Nevertheless, Lee ends up by liking the oh-so-polite secret agent, if not quite trusting him or his country "I believe honestly that if Mr. Moto, a most accomplished gentleman, and I were to meet today that we might enjoy each other's company, and I should be glad to drink with him in one of his minute wine cups to the future of Japan. I have an idea that he would agree with me heartily in wishing for perpetual amity between Japan and the United States, as long as that amity did not interfere with what he and his own political faction conceive to be his nation's divine mission to establish a hegemony in the East."[21]

Along the way to this ambivalent conclusion, Casey Lee meets the equally ambivalent Sonya Karaloff: "She was a tall girl, almost lanky. Her hair was reddish gold. Her eyes, dark blue, gave the combined impression of being both shrewd and seductive. Her lips were painted a deep red, and her hands were very long and slender. She had the social poise and the adamantine quality of a more sophisticated world. I knew that she was a Russian, because I had seen her type often enough during my short stay in the Orient. They were all aloof, but all charming companions, able to be agreeable in any mood, able to give one an adventurous sense of competence, and displaying at the same time their own sadness, for they were sad people who wandered without a country."[22]

Needless to say, the All-American Boy and the White-Russian Girl become romantically reconciled with one another. But not before Casey suspects Sonya of being a *femme fatale* international spy. It turns out, however, that her late scientist father—Alexis Karaloff—had invented a powerful new fuel oil for naval vessels. The Red Russians want it. The Americans want it. The British want it. The Japanese want it. *Everybody* wants it.

No Hero/Mr. Moto Takes a Hand/Your Turn, Mr. Moto firmed up the foundations for the series as a whole. Marquand's formula allows for the occasional random variable. But the main and invariable constant is the strategic distance Moto keeps from every other character, making his longest appearance at the obligatory dénouement.

Nobody ever sees inside Moto's head, and we only know what little he chooses to tell us about himself or what he's been ordered to do on His Emperor's Secret Service. Moto seems to enjoy more freedom of action than most secret agents, and he might resemble M and James Bond rolled into one. Unlike Charlie Chan, Moto speaks articulate Standard English, apart from the idiosyncratic "so very sorry" every now and then. Nothing is revealed about his social background or academic history, but his aristocratic bearing and wide-ranging erudition shine through. The effortless superiority of an Ivy League and/or Oxbridge graduate—which he could very well be. "I can do many, many things. I can mix drinks and wait on tables and I am a very good valet. I can navigate and manage small boats. I also know carpentry and surveying and five Chinese dialects. So very many things come in useful."[23]

The stories are narrated by a series of young American men who—despite having shady reputations back home—are innocents abroad whenever Fate directs them to the Far East. Casey Lee is unique in doing double duty as a chronicler for both Mr. Moto and Commander James Driscoll, one of the few professional Western secret agents to play a leading role. These happy amateurs not only find themselves hapless in exotic foreign parts, but also fall under the spell of attractive women who are involved either directly or indirectly with espionage and other international intrigues. After many misadventures, they all find their way out of these immoral mazes and win the love of the actually guilt-free women. Helped, in no small measure, by the wily Japanese super spy. Annotated checklist:

Thank You, Mr. Moto (1936). Narrated by Tom Nelson, an expatriate American "gone native" in China, who becomes involved with the Imperial Japanese expansion into Manchuria and is jolted out of his apathetic complacency. "There is [Mr. Moto tells Nelson] a group in my country, somewhat bigoted and fanatical. It feels our nation is not moving fast enough. Frankly, this group has been a source of very bad annoyance. My mission out here is to curb its activities…. Yes, I am afraid there are certain of my countrymen behind this. I have failed in preventing their rash actions. Therefore I think that they will kill me. I do hope that you understand me now."[24]

Think Fast, Mr. Moto (1937). Young Wilson Hitchings, of the Hitchings Brothers merchant bank in Shanghai, is reassigned to Hawaii. He must troubleshoot the Hitchings Plantation, a gambling house in Honolulu. "Excuse me, please, if I did not make myself clear," he said, "perhaps I was excited. Please, I am not excited now." Mr. Moto's eyes were bright and steady, he was breathing fast through his closed [gold-filled] teeth. "A shot was fired at me through the open window. I'm very very sorry—I did not expect one so soon. Attempts have been made to liquidate me before, Mr. Hitchings. Enough of them so that I should have been more careful. I had not thought I had been asked to this room to be murdered. Please, I shall be going now."[25] "Many more mysteries to solve, Mr. Moto! You are, please, so very very charming" (*Boston Transcript*).

Mr. Moto Is So Sorry (1938). For the first and only time, Mr. Moto takes part in almost every scene of this particularly suspenseful novel. Calvin Gates (the third-person viewpoint character) is a somewhat shady American who makes his way through Japanese-dominated northern China to Inner Mongolia. He joins an archaeological expedition, along with Shirley Galloway, a lovely young technical artist (also American). But there is danger everywhere. Mr. Moto explains the strategical situation to Gates: "Excuse me, your own great country has taken territory. The British Empire has taken nearly half the globe. Why should not Japan? It is the manifest destiny of stronger nations. Nevertheless, we do not wish to grab. We only desire a partnership, a cordial co-operation, an understanding with the Chinese.... We have offered them our army to pacify the country, yet they grow difficult, particularly the American-educated Chinese. If I am rude, I am so sorry."[26]

Last Laugh, Mr. Moto (1942). With half the world now at war, and the other half on tenterhooks, *The Saturday Evening Post* declined to serialize Marquand's latest novel about a Japanese master spy. It was accepted by *Collier's* magazine, but they insisted upon a title change to the Mr. Moto–free *Mercator Island* (September 6 to October 25, 1941). The titular island is in the Caribbean, near Jamaica, which makes the story read as if it had been written by F. Van Wyck Mason. Moto appears surplus to requirements for most of the time, and his summing up is a lot more cursory than usual. Then he makes this rather menacing statement: "So nice to have met you. Some other time again, when it is pleasanter, I hope. You must step aboard at once, please. The farther you are away so much the better for you I think."[27]

Fox (later Twentieth Century–Fox) Studios had struck Oriental-detective gold with their audience-friendly Charlie Chan films, most of which bore little or no relation to the character created by Earl Derr Biggers. Then, beginning with *Think Fast, Mr. Moto* (1937), they made eight Mr. Moto films within a two-year period, most of which bore little or no relation to the character created by John P. Marquand. Producer Sol M. (Solomon Max) Wurtzel (1890–1958) had acquired the rights to *No Hero* in 1935, but it was never filmed. Moto was played superbly by the Hungarian-born actor Peter Lorre, who—with few facial changes apart from thick spectacles and slicked-down hair—was a more convincing Japanese than the over-made-up

Swedish-born actor Warner Oland (1879–1938) managed in his "Charlie Chan" mode. Lorre accepted the B-movie role because it gave him the chance to play the hero, for a change.[28] William K. Everson wrote this brisk overview:

> Moto operated rather differently from Chan, employing disguises, working undercover [for a kind of Interpol organization], watching and waiting, and then pouncing in the last reel. There was much more scope to the Moto adventures, and murder was often only an incidental. Moto was also a small lithe man, and an expert at jujitsu, with the help of a double, of course, Peter Lorre engaged in some extremely lively fight scenes which often brought the films to a much more rousing conclusion than the predictable confrontations of the Chans.[29]

Film rights to *Think Fast, Mr. Moto* had been bought by Fox in July 1936, though the novel itself wasn't published as a book until May 1937. Actual filming began on February 11, 1937, with a release date of July 27 (USA). Marquand had, reportedly, sold four unwritten Mr. Moto stories to Fox at $8,000 apiece (*The New York Times*: June 11, 1937).

The movie Mr. Moto was given the first name of Kentaro, not the novelistic initials I.A. Apart from Lorre, the main cast included Thomas Beck (1909–1985: Bob Hitchings, Jr.); Virginia Field (1917–1982: Gloria Danton); Sig Ruman—as Sig Rumann (: 1884–1969: Nicholas Marloff). N.B.J. Carrol Naish (1896–1973) would star in the Anglo-American TV series *The New Adventures of Charlie Chan* (syndicated in the USA, 1957–58). Although Marquand was more than happy to take the screen-rights money, he didn't mind all that much how the film-makers handled his written-for-the-market character. Director Norman Foster (1803–1976) knocked a script by Howard Ellis Smith into final form, with the help of mystery writer Philip MacDonald (1899–1981).

There is only a passing resemblance between the plot of the book (see above) and the film version of *Think Fast, Mr. Moto*. In hot pursuit of diamond smugglers, special investigator Moto takes passage aboard a tramp steamer from San Francisco to Shanghai, by way of Honolulu. The screenwriters rectified Marquand's general lack of inconsequential humor. For example, this digression about college educations between (a) Hitchings and (b) Moto:

> "Stanford, '34."
> "Stanford, '21. Honorary member."
> "What do you know about that! Moto, '21, let's see…. Oh, I remember reading about you. You broke a pole-vault record, didn't you?"
> "Now I would only break the pole."

Thank You, Mr. Moto was both the second Mr. Moto novel to be written and the second to be made into a feature film (but see below). Release date: December 24, 1937. Thomas Beck again played the guileless American expatriate secondary hero—Tom Nelson, this time. Other cast members included Jayne Regan (1909–200: Eleanor Joyce); Sidney Blackmer (1895–1973: Herr Koerger); Sig Ruman/Rumann (Colonel Tchernov); John Carradine (1906–1988: Pereira). Philip Ahn (Prince

Chung). N.B. Ahn would appear in *Charlie Chan in Honolulu* the following year, as Wing Fu. Ahn achieved more lasting fame playing Master Kan, in the cult TV series *Kung Fu* (1972–75). Penzler and Steinbrunner: "A Chinese prince kills himself when the dowager queen is murdered by enemies of the throne who are looking for some ancient scrolls that show the location of Genghis Khan's treasure. There are other deaths, and Moto dispatches two of the villains himself, before he manages to steal the scrolls."[30] Mr. Moto acted more like a professional secret agent in this film—and one who held a Bond-style license to kill. *The Christian Science Monitor*—of all publications—rated *Thank You, Mr. Moto* as "well made and fairly exciting" (January 22, 1938). Lorre was now well on the way to being typecast. The films had become so popular—and lucrative—that Fox producer Darryl F. Zanuck (1902–1979) refused him a leave of absence to act opposite Miriam Hopkins in S.N. Behrman's play *Wine of Choice*, a Theatre Guild production set for Broadway in December 1937.

It will take a good few sentences to straighten out what happened next. The "real" third Mr. Moto film had been shot in mid–1937, as *Look Out, Mr. Moto*, but its release was delayed until the following year (see below). Fox rescheduled with *Mr. Moto's Gamble*. *Charlie Chan at Ringside* had gone before the cameras in January 1938, starring Warner Oland as Chan and Keye Luke as his Number One Son. But Oland fell sick, forcing the production to be suspended. Although Fox announced, in March 1938, that Oland would return in *Charlie Chan on the Clipper Ship*, he never fully recovered from his illness and died in August 1938. Sidney Toler (1874–1947) took over the role, from *Charlie Chan in Honolulu* (release date: January 13, 1939). Since at least $100,000 had already been spent on the aborted Chan film, Sol Wurtzel had the script rewritten for Moto. Shooting resumed on 22 January, ended in late March, and the film had an unusually fast release date (April 7, 1937). There is absolutely no espionage involved. Max ("Slapsie Maxie") Rosenbloom (1904–1976) provides heavy-handed comedy relief as "Knockout" Wheeler, a kleptomaniac pugilist training to be a private detective—so that he can arrest himself! Keye Luke (Number One son, Lee Chan) essays a cheeky "crossover" role as a student in Moto's criminology class.

Look Out, Mr. Moto was finally released on June 24, 1938, as *Mr. Moto Takes a Chance* (a poster had been produced with the original title). Norman Foster took back his directorial chair, co-writing the screenplay with Lou Breslow (1900–1987) and John Patrick[31] (based upon a story by Willis Cooper [1895–1955], and the character "created by J.P. Marquand"). The cast list featured Rochelle Hudson (1916–1972: Victoria "Vicki" Mason); Robert Kent (1908–1953: Marty Weston); J. Edgar Bromberg (1903–1951: Rajah Ali). The film opens with round-the-world flying aviatrix Victoria Mason flying over stock footage of Angkor Wat (a ruined temple in Cambodia, then part of French Indochina). Vicki, for short, is actually a British agent, sent to spy upon the politically overambitious Rajah Ali, in the never-never Kingdom of Tong Moi. Her plane crashes—accidentally on purpose. She is duly "rescued" by Mr. Moto, who is pretending to be an archaeologist, on much the same secret but separate mission. He also disguises himself as a white-bearded jungle hermit. (Lorre's "Asian" make-up took almost three hours to be applied.) It's all very much in the Van Wyck Mason vein, and Hugh North could easily have been substituted for Mr. Moto.

Mysterious Mr. Moto (October 14, 1938) opens with the fastest-ever escape from the former French Penal Colony of Devil's Island, off the South American coast. In next to no time, Mr. Moto—undercover as Ito Matsuka, a Japanese murderer— and his fellow convict, Paul Brissac (Leon Ames: 1902–1993), move from Cayenne (French Guiana) to Lisbon and, finally, to London. Brissac (alias Romero) belongs to an international group calling themselves the League of Assassins. They are intim- idating Anton Dorvak (Henry Wilcoxon: 1905–1984), a Czechoslovakian pacifist industrialist, who refuses to part with yet another new super-steel formula. Moto now acts as a gentleman's gentleman for the most ungentlemanly Brissac/Romero. ("Oh so. Suiting you?") N.B. Moto shows his warrant card to Sir Charles Murchison, a Commissioner at Scotland Yard (played by Lester Matthews: 1900–1975). Held up to the camera, it reads: "International Police. Kentaro Moto. Agent General."

Mr. Moto in Egypt was the relevant working title of the irrelevantly retitled *Mr. Moto's Last Warning* (release date: January 20, 1939). Norman Foster directed and co-wrote the screenplay, again with Philip MacDonald. The particularly strong cast list includes Ricardo Cortez (1900–1977: Fabian the Great); Virginia Field (Connie Porter); John Carradine (Danforth: aka Richard Burke, British Secret Agent S-14); George Sanders (Eric Norvel); Joan Carroll (1932–2016: Mary "Marie" Delacour); Robert Coote (1909–1982: Rollo Venables); Margaret Irving (1898–1988: Madame Delacour); Teru Shimada[32] (Fake Mr. Moto). *Last Warning* has all the right ingredi- ents for a highly spiced espionage thriller. A Royal Navy flotilla based in Port Said, Egypt, is assigned to maneuvers with the French fleet. But a short delay is forced when the British Secret Service issues a warning about potential sabotage. Mean- while, a passenger ship docks carrying Madame Delacour (wife of the French admi- ral in joint command of the naval exercise), her daughter Marie, the over-suave Eric Norvell (of indeterminate nationality), the silly-ass Englishman, Rollo Venables, and someone who is not Peter Lorre calling himself Mr. Moto. Before long, Norvell has "Mr. Moto" killed. The real Moto is posing as Mr. Kuroki, the owner of a tourist-trap curio shop.

Mr. Moto in [not *on*] *Danger Island* (April 7, 1939) was a frantic affair—both on-screen and off. Director Herbert I. Leeds (1907–1954), with producer John Stone (1888–1961), had to interweave the work of no fewer than five screenwriters: Peter Milne; John Reinhardt; George Bricker; Jack Jungmeyer; Edith Skouras. (Marquand received his usual courtesy credit as the "creator" of Mr. Moto.) The whole cine- matic ball of wax had been "inspired" by a *sixth* writer, John W. Vandercook (1902– 1963), and his novel entitled *Murder in Trinidad*.[33] Fox had already filmed *Murder in Trinidad* (release date: May 16, 1934), under its original title. Director: Louis King (1902–1974). Writer: Seton I. Miller. Cast list includes Nigel Bruce (Bertram Lynch);

Heather Angel (1909–1986: Joan Cassell); Victor Jory (Howard Sutter). Simply put, League of Nations investigator Lynch is sent to Port of Spain, the capital city of Trinidad and Tobago, to track down a gang of diamond smugglers. Which he does, after some tense moments in a crocodile-infested swamp. It does not lie beyond the bounds of plausibility that Ian Fleming saw this film, and /or read the novel, when he was a callow youth. Not necessarily within those bounds, either. N.B. *Murder in Trinidad* was filmed for a third time—almost unrecognizably—as *The Caribbean Mystery* (1945).

Despite having been announced in July 1938 (*The New York Times*: July 18, 1938), the eighth Moto film—*Mr. Moto Takes a Vacation* (release date: July 7, 1939)—was actually the seventh to go before the cameras. Norman Foster directed and co-wrote the original screenplay, again with Philip MacDonald. The story opens in Arabia, where Howard Stevens—a young American archaeologist—unearths the legendary crown of the equally legendary Queen of Sheba. Mr. Moto, posing as an Austrian archaeologist called Professor Heinrich von Kleinkof, validates the discovery. Ostensibly on vacation, Moto has made himself responsible for guarding the crown from being stolen by Metaxa, a master criminal long believed dead—mistakenly, in Moto's professional opinion. Foster and MacDonald graced *Vacation* with a good comedy-action sequence, only to disgrace it with several "gag" scenes that are gagging in more ways than one. However, they redeemed themselves by including a *Wacky Races* car chase that was stolen by Black actor William ("Willie") Best (1916–1962), who went disgracefully uncredited. Although Best had stereotypical language foisted upon him, his lines made perfect sense and he came out as very much the hero of the hour. But it's Peter Lorre who delivers the last wry words: "Oh, well. Perhaps I wasn't meant to have a vacation."

There is truth in the conventional wisdom that impending Far Eastern hostilities killed off the Mr. Moto book series (see above). Ditto the film series, though Fox had announced the making of four more Moto films during the period April 1939 to April 1940. Apart from that, however, the novelty of "heroic" stardom had finally worn off for Lorre, who also wanted to avoid typecasting in B movies—no matter how well-made or well-received. Lorre was also suffering from the after-effects of morphine addiction (the drug had been prescribed to alleviate his chronic gall bladder problems). Having extricated himself from his Fox contract, in July 1939, he went on to make a string of classic film noirs at Warner Brothers, including *The Maltese Falcon* (1941), *Casablanca* (1942), and *The Mask of Dimitrios* (1944). See *The Films of Peter Lorre*,[34] by Stephen D. Youngkin, Jones Bigwood, and Raymond Cabana, Jr.

Lorre might not have been disgruntled over the Mr. Moto films, but he was certainly far from being gruntled (with apologies to P.G. Wodehouse). The necessary stunt work had also taken its toll, with a dislocated shoulder during his filming of *Vacation*. In 1939, Lorre attended a lunch given by visiting Japanese officials. He wore a badge saying: "Boycott Japanese goods." During the Second World War, the name "Mr. Moto" became a pejorative nickname for all "Japs" used by American service personnel. Civilian vilification was just as bad—if not worse. For example, the Aeronca Aircraft Corporation (Middletown, Ohio), published this stridently xenophobic "Ode to Mr. Moto!" (*Collier's* magazine: July 11, 1942).

> "Hell, shipmates—there's only one."
> One lone Jap on the Carrier intent, to crash decks aft—or fore,
> But our lad in the fighter wasted no time with this blighter
> Now Moto doesn't live here anymore.

With his closest competitor—Mr. Moto—out of the way, Charlie Chan carried on as the preeminent cinematic Oriental detective. But another putative rival existed in the form of James Lee Wong, generally known as Mr. Wong. Tall and lean, the physical opposite of Chan, not much given to spouting Confucian aphorisms. Wong had been created by Hugh Wiley (1884–1968) for *Collier's* magazine, in 1934. Four years later, the Poverty Row studio Monogram Pictures brought Wiley's character to the big screen in the flatly entitled *Mr. Wong, Detective* (release date: October 5, 1938). The screenplay, by Houston Branch (1899–1968) and Hugh Wiley, had Wong uncovering an international spy ring that is after a secret formula (for poison gas, this time). But the main attraction was undoubtedly Boris Karloff,[35] then at the height of his fame as a horror-film star. Five more Mr. Wong films followed, none of which had any real cloak-and-dagger content: *The Mystery of Mr. Wong* (1939); *Mr. Wong in Chinatown* (1939); *Doomed to Die* (1940); *The Fatal Hour* (1940); *Phantom of Chinatown* (1940). Karloff was replaced by Keye Luke in the final film, thus becoming the first Chinese-American actor to play a Chinese leading man in an American motion picture. He portrayed "Jimmy" Wong—a younger version of James Lee Wong. The politically correct experiment failed, however, and Monogram gave up on Oriental detective heroes until taking over the moribund Chan Family franchise in 1944 (beginning with *Charlie Chan in the Secret Service*).

Oriental detectives—whether of American or actual Far Eastern origin—fell out of favor in the post–Second World War and quite soon to be post-colonial world. There was, however, a strong market for fiction about Americans living, working, and—especially—loving in the "new" Japan. Two otherwise very different authors led the field: Pearl S. Buck (1892–1973), e.g., *The Hidden Flower* (1952); and James A. Michener (1907–1997), e.g., *Sayonara* (1954).

Ergo: Stuart Rose, then editor of *The Saturday Evening Post* (also an "intellectual property consultant" for Twentieth Century–Fox), persuaded Marquand to write another Mr. Moto novel—after a lapse of 15 years. Once again, Marquand was given lavish traveling money ($5,000) for a month-long stay in Japan, along with an even more lavish $75,000 advance. He had spent considerable time in the Far East during 1944–45, both as Special Consultant for the Secretary of War and as a War Correspondent for the United States Navy. Then, in 1947, came an extended tour with the Commander of the Pacific Fleet. But to write an up-to-date novel set in Japan, Marquand felt it necessary to become more closely acquainted with the bombed-out city of Tokyo and its environs. "It seemed to me that the era of change is altering the East more markedly than any other part of the world. It is always difficult to give an adventure story an illusion of reality; I'd like to think that my contemporary background of Japan does that; it is authentic through my eyes at least."[36]

Apart from the obvious financial gain, why should a well-respected mainstream author—ranked alongside Hemingway and Faulkner—revert to middlebrow thriller writing? Marquand himself provided the answer: "I wanted a change of pace from the series of novels I had been writing about New England and New York people for the last twenty years. And above all I wanted to know whether or not I was still able to write a mystery, one of the most interesting forms of literary craftsmanship, if not art, that exists. I like to think that this is better than my earlier mystery stories; it ought to be, because I am twenty years older and I hope know my way around better than I used to."[37] But he wisely left that for his readers to judge, one way or the other.

Rendezvous in Tokyo was first serialized in *The Saturday Evening Post* (November 24, 1956, until January 12, 1957), then published in book form as *Stopover: Tokyo*[38] (the colon being omitted from the subsequent Bantam paperback edition). Other title changes would follow over the years: *The Last of Mr. Moto* (Berkley, 1963) and *Right You Are, Mr. Moto* (Popular Library, 1977). Marquand made the most of his refresher crash-course in postwar Japanese history and then present-day culture. For a single example: "Tokyo was not a romantic city. It lay sprawling over a large area, divided by a muddy river and canals—a dusty, smoky city that sweltered in the summer and shivered in the winter. Except for the areas contiguous to the Imperial Palace, all the districts of that immense city were joined together planlessly like a deck of cards thrown on a table, so that dwellings, shops, temples and factories were shuffled into an indiscriminate confusion. There were districts, but there were no street names except for those that had been set up by the American Army of Occupation. It was fortunate that most of the dwellings in Tokyo were of fragile frame construction, with paper windows, because they caught fire so easily in the winter, thus making better city planning possible when they were rebuilt."[39]

Although *Stopover: Tokyo* was the last of Marquand's Mr. Moto novels, it was far from being the least. Arguably the best, in fact, with a darker tone and sharper edge that matched the nerve-wracking Cold War times. Marquand does a brilliant le Carré–before-his-time job of describing the constant tension and danger faced by a secret agent in the field. Gone are the lost and lonely American souls who have no real reasons to be anywhere east of Suez, blundering into foreign intrigues they never fully understand and needing to be helped out by kindly Mr. Moto. The Men in Gray—if not Black—have taken their place. Men like "The name is Rhyce," he said. "John O. Rhyce (pronounced *rice*: the middle initial = zero), from Washington, D.C."[40]

Jack's next mission will be to break up a Communist-run espionage ring in Tokyo posing as the Asian Friendship League and headed by an American front man "do-gooder" called Charles K. Harrington. Intelligence reports indicate that they are planning anti–American demonstrations in Tokyo and the assassination of an as yet unidentified Japanese politician. But the Chief has some incomplete knowledge of another renegade American (Benjamin "Big Ben" Bushman) working behind the scenes, and his Russian spymaster (Skirov). Bill Gibson is Our Man in Tokyo. He is partnered with an Intelligence colleague named Ruth Bogart, who will pretend to be his secretary: "She was very pretty, which did not surprise him. He would have estimated her age at not over twenty-five, until a glance at her hands made him doubtful. Her height was five feet six, hair dark brown, eyes grey green."[41] The couple don't fall in love at first sight, but their increasingly close personal relationship makes the chance of a fatal mistake during this complex mission all the more likely.

After two short but story-significant stays in Honolulu and Wake Island, Jack and Ruth make their final landfall at Tokyo airport. The first time Rhyce had seen Japan was when he had flown over it as an observer on a B-29 bombing mission. Mr. Moto makes his usual self-effacing and enigmatic first bow just under a third of the way through the book:

"Excuse me, sir. Do I speak to Mr. Rhyce?"
"Why, yes. I'm Mr. Rhyce."
"I am so very glad, sir. May I introduce myself?" [His] hand moved with astonishing rapidity as he snatched a wallet from inside his purplish blue coat and whipped a name card out of it.
"Please," he said, holding out the card.
"I.A. Moto" [Jack read aloud] "Well, let's see—that name rings a bell somewhere."[42]

Although Mr. Moto comes across here as his familiar serious-comic self, the scenes that follow show that—like Japan itself—he has emulated the "supple bamboo bending with the typhoon" and never broken. Nothing explicit is told us about his wartime career, but it's hard to believe that the essentially humane Moto ever went over to the Dark Side of prison-camp interrogation atrocities. One thing is for sure, however. Japan's army, navy, and air force may be gone, but its "national will to live" is exemplified by the still-intact Secret Service. Mr. Moto is still serving his Emperor, and—perforce—the firm-but-fair American overlords. Jack Rhyce had "often heard older men in the bureau, including the Chief, say that pre-war Japanese agents were tops in the field. They loved intricacies, and if they knew what they wanted, their patience was inordinate."[43] Marquand builds up a composite picture of the "new" Moto as the novel goes along:

"Oh," Jack Rhyce said, "so you're a cop, are you?"
Mr. Moto looked grave and shook his head. "Not what you call a cop," he said. "I am just what you are, Mr. Rhyce, and you and I do not want cops, do we? I only want a quiet talk with you. It would be a pity if I were to call the police."[44]
"To happy peace between the United States and poor Japan," Mr. Moto said. "Very foolish men made the war. Ha-ha. Nearly all of them are dead."[45]
"I am not anti–American," Mr. Moto said. "I hope so very much that you are not anti–Japanese, Mr. Rhyce."
"Not at the minute," Jack Rhyce said. "I'm anti–Communist right now."
Mr. Moto drew in his breath again very carefully.
"Americans are so very nice, but sentimental sometimes."[46]

Stuart Rose, at *The Saturday Evening Post*, did not approve of the downbeat ending (spoiler alerts: Ruth Bogart is tortured to death and Jack Rhyce gives up Intelligence work as a bad job), but *Stopover: Tokyo* hit all the bestseller lists. The critical response was equally positive, e.g., "Superlative suspense thriller—unmistakably Marquand" (*The New York Times*).

Twentieth Century–Fox turned *Stopover: Tokyo* (minus the colon) into a "major motion picture" almost before the ink had dried on its first book publication (the film rights having been bought in March 1956, before the novel came out). They made it in De Luxe color and the new Cinemascope widescreen process, which produced an image twice as wide as it was high by using special projection equipment. Like many such "letterbox" formats—VistaVision, Todd-AO, etc.—Cinemascope was ideal for historical spectacles, but unsuited to more intimate, small-scale domestic dramas or film noirs. And that was the sad case with *Stopover Tokyo*, despite being a singular success on the technical level. Cinematographer Charles G. Clarke (1889–1983) carried out lavish location filming in Kyoto, a sacred Shinto city that had been spared heavy wartime bombing and had been taken off the atomic hit-list because of its rich cultural heritage. However, any resemblance between Marquand's novel and its cinematic offspring was purely tangential.

To begin with, Jack Rhyce and Bill Gibson have been granted one measly name-check each. Rhyce has become Mark Fannon, an Intelligence agent—code clerk, really—played by the then 27-year-old and looking ten years younger Robert Wagner (1930–). There is no visible Chief. Fannon works alone, without the lovely but ill-fated Ruth Bogart. Her place is taken by a Welsh (!) airport receptionist named Tina Llewellyn, played by the then 24-year-old and looking even younger Joan Collins (1933–).

To end with, this film based upon a Mr. Moto novel leaves out Mr. Moto. "So sorry, Lorre *san*." It would seem that Fox saw more profit in making a *Look-at-Life*-type travelogue than faithfully transcribing Marquand's novel into cinematic form. They were also, of course, keen on promoting the careers of their fresh young contract stars. There can be no reasonable doubt that Lorre's comeback performance as Mr. Moto would have up-screened every other actor in the film. Apart from that, the American (and European) cinema-going public might not yet have been ready for a Japanese character playing such a high-profile role. There are three Japanese characters in *Stopover Tokyo*, who—put together—could be seen as a composite of Mr. Moto: Lt. Afumi (police officer: Heihachiro Okawa); Captain Masao (Afumi's boss: Denmei Susuki); Nobika (informer: Solly Nakamura).

Seven years later, Ian Fleming wrote his own "Japanese" novel, *You Only Live Twice*—and a very strange novel it was, too. John Brosnan summarized it as follows: "At the beginning we find Bond recovering from a breakdown which resulted from his wife being murdered by Blofeld at the end of [*On Her Majesty's Secret Service*]. Bond has gone to seed and good old M is prepared to throw him out of the Service, but he relents and instead sends him on a minor mission to Japan as a last chance.

Here, for most of the book, Bond wanders around soaking up the atmosphere of the place [as Fleming himself did in *Thrilling Cities*[47]] and generally acting like a tourist. Not until the last third of the novel is there any real action" (*James Bond in the Cinema*[48]). The 1967 film version—scripted by Roald Dahl (1916–1990)—veered even further away from the source material than *Stopover Tokyo* had done: "The film opens in outer space...."[49]

N.B. Another cinematic connection between *Stopover Tokyo* and Ian Fleming concerns the "steam room" scene (Mark Fannon almost fried to death) and the Shrublands Health Farm episode in *Thunderball* (1965), where 007 turns up the heat on SPECTRE secret agent Count Lippi.

Mr. Moto made his last literary bow in *Stopover: Tokyo*. If Marquand had a further novel lined up for his iconic Japanese hero, he never got round to writing it. But Moto would be granted one final—to date—movie go-round with *The Return of Mr. Moto* (1965): aka *Mr. Moto and the Persian Oil Case*. "The most famous secret agent of them all is back in a new adventure!" screamed the poster tagline. A defiant and/ or desperate assertion, considering that the film would be running in films against James Bond and *Thunderball*, at the exact same time. Twentieth Century–Fox—who still owned the screen rights—distributed this British-made film on behalf of Lippert Pictures, an American company founded by Robert L. Lippert (1909–1976) in the late 1940s. Director: Ernest Morris (1913–1987). Release date: October 18, 1965 (UK). Filmed at Shepperton Studios.

The latest but hopefully not last actor to play Mr. I.A. Moto was Henry Silva (1928–2022), whose vaguely "Oriental" features led to his being cast as Chink in *The Tall T* (1957) and the martial-arts villain Chunjin, in *The Manchurian Candidate* (1962). Silva provided an audio commentary for the Twentieth Century–Fox DVD boxed set, *The Mr. Moto Collection, Volume 2* (2007), in which *The Return of Mr. Moto* appears as a featured extra. From his IMDb Website Biography section: "While making minimal comments about [*The Return of Mr. Moto*], Silva does address the issue of his heritage. Wryly noting that he had been assumed to be everything, including Russian, he specifically denied being of Puerto Rican heritage, which is the most commonly reported origin. His mother was from Northern Spain and his father was Italian. He was born in Brooklyn [September 15, 1928] but left there when he was only five months old."

Mr. Moto—now a Special Agent for Interpol—is called in to help the British Secret Service investigate the sabotage of oil wells belonging to the Beta Oil Corporation in the Iranian province of Wadi Shammar. The same thing has been happening to other international petroleum companies in that region. A secret cartel plans to take over the oil leases when they become due for renewal. Moto goes undercover as a Japanese conference delegate called Mr. Takura, after an attempt on his life fails but he is believed dead. How Moto escaped from the weighted sack thrown into the river Thames is left unexplained. Henry Silva does a passable impersonation of Peter Lorre, but it confounds belief that not even the antagonists who have met him at close range don't see through his minimal false-beard-and-glasses disguise. Spoiler alert: the most likeable and least likely suspect character turned out to be the mastermind behind it all.

Critical reactions to *The Return of Mr. Moto* were mainly on the adverse side. A.H. Weller, for one, called it "extremely garrulous and inane" (*The New York Times*: December 2, 1965). Any chance of a sequel was undercut by its being made in monochrome and released as the bottom half of double bills. It might have been better to pitch it as the pilot episode of a TV series. In fact, an episode of *Pulitzer Prize Playhouse* (season 2, episode 11: May 7, 1952), was entitled "The Return of Mr. Moto." Based on a story written by Marquand himself, it starred James Daly, Elmer Davis (narrator), Eva Gabor, and Harold Vermilyea.

Before, during, and after his wartime service, Marquand had been establishing himself as one of America's most successful middle-to-highbrow novelists: In particular: *Wickford Point* (1939); *H.M. Pulman, Esquire* (1942); *B.F.'s Daughter* (1947); *Point of No Return* (1949); *Melville Goodwin, U.S.A.* (1951). *B.F.'s Daughter* was filmed—not very well—in 1948. Ditto *Melville Goodwin, U.S.A.*, unrecognizably filmed as *Top Secret Affair* (1957). At least *Stopover Tokyo* (see above) had Cinemascope going for it—if not Mr. Moto. Marquand's rather fraught relationships with the opposite sex—married twice, divorced twice—were reflected in his final novel, *Women and Thomas Harrow*.[50]

Marquand kept his short-form fiction hand in during the mid–1950s with the occasional funny-peculiar story for *Sports Illustrated* magazine about the friction between an "old-line" country club and its adjacent "upstart" rival (collected in *Life at Happy Knoll*). He had, it seemed, a bright late-period career in front of him, airily walking the tightrope between popular success and critical acclaim. Even the Nobel Prize for Literature might have been a faint—if outside-chance—possibility. But it was not to be. The 66-year-old Marquand suffered a sudden fatal heart attack at his Newburyport home in the summer of 1960. N.B. John Philips Marquand, Jr. (1923–1995), followed in his father's literary footsteps with an only novel, *The Second Happiest Day*[51] (a tribute to returning Second World War veterans).

Literary and motion-picture Oriental detectives fell out of favor during the 1950s—right up until the present day, in fact. The only venerable exception is Charlie Chan. As mentioned above, J. Carrol Naish starred in *The New Adventures of Charlie Chan*, a syndicated TV series of which the first five episodes were made by Vision Productions in the United States. First broadcast: August 9, 1957, USA. Production was then moved to the United Kingdom, under the aegis of ITC Entertainment and Television Programs of America (finishing in mid–1958). Thirty-nine 25-minute black-and-white episodes were made altogether. The British episodes were mostly set in London. From *Halliwell's Television Companion*[52]: "Rather scruffy cases for the Oriental detective, with a star plainly unhappy in the role."

Masao Masuto, created by E.V. Cunningham (i.e., Howard Fast) is a significant exception to the Decline of the Oriental Detective rule. This American-born Mr.

Moto clone first appeared in *The Case of the One-Penny Orange*.[53] From *Encyclopedia Mysterioso*: "A Zen Buddhist in the Los Angeles Police Department, Masuto [like *Columbo*], has cases that tend to take him to the sprinkled lawns rather than to the mean streets. The Nisei (first generation of Japanese-Americans born in the United States) detective is a karate expert who grows roses and is a devoted family man. He has a sense of humour, too, putting on a stereotypical World War II movie Japanese accent for the benefit of the prejudiced." But a *real* Chinese detective—Inspector Chen Cao of the Shanghai Police Department—created by a *real* Chinese writer—Qui Xiaolong (1953–)—has assumed significance in recent years. Qui (born in Shanghai, 1953) is an English-language poet, literary translator, and academic who now lives in St. Louis, Missouri. He first visited the United States in 1988 to write a book about T.S. Eliot. After the Tiananmen Square protests in 1989, however, he stayed in the USA to avoid persecution by the Chinese Communist Party. His first Inspector Chen novel, *Death of a Red Heroine*, came from Random House in 2000. Industrial espionage is a frequent plot concern.

In quick conclusion. Like Sir Arthur Conan Doyle, John P. Marquand wanted to be remembered for his "serious historical novels" rather than the "down-market" Sherlock Holmes. But—like Conan Doyle with Holmes—he had no need to say "So sorry" about his creation of Mr. Moto, one of the most well imagined and best-loved secret agents in all popular fiction. As a matter of associational interest, Stuart M. Kaminsky (1934–2009) wrote a novel about his Hollywood private detective, Toby Peters, entitled *Think Fast, Mr. Peters*.[54] "Quickly—and bizarrely—a cityful of [Peter] Lorre look-alikes become targets of invisible assassins and Toby is framed for murder" (blurb).

Chapter Six

The War That Changed War

"I have to tell you that no such undertaking has been received, and that consequently this country is at war with Germany" (Prime Minister Neville Chamberlain: September 3, 1939). "I ask that the Congress declare that since the unprovoked and dastardly attack … a state of war has existed between the United States and the Empire of Japan" (President Franklin D. Roosevelt: December 8, 1941). Hardly a day—or perhaps even an hour—goes by without a new book of fiction or nonfiction being published about the Second World War. From Dunkirk to D-Day, from Prague to the Philippines, from Churchill to Chiang Kai-shek, from Blitzkrieg to Bouncing Bombs, from everywhere to everyone and everything else. Max Hastings's *All Hell Let Loose: The World at War 1939–45*[1] is a more recent one-volume history, with much updated and newly discovered information. A second world war had long been anticipated by spy-fiction writers, particularly in the United Kingdom.

Leslie Charteris had Simon Templar pitting his wits and sinews against warmongering industrialists and mythical European statesmen during most of the 1930s. *Prelude for War*,[2] later retitled *The Saint Plays with Fire* (Triangle, New York, 1942), can stand as a prime example of pre–Second World War it-*can*-happen-here popular fiction. Simon Templar acts more like a counterspy than ever before. The point is trenchantly made that Fascism and Nazism were not necessarily confined to Italy and Germany. France—and the United Kingdom—had no special immunity from the totalitarian "virus" that was then spreading across Europe. Fascist parties existed in both countries, led by (a) Jacques Doriot and (b) Sir Oswald Mosley. There is even a direct reference to the stage-managed Reichstag Fire (February 27, 1933) that helped Hitler gain absolute power and establish the Third Reich: "Of course the Nazis said that the Communists had done it; but a good many people have always believed that the Nazis arranged it … to give themselves a grand excuse for what they went on to do afterwards."[3]

At about the same time, however, Eric (Clifford) Ambler[4] came to "own" the pre–Second World War British spy thriller. As Hugh Hebert wrote, in his obituary for *The Guardian* newspaper (October 16, 1998): "Ambler's central characters were amateurs of a kind closer to Somerset Maugham's Ashenden—neither heroes nor anti-heroes. They had little or no experience of the military or secret worlds and no strong ideological commitment. Not all of them were even British. They might be a writer/journalist, as in *The Mask of Dimitrios* [1939], rated one of Ambler's best and most influential works. They might be a refugee teacher, a businessman, or a medic—like *Dr. Frigo* [1974], Ambler's own favourite. They stumbled into complex situations, where they had to make tough choices under pressure."

The tight plotting, narrative drive, and moral ambiguity of Eric Ambler's prewar novels paved the way taken by Graham Greene.[5] Greene went so far as to say: "Mr. Ambler is our greatest thriller writer." As a matter of chronological fact, however, Greene had a four-year head start on Ambler when it came to writing quasi-realistic espionage thrillers. Henry Graham Greene was born in Berkhamstead, Hertford-shire. The autobiographical *A Sort of Life*[6] gives next to nothing away concerning his early life. Recommended reading: *The Life of Graham Greene*,[7] in three volumes, by Norman Sherry.

A Gun for Sale[8] could be described as Greene's breakthrough novel—especially in the United States, where it had appeared a month earlier than the British edition (with the more "American" title of *This Gun for Hire*). Robert Macfarlane summarized the plot in his introduction to the Vintage Classics paperback edition: "The 'gun' is an assassin called Raven, who is hired to kill the Czech Minister for War. Raven returns to England after a successful hit, only to be paid off in stolen notes by his contact, Cholmondeley [pronounced Chumley], and nearly arrested as a consequence." Paramount Studios bought the film rights to *This Gun for Hire* within a year of publication, and it was eventually made in 1942, with Alan Ladd (1913–1964) as Philip Raven.

The Ministry of Fear[9] is one of the best—and most frightening—spy novels to be written during the Second World War. Its quasi–Orwellian title is explained as follows: "[The Germans] formed, you know, a kind of Ministry of Fear—with the most efficient under-secretaries. It isn't only that they get a hold on certain people. It's the general atmosphere they spread, so that you can't depend on a soul."[10] *The Ministry of Fear* (1944) is one of the best—and most frightening—spy films to be made during the Second World War. For one thing, it was directed by Fritz Lang (1890–1976), an Austrian-born *émigré* with German-language Expressionist classics like *Metropolis* (1927), *Spione* (*Spies*: 1928), and *Das Testament du Dr. Mabuse* (*The Testament of Dr. Mabuse*: 1933) to his credit. For another thing, it could boast a fine central performance from Ray Milland (1907–1986) as Stephen Neale (formerly Arthur Rowe).

Dennis Wheatley's entry into Top Secret war-work was remarkably smooth and easy. In early 1939, he toured England as part of the National Recruiting Panel. Two years later came an offer to join Churchill's War Cabinet as the only civilian member of the Joint Planning Staff (1941–44), located in a subterranean bunker off White-hall. He also found the time to write five new Gregory Sallust novels. From a future author's note:

With regard to the present series, the sequence of titles is as follows: *The Scarlet Impostor* [1940], *Faked Passports* [1940], *The Black Baroness* [1940], *V for Vengeance* [1942] , and *Come into My Parlour* (1946). Each volume is a complete story in itself, but the series covers Gregory's activities from September the 3rd, 1939, to December the 12th, 1941, against an unbroken background incorporating all the principal events of the first two and a quarter years of the Second World War. Gregory also appears in *Contraband* [see Chapter Two], an international smuggling story of 1937, and *The Island Where Time Stands Still*, an adventure in the South Seas and Communist China during the year 1954.

Like James Bond, Sallust is often threatened with physical torture. From *The Scarlet Impostor*:

"It is unfortunate, Mr. Sallust," [said Gruppenführer Glauber] "that only by applying a very stringent test of your veracity can I ascertain whether or no you are speaking the truth. If you still maintain that you know nothing more when both your eyeballs are charred I shall have to accept your statement, but I should be failing in my duty were I to neglect any measure which might induce you to remember a little more."

With a swift, unexpected movement he jabbed the cigar lightly at Gregory's right eye, brushing its ash off on the eyelid, so that although Gregory was not burnt he felt the heat of the glowing end as he jerked back in his chair.[11]

Unlike James Bond, however, threatening is usually as far as it goes. Although Sallust does have the same kind of manly facial disfigurement: "Gregory frowned and the old scar on his forehead went white."[12] But the torture-porn worst is yet to come, in *Come into My Parlour*, meted out to a stark naked German prostitute who had helped in the attempted escape of a shot-down British airman: "Erika [von Epp] saw with horror that the ['kind of wooden'] throne was a form of electric chair but that instead of the shock being administered as usual by knee pads and a headband the terminals were designed for the impalement of the wretched woman. The two troopers stood by making lewd jokes while the other man thrust them into her writhing body."[13]

Seven years later, an equivalent but comparatively tame torture scene would feature in *Casino Royale*. The villain, Le Chiffre, watches from a "throne-like chair" as James Bond is tied to another, bottomless chair, with his naked "buttocks and the underpart of his body" protruding beneath it. Le Chiffre then applies a cane carpet-beater to 007's now far from being private parts. The result was, as Fleming so delicately put it, startling.

At a much less "stratospheric" level of Second World War British spy fiction than Wheatley, we find Peter Cheyney (1896–1951). Born in the East End of London, Reginald Evelyn Peter Southgate Cheyney trained as a lawyer, but soon grew tired of routine office work. Cheyney's first mystery novel, *This Man Is Dangerous*,[14] kicked off a ten-book series featuring American FBI agent Lemmy Caution (who later moved to London). Caution would find himself on the fringes of intrigue every once in a blue moon. But Michael Kells, in *Sinister Errand*,[15] is the real secret-agent deal. His mission is to chase Nazi spies who are evaluating V1 "flying bomb" target sites all over London. *Sinister Errand* was filmed as *Diplomatic Courier* in 1952. It was updated to early postwar times and starred Tyrone Power (1914–1958) as "Mike" Kells, a courier for the American State Department, now drafted by Counterintelligence to find an important Russian document. Kells returned in *Ladies Won't Wait* (1951).

Stephen Mertz, the American writer and critic, maintains that "Cheyney's most original, and most critically acclaimed, work was his so-called 'Dark' series of espionage novels, all of which feature 'dark' in the title, concerning a top secret British counter-intelligence unit operating against Nazi agents in wartime England and abroad [neo–Nazis are hunted down after 1945]. [The] first two books of this series, *Dark Duet* [1942] and *The Stars Are Dark* [1943] represent Peter Cheyney at the very top of his form."[16] Further reading: *Peter Cheyney, Prince of Hokum*, by Michael Harrison.[17] The kinetic "Kane" is the one-book wonder of *Dark Duet*.

However, the officially neutral and isolationist-inclined United States had not stood idly by from mid–1939 until late 1941. Two of the five relevant-period films cited by Leonard Rubenstein in *The Great Spy Films*[18] are British: *The Lady Vanishes* (1938), directed by Alfred Hitchcock, and *The 49th Parallel/*aka *The Invaders* (1941), directed by Michael Powell. (1905–1990). The other four were American: *Confessions of a Nazi Spy* (1939), directed by Anatole Litvak (1902–1974), *Foreign Correspondent* (1940: Hitchcock again), *The Seventh Cross* (1944), directed by Fred Zinnemann (1907–1997), and *Across the Pacific* (1942), directed by John Huston (1906–1987). *The Lady Vanishes*, a jokey take on Ethel Lina White's 1936 novel *The Wheel Spins*, takes place in a generic mid–European totalitarian state. But *Foreign Correspondent* is made of very much sterner stuff.

Foreign Correspondent starred Joel McCrea (1905–1990) as two-fisted crime reporter John ("Johnny") Jones, whose editor has assigned him—very much against his will—to report upon the imminent outbreak of war in Europe. The script was written by Hitchcock regulars Charles Bennett and Joan Harrison, with additional (uncredited) dialogue by James (*Lost Horizon*) Hilton, Robert Benchley (who also plays a journalist named Stebbins), Ben Hecht, and Richard Maibaum (who would later work on many a James Bond film). McCrea's character begins by representing the typical couldn't-care-less American attitude to international affairs in general and European unrest in particular. But he is forced to learn and act better, as demonstrated by his rousing final speech from a radio station in bomb-blasted central London, à la real-life American broadcaster Edward R. Murrow (1908–1965). Abridgement:

> JONES: I can't read the rest of this speech I have because the lights have gone out. You can hear the bombs falling on the streets and homes. Don't tune me out—hang on—this is a big story—and you're part of it. It's too late now to do anything except stand in the dark and let them come as if the lights are all out everywhere except in America.
> MUSIC. "America" plays softly as background to the speech and throughout the end credits.
> JONES: Keep those lights burning, cover them with steel, build them in with guns, build a canopy of battleships and bombing planes around them and, hello America, hang onto your lights. They're the only lights in the world.

This scene was filmed on July 5, 1940. Five days later, the first German bombs fell on London. The United States would be forced into entering the war nearly a year and a half after the release of *Foreign Correspondent*. Hitchcock did his bit for the Allied cause with two more flag-waving films: *Saboteur* (1942) and *Lifeboat* (1943). Further reading: *A Pictorial History of War Films,*[19] by Clyde Jeavons. For the most part, however, major Hollywood studios made very few A-films about spies and counterspies until after both the European and Far Eastern wars had come to an end. But this *de facto* abstention policy did not apply to the mass manufacture of B movies, from major, minor, and downright Poverty Row studios. For example:

Enemy Agents Meet Ellery Queen (Columbia Pictures, 1942). Director: James P. Hogan. (1890–1943). Scripted by "Ellery Queen" (see below). Queen, played by William Gargan (1905–1979) helps Free Dutch agents fight Nazi spies over industrial diamonds in this "final entry to an undistinguished series" (Maltin).

Sherlock Holmes and the Secret Weapon (Universal Pictures: 1942). Director: Roy William Neill (1887–1946). Scripted by W. Scott Darling (based upon 'The Dancing Men,' by Conan Doyle). "Holmes [Basil Rathbone] is hired to protect the inventor of a new bombsight from the deadly clutches of Moriarty [Lionel Atwill]" (Maltin).

The Falcon Strikes Back (RKO Radio Pictures: 1943). Director: Edward Dmytryk. Scripted by Edward Dein and Gerald Geraghty. Story: Stuart Palmer. Based upon the character created by Michael Arlen. "The Falcon [Tom Lawrence, played by Tom Conway: 1904–1967] is framed for murdering a banker as part of a war-bond racket and tracks down the real culprit in this breezy entry" (Maltin). N.B. Conway was the elder brother of George Sanders, who had played the Falcon's brother (Gay Lawrence) in the first four films.

Charlie Chan in the Secret Service (Monogram Pictures: 1944). Director: Phil Rosen (1888–1951). Scripted by George Callahan (1902–1989). "The Oriental sleuth [played by Sidney Toler] probes the murder of an inventor [anti-torpedo device] in this initial *Charlie Chan* film for low-budget Monogram studios, which resulted in an obvious drop in production values and the addition of [Mantan] Moreland in the stereotyped role of Birmingham [Brown], a frightened cab driver" (Maltin). N.B. Highlighted by the performance of Marianne Quon (1917–1991: as Iris Chan, daughter of Charlie).

This annotated list could be extended to take up an inordinate amount of page space. But even the plethora of espionage-related second features were easily outnumbered by the serial superstars. The Shadow and the Spider came from pulp magazines, Dick Tracy and Secret Agent X-9 from the slightly more respectable newspaper comic strips. They, in their turn, faced stiff box-office competition from serials based upon the shenanigans of those insurgent comic-book "superheroes." The differences between newspaper comic strips and separately published comic books are succinctly explained by Bradford W. Wright in his landmark study, *Comic Book Nation: The Transformation of Youth Culture in America.*[20] "Although there is some overlap between the two (comic strips have been packaged as comic books, and a few comic book features have been syndicated as comic strips), these different marketing practices and target audiences have given each medium its own distinctive look and character."[21]

Superman and Batman were the great super-heroic originals, with Superman, alias Clark Kent, making his debut in the first issue (June 1938) of *Action Comics* (National Periodicals). He was created by two young men from Cleveland, Ohio: writer Jerry Siegel (1914–1996) and artist Joe Shuster (1914–1992), who had spent several years trying to persuade newspaper-syndicate and comic-book editors to publish the exploits of their red-and-blue-costumed hero. Batman, alias Bruce Wayne, was the joint creation of artist Bob Kane (1915–1998) and writer Bill Finger (1914–1974). The "Caped Crusader" first appeared in *Detective Comics* #27 (May 1939). He was later joined by Robin, alias Dick Grayson—the ever-youthful "Boy Wonder."

Wright's second chapter is entitled "Race, Politics, and Propaganda. Comic Books Go to War, 1939–1945." He opens it with the creation of that literally emblematic American superhero, Captain America (in *Captain America Comics* #1, March 1941): "A patriotic young American named Steve Rogers, too sickly and weak to qualify for standard enlistment, volunteers for a dangerous scientific experiment conducted by the nation's top scientist, Professor Reinstein. Injected with a strange, seething liquid, Rogers undergoes a startling transformation. Growing in height and mass, Rogers's muscles expand and tighten to the peak of human perfection. No longer a frail patriot, he now has a massive physique, a proud new name, and a bold mission. The nation's newest 'super-soldier,' Captain America, is born."[22] Bodybuilder Charles Atlas—raised to the *n*th power.

Captain America, however, was not the first American superhero to take up the fight against Fascist dictatorships. As Roy Thomas points out, in *Superman: The War Years 1939–1945*[23]: "[despite isolationism] war images from China and Spain and of the new technologies of which war Hitler and Mussolini and General Tojo were employing in their modern-day sabre-rattling, were omnipresent in the magazines, newspapers, and newsreels of the day. So it was all but inevitable that several covers of *Action Comics* and the quarterly *Superman* title that debuted in the spring of 1939 would depict the Man of Tomorrow smashing an airplane or tank—even if the alleged 'enemy' was coyly unidentified."[24] But the "sneak attack" on Pearl Harbor would change all that. A few days after President Roosevelt declared war on Japan, Hitler and Mussolini declared war on the United States of America. It now truly was the Second *World* War—for comic books, along with everything and everyone else.

Superman protected an Allied transatlantic convoy from an infinitely more fantastic threat in *Superman* #20 (January–February 1943). Cue another burbling blurb: "Only the warped, fiendish minds which conceived the bombing of Poland, the execution of innocent millions, the crushing of peaceful nations, could have launched the most terrible horror of the war ... *sea serpent terror!* SUPERMAN, *champion of democracy*, clears the sea-lanes of Hitler's monstrous slave-creatures in the action-packed adventure of ... 'DESTROYERS FROM THE DEPTHS'"! They are under the control of two-toothed, bald, knobby-headed Herr Doktor Fange: "HA! HA! HA! Nice vork, mine pretty pets! Smash der convoy for our glorious Fuehrer HA! HA! HA!"

The closest thing to a "real spy/counterspy" in Second World War-time comic books had the apt cognomen of *Spy Smasher*. He was created for Fawcett's *Whizz Comics* (#2, February 1940) by artist C.C. (Charles Clarence) Beck (1910–1989) and writer Bill Parker. (1911–1963). Ron Goulart explains: "Spy Smasher, in reality wealthy [Virginia] sportsman Alan Armstrong, lived up to his name and specialized in combating spies, saboteurs and would-be invaders. His fiancée Eve was the daughter of Admiral Colby, head of Naval Intelligence, a relationship that kept Alan up to date on Axis activities. He had no superpowers, and when he wanted to fly, he had to hop into his gyrosub—'a super craft which travels as fast as light on the ground, in the air and underwater.' Initially his costume and goggled helmet were brown, but later on he switched to a tighter-fitting green ensemble."[25] Arch-villains included America Smasher, a poisonous Nazi dwarf, and the super spy/scientist known only as the Mask. *Spy Smasher* provided an early writing opportunity for Patricia Highsmith (1921–1995), who was later to become the acclaimed author of *Strangers on a Train* (1950) and *The Talented Mr. Ripley* (1955). See *The Talented Miss Highsmith,*[26] by Joan Schenkar.

A 12-episode film serial version of *Spy Smasher* was released by Republic Pictures on April 4, 1942. Producer: William J. O'Sullivan (1913–1994). Director: William Witney (1915–2002). Kane Richmond played the title role. The musical score, by Death ("Mort") Glickman (1898–1953), effectively employed the V for Victory (*Da-da-da-daaaa*) theme from Beethoven's Symphony No. 5 in C Minor (Opus 67). This V-sign formed part of Spy Smasher's belt, together with the … Morse code symbol for the letter. Harmon and Glut: "As the mysterious foe of all spies, Alan Armstrong wore a dark uniform very similar to the one in the [comic books]. There was a flowing cape, a diamond-shaped chest emblem, and gloves. (In the comic magazine, the outfit had originally been a brown aviator's uniform. Later, the costume seemed to shrink to standard tight-fitting long underwear and to turn bright green, all due to wartime soap substitutes, one might suppose.)"[27]

Further reading: *The Adventures of Spy Smasher in the Comics and the Movies*, by Eric Stedman.[28]

Republic Pictures also created a secret-agent hero who had no connection with radio, pulp magazines, newspaper comic strips, or comic books. The 15-episode *G-Men vs. the Black Dragon* was released on January 16, 1943. Producer: William J. Sullivan (also a co-director). Other directors: Spencer (Gordon) Bennet and William Witney. Federal agent Rex Bennett was played by superhero-sized (6 feet 4 inch/1.96 centimeters tall) Canadian actor Rod Cameron (1910–1983), who towered over everybody else in every scene. Cameron had previously been employed by Paramount Pictures, standing in for their A-movie star Fred MacMurray (1908–1991). Oyama Haruchi played a Japanese spy and leader of the Black Dragon Society.

The screenwriting team of Ronald Davidson, William Lively, Joseph O'Donnell, and Joseph Poland delivered on the promise of Republic's typically overwrought trailer: "JAP PERIL—COME TO LIFE! EVERY MOMENT ELECTRIC WITH THRILLS!

EVERY SCENE BURSTING WITH ACTION! 15 PULSE-POUNDING HIGH-TENSION CHAPTERS!" Oyama Haruchi gives an introductory pep-talk to his subordinates: "Keep in mind that our aim is to spread terror and confusion, to cripple America's war effort, and undermine her morale." His methods are terrorism, sabotage, and corruption, with the Black Dragon Society smuggling enemy agents into the United States—cunningly disguised as Egyptian mummies. American Rex Bennet, Chinese Chang Sing, and British Vivian Marsh fight valiantly to defend Truth, Justice, and the United Nations Way from the Fanatical Fascist Fiends.

G-Men vs. the Black Dragon made pots of money for Republic, who duly rushed a sequel into production. The shooting schedule for *Secret Service in Darkest Africa* lasted an unusually long 45 days, from April 12 until May 23, 1943 (July 24). Rod Cameron reprised his rowdy role as Rex Bennet (also, briefly, the fake German secret agent G27, hotfoot from Stalingrad). As per John Buchan's *Greenmantle*, the Germans are misusing religion in an attempt to control the Middle East with the help of deluded Islamic fanatics. The action was even more fast and furious than in *G-Men*, with stuntman Tom Steele standing in for Cameron during the more ferocious fight scenes.

Other and more "respectable" heroes from "real" hardcover books also pitched in to aid the Allied war effort. Simon Templar had taken an early hand in this Great Counterspy Game, before relocating to the USA (like his creator). The chronicles are remarkably silent on the part that Simon Templar played in the early war years, although one feels that he must have done *something* to help the Old Country in her hour of need. Then along came *The Saint in Miami*.[29] Having decided not to enlist in one of the armed services—British or American—the Saint now works for a shadowy Government security agency, under the guidance of the hardly less shadowy Hamilton ("Ham," for short). The NYPD and the FBI are also in on the act. No undue stress is ever placed upon his Englishness, so that he becomes more and more "transatlantic" in character.

The Saint Steps In (1943) takes place in Washington, D.C., where Madeleine ("smiling brown eyes and hair the colour of old mahogany") Gray begs Simon Templar for help. Her father, Calvin Gray, has invented a revolutionary new form of synthetic rubber, the formula for which has been stolen by a predatory industrialist named Frank Imberline. In very short order, Templar is up against what seem to be gangsters but who turn out to be Fifth Columnists of a peculiarly American kind. As the Saint ends up pontificating: "Simply because [Hobart Quennel] is a man like that. Because he's more dangerous than any fifth columnist or any outright crook, because he sincerely believes that he's a just and important and progressive citizen. Because he can talk contemptuously about Café Society and the playboy class, and really believe it and feel sincerely superior to them, and sandwich it in between mentioning his new strings of polo ponies and the parties he throws for his daughter [Andrea] when they drink thirty cases of champagne. 'They're dead but they don't know it'—but he's one of them and he doesn't know it…."[30]

Steps In was bracketed by two short-form collections: *The Saint Goes West* (1942) and *The Saint on Guard* (1944). In "Arizona" (*Go West*), the Saint is up against Ludwig Julius, a Nazi scientist plotting to mine the quicksilver deposits beneath the Circle Y for use in the manufacture of German munitions. If *Goes West* panned out at only 33⅓ percent espionage fiction, then *The Saint on Guard* came so close to 100 percent as to make no difference. The two stories also mark the end of Simon Templar's officially sanctioned counterspy activities during the Second World War. "The Black Market" (*Black Mask*, March 1944) sports a banner headline from the New York *World Telegram*: SAINT TO SMASH IRIDIUM BLACK MARKET.

"The Sizzling Saboteur" (*Flynn's Detective Fiction*, November 1943, as "The Saint in Trouble") is—figuratively speaking—Olga Ivanovitch: "Beauty of a stately kind that had no connection with the common charms of the other temptations there.... By her birth certificate she might have been any age; but by the calendars of a different chronology she had been old long ago—or ageless."[31] But the term "sizzling saboteur" could *literally be* applied to Henry Stephen Matson, whom Simon Templar had been tailing from St. Louis, Missouri, to Galveston, Texas: "His hair was all burned off [by gasoline], his hands were barbecued from trying to beat out the flames of his own pyre, and the few remnants of his clothes were charred to him in a hideous smelting."[32]

Of the contemporary and "indigenous" American mystery writers, Raymond Chandler alluded *en passant* to the war effort throughout *The Lady in the Lake*.[33] For example: "The Puma Lake dam [San Bernardino] had an armed sentry at each end and one in the middle. The first one I came to had me close all the windows of the car before crossing over the dam. About a hundred yards from the dam a rope with cork floats barred the pleasure boats from coming any closer. Beyond these details the war did not seem to have done anything much to Puma Lake."[34]

Another mystery writer, Davis Dresser (1904–1977) did very much the same thing, under his more famous pseudonym of Brett Halliday. Dresser was born in Chicago, Illinois, but was raised in Texas. After many adventures, he finished high school and earned a certificate in Civil Engineering from Tri-State College, Angola, Indiana. Dresser then turned his hand to writing pulp fiction—without notable success, until Michael ("Mike") Shayne came along. Appearance-wise, Mike never changed much from chapter 1 of *Dividend on Death*:[35] "His rumpled hair was violently red, giving him a little-boy look curiously in contrast with the harshness of his features. When he smiled, the harshness went out of his face and he didn't look at all like a hard-boiled private detective who had come up to the top the tough way." Like Philip Marlowe, his own near contemporary, Shayne was not called up for the draft. Nor did he ever get officially involved with the war effort—again, like Philip Marlowe. However, since Pearl Harbor was bombed six months before *The Corpse Came Calling*,[36] there is a lot of anxiety expressed about Fifth Columnists, potentially disloyal German expatriates, and emergency rationing. In many ways, Mike Shayne operated in a more realistic wartime American world than Philip Marlowe. And

Blood on the Black Market[37] does for the state of Florida what *The Lady in the Lake* did for California:

> Accustomed for many months to the dimout and gasoline restrictions, Shayne no longer noticed the paucity of vehicular traffic, but this, coupled with deserted business build-ings on the Trail beyond Coral Gables, gave added protection to criminals who took advantage of the wartime necessities to rob and murder.[38]

At the far end of the spectrum from Michael Shayne lies the mystery writer/pri-vate detective Ellery Queen, the creation of two cousins who wrote together under the pseudonym of Ellery Queen. Frederic Dannay (1905–1982) and Manfred B. (for Bennington) Lee (1905–1971) were both native New Yorkers (Dannay from Elmira, Lee from Brooklyn). Their first novel, *The Roman Hat Mystery*,[39] introduced Queen as only a slightly less insufferable clone of Lord Peter Wimsey, prone to lecture everyone within range on every subject under the sun. However, Ellery does become more mellow and agreeable with the passing years—not unlike Lord Peter himself, to be fair. Apart from appearing in over 50 books, Ellery Queen became a star of films, radio, comic strips, and television. Recommended reading: *Royal Bloodline: Ellery Queen, Author and Detective*,[40] by Francis M. Nevins, Jr.

Q.B.I: Queen's Bureau of Investigation (1954) commences with a MEMO from Ellery himself: "Here and there in the closed-case records of Queen's Bureau of Investigation will be found a case marked *Special....*" But a Q.B.I. Espionage Dept. is conspicuous by its absence. Even the three Ellery Queen novels published during between 1942 and 1945—*Calamity Town* (1942), *There Was an Old Woman* (1944), and *The Murderer Is a Fox* (1945)—might as well have been set in peacetime. The *Ellery Queen* radio series (1939 to 1948), every script of which had been written by Dannay and Lee, did feature some few-and-far-between counterspy dramas, but they never amounted to much. Only one of the seven EQ feature films made any explicit reference to espionage: *Enemy Agents Meet Ellery Queen* (see above).

Nero Wolfe—the super-heavyweight, orchid-growing, beer-drinking, book-collecting, woman-hating, and exercise-averse Manhattan-based private detective created by Rex Stout (1886–1975)—took a more active part in espionage than Michael Shayne and Ellery Queen, put together. The same occasional counterspy thing goes for Archie Goodwin—his athletic, handsome, and definitely not woman-hating Young Man About Town assistant. Recommended reading: *Rex Stout: A Biography*,[41] by John McAleer.

Stout's first-written but second-published novel, *The President Vanishes*,[42] is not without interest to students of spy fiction. It was published anonymously. McAleer: "Not until 1939, when he began to take an active role in national affairs, did Rex acknowledge *The President Vanishes* as his own."[43] The vanishing president is Craig Stanley, who had been facing a political crisis—perhaps even impeachment—over potential American embroilment in an impending second European Great War. The countries are unidentified. At first the Secret Service treat it as a kidnapping case, but no ransom note is received and no demands of any kind are made. It gradually becomes evident that President Stanley has arranged his own disappearance to help nip a military coup by a fascistic cabal of "Grey Shirts," allied with Big Business, in the bud.

Meanwhile, Stout had been laying the foundations for his first Nero Wolfe novel, *Fer-de-Lance*,[44] which saw publication a month (September over October) before *The President Vanishes*. Further verifiable facts—and fanciful speculations—are to be found in *Nero Wolfe of West Thirty-Fifth Street: The Life and Times of America's Largest Private Detective*,[45] by William S. Baring-Gould (1913–1967). Baring-Gould (the S = Sabine) had previously written *Sherlock Holmes of Baker Street: A Life of the World's First Consulting Detective*,[46] in which he gave credence to the theory that Nero Wolfe was the illegitimate son of Sherlock Holmes and the American opera singer Irene Adler (q.v. "A Scandal in Bohemia": *The Strand*, July 1891). More to our present case, however, is the chapter boldly entitled "Wolfe and Archie Go to War":

> When the [Second World] war came, it was Major Archie Goodwin, United States Military Intelligence. His first assignment, early in 1942, was to straighten out a "mess down in Georgia," and he did pretty well at it, too, according to the department's top mackaroo.
>
> Army Intelligence wanted Nero Wolfe to go to work for them also, of course, in connection with undercover enemy activities in this country, but Wolfe had other plans and refused to cooperate. So Archie's next assignment was to convince him.[47]

Not that the timber-wolfish Wolfe took much convincing. Baring-Gould uses this line from *Not Quite Dead Enough* (1944) as a chapter-heading epigraph: "I am going to kill some Germans. I didn't kill enough of them in 1918." It has become Wolfe's "working hypothesis" that two million Americans should kill ten Germans apiece, and he fully intended to play his homicidal—even genocidal—part. Wolfe was finally persuaded to give up his mad scheme to kill Germans personally, of course, and the "log entry" continues: EXT? "The first recorded case [Wolfe] and Archie shared together as wartime assistants to the military is described in *Not Quite Dead Enough* (title novella of collection: first published in *The American Magazine*, December 1942). It took place on a Monday to Wednesday in early March 1942, and it was followed in the new year by 'Booby Trap' (second novella of same: first published in *The American Magazine*, August 1944). Archie's special assignment for most of the rest of the war was to assist Wolfe in the various projects entrusted to him by the army. This was not very much to his liking: three times he requested overseas duty, and three times he was turned down."

The last recorded wartime case of Wolfe and Goodwin began—according to Baring-Gould's chronology—on a Tuesday in May 1944. Archie gave it the title "Help Wanted, Male" (*The American Magazine*, August 1945). It was reprinted in *Trouble in Triplicate* (1949) , along with "Before I Die" (*The American Magazine*, April 1947) and "Instead of Evidence" (ditto, May 1946, as "Murder on Tuesday"). "'It was merely a job,' Wolfe murmured, as if he knew what modesty was."

Of associational interest only are the Bertha Cool and Donald Lam novels written by Erle Stanley ("Perry Mason") Gardner (as A.A. Fair). They were obviously "inspired" by Nero Wolfe and Archie Goodwin, but that is about all that the two series have in common. Steinbrunner and Penzler: "The senior member of this unlikely detective team is Bertha Cool, a large gray-haired woman in her sixties. Her weight (as much as 275 pounds) is a constant problem. Lam is a disbarred lawyer who has had many brushes with the police. The Cool-Lam team is formed at the outset of *The Bigger They Come*,[48] when Donald, hungry and desperately in need of work, convinces Mrs. Cool that despite his diminutive appearance (5 feet 6 inches tall and 125 pounds) he is man enough to be a detective." Lam become a full partner in *Double or Quits* (1941). They spend little or no time on espionage work, even during wartime, when Lam does naval service in the South Pacific. Bertha takes over telling the tale of her now # cases. Lam receives a medical discharge in *Give 'Em the Ax* (1944), after contracting a tropical disease. He duly returns to the agency fold—only to become the prime suspect in a murder case.

But the most incongruous, not to say incredible, fighter against Fascism must surely be John Clayton, Lord Greystoke—better known to the world as Tarzan, Lord of the Jungle. Like Sherlock Holmes and James Bond, Tarzan has become such an iconic figure that it is often difficult to remember that he was created in the mind of an American writer called Edgar Rice Burroughs (1875–1950). *Tarzan of the Apes* (the lost son of an ape-murdered English lord) first appeared in *The All-Story* pulp magazine for October 1912, and in book form two years later. Twenty-three more Tarzan novels would flow from the author's overworked typewriter. Burroughs himself was born in Chicago, Illinois. Before writing came to his financial and emotional rescue, he had failed at just about everything. Recommended biographical reading: *Edgar Rice Burroughs: The Man Who Created Tarzan*,[49] by Irwin Porges.

Tarzan of the Apes turned into *Tarzan of the Movies*[50] (by Gabe Essoe) in 1918, as given personage by the portly Elmo Lincoln (1889–1952). Enid Markey (1904–1981) took the part of Jane Porter, a beautiful 19-year-old girl from Baltimore, Maryland, who would—in the fullness of time—become Tarzan's "mate." Over time, Tarzan himself came to be regarded as American rather than British—especially since he would be portrayed by a long string of American actors. Ironically, though, Johnny Weissmuller (1904–1984)—the first talking-picture Tarzan—actually hailed from what is now Romania. Weissmuller played the character in twelve films, from *Tarzan the Ape Man* (MGM: April 2, 1932) until *Tarzan and the Mermaids* (RKO: May 19, 1948). The Irish-born actress Maureen O'Sullivan (1911–1998) partnered him as Jane.

Espionage as such does not figure largely in the novels, although the Tarzan family is plagued by Bolshevik blackguards Nikolas Rokoff and Alexis Paulvitch in *The Return of Tarzan* (1915), *The Beasts of Tarzan* (1916), and *The Son of Tarzan* (1917). *Return* ends with Tarzan landing the job of Special Agent in the French Ministry of War and posted to Algeria. The films, however, took a strongly proactive attitude with regard to the ongoing Second World War, as Gabe Essoe explained:

During the early stages of production on *Tarzan Triumphs* (MGM: February 19, 1943), producer [Sol] Lesser (1890–1980) was contacted by the State Department, which considered Tarzan an important propaganda weapon.

Carroll Young wrote an original story in which he tried to make Tarzan a symbol of freedom and the spokesman for the American idea. He and Roy Chanslor (1899–1964) adapted the screenplay, which began with Zandra (Frances Gifford [1920–1994]), white princess of a lost civilization, coming to Tarzan for help. The Nazis had invaded the jungle intent on conquering her peaceful people in order to take possession of their wealth in tin and oil.

At first Tarzan, playing the supreme isolationist, merely said, "Nazis go away." To which Zandra replied, "You don't know them. Once they conquer us, they will spoil everything you stand for." Tarzan got the message and came across with this line: "Now Tarzan make war!"[51]

Tarzan Triumphs was a box-office triumph, too, earning over $1,500,000 in U.S. rentals alone (Edgar Rice Burroughs, Inc., made a healthy profit of $208,000).

Pulp-magazine characters like Doc Savage and the Shadow (see Chapter Six) kept their distance from the "real" Second World War, confining themselves to the occasional spy-ring busting. As in comic books, cinematic chapter plays, and B movies (see above), Germans and "Japs" had become the generic villains, just as Russians and Chinese had been before that, and Germans and—well—Chinese before that. It was all part of the constant struggle to keep the clichés current. Too many magazine writers were also content to re-fight the last war, with impossible characters using ever more impossible weaponry (flying buzz saws, supersonic vampires, and the unlikely like). One by one, the anachronistic "air-adventure" pulps were shot out of the newsstand sky.

The actual Second World War ended with (a) the surrender of Germany on May 7, 1945, and (b) the surrender of Japan on August 14, 1945. Max Hastings: "Practically all those who participated, nations and individuals alike, made moral compromises. It is impossible to dignify the struggle as an unalloyed contest between good and evil, not rationally to celebrate an experience, and even an outcome, which imposed such misery upon so many. Allied victory did not bring universal peace, prosperity, justice or freedom; it brought merely a portion of those things to some fraction of those who had taken part. All that seems certain is that Allied victory saved the world from a much worse fate that would have followed the triumph of Germany and Japan. With this knowledge, seekers after virtue and truth must be content."[52]

Further reading: *The Star-Spangled Screen: The American World War II Film*,[53] by Bernard F. Dick.

"Extravagant fiction today—cold fact tomorrow" was the masthead slogan on the first issue of *Amazing Stories* (April 1926), which was also the first magazine entirely devoted to science fiction (or "scientific romance" as it was then known). Recommended reading: *Trillion Year Spree: The History of Science Fiction*,[54] by Brian W. Aldiss, with David Wingrove. Conan Doyle and H.G. Wells had successfully forecast how relatively new weapons like fighter-bomber planes, submarines, and "land ironclads" (i.e., tanks) would be put to aggressive use in the Great War. The major powers would develop these weapons to a high degree of efficiency during the next twenty-odd years, unaware—or, in some cases, unheeding—of the even more terrible technological threats that were then about to be unleashed upon the world. Moreover, the changes in waging open warfare were matched by concomitant changes in the running of covert intelligence operations. Old allies became new enemies and old enemies became new allies, almost overnight. If "spy fever" had died down for a while after the First World War, it went increasingly viral after the Second. Both in fact and in fiction.

Like its 1914–1918 predecessor, the 1939–1945 conflict overstimulated the growth of applied military science. Guided missiles had long been a familiar science fiction trope. But German scientists—including Wernher von Braun (1912–1977), who later worked on the American space program—would engineer-up those all-too-real "vengeance" weapons the V1 flying bomb and V2 longer-range rocket. Recommended reading: *Target London: Under Attack from the V-Weapons During World War II*,[55] by Christy Campbell. The Manhattan Project led to atomic bombs being dropped on the Japanese cities of Hiroshima (August 6, 1945) and Nagasaki (August 9, 1945). See *Brighter Than a Thousand Suns: A Personal History of the Atomic Scientists*,[56] by Robert Jungk.

The ink was barely dry on the surrender documents countersigned by Germany and Japan when George Orwell (1903–1950) coined the term "cold war" to describe the new geopolitical standoff between East and West, in an article for *Tribune* entitled "You and the Atomic Bomb" (October 19, 1945). He would later give it definitive fictional form in his classic dystopian novel *Nineteen Eighty-Four*.[57] Another iconic term was coined by the now ex–prime minister Winston Churchill, in a speech he delivered at Westminster College, Fulton, Missouri: "From Stettin in the Baltic to Trieste in the Adriatic, an iron curtain has descended across the continent" (March 5, 1946). Churchill's rhetoric made an already paranoid Stalin believe that the West had always looked upon the Soviet Union as an unfriendly power. President Harry S. Truman[58] (term of office: April 12, 1945, to January 20, 1953) added fuel to the flames with an address before a Joint Session of Congress (March 12, 1947): "The free peoples of the world look to us for support in maintaining their freedoms. If we falter in our leadership, we may endanger the welfare of our own nation. Great responsibilities have been placed upon us by the swift movement of events. I am confident that the Congress will face these responsibilities squarely."

The wartime alliance was fast becoming a thing of threads and patches. Before long, those "swift movements of events" included the Berlin Airlift (1948–49): a large-scale operation to supply West Berlin during a Soviet blockade; the Communist takeover of China in 1949; and the Korean War (which lasted from June 25, 1950, until July 27, 1953). The North Atlantic Treaty Organization (NATO) military alliance was formed in 1949, with the rival Warsaw Treaty Organization (aka the Warsaw Pact) following six years later. Recommended reading: *Cold War*,[59] by Jeremy Isaacs and Taylor Downing, based upon the 1998 television documentary series made for Turner Broadcasting Incorporated (initially shown on CNN and BBC 2). Tagline: *For 45 years the world held its breath....* W.H. Auden (1907–1973), the Anglo-American poet, anticipated what was to come in his long poem entitled *The Age of Anxiety: A Baroque Eclogue.*[60] Meanwhile, the spying game was now increasingly more a matter for "players" than "gentlemen"—as in the early days of cricket and lawn tennis. The British would "muddle through" the longest, exemplified by Graham Greene in *Our Man in Havana.*[61]

"Since the United States had never had any co-ordinated secret intelligence service," wrote Constantine FitzGibbon, "save briefly and not too happily in time of war, and since well-informed men foresaw the duration of USSR-USA hostility at least as early as 1945, it was clear that an efficient, peacetime intelligence service was both essential and of high priority. The Americans looked first, and obviously, to the British model, then to the German ... and only belatedly to what the Russians were up to in this murky world."[62] The CIA evolved from the World War II OSS (Office of Strategic Services), an espionage and sabotage organization. It was constitutionally restricted to just operating overseas, leaving all domestic counterspying to the FBI. In theory, at any rate. Recommended reading: *The CIA and the Cult of Intelligence,*[63] by Victor Marchetti and John D. Marks. Every politician and soldier who had been anybody immediately started work on his memoirs or potted histories of the most recent world war. Churchill's six-volume history of *The Second World War*[64] can stand as the prime example.

Alfred Hitchcock's *Notorious* (1946) is far and away the best American spy film to come out of the immediate postwar years. Following the conviction for treason of her Nazi-sympathizer father, Alicia Huberman (Ingrid Bergman: 1915–1982) is recruited by a handsome but aloof government agent named T.R. Devlin (Cary Grant: 1904–1986) to infiltrate a neo–Nazi group operating in Rio de Janeiro. Leonard Rubenstein: "The espionage involved was deliberately vague: a bottle full of uranium ore and several refugee German scientists flitting about in dinner jackets could have added up to an atomic bomb project somewhere in the Brazilian mountains, but [Ben] Hecht's screenplay kept the intrigue at the level of a simple plot device."[65] *Notorious* rivaled the box-office success of *Casablanca* (1942), which had also starred Ingrid Bergman (and Humphrey Bogart).

The espionage element was even more skimped in *Blackhawk*, the fifteen-chapter serial made by Columbia Pictures (1952). Harmon and Glut: "For the part of Blackhawk, [Sam] Katzman [producer] and [Spencer G.] Bennett [co-directed, with Fred F. Sears] decided to hire none other than Superman himself, or at least Kirk Alyn (1910–1999), the actor who had played the Man of Steel in their two previous chapterplays (1948 and 1950). Surprisingly, the actor looked as much like Blackhawk, with his blue military uniform and black hawk insignia over a yellow background, as he did like Superman."[66] As for the plot, it had something to do with an enemy sabotage ring that possessed the standard-issue "electronic" death ray. Some of the Blackhawk World War II exploits were chronicled in a paperback-original novel written by

William Rotsler.[67] The heroic but anachronistic team was brought bang up-to-date by DC Comics (*Blackhawk* #108, January 1957), and went on to fight many a fantastically formidable foe until their final honorable discharge in the summer of 1990.

Meanwhile, radical and far-reaching changes were taking place in marketing of popular fiction. Pulp magazine publishers had to contend with rising production costs, which increased by seventy-two percent between the end of 1944 and the middle of 1947. It turned out to be a losing fight. For example, three of the largest science fiction pulps—*Planet Stories, Startling Stories,* and *Thrilling Wonder Stories*—folded before the end of 1955. Other, cannier publishers converted to the more cost-effective "digest" magazine size (approx. 5½" × 7½"), e.g., *Astounding Science Fiction* (1943) and *Amazing Stories* (1953). Several mystery and western pulps prudently followed suit. Slick magazines such as *Collier's* and *The Saturday Evening Post* continued to provide lucrative markets for poplit writers. But it was the so-called Paperback Revolution that really drove pulps and slicks to the wall.

Paperbacks are the lineal descendants of the late nineteenth-century dime novels (see Chapter Two), which had themselves been anticipated by the German publisher Bernardt Tauchnitz (1816–1895). Based in Leipzig, Tauchnitz issued softcover editions of British and American authors, from 1841 until 1943, with the occasional unsuccessful revival. The long-running story is told in *Tauchnitz International Editions in English 1841–1955: A Bibliographical History,*[68] by William B. Todd and Ann Bowden. But the mass-market paperback phenomenon really began with the formation of Penguin Books in July 1935. It was the brainchild of (Sir) Allen Lane (1902–1970), who then worked for The Bodley Head, a British hardcover publisher. The first batch of Penguins sold for sixpence (roughly equivalent to an American quarter, in those days), which made "highbrow" books more readily available to the general public. American publishers Robert F. DeGraff (1895–1981), M. Lincoln Schuster (1897–1970), Leon Shimkin (1907–1988), and Richard L. Simon (1899–1960) founded Pocket Books in June 1939. Allan Lane opened an American branch of Penguin at about the same time. It was run by Ian Ballantine (1916–1995), who would later leave to found Bantam Books (1945) and then his own company, Ballantine Books (1952).

"With few exceptions," wrote Thomas L. Bonn, "most of the [American] paperback publishers who followed Pocket Books in the 1940s and 1950s had extensive experience in the magazine business, as opposed to the book business. Dell and Fawcett were among the largest periodical publishers in the country when they began their book programs. Ace, Avon, Berkley, Popular Library, and Pyramid all were directed by men with mass circulation magazine experience."[69] Recommended— and lavishly illustrated—reading: *The Great American Paperback,*[70] by Richard A. Lupoff.

Fawcett Publications enjoyed a particularly strong distribution network, carrying such popular magazines as *True* and *Mechanix Illustrated*. Also a wide range of comic books, from *Captain Marvel* to *Hopalong Cassidy*. The company had been founded in the 1920s by two brothers: Wilford Hamilton Fawcett (1885–1940) and

Roscoe Kent Fawcett (1913–1999). Comic book and magazine sales had both taken a nosedive after World War II, however, and the Fawcetts decided to follow their competitors into the lucrative paperback market. The snag was that those more established pulp-into-paperback publishers had already lined up reprint deals with major hardcover companies. Then, in September 1949, Fawcett contracted with New American Library (a continuation of U.S. Penguin Books) to distribute their Signet (fiction) and Mentor (nonfiction) titles. The contract prevented Fawcett from publishing reprints of hardcover books, but permitted them to produce paperback originals.

Fawcett were not only sharing in the success of Signet (especially Mickey Spillane's "Mike Hammer" novels), but they had now added the Gold Medal second string to their bow. *The Persian Cat* (#103), by John Flagg, was the first Gold Medal original fiction title (courtesy of a new contractual arrangement with New American Library). Ron Goulart, in *The Dime Detectives*[71]: "What Gold Medal specialized in was original novels. Some were merely sleazy, but others were in a tough, hardboiled style that seemed somehow more knowing and more contemporary than that of the surviving pulps."[72] Further reading: "The Golden Era of Gold Medal Books," by George Tuttle, in Gary Lovisi's *Paperback Parade* (No. 33, March 1993). They went on to publish some of the best genre fiction ever written in the USA, from mysteries to westerns, historical fiction to science fiction, Gothic novels to spy fiction. As for the latter category, Edward S. Aarons would take a long head start in the Cold War Espionage Stakes.

CHAPTER SEVEN

Assignment—Edward S. Aarons

As related in the Introduction, Ian Fleming's first four James Bond novels were given their initial American paperback publication by Popular Library (*Casino Royale*: as *You Asked for It*) and Perma Books (*Live and Let Die*; *Moonraker*: as *Too Hot to Handle*); *Diamonds Are Forever*. Eric Ambler and Graham Greene were often reprinted, as were F. Van Wyck Mason and John P. Marquand, but paperback-original spy novels were a bit thin on the ground. Then, midway through the decade, Fawcett introduced a CIA secret agent named Sam Durell, created by Edward S. Aarons.[1] It would prove to be the first of just over forty volumes in a globally popular series that lasted for just over two decades.

Edward Sidney Aarons was born in Philadelphia, Pennsylvania. Aarons graduated from Columbia University, New York City, with degrees in Ancient History and Literature. According to an autobiographical sketch, he once "covered five-alarm fires, police stations, and the morgue" as a Philadelphia newspaper reporter. Other occupations included mill-hand, salesman, and professional fisherman. In December 1941, one week after the Japanese aerial bombardment of Pearl Harbor, he joined the U.S. Coast Guard.

Ex-Chief Petty Officer Aarons became a full-time writer soon after his discharge from the Coast Guard in late 1949. It was no snap career decision. His literary ambitions were set after winning a collegiate writing contest in 1933. Aarons's first novel, *Death in the Lighthouse*,[2] followed five years later, one of twenty-eight titles to be published under his Edward Ronns pseudonym. Aarons was one of the few "name" writers to be picked up by Phoenix Press, a lending-library firm that paid next-to-no royalties. Next came *Murder Money* (1938) and *The Corpse Hangs High* (1939). Of the latter novel, Lee Server wrote (in *Encyclopedia of Pulp Fiction Writers*[3]): "Aarons's work for [Phoenix Press] was crude, if colorful. In *The Corpse Hangs High*, for example, private eye 'Beauty' Black gets slugged unconscious in a classic sub–Chandler riot of metaphors that verge on the ridiculous: "A red, red rose blossomed before my eyes, spread out until it filled the universe, and then turned rotten and decomposed into a mountain of red worms that wriggled wildly away into the darkness."[4]

Twenty-five other novels as by "Edward Ronns" followed over the years that lay ahead. Two of them—*No Place to Live*[5] and *Gift of Death*[6]—concerned a private detective named Jerry Benedict. Another pseudonym, Paul Ayres, was appended to *Dead Heat*.[7] Aarons also sold a baker's dozen of pulp-magazine stories (all as Ronns), including: "A Corpse for Carol" (*The Shadow*, December 1945) and "Noose Around my Neck" (*Scarab Mystery Magazine*, November 1950).

Aarons's first novel to be published under his own name was *Nightmare*.[8] "Tough, moving and amply exciting tale" (*Saturday Review of Literature*). But his big breakthrough came with a quick flurry of novels he wrote for Fawcett/Gold Medal, initially bylined Edward Ronns. In 1950 alone: *Catspaw Ordeal*; *Million Dollar Murder*; *State Department Murders*; *The Decoy*; *I Can't Stop Running*. Then: *I Can't Stop Running* (1951) and *Don't Cry, Beloved* (1952). After that, Fawcett switched exclusively to Edward S. Aarons: *Escape to Love* (1952); *Come Back, My Love* (1953); *The Sinners* (1953); *Girl on the Run* (1956). *The Sinners* prefigures many a nautical melodrama by Charles Williams: "Two men, friends since college, had set off with their wives for a basking, leisurely year's cruise of the Caribbean. But the storm had ended all of that—as if the wind itself had ripped away the masks of convention and courtesy to show them the primitive terrors and passions that only haunt the edges of our dreams" (blurb).

Aarons might have carried on as a "valued contributor" to the Gold Medal assembly line of original pulp-fiction paperbacks. However, the Fates and/or Fawcett Publications had something much more substantial in store for him. The Gold Medal list ran the gamut of poplit genres (see Chapter Eleven), with the conspicuous exception of a regular spy-hero series. Whether by accident or design, Aarons would rectify that omission in mid-decade, with *Assignment to Disaster*,[9] his first novel to feature the imperturbable Sam Durell. It would later be retitled *Assignment—To Disaster* (1959), after *Assignment* became a handy series-identifier tagline. But inconsistent formatting meant that sometimes a colon or an ellipsis replaced a dash or—as with most of the later printings—no punctuation marks were used at all. The "dash" form will become the standard usage here.

Disaster (for short) gets off to a breakneck start. From chapter 1 (redacted):

It came to [Sam] Durell at the K Section of the Central Intelligence Agency this way:
Calvin Jackson Padgett disappeared.
Get him!
A score, a hundred, a thousand men began to fan out from the desert experimental base, from Las Tiengas, from the whole state of New Mexico, from the entire South-west.
If necessary, kill him!
Calvin Padgett, M.S., Maryland born, electronics technician, age twenty-eight, six feet even, weight 155, sandy hair, blue eyes, small scar on right jaw, soft-spoken. Dangerous. Armed. Rebellious.
One clue, finally: Padgett called his sister in Washington, D.C.
So it came to Sam Durell:
Get to the girl. See if she knows where he is, why he ran. There isn't much time. Five days. He knows too much about Cyclops.
And what is Cyclops?
Nothing you need to know, Durell. Get to the sister. Work fast. Find Calvin Padget!

This extract may be taken as a template for every subsequent Sam Durell novel. Or, indeed, many another serial spy-novel character. Secret agent (and the reader) is given a terse but accurate briefing about some new existential threat to national/ international security and then sent off on his not-so-merry way. The accelerated, matter-of-fact style is jettisoned after chapter 1, although Durell does act more like a lone-wolf private eye than a government-issue secret agent for much of the time. Aarons still had a lot of character-building and structural work ahead of him.

Durell resents his immediate superior, Burditt Swayney, who resents him in turn—doubled. "[Burritt] Swayney was round and plump and pale, with a habit of making sucking sounds with his small mouth. His eyes were the coldest pale blue Durell had ever seen. The man was a human memory machine and a confirmed lecher. Durell did not like him, but for the sake of the work, he got along with him."[10] But Sam gets on well enough with the boss of all his bosses, General Dickinson McFee. "McFee was a small man, narrow-shouldered, with a bulging intellectual forehead and pale-brown, tired eyes. You forgot how small he was physically after you were with him any length of time. After a moment he seemed to fill the room. He waved Durell to a metal chair while he continued talking into a tape recorder. Durell smoked and waited."[11]

K Section H.Q. is located at Rock Creek Park and 20 Annapolis Street, Washington, D.C. "The brass plaque on the grey-stone front of the big Georgian house read simply, 'The Johnson-Kimball Company,' in dignified letters. [Durell] felt gritty and tired, his shirt already sticking to his back as he entered. As he went through the Italian marble foyer he heard the busy rattle of office machines in the cover offices that formed a façade for the real business conducted in the building."[12]

We are vouchsafed no detailed physical description of Samuel Cullen Durell in *Disaster*, but Aarons was more forthcoming in future novels. For example, *Assignment—Angelina*[13]: "Durell was a tall man in his thirties, with thick black hair, a small, trim mustache and dark blue eyes that reflected the quickness of his Cajun temper. He was powerfully built under his conservative gray summer suit, and he moved with deceptive ease and grace. His fingers were long and slender, adept with a gun, knife, or a hand in a poker game."[14] Apart from a few photogenic gray hairs, Durell showed no perceptible aging over his thirty-odd years of secret service. He usually wore dark blue suits, white shirts with button-down collars, and non-violent neckties. In stark contradiction, the standard Gold Medal head-shot of Sam Durell showed him as an apparently down-on-his-luck PI wearing a black pork-pie hat. And clean-shaven, if perhaps a bit stubbly. Fortunately, it was mostly relegated to the back covers, with a more suitable spy-hero figure taking the front-cover spot (accompanied by the obligatory beautiful blonde/brunette/redhead).

Also from *Angelina*: "[Durell] had been brought up by his Grandfather Jonathan, one of the last of the old Mississippi gamblers. The old man had worked the side-wheelers from St. Louis to New Orleans, and Durell's boyhood had been spent in the hot, green silences of the bayous around Peche Rouge in the delta country. His accent no longer betrayed him, thanks to his years at Yale and the war and his tours with G-2, the old OSS, and more recently, the CIA."[15]

Hence Durell's agency code name—Cajun (a Louisianian descended from French-speaking immigrants from Arcadia, i.e., Nova Scotia). Durell would generally begin each two-per-year novel in a situation involving violence and/or mystery, being sent to exotic foreign parts, following a trail of false leads and betrayal, finally catching up with and defeating the archvillain, then bowing out with world peace temporarily restored and the leading lady in his arms.

"Ripped from Today's Headlines"—the publicity slogan used by Warner Brothers back in the 1930s—could have been amended to read "Tomorrow's Headlines" concerning the Sam Durell novels. *Disaster* opens the ball in no uncertain terms. The runaway Calvin Padgett (mathematician) and his seemingly more stable elder brother, John (Project Manager and computer expert), are key scientists in the development of Cyclops, an artificial satellite to be launched into orbit a year before the Russian Sputnik I did it for real on October 17, 1957. The nuclear-armed Cyclops is to be fired into a thousand-mile-high orbit around the Earth. It will become what Durell "quietly" calls "the conscience of humanity"[16]—ensuring a benevolent Pax Americana. Lift-off has been set for 16.00 hours on the Fourth of July. But "somebody gimmicked the relays in Cyclops' brain so it will run amok. It won't orbit. It will go up in an arc and come down somewhere on the continental United States and its warhead will spray bombs over a wide area. It can destroy us all."[17] Less than four days left until Doomsday for America....

Aaron's penchant for impeccable research also enabled him to describe the geography and culture of "exotic foreign parts" without getting bogged down in guide-book banalities or letting too many of his personal observations impede the story. Durell made James Bond look like a comparative stay-at-home, as these *Assignment* titles can bear witness: *Budapest* (1957); *Ankara* (1961); *Lowlands* (1961: Lowlands = Holland); *Burma Girl* (1961); *Karachi* (1962); *Sulu Sea* (1964); *The Girl in the Gondola* (1964); *Palermo* (1967); *Peking* (1969); *White Rajah* (1970); *Tokyo* (1971); *Bangkok* (1972); *Maltese Maiden* (1972); *Ceylon* (1973); *Sumatra* (1974); *Afghan Dragon* (1976). Random example, from *Sorrento Siren* (1963): "The day was hot and sultry. A haze hung over the Bay of Naples and the mountains toward Pompeii. Durell had a quick breakfast at the air terminal and took a taxi to the Hotel Sentissi on the Via Partenope. The harsh *espresso* coffee made him wish for the Louisiana blend he preferred. The driver swung down to the waterfront and passed the big luxury hotels in the Santa Lucia area, with its terraced restaurants and docks and the massive bulk of the Castell dell'Ovo looming against the blue sky. As this early hour, the streets were still relatively empty."[18]

In his first written-up *Assignment*, Sam Durell never sets foot outside the United States. The same thing applies for number six, *Assignment—Angelina*, which takes place in Arizona, Indiana, New York, and Louisiana. But these would prove exceptions to the general globe-trotting rule.

The fair sex is represented in *Disaster* by Hazel (no surname given), Cori Neville, and Deirdre Padgett. Hazel has the underwritten—almost *non*-written role of Girl Friday to General McFee. Cora Neville is the rich-lady owner of the Salamander hotel in Las Tiengas. She has, it would seem, enjoyed a romantic dalliance with Calvin Padgett. Durell pays her a surprise visit: "[Cora Neville] sat at a vanity table, studying her blonde erotic beauty. From the waist up she was nude, and around her swelling hips was a slithered heap of silk, nothing more. Her nakedness did not seem to be a conscious matter with her, or designed to gain any overt reaction from the man who was with her."[19] That man is George West, the general manager of the Salamander, who—despite his All-American Boy name—soon reveals himself to be as Slavic as blintzes. But Deirdre Padgett makes the most traumatic entrance:

> The girl appeared suddenly from round the dark corner. One moment the street was empty, wide, peaceful, pooled with shadow under the poplar trees. The next, here she comes, almost running, wearing a light tan topper over her shoulders. From the window, Durell watched her walk, almost skipping in her haste, from shadow to shadow on the old brick sidewalk. Long legs, red hair. Right. He glimpsed her face. Good bones, wide eyes shining. Shining with what? He saw her run now. Fear. Fright was in her.[20]

Apart from being Calvin Padgett's younger sister, Deirdre is the scionette of a poor-but-proud Maryland aristocratic family. She works as a fashion editor for one of the D.C. daily newspapers. Durell saves her from being abducted by ruffians between pages 9 and 10. She is then persuaded to join his rendezvous with Calvin in New Mexico. They are—alas!—taken prisoner almost immediately upon their arrival. But all's well that ends well:

> Her eyes questioned him. He smiled. He kissed her.
> "Come closer," he said.
> "Sam?"
> "I'll never let you go," he said.

But things don't work out that way—nowhere near it, in fact. Deirdre Padgett leaves Durell at the outset of his very next case, *Assignment—Treason* (1956), for the very good reason that he has become emotionally distant and canceled their wedding. No explanation given. To be fair, Sam has just become embroiled in a complicated operation to expose rogue CIA agents—and even he comes under suspicion from General McFee. *Assignment—Suicide* (1956) begins with the unequivocal statement that Sam and Deirdre have split up for good—a statement that is later contradicted in *Assignment—Budapest*. Deirdre expresses a wish to join the CIA, but Durell flatly vetoes the idea of her working as a secretary, let alone as an agent. The on-again, off-again relationship lurches along until Deirdre finds herself attracted to Adam Stepanic, potentially the first American astronaut, in *Assignment—Mara Tirana* (1960). There is, however, a permanently on-again happy ending:

> [Durell] wanted to tell Deirdre [nicknamed "Dee" by this time] that there was a time in their lives when caution could prove a tragic trap to deprive them of happiness forever. She wanted to share his world. He would open the door, then, and let her in, and hope it

would not end for them as it had for the centurion on Zara Dagh [whose wife had joined him on campaign]. And if it did—well, there would be a time behind them, and this time right now, when he looked at how beautiful she was and wanted her.[21]

It became clear to Fawcett and Aarons himself that putting Sam Durell into a serious romantic relationship from the very first book would impede his career as a freewheeling secret agent. This led to the subsequent downplaying of Deirdre Padgett and the concomitant up-playing of what might be called female targets of opportunity. Several of the novels were given "named woman" titles. Apart from *Angelica* and *Mara Tirana* (see above): *Stella Marni* (1957); *Madeleine* (1958); *Carlotta Cortez* (1959); *Helene* (1959); *Lili Lamaris* (1959); *Zoraya* (1960). Cora Neville, from *Disaster*, is an already cited convenient example. Others include the Fleming-esque Pleasure Kendall (*Carlotta Cortez*), Jasmine Jones (*Nuclear Nude*: 1968), and Queen Saldava of Pakura (*Golden Girl*: 1972 and *Amazon Queen*). For the record, Durell races to Deirdre's rescue in *Budapest* and *Assignment—School for Spies*: 1966 (where she has supposedly married a Soviet sleeper agent named Bruno Faulk and defected with him to East Germany).

Like Bond in the books but not in the films, Durell does not force his sexual attentions upon unwilling women, not even in the line of duty. Moreover, Aarons had the good taste to avert his authorial gaze away from anything but the most innocuous of "heavy petting" scenes. He really let rip, however, in *Assignment—Manchurian Doll* (1963), with the particularly repellent villain Omaru, a "bastard Irishman, neither European nor Japanese [whose] mountainous physique and appearance of a *sumo* wrestler attracted none of the women. [But he amused himself] without outside interests. [Baroness] Isome saw to that."[22] Not for readers of a shockable disposition:

> One of Isome's maids knelt in swift silence at Omaru's side, bowing beside his big, special chair. He shivered, looked down at the pale, smooth nape of the maid's neck, seeing the tender wisps of dark hair that escaped her exquisite coiffure. He put his thick thumb in the small indentation just below the hairline....
> Omaru's breath hissed. His rotating thumb quickened on the maid's neck as she knelt beside him. His grip hurt her, but he did not know or care. His bulk trembled in response to Isome's increasing passion. Omaru's breath hissed. His rotating thumb quickened on the maid's neck as she knelt beside him. His grip hurt her, but he did not know or care.
> A small shudder shook Omaru. He sighed, leaned back, released the kneeling maid's neck. She got up at once, handing him what was needed.[23]

Omaru comes across as an "X Certificate" presentiment of Jabba the Hutt. Aarons didn't usually go in for such Mr. Big or Goldfinger villains, opting for realistic—or at least plausible—protagonists like *Manchurian Doll*'s Colonel Alexei Kaminov. His adversaries range from mere bullies *à la* L'Heureux (*Madeleine*) to the criminal mastermind Dr. Van Handel (*Star Stealers*: 1970). Dinov (*The Girl in the Gondola*) combines both "qualities" in one surprise package after another. Sometimes Durell meets up with a female villain, most notably Jesse Corbin in *Angelina* and the eponymous *Stella Marni* (1957).

Although Sam Durell talks the talk about being the patriotic stone-cold killer who places his current mission above mere humanitarian concerns, he seldom walks the walk. Violence from the bad guys—and gals—is invariably sadistic. Durell, on the other hand, kills quickly and with no evident pleasure. "The cleanest fighter in spy fiction" (to make free with an old Bulldog Drummond tagline). Durell himself takes an inordinate amount of punishment, invariably emerging bloody if not quite unbowed. He can both dish it out and take it back. Two examples, each from *Manchurian Doll*:

> One of the first things you learn while when training for K Section at the Farm is how much distance to keep when you cover a man with a gun, and especially how tight a grip to keep on your weapon. The Japanese hood was not professional in Durell's world. Smiling, Durell turned and smashed the gun from the man's hand. The man screamed, wringing a broken wrist, and Durell kicked the heavy gun aside.[24]
> He felt Omaru's breath explode in his face and his body was lifted from the ground in the man's violent, sweeping grip.[25]

Durell wins—eventually—but he surely knows that he's been in a fight to the near-death.

N.B. The *Manchurian Doll* is Nadja Osmanovna, who runs the KGB operation at the Soviet embassy in Tokyo, with a sad backstory based upon her girlhood in China.

The ending of *Disaster* was more suited to a one-off novel than the first volume of a hopefully long-running series. It proved easy enough to finesse the fluctuating relationship between Durell and Deirdre over the course of so many books. But if the all-seeing eye in the sky Cyclops nuclear-capability satellite had turned out to be viable, then secret agents like Sam Durell would have lost most of their usefulness. In the event, it was never even mentioned again. Durell's third mission, recounted in *Suicide*, concerns the imminent Russian development of an ICBM (Inter Continental Ballistic Missile), giving them the means to launch an unanswerable first strike against American targets. A fully operative Cyclops satellite would have nipped that idea in the bud. Another problem with *Disaster* was that Durell had been treated more like a rookie than a secret agent with at least ten years of exemplary service. James Bond would never take a crack like "You look beat, you stupid Cajun" from Felix Leiter, even when said in fun (by friendly fellow agent Lew Osbourn). General McFee, who should know better, won't cut him even an inch of slack. But he is accorded infinitely more respect from the second novel on.

Aarons knuckled down to a remunerative routine of one new Sam Durell novel every six months or so. The period 1965–66 was particularly busy, *Assignment*-wise: *The Cairo Dancers* (1965), *School for Spies*, *Cong Hai Kill* (1966), and *Palermo*.

Cong Hai Kill (along with *Bangkok*) is the closest Durell ever got to the Vietnam War, then coming up to the boil in that part of Southeast Asia. Too controversial for Fawcett, it would seem. But the Viet Cong do rate an oblique mention: "Snakes were the symbol, the method of life, of the Cong Hai. Silent, secret, and venomous, they were cousins to the V.C. across the peninsula in Vietnam, infiltrating the jungles and mountains here on the Gulf of Siam as sinuously as the snakes that were their totems."[26] Deirdre must perforce join him on this mission, to the tacit objection of McFee: "Deirdre loves you, Cajun. You've known many women, but you always return to her. She's too damned good for you, of course. We have no rule against married men, but it's easier on bachelors in this business, and we prefer men who don't have their minds on wives and families back home. You've always agreed with this, I know."[27] As Durell mentally acknowledges.

Then, after the so-so *School for Spies*, Aarons had Durell make a few trips into the light-headed fantastic. In *Moon Girl* (1968), the Soviet Union has seemingly stolen a march on America where lunar exploration is concerned. Tanya Ouspanaya, a half–Chinese and semi-amnesiac Russian cosmonaut whom Durell has rescued from solitary imprisonment in Tehran might or might not have just come back from living in a pressure-domed Moon Base with her scientist father (a slight acquaintance of Durell). The plot thickens even further as time goes woozily by. *Nuclear Nude* involves a painting called *The Nuclear Nude* that conceals a coded message that has got something to do with the military applications of neutrino research. On top of that, a SPECTRE-type group calling itself the Sentinels are working behind the scenes to provoke a Third World War, for the usual divide-and-rule purposes. *Assignment—Black Viking* (1967), however, makes even the film version of *You Only Live Twice* look like a piece of grim documentary realism.

Whoever wrote the front-cover blurb for *Black Viking* got it spot on: "The Chicoms [Chinese Communists] make an odd alliance with a half-crazed genius to give SAM DURELL his most dangerous and bizarre case to date." Something damned strange is happening to the weather (adapted from the back-cover blurb). Not just freakish blizzards in the Sahara, but unseasonable monsoons and typhoons in the East, hurricanes and tornadoes in the USA, and—in Europe—torrential floods and unending snow. Meteorologists predict a new Ice Age. The CIA/KGB "masters of deceit" sink their differences to meet in Belgium (the apparent epicenter) and select an elite task force to combat this man-made ecological disturbance. Durell leads the team and their search leads them far up the Baltic to the far north of Sweden, in pursuit of eccentric Professor Peter Gustaffson, who is ostensibly behind all these stormy shenanigans. His beautiful niece, Swedish secret agent Sigrid Gustaffson (alias Bjornson), has also joined in the hunt. Ditto his equally eccentric archaeologist brother, Eric.

Authorial scene-setting (in italics): "*The city of Bruges in Belgium, like several other cities in Northern Europe that take pride in the beauty of their canals, calls itself the 'Venice of the North.' It has no need for comparisons, for Bruges has a singular beauty of its own.... Bruges was founded in the seventh century as a Viking settlement and named 'Brucken,' which means The Landing Place. It was fortified in the ninth century and three hundred years later became the greatest port of northern Europe, the chief entrepôt of the Hanseatic League. Today it is the capital of West Flanders. Its*

port is silted up and it is nine miles from the North Sea coast.... Here and there one
can still spot the strain of Viking blood from the wild Norsemen who roared down from
Scandinavia with bloody swords, screaming oaths, for arson, robbery and rape."

The titular *Black Viking* is Durell's nickname for the rapscallion sea captain
Olaf Jannsen, who shares the same obsession with all things Viking as Dr. Eric Gustaffson (spoiler: Eric is the real "half-crazed genius" of the front-cover blurb). Durell
and Jannsen come to anachronistic blows:

> The big, black-haired man grinned and stood with his feet slightly spread for balance, his
> strong arms uplifted as he continued to whirl the mace with a deceptively lazy swing.
>   "Do you know the term 'berserker,' Mr. Durell? I am a berserker. A Viking filled with
> the lust for blood. Your blood."
>   The whirling iron ball came closer, almost grazed [Durell's] face. He turned his head
> instinctively aside, and Olaf laughed. Durell saw that the apartment was like a museum,
> cluttered with Viking weapons. His cheeks touched cold iron as his head was forced
> against the wall by the approaching mace. The iron ball sang as Olaf spun it slightly
> higher above his head. The strange light in his eyes brightened.[28]

Black Viking is a particularly demented example of spy-fi—adapted from the
term sci-fi—used to describe the lower-brow forms of science fiction. Abandon logic,
all ye who enter here. *Moon Girl*, *Nuclear Nude* (featuring another Chinese villainess, Madame Hung), and *Star Stealers* lowered the imaginative temperature to
infinitely more plausible levels. *White Rajah* (1970), which appeared just before *Star
Stealers*, made the best of both stylistic worlds. American naval jets have been violat-
ing Malaysian air space. *Hijacked* American naval jets, in squadron strength. If Sam
Durell can reach a remote mountaintop he might find the answer. But between him
and this mountain lies a countryside aflame with bloody riots, freelance assassins,
a CIA buddy (George Hammond) gone rogue, and an "unknown subject" traitor.
His lethally wild-card ally is Pala Mir, granddaughter of the enigmatic White Rajah
(Anthony Merrydale), who lives on and rules over that very same mountain-top.

After that, Aarons the writer and Durell the character wrote and enlivened a
string of well-above-average spy novels, including *Silver Scorpion* (1973), *Quayle
Question* (1975), *Black Gold* (1975), and *Afghan Dragon* (1976). But *Unicorn* (1976),
his 43rd and last-written novel, was yet another exercise in spy-fi. Dr. Alexander
MacLeod, a deranged Scottish scientist, has created an army of drug-empowered
supermen. These "unicorns" will be used to impose a new and mercilessly discipli-
narian world order: "The term 'unicorn' is an apt one. It was not chosen by accident. The symbol was picked deliberately. The unicorn is, according to mythology ...
inevitably drawn to virtue, purity and decency. They say the unicorn's hooves never
touch grass." Dr. MacLeod grinned, but his eyes were hard. "So we leave little or no
trace, we unicorns. You have noticed, of course, our connections with, or against,
various national security forces. An elite body, scattered around the world, will soon
enough put things right."[29]

A direct reference is finally made to Vietnam: "Hugh Donaldson was an old Far

East hand. There had been a time when he had run a string of networks up through British Malaya, when the Communists there first began sharpening their tactics for guerrilla warfare.... His other networks later ran through Indonesia during the Sukarno years, and finally into French Indo-China, where he was covered as an import-export man and also handled foreign aid. When the French left after Dien Bien Phu and turmoil followed, before the U.S. blundered into its own agony in South Vietnam, Donaldson had quite properly headed detachments of Green Berets among the hill people and afterward enjoyed certain privileges as adviser to Saigon's GGK, the intelligence apparatus designed to help check the tide of materiel flowing south along Uncle Ho's jungle trail from Hanoi."[30] It is not beyond the bounds of possibility that Sam Durell would have taken an active part in the Vietnamese conflict, had his creator been spared.

The Sam Durell Dossier would reveal little more about Cajun's private live than what has already been revealed in these pages. Durell is a dour man who never cracks a joke—at least not on the firm's time. He drives a car every now and then, in the line of duty, but without fixating on the make or model. No vodka martinis for him—shaken or stirred—not even a mint julep. Bourbon, perhaps, followed by a beer chaser. There are no "product placement" brand names. In *Assignment—Zoraya*, however, Durell reflects upon his college friendship with Prince Amr of Maari—nicknamed Bogo—and the "child-woman, Zoraya." He had finally taught Bogo how to play poker. But all that has been swept away in the swirling mists of time:

> Whatever Amr was today, the Yale undergraduate was gone. And whatever Durell had become, as he drove his Fiat along the fine Swiss highway toward Lausanne, he was a far distance from his Bayou boyhood and his years in New Haven. He had even come a long way from the relatively simple days of service with G2 and the old OSS. He had been manipulated, by time and circumstance. He had been at war too long, he thought, fighting in this secret war of sudden death in obscure parts of the world.
>
> Like his opposite number here in Geneva, Major Kolia Mikelnikov, Durell had become a professional, a finely honed weapon for defence, a deadly mechanism for assault. He would probably stay in the business, he thought, until he ended, through a tiny, momentary error, like John Blaney, in Jidrat.
>
> Very dead.[31]

But Sam Durell novels would live on after the death of their original author. *Assignment—Sheba* (1976) came out first, attributed to one Will B. Aarons. William L. DeAndrea, in *Encyclopedia Mysteriosa*:

"Declared by some published sources[32] to be the son of Edward S. Aarons, this was instead a house name used by Fawcett Publications.... The pun involved was obvious—the anonymous writers 'Will B.' (or at least attempt to be) Aarons." Very simple was this explanation, and plausible enough—as most wrong theories are! (To paraphrase the protagonist of *The Time Machine*). The facts were revealed by Jeff Falco and Al Hubin in Doug Barrett's "An Introduction to Edward S. Aarons' Assignment Series."[33]

Falco checked the obituary of Aarons in *The New York Times* (June 20, 1975), which told him: "Surviving are his widow, Grace Dyer Aarons, and a brother William Aarons." A copyright search for *Assignment—Death Ship* (1983), the sixth and last posthumous Sam Durell novel, revealed that copyright had been assigned to "Lawrence Hall and Will B. Aarons (Executor for the Estate of Edward S. Aarons")." *Assignment—Tiger Devil* (1977) placed "(pseud.)" after "Will B. Aarons," the claimant being listed as "Fawcett Publications." For Edward's *Amazon Queen*, the claimant was given as "William B. Aarons, Jr. (Executor)." *Maltese Maiden* (with Madame Hung) and *Golden Girl* are credited to "William B. Aarons & William B. Aarons, Jr. (Executor)." It would appear, Falco concluded, that there had indeed been a Will B. Aarons, if not two of them, the brother and nephew of Edward S. Aarons. Confusion reigned supreme.

Hubin consulted Social Security Death Benefit Records, finding a William B. Aarons. He passed away in Atlantic City, but his Social Security number was issued in Pennsylvania, as was that of Edward S. Aarons (listed as E.S. Aarons in the Death Benefit records). A letter to Will B., Jr., elicited the following response: "Will B. was indeed my father. Regarding the author of the six books in question, I can tell you that for each of the books there was a primary author who was not my father. I really do not know if my father had any role in the development, editing, or other activities related to those books, but my sense is that he had no role. You may get additional information from our agent." The Mystery File article ends with this unequivocal statement: "AARONS, WILL B. This was a real person, William B. Aarons, 1914–2002, the brother of Edward S. Aarons. But according to WBA's son, and confirmed by their agent, WBA did not write any of the six books; they were all penned by Lawrence Hall."

The other authorized-sequel *Assignment* novels are *13th Princess* (1977), *Mermaid* (1979), and *Tyrant's Bride* (1980). "© CBS Publications, The Consumer Publishing Division of CBS, Inc." And the prose does have a clunky, corporate feel about it, though never falling below the level of basic thriller-writing competence. From the opening pages of *13th Princess*:

> The man gestured impatiently with a Beretta automatic that was aimed at Durell's chest. Durell had no fear of the gun.
>
> Nor of the open window, seven stories above a London street.
>
> Not even of the note he had compliantly written, which stated simply: "I can't go on."
>
> Ordinarily Durell saw himself as a small cog in the machinery that kept the earth turning a spin or two ahead of the madmen and zealots whose schemes could leave it a nuclear cinder.
>
> But now he was a vital cog.
>
> If he died in this sedate Oxford Street hotel room, the Western world literally could spin to a halt. Commerce and industry might wither, cities die. Nations would lie enfeebled, an invitation to the conqueror's rape and sword.
>
> All because of greed and parochial politics?
>
> Because of oil.

UK readers became aware of Aarons and Durell through the "British" Gold Medal paperbacks that were published by Frederick Muller from 1955 until 1964 (when Fawcett merged with Coronet Books, the paperback division of Hodder & Stoughton). This probably accounts for Sam Durell's only comic-strip appearance, in *Passport to Peril*, #172 in the Super Detective Library (London: Fleetway Publications, April 1960). The script was written by Joan Whitford (whose pseudonyms included Barry Ford and Rex James), loosely based upon *Assignment—Helene*. Cover artist: Giorgio De Gaspari. Interior artist: Alberto Breccia.

An estimated 23 million Sam Durell novels were sold in the USA and UK, with who knows how many more in foreign-language markets. Why none of them were ever turned into "major" or even "minor" feature films is a mystery in itself. Fawcett had a higher hit rate with Hollywood than any other paperback publisher of that so near and yet so remote aureate era. Adapted from George Tuttle's article entitled "Gold Medal at the Movies" (*Paperback Parade* #33): "In the April 21, 1956 issue of *Publisher's Weekly*, Fawcett Publications published a two-page ad with the headline: '18 GOLD MEDAL BOOKS CURRENTLY BEING MADE INTO MOTION PICTURES.' Along the border, there were 15 Gold Medal covers to highlight the ad.... The eighteen books currently being made into movies bring to thirty-nine (39) the number of Gold Medal Books purchased to date by the film industry. Of these eighteen, it seems that only eight, maybe nine, were released as completed motion pictures."

Tuttle worked out a timeline of 1950s film projects that had been derived from original Gold Medal books (October 1950 to November 1959). He compiled it by using the *International Motion Picture Almanac* and Paul Nathan's "Rights and Permissions" column in *Publishers Weekly*. The only Aarons-related entry is for November 1958: "National Films has bought Edward Ronns' *State Department Murders*." If an option was signed, however, it was never taken up.

The closest Aarons got to Hollywood recognition was writing proficient novelizations for three films and one TV series. In chronological order: *The Black Orchid*, as by Edward Ronns.[34] "Fabricated soaper of bumbling businessman [Anthony Quinn] romancing criminal's widow [Sophia Loren] and the problem of convincing their children that marriage will make all their lives better" (Maltin). Screenplay: Joseph Stefano. *But Not for Me*, as by Edward Ronns.[35] "22-year-old secretary/aspiring actress [Carroll] Baker falls for her has-been theatrical-producer boss [Clark] Gable, who won't admit that he's on the dark side of 50" (Maltin). Screenplay by John Michael Hayes, from the stage play *Accent on Youth* by Samson Raphaelson. *Hell to Eternity*[36]: "Straightforward drama based on true story of WW2 hero Guy Gabaldon [played by Jeffrey Hunter], who was raised by Japanese foster parent" (Maltin). Screenplay: Ted Sherdeman and Walter Roeber. Story: Gil Dowd. *The Defenders*.[37] Original novel, based upon the TV series (September 16, 1961, to September 9, 1965). Created by Reginald Rose, starring E.G. Marshall and Robert Reed.

An *Assignment* novel like *Black Viking* adapted for the silver screen would have given any spy-fi film of the mid- to late 1960s a good run for its box-office money.

Sam Durell, the all–American equivalent of James Bond. With some justice, Aarons has been criticized for his frequently outlandish plots, overreliance upon coincidence, illogical decision-making, faulty mission preparation, slapdash structure, one-dimensional characters, and rushed *deus ex machina* endings. Deadlines loomed up on a six-monthly basis; Aarons had to go with whatever he'd got when the allotted time was up. However, a fortunate few Gold Medal authors managed to break free of this typewriting treadmill, including John D. MacDonald, Louis L'Amour, and—where espionage fiction was concerned—Donald Hamilton.

CHAPTER EIGHT

Hamilton and Helm

"If President Kennedy is a fan of British secret agent James Bond, he should switch his allegiance to Matt Helm. For there isn't a thing the incredible Bond can do that U.S. agent Helm can't do better," ran a patriotic notice in the *Buffalo News*.

Matt Helm was created by Donald (Bengtsson) Hamilton.[1] He was born in Uppsala, Sweden, the son of Dr. Bengt Leopold Knutsson Hamilton and Elise Franzisca Hamilton (née Neovius). His family immigrated to the United States when he was eight years old, where they settled in Boston, Massachusetts. Hamilton graduated from the University of Chicago in 1938, with a bachelor of science degree in chemistry. During the Second World War, he served in the U.S. Naval Reserve, as a chemist, rising to the rank of lieutenant. He was married to Kathleen Hamilton (née Stick) from 1941 until she passed away in 1989. They would have four children: Hugo, Elise, Gordon, and Victoria. The family made their home in Santa Fe, New Mexico.

Immediately after the war, Hamilton sold an article to *Yachting Magazine*, a short story to *Collier's* ("Stranger's Return": June 1, 1946), and a counterspy novel entitled *Date with Darkness*.[2] Then came *The Steel Mirror*[3] and *Murder Twice Told*,[4] a collection of two novellas ("The Black Cross" and "Deadfall"). Hamilton didn't produce another book for nearly four years, during which time he concentrated upon writing huntin', shootin' and fishin' articles while pursuing his avocation of freelance photography. Then Dell Books published a western novel, *Smoky Valley* (1954), which was filmed as *The Violent Men* in 1955. Directed by Rudolph Maté, it starred Barbara Stanwyck, Glenn Ford, and Edward G. Robinson. But he really hit pay dirt with *The Big Country* (1957), another Dell western range-war novel that had appeared as a four-part serial in *The Saturday Evening Post* (beginning February 9, 1957: as *Ambush at Blanco Canyon*). William Wyler directed the classic 1959 film version, starring Gregory Peck, Charlton Heston, and Jean Simmons, with even more classic theme music by Jerome Moross.

Dell published three more westerns by Hamilton: *Mad River* (1956); *The Man from Santa Clara* (1960); *Texas Fever* (1961). They also published two of his best stand-alone mystery novels: *Line of Fire* (1955) and *Assignment: Murder* (1956), which Gold Medal reprinted as *Assassins Have Starry Eyes* (1966), probably to avoid confusion with Edward S. Aarons. This internal blurb from the 1958 British Panther paperback edition of *Line of Fire* was indicative of many more Hamilton novels to come:

The opening pages of this tense and exciting crime thriller set the scene for one of the subtlest and intriguing situations the reader will have come across.

For here is a man with all the obvious attributes of a hero, setting up a gun with a telescopic sight in an upper window of an office building, with the obvious intention of murdering the Governor of the State as he passes by.

From here on the story takes an astonishing turn, although just how, and in what direction, it would be unfair to reveal. It is sufficient to say, however, that the whole chain of events is interwoven with the most extraordinary knowledge of ballistics, in which the chief character is an expert. A first-rate thriller by an important American author.

The never-named chief character reveals his expertise with firearms in the very first paragraph: "I had a sandbag rest for the gun just inside the window and a six-power telescopic sight. The gun itself was a star-gauge Springfield they had picked up for me; it would shoot better than inch groups at a hundred yards now that I had tuned it and learned what ammunition it liked. Most people don't seem to know it, but guns are very particular about what you feed them; what'll shoot like a dream through one rifle will spray all over the landscape from another. This particular gas pipe liked the hundred-and-eighty grain bullet in front of a hot load of forty-seven and a half grains of Hi Vel No. 2 powder which pushed it along, I figured, at better than twenty-eight hundred feet per second."

When editor *extraordinaire* Knox Burger (1922–2010) left Dell for Gold Medal in 1959, replacing the deceased Richard Carroll as Editor-in Chief, he took Donald Hamilton with him. It soon turned out to be a very good mutual career move. Fawcett was then in the painful process of losing Richard S. Prather (1921–2007), whose Hollywood P.I. Shell Scott books had sold over 20,000,000 copies and counting. Burger later explained (in *Mystery Scene* #34, 1991): "[Hamilton's] first book about Matt Helm was called *The Wrecking Crew* and he'd killed him off at the end. So I said, 'Don't kill the guy off. Keep him alive and put him into a series.'" The hole left by Prather's defection to Pocket Books/Simon & Schuster was duly filled, though the Shell Scott novels already published by Gold Medal continued to sell in their tens of thousands.

The first-published Matt Helm novel was actually *Death of a Citizen*.[5] It takes place in 1958, thirteen years after the end of World War II. Like his creator, Matthew Helm is a freelance popular-fiction writer and a huntin', shootin' and fishin' photographer. Under the code name Eric, he had once worked for a deep-dark military intelligence organization. Then he is pressed back into secret service by his former boss-man, known simply as "Mac." Gold Medal were kind enough to provide a CONFIDENTAL file-card blurb. "REMARKS: A citizen dies—and a wartime special agent is reborn, as the girl with the code name Tina walks into a cocktail party and 15 years of Matt Helm's complacent postwar life slips away. Suddenly the old automatic reactions take over, and Helm is thrust back to the time when he'd been a lethal young animal trained to kill—and she had been his partner." And, from the first chapter:

But it was Tina, all right. She looked at me for a moment without expression ... and I couldn't tell if she recognized me or not. There was more meat on my bones and less hair on my head. There were the other changes that must have left visible traces for her to see; the wife [Beth] and three kids [Matt, Jr., Warren, and Betsy]....

I was an ardent fisherman these days ... but at the back of a desk drawer was the little worn Colt Woodsman with the short barrel, and it was still loaded. And in my pants was the folding knife of Soligen steel that she'd recognize because she'd been present when I'd taken it from a dead man to replace the knife that he'd broken, dying.[6]

Matthew L. Helm was born c. 1921. He is 6′ 4″ tall, weighs just under 200 pounds, and carries it on a "beanpole" frame. His mono-named master, Mac, delivers a "little lecture" to all spy-school graduates:

"Remember that dignity is the key to any man's resistance, or any woman's. Take, for instance, a soldier in a clean uniform, lead him politely to a desk, set him decorously on a chair, request him to place his hands before him, stick splinters under his fingernails, and set fire to them ... and you'll be surprised how often he'll watch his fingertips cooking and laugh in your face. But if you take the same man, first, and work him over to show that you don't mind bruising your knuckles and don't have a bit of respect for his integrity as a man—you don't have to hurt him much, just mess him up until he can no longer cling to a romanticized picture of himself as a noble and handsome embodiment of stubborn courage ... "[7]

James Bond may have been given a license to kill in the line of duty, if necessary, but "killer" is Matt Helms's main job description—or "assassin," to put it politely. By the end of Book One, the once-more homicidal Helm has tortured an admittedly not-very-nice woman and also become estranged from his wife and family. Unusually for a paperback-original genre novel, *Death of a Citizen* received warm praise from the national press. "A harsh and sometimes shocking story, told with restraint, power and conviction" (*The New York Sunday Times*). Ditto *The Wrecking Crew* (1960: nickname given to the organization that employs Helm, because of its high rate of assassinations): "Well-plotted action, interesting ambivalence and uncompromising harshness ..." (ditto again). Back-cover casefile blurb: "Helm has been sent halfway around the world to find and destroy the mythically elusive agent they called Caselius. His only lead to him is a woman, who might or might not be a double agent. Before Helm finally faces Caselius up in the bleak north woods of the Swedish ore country, two women will die, two more souls will be charged up to Matt Helm's account, in heaven or in hell." N.B. Helm shares the Swedish background of his only begetter.

The Removers (1961) opens with another glimpse into Helm's fractured private life. He travels to Reno, Nevada, answering a written request from his now ex-wife, of six months or two years duration. (Hamilton is somewhat vague on the time span). Beth has married a rancher named Lawrence Logan since leaving Helm whenever, and they have apparently fallen out of contact. But the personal mission turns lethally official after Helm learns that Sal is connected with Vladimir Martell, an enemy assassin currently operating in the USA. Drug smuggling turns out to have been a convenient cover-up for something even more sinister. N.B. Helm met the Connecticut-born Elizabeth ("Beth") while he was recuperating from war wounds in a D.C. hospital. She had been working for the USO (American Service Organization).

In *The Silencers* (1962), Helm has been ordered to Juarez, Mexico. His mission: Extricate an agent, Mary Jane Springer, who might or might not wish to return with him voluntarily. Dead or alive, in plain English. By this time, it has been well-established that Matt Helm "...makes British spy James Bond seem like a powder-puff" (*Denver Post*). But he seems to have gone completely over to the Dark Side in *Murderers' Row* (1962)—the unofficial designation of "Wrecking Crew" headquarters in Washington, D.C. His unsavory assignment is to rough up a young female American agent known only as Jean. She has infiltrated an enemy spy ring, bent on obtaining AUDAP (Airborne Underwater Detection System), which can locate Polaris submarines at sea. Dr. Norman Michaelis, its inventor, has disappeared while sailing alone on the Chesapeake Bay. No body was found. Kidnap victim—or defector? The "fake" assault and battery is meant to allay any suspicions they might entertain about her loyalty. But it all goes horribly wrong:

> I took another long breath, and knelt down and made a brief examination. There was nothing fundamentally wrong, that I could see, except that she was dead. She was kind of a mess by this time, of course. She was supposed to be. That was what I was there for. The idea had been for her to look spectacularly beat-up—to show how seriously we took her disloyalty—without having anything really broken except a certain bone in the forearm. As Mac had said, she had to have at least one broken bone or they wouldn't buy it. Besides, a nice big cast makes a person look very harmless and helpless, while at the same time it affords concealment for a number of small emergency tools and weapons, properly designed. The surgeon at the local hospital had his instructions....[8]

Helm goes on to treat the brutal killing of just–Jean with all the emotional engagement of a speak-your-weight machine: "I looked back. If you can do it, you can damn well look at it, no matter how badly you've loused it up. I never trust these delicate chaps who are hell behind a telescopic sight at five hundred yards but can't bear to come up close and see the blood. I gave her a long look, lying there among her spilled pearls. What did I think about—besides wondering, again, what the hell went wrong? Well, if you must know, I thought it would be nice to be in Texas, which is a hell of an attitude for a good New Mexican."[9]

James Bond, Sam Durell, Colonel Hugh North—even bluff old Bulldog Drummond—might have shed a manly tear or two at such an affecting sight. Mac takes the view that Agent Eric could have gone too far this time. From the back-cover blurb: "He is on a dangerous mission it is true ... but his own callousness seems to have reached a point of absolute savagery. He has apparently murdered one of our own agents. Helm is on or near [the] Chesapeake Bay. He is armed and dangerous, and must be located, kept under surveillance, and removed from active service...." Needless to say, Matt Helm clears his name and foils the fearsome foe in the very nick of time, but a black mark will no doubt be affixed to his personal file. N.B. The term Murderers' Row was coined in 1918 to describe a particularly intimidating section of the New York Yankees' batting lineup.

Matt Helm mellows a bit with the passing books and years, while the increasingly long-ago Second World War is written out of his backstory. However, he remains essentially a killing machine for Mac and Uncle Sam. Hamilton himself characterized Helm as (A) He's actually a pretty good guy. (B) He kills." The parallel between Helm and the anonymous gunman in *Line of Fire* is constantly made clear. From *The Ambushers* (1963): "Four and a quarter inches with the 150-grain load. A bolt-action rifle that won't group within two inches at a hundred yards isn't worth having, and we ought to get one and a half even with factory ammunition."[10]

The usually Homeland-based Helm goes a little further afield in *The Ambushers*. He has been posted to one of those generic nonexistent island countries that speckle the former Spanish Main. "I couldn't help thinking that there was a certain remarkable resemblance in names between the River of Goats [*Rio de las Cabras*] here in Costa Verde—let's call it Costa Verde—and the Bay of Pigs over in Cuba, where some other men had been put ashore not too long ago under somewhat similar circumstances [April 17–19, 1961]. They'd been trying to start a revolution and I was supposed to stop one, but the basic situation was about the same. I couldn't help remembering that they hadn't had much luck at the Bay of Pigs."[11] Same old, same old covert subversive story.

Helm is operating under the Hispanic cover name of Miguel Hernandez. As he is quick to explain: "The blood of the *Conquistadores* does not flow in my veins. I was born in Minnesota, and while I moved to the state of New Mexico at an early age, and picked up a little Spanish there, I still get along better in some Nordic tongues, not to mention English. However, for this occasion, I'd had my face and hands stained and my hair dyed. I wasn't supposed to have to fool anybody up close. On the other hand, it was considered inadvisable to advertise too widely the fact that I was a foreigner. Besides, a dark face shows up less conspicuously in the forest."[12] His initial contact in Costa Verde is Colonel Hector Jiminez, who (spoiler alert) finally replaces the assassinated *El Presidente*.

An integral part of Helm's mission is to rescue another unfortunate—and again un-surnamed—female agent, Sheila, the first assassin sent to "terminate" El Fuerte. She had been captured, tortured, and raped. Helm makes a qualified attempt at sympathy: "The sun was bright on her short-cut hair as she lay there, firing [a rifle in target practice] steadily. I could remember when it had been even shorter, hacked and ragged. Well, that had nothing to do with sighting a rifle, or with her marksmanship in general. What was important was that she seemed to know what she was doing. They all get rifle training, but it doesn't always take."[13]

Helm does, however, escort Sheila to a secret treatment facility in Arizona known simply as the Ranch. But that act of mercy coincides with his follow-up mission: Locate and destroy Heinrich von Sachs, a very much *not* ex–Nazi scientist whose diabolical plan is to destroy El Paso with a nuclear missile smuggled into northern Mexico from Cuba. Destructive superpower conflict followed by the formation of a Fourth Reich in Western Europe. *Moonraker*—American style.

Gail Hendricks, Matt Helm's once-in-while sexual partner (since *The Silencers*) is killed off in an off-page car accident at the very beginning of *The Shadowers* (1964). It inspired this vaguely misogynistic interior monologue: "I bent down and pulled the blanket back and had my look, then replaced the cover and walked off a little ways until I stood looking down at something gleaming in the rank grass. It was a silver evening pump to go with the dress she'd worn. I reflected on women's shoes and how they never could seem to stay on in a crisis. If the final cataclysm overtakes the human race, I decided, the last trace of womankind left behind in the smouldering wreckage will be scorched, radioactive slipper with a high, slim heel."[14]

By that time, the Hamilton/Helm template had been firmly set, right down to the definite article + single-word tagline titles (which were generally meant more for convenient series identification than descriptive accuracy). *The Ravagers* (1964), *The Devastators* (1965), *The Betrayers* (1966), *The Menacers* (1968), and *The Interlopers* (1969) saw out the first decade of Matt Helm novels. Scotland is the European setting for *The Devastators*, and Helm demonstrates a previously unknown knowledge of Caledonian couture: "[Nancy Glenmore] was wearing a buttoned-up cardigan sweater and one of those pleated kilt-skirts that close with a big safety-pin, and it was the Glenmore all right: not the dress tartan, which is chiefly red, but the hunting, which is light blue and green. Unfortunately, they're doing all kinds of sissy things to the brave old plaids these days—I guess some people feel they're too garish for good modern taste—and these were no longer the honest, bold Highland colours so dear to the heart of the butterfly boys."[15]

It was nigh on two years before Mission #13, *The Poisoners* (1971) hit the bookstores. From the back-cover file card: "When Helm is despatched to Los Angeles to investigate the shooting of an agent named Annette O'Leary, it wasn't just an official assignment—it was personal. Helm and the girl had worked at very close quarters in the past [*The Menacers*: 1968] and he was determined to find her killer. He then stumbled into his most fantastic investigation ever—leading to encounters with two-bit hoods, a trio of beautiful women, a bunch of drug-traffickers and his old friend [Chinese secret agent Mr. Soo, from *The Betrayers*: 1966 and *The Interlopers*: 1969], whose government has ideas about polluting America to death. *The Poisoners*—a very apt title, to be sure—is one of Hamilton's few forays into spy-fi, following Edward S. Aarons."

Normal scribbling service resumed with *The Intriguers* (1973), *The Intimidators* (1974), *The Terminators* (1975), *The Retaliators* (1976), and *The Terrorizers* (1977)—in which Helm starts his account by explaining how he had been fished out of Hecate Strait, off the coast of British Columbia. Then, on the second page: "In some respects, the mental computer seemed to be quite cooperative. It simply balked at handing out data on one subject. Me." Helm's amnesia is temporary, but—after many near-miss adventures—he spends the last chapter in hospital, wondering if he's finally getting too old for this kill-or-be-be-killed game. Mac seems to have put Helm on sick leave for almost five years. Hamilton himself wrote only one novel during that lay-off period—a would-be "Robert Ludlum" blockbuster entitled *The Mona Intercept*.[16] The title alone invited comparison with the bestsellers of Robert Ludlum (whose time here will surely come). Gold Medal accorded it a burbling cast-of-characters blurb:

> THE DOOMSDAY PEOPLE—FIGHTING FOR POWER, LIFE, AND LOVE ON THE TRECHEROUS SEAS!
>   JIMMY COLUMBUS. King of the Cuban Mafia, he defied Castro—and declared war on the U.S. government.
>   PHILIP MARTIN. His Vietnam experience and his hot Spanish blood combined to make him a deadly specialist in anti-terrorism.
>   LUCIA BARNES. The pretty little girl brought a special abandon to the bedroom—and a murderous jinx.
>   HAROLD ULLMAN. He felt a keen guilt about his wife—and rose to astonishing heights of heroism to redeem himself.
>   ELIZABETH CAMERON. She rose from Iowa farm-girl to high-grade Washington civil servant—before her blistering baptism under fire.
>   SAIL ON A VOYAGE OF DEATH, DEFIANCE, AND DISCOVERY—TO THE MONA INTERCEPT!

The Mona Intercept sold well enough, but it neither challenged Ludlum nor pre-empted Tom Clancy's phenomenal techno-thriller success. Not even the gold-leaf title lettering could make a commercial difference. Hamilton "ran for cover" with a one-a-year string of Matt Helm novels: *The Revengers* (1982); *The Annihilators* (1983); *The Infiltrators* (1984); *The Detonators* (1985); *The Vanishers* (1986); *The Demolishers* (1987). *Revengers*, at 200+ pages, was Hamilton's longest and most padded-out novel to date. Helm is initially assigned to look after Mac's daughter, Martha, whose retired agent husband Bob Devine has been murdered for no apparent reason. His next assignment takes him to Florida, where he forms a significant-other relationship with a reporter named Eleanor Brand. It carries over into *The Annihilators* (1983: set in Costa Verde: see above): "Marriage wasn't outside the realms of possibility, although we were neither of us particularly good matrimonial material. On the other hand, for the time being, either party was free to terminate the relationship at will, no explanations required, no questions asked."[17] But the relationship is soon permanently terminated—by the abduction and killing of Eleanor Brand.

After another two-year break came *The Frighteners* (1989), *The Threateners* (1992), and *The Damagers* (1993)—the twenty-seventh and last Matt Helm novel to be published during Hamilton's lifetime. The chief villain is Roland Caselius, the son of Raoul Caselius, from *The Wrecking Crew* (see above). Roland heads an international sabotage organization calling itself DAMAG, Incorporated. Like father, like son. Helm has one of his infrequent hand-to-hand combats with Siegelinda ("Ziggy") Kronquist (née Greta Larsson), their agent number DAMAG004:

There was a testing moment during which [Ziggy and I] just lay there straining against each other. She was in better condition, but I was bigger and she couldn't force the knife point any closer to me. I let her expend part of her strength keeping the dart launcher twisted aside. It didn't matter since the thing was strictly a one-shot proposition. Suddenly she broke free and rolled away and stood up, or tried to, forgetting where she was. Her head hit one of the wooden battens that held the cabin's elaborate quilted headlining, dazing her for a moment, giving me time to switch on the little bedside light. She crouched there naked, still holding the knife; after a moment, she looked down at the bright little tuft of plastic sprouting from her left breast.[18]

N.B. There is an agent DAMAG008, but no 007.

Like his Fawcett predecessor, Sam Durell, Matt Helm became a potent American answer to James Bond. Unlike Cajun, however, Eric joined 007 on the silver screen—even if only in madly mutated form. The four Columbia film versions (see below) had the miscast Dean Martin[19] playing Helm, in his patent boozy-woozy persona. Martin would have been perfectly cast as Shell Scott, Richard S. Prather's "happy go looky" private eye, which the studio initially had in mind for cinematic adaptation. But the producers decided to make box-office hay while the Bond sun shone, combining quirky Shell Scott humor with Matt Helm super-spy spectacle. Which begged the question: "Have they overpowered the *real* Matt Helm and left him for dead?"

The movie rights to Matt Helm had already been snapped up by independent producer Irwin Allen (1905–1987), who had co-founded Warwick Productions with Albert R. Broccoli in 1951. Broccoli had been keen on filming the James Bond novels, but Allen disagreed and they went their separate ways. He then saw Hamilton's hard-man hero as a means of getting himself into the gainful spy-film game. Having read one of the Helm novels at an airport terminal—"*The Silencers* or *The Death of a Citizen* (sic), I forget which" (*Los Angeles Times*: July 6, 1967)—he optioned the whole series inside twenty-four hours. "…and it was a sizeable amount" (ditto). A deal was struck with Columbia Pictures in 1964, with *The Silencers* chosen to be the first novel put before the cameras.

The Silencers (U.S. release date: February 18, 1966) ended up as an uneasy amalgam between the putative source novel and *Death of a Citizen*. Ex–secret agent Matt Helm has become a hedonistic photographer of glamour girls. He enjoys a friend-with-benefits relationship with his Bond Girl-ish assistant, Lovey Kravezit, played by Beverly Adams (1945–). But Helm is lured back to the ICE (Intelligence Counter Espionage) off-colors by his former boss, MacDonald ("Mac"), in the irascible form of actor James Gregory (1911–2002). The non-canonical villain and head of the Big O (Bureau of International Government and Order) organization, Tung-Tze (Victor Buono: 1938–1982), has masterminded Operation Fallout. A missile will disrupt an underground atomic-bomb test being held at Alamogordo, New Mexico, thus instigating World War III (which always seems like a good idea to some people). Helm sets out to stop him, with the welcome help of Tina (Daliah Lavi: 1942–2017) and unwelcome interference from Gail Hendricks (Stella Stevens: 1938–), a beautiful but klutzy redhead who might—improbably enough—be an enemy agent.

Although savaged by the critics and many disappointed Donald Hamilton fans, *The Silencers* made a healthy $7,000,000 profit in American box-office rentals alone. As Allen told *The Los Angeles Times*: "[It was] great timing that Helm caught on the same time Dean's TV series took off." Sample tagline: "Meet Matt Helm and his Slaygirls!"

If *The Silencers* kept only about 20 percent of their two source novels combined, then the sequels came as near as damn it to zero percent, taking the main character names into account. *Murderers' Row* (U.S. release date: December 20, 1966) was directed by Henry Levin (1909–1980) Producers: Irving Allen and Euan Lloyd (1923–2016). Screenplay: Herbert Baker. The movie Matt Helm fakes his own funeral to facilitate an undercover mission to the French Riviera, where Julian Wail—a key operative of Big O—has kidnapped a scientist named Dr. Norman Solaris. Wail plans to use the good doctor's "heliobeam" solar-powered death ray to incinerate Washington, D.C. (the opening sequence features the destruction of a scale-model Capitol building). James Gregory and Beverly Adams reprise their roles as "Mac" and Lovey Kravesit. Other cast members included Ann-Margret (1941–: Suzie, daughter of Solaris); Karl Malden (1912–2009: Julian Wail); Camilla Sparv (1943–: Coco Duquette); Richard Eastham (1916–2005: Dr. Norman Solaris); Tom Reese (1928–2017: Ironhead). Gadgets abound. Helm uses a cigarette-cum-dart gun and Wail a Gyrojet spear-pistol—shades of the 1965 *Thunderball* film. N.B. Helm drives a 1966 Ford Thunderbird Landau Special.

The Ambushers (December 22, 1967) was very loosely based upon Hamilton's novel of that title and less loosely based upon *The Menacers*, although it had first been entitled *The Devastators* (upon which it wasn't in the least based). "What better man to track down a flying saucer scare than a hardhead like MATT HELM?" (*The Menacers* blurb). In the film version, an experimental USAF "UFO" is tractor-beamed down in Central America by operatives of Big O. Matt Helm meets the now amnesiac pilot, Sheila Sommers, while seeking out a mole at ICE Training Headquarters. For some spy-fi reason, only women can pilot this radical new air- and spacecraft; men are killed by its "electromagnetic force field" (or whatever). Helm (posing as a photographer) and Sommers (posing as his wife) are assigned to recover the hijacked government property, following a hot lead in sunny Acapulco.

Tagline: "MATT HELM RIDES AGAIN!" He rides a Triumph motorcycle (plus sidecar, to start with) in hot pursuit of a runaway railroad flatcar with flying saucer (and trapped female pilot) aboard. At one point, Helm zooms the bike underwater across a riverbed, foreshadowing by almost ten years 007 and his amphibious Lotus Esprit in *The Spy Who Loved Me* (October 27, 1977). In another Bond-anticipatory scene, from *Live and Let Die* (release date: June 27, 1973), Helm strips the dress off Sheila Sommers using a hand-held magnetic device. Judith Crist pulled no critical punches: "The sole distinction of this vomitous mess is that it just about reaches the nadir of witlessness, smirky sexiness and bad taste—and it's dull, dull, dull to boot" (*The St. Petersburg Times*: September 15, 1978).

If not quite going from the ridiculous to the sublime, *The Wrecking Crew* (December 25, 1968) did at least have a comparatively sensible plot. No surprise there, since the script was written by the eminent mystery author, William P. McGivern (1918–1982). Herbert Baker had been seconded to co-writing (with William Bast: 1913–2015) Irving Allen's more ambitious made-in-Britain spy movie, *Hammerhead* (1968). Director: David Miller (1931–2019). It was based on the novel by James Mayo[20] and starred Vince Edwards (1928–1996) as art dealer/part-time secret agent Charles Hood. Helm's mission for ICE is to prevent Goldfinger-lite Count Contini (Nigel Green: 1924–1972) from crashing the global economy by stealing a billion dollars in gold. His main helpmate is Freya Carlson (Sharon Tate: 1943–1969), a Danish tour guide who turns out to be a British secret agent. His lethal female adversaries are the Russian Linka Karensky (Elke Sommer: 1940–) and the Chinese Wen Yu-Rang (Nancy Kwan: 1939–). Contini loads the hijacked bullion upon a train heading for Luxembourg, but Matt and Freya hunt him down by helicopter. Phil Karlson (*The Silencers*) returned as director, and his energetic style lent the film an air of urgency not much seen in either *Murderers' Row* or *The Ambushers*.

Beverly Adams did not appear as Lovey Kravesit because she was playing "Ivory" in *Hammerhead*. Nor did James Gregory come back as MacDonald. Gregory later said that the budget had been significantly cut and he wouldn't accept the smaller fee offered to him (*Filmfax* #84, April 2001). John Larch (1914–2005) took over, although his part was far from being overwritten. The working title had been the non–Hamiltonian *House of the Seven Joys*, which survives in the theme song composed by Mack David and Frank DeVol. Leonard Maltin gave *Wrecking Crew* a 1½ grade, adding that "Chuck Norris [1940–] has one line with Dino in a bar and Bruce Lee [1940–1973] is listed as film's 'karate advisor.'" Critics either liked or disliked *The Wrecking Crew*. "It was the best Matt Helm film, it was the worst Matt Helm film" (with apologies to Charles Dickens). Box-office takings took a deep nose-dive—just $2.4 million in U.S. and Canadian rentals (*Variety*: January 7, 1970).

Nevertheless, a fifth Matt Helm film—to be entitled *The Ravagers*—was announced after the credit list of *Wrecking Crew* (as with "James Bond will return in ..."). *Hammerhead* had made a tidy profit in Western Europe, but it failed to nail the all-important American market. Matt Helm remained an exploitable cinematic property, despite the diminishing receipts. Dean Martin, however, was so distraught over the ritual murder of Sharon Tate by the Charles Manson "Family" (August 9, 1969) that he couldn't bring himself to play the part again. Columbia retaliated by withholding Martin's share of the profits on *Murderers' Row*,[21] and the project was duly canceled. In any case, the spoof spy-film genre had almost run out of super-heated steam at that time.

Matt Helm was further transmogrified into a 13-episode TV entitled *Matt Helm*. It ran on the ABC network from September 20, 1975, until January 3, 1976. Richard Meyers, in *TV Detectives*[22]: "Just as the book and film Matt Helm were different, so too was TV's Matt Helm. Executive producer Irving Allen, producer [Seymour]

Buzz Kulik [1922–1999], and writer Sam Rolfe [1924–1993] tried to make the tele-flick Matt a combination of both the book and the film Helm. When he appeared in the TV movie [May 7, 1975], he was played by [Anthony] Tony Franciosa [1928–2006] and was now a former spy turned private eye. Though it was a nice try, no one was fooled. *Matt Helm* lasted all of three months as a series."[23]

The *Matt Helm* (sole title) pilot episode was directed by Buzz Kulik. Helm's backstory as a former secret agent with the Machine, the GIA (?) and ICE doesn't really square with his new bright-and-breezy LA-based PI persona, embodied by the Italianate Tony Franciosa. He might as well—or better—have been called Shell Scott (which is where we came in). Of the succeeding thirteen episodes, only three have any connection with espionage: "Squeeze Play" (November 1, 1975); "Think Murder" (December 6, 1975); "Die Once, Die Twice" (January 3, 1976). Matt Helm's film and TV incarnations may not be as one with Nineveh and Tyre, but they don't have much of a cult following—if any. The movies, however, are at least of footnote significance in spoof spook-film history. See *Booze, Bullets and Broads: The Secret of Matt Helm!*,[24] by Bruce Scivally

The Silencers was beaten to the box-office punch by *Our Man Flint* (January 16, 1966), which starred James Coburn[25] as a former agent of Z.O.W.I.E. (Zonal World Organization Intelligence Espionage) who is pressed back into not-so-secret service work by his ex-boss, Floyd C. Cramden (Lee J. Cobb: 1911–1976). Director: Daniel Mann (1912–1991). Producer: Saul David (1921–1996), for Twentieth Century–Fox. Original screenplay by Hal Fimberg (1907–1974) and Ben Starr (1921–2014). Jack Pearl wrote the tie-in novelization.[26] Flint's mission is to prevent the Galaxy cabal from extorting the world with their weather-control machine. The plot is as way-out as it gets, but it makes imperfect sense on its own terms. Unlike the sequel, *In Like Flint* (March 15, 1967), which makes *The Silencers* look like a kitchen-sink docudrama. Director: Gordon Douglas (1907–1993). Fimberg took sole screenwriting credit—or discredit—this time. Tie-in novelization by Bradford Street.[27] "Weak sequel to *Our Man Flint* finds our hero going against secret society of women [the Fabulous Faces] plotting to take over the [patriarchal] world" (Maltin). N.B. The title is an arch reference to the saying "in like Flynn," extolling the sexual prowess of Australian-born actor Errol Flynn (1909–1959).

Over the Pond, ex–Captain Hugh "Bulldog" Drummond—or a reasonable facsimile thereof—returned in the British-made film *Deadlier Than the Male* (UK release date: February 21, 1967). The title was taken from the same Kipling poem as Sapper's 1928 novel, *The Female of the Species*. Director: Ralph Thomas (1915–2001). Drummond (now a Korean War veteran working as an insurance company investigator) was played by Richard Johnson (1927–2015), who was no fan of the Great Original: "It was an entirely new creation that was not in the Drummond books. I couldn't respect the man. He was bigoted and brutal. A Nazi character. I didn't attempt to make myself into that character. We started with a fresh page" (*Los Angeles Times*, September 25, 1966). Johnson had been director Terence Young's first choice as James Bond, but they never came to terms. Nigel Green, who would later appear in *The Wrecking Crew* (see above), was a suitably sinister Carl Peterson (here spelled Petersen)—that most arch of all arch-enemies. The plotline had more than a little method in its madness. But the sequel, *Some Girls Do* (January 23, 1969), took leave of its interesting premise (the sabotage of a prototype British supersonic airliner)—and its senses—within the first half hour. Novelizations by Henry Reymond.[28]

N.B. Hugh Drummond was never once referred to as Bulldog, in either film.

If the Matt Helm films are known to anyone today, apart from Hollywood historians (official and happy amateurs) it's mainly because of the Dean Martin connection—and even that might be overstating the case at present. Nevertheless, they—along with the Derek Flint and Hugh Drummond movies—mark the "spoofification" that crept into the sub-genre during the late 1960s and all through the 1970s, both on the small (e.g., *The Man from U.N.C.L.E.*) and large screens. Even James Bond came to resemble a more upmarket Matt Helm during the "Roger Moore" years. The tommyrot had already set in with the left-field 1967 film version of *Casino Royale.* "Considering the talent pooled on [David Niven, Peter Sellers, Ursula Andress, Orson Welles, Deborah Kerr, etc.] and off [Directors: Val Guest, Kenneth Hughes, John Huston, Joseph McGrath, and Robert Parrish. Writers: Wolf Mankowitz, John Low, Michael Sayers, among uncredited others] screen … it should have been a triumph. Instead it's a double oh dear."[29]

Donald Hamilton kept himself at a safe distance between the book and film Matt Helms. He made no comments one way or the other—in public, at any rate. There wasn't much of a "crossover" effect, with readers and cinemagoers comprising fundamentally different and downright incompatible markets. Hamilton's only produced screenplay was for *Five Steps to Danger* (1957), in collaboration with its director Henry S. Kesler (1907–1997) and Turnley Walker (1913–1997). It was freely adapted from *The Steel Mirror.* "By-now clichéd spy drama, enhanced by [Ruth] Roman and [Sterling] Hayden" (Maltin). Fawcett eventually reprinted all his pre–Matt Helm novels, e.g., *Night Walker,*[30] which had once been a five-part serial in *Collier's* (June 16 to July 14, 1951), as *Mask for Danger.* They also published *On Guns and Hunting* (1970), a collection of articles on those subjects, and an anthology of western short stories entitled *Iron Men and Silver Stars* (1970). The non–Fawcett hardcover, *Cruises with Kathleen,*[31] recounted his cruises on the 27-foot cutter *Kathleen.*

After leaving Santa Fe, Hamilton lived on his yacht for a few years, before settling down in Sweden with his son, Gordon. He passed away, peacefully at sleep, in November of 2006, aged 90. The Donald Hamilton papers (1945–1995) are housed at the Charles E. Young Research Library, University of California, in Los Angeles. Hamilton had completed a final Matt Helm novel, *The Dominators,* in 2002. But it remained unpublished, for whatever reason. Keith Wease later produced an edited version on CreateSpace.[32] Wease also wrote *Matt Helm: The War Years*[33]: "I wrote about Matt Helm's wartime experiences and his pre-war life. Incorporating direct quotes from the books, and my own imagination, I filled in many of his mission details [including Tina from *Death of a Citizen*] and added several of my own, trying to keep the narrative authentic to Donald Hamilton's style." Many of the original Helm novels are now back in print. DreamWorks optioned them all for filming in 2002, but they have languished in Development Hell ever since.

CHAPTER NINE

Killmasters—and Mistresses!

Dedicated to
The Men of the Secret Services
of the
United States of America

So ran the dedication to every one of the 160 "Killmaster" novels published from 1964 until 1990. They were all purportedly written (mostly in the first person) by Nick Carter, a lineal descendant (?) of the original Nicholas Carter, Master Detective. This direct response to the James Bond phenomenon was the brainstorm of a Canadian "book packager" named Lyle Kenyon Engel.[1] See "The Fantastic Novel Factory Paperback Impresario: Cranking Out Books, Raking in the Money," by Joseph McLellan (*The Washington Post*, February 12, 1979). His only known connection to spy fiction had been *American Agent: The Magazine of the Secret Services* (two issues: Spring and August 1957). Issue No. 1 featured the novella *Operation Zero*, by John Jakes (1932–), who would later write *On Secret Service*,[2] about the exploits of Lon Price (a fictional operative for the Pinkerton Detective Agency during the American Civil War).

The most noteworthy "non-literary" American postwar American spy-fiction hero was U.S. Special Agent Steve Mitchell, played by Brian Donlevy (1901–1972). Donlevy's own production company made the *Dangerous Assignment* radio series (160 episodes: 1949–1953). There was an Australian version, that lasted from 1954 until 1956, which adapted the original scripts. A syndicated 39 × 25m TV film series of the same title appeared in 1952. "The Commissioner" (Herb Butterfield: 1895–1975) sent the strong-but-stolid Steve Mitchell perambulating all over the world—without leaving the NBC studio backlot.

Of more lasting importance than Steve Mitchell in *Dangerous Assignment* was John Drake in *Danger Man* (see Introduction), played by Patrick McGoohan (ditto).[3] Drake was a lone-wolf American security operative for NATO. The British-made series of 39 × 25m black-and-white episodes had been created in 1960 for Lew Grade (1906–1998) and ITC (Incorporated Television Company) by writer-producer Ralph Smart (1906–2001). Smart had scored an international success with *The Invisible Man* TV series (September 1958 to July 1959: CBS network from April 5, 1961, until September 13, 1961), which leaned heavily in the direction of espionage. Richard Telfair (alias Richard Jessup: 1925–1982) wrote a tie-in novel entitled *Target for Tonight.*[4] From chapter 1: "We're known as Danger Men." It's a pretty apt title. It is necessary to run constant checks and double-checks on the operations of NATO, making sure that, should trouble come, NATO would be ready for it. In each of us there is a hardened pride at being a Danger Man. We know we're tough. But more importantly, *they* know we're tough."

A devout Roman Catholic, McGoohan had laid down hard-and-fast ground rules before he would accept the role of John Drake, which also led him to reject both the Saint and James Bond. From *Cult TV: The Golden Age of ITC,*[5] by Robert Sellers: "Undoubtedly the most controversial aspect of Drake was his attitude towards sex. Believing promiscuity should not be encouraged on television, McGoohan decreed that Drake must never be involved sexually with his leading ladies."[6] It soon became clear that the "Killmaster" incarnation of Nick Carter stood for everything that McGoohan, and John Drake, set themselves against. Lyle Engel's "reboot" of this vestigially brand-recognition character factored in sex-and-sadism elements from the Bond/Durell/Helm franchises.

The traditionally freelance Nicholas J. Huntington Carter has become an Organization Man working for AXE, the assassination and troubleshooting branch of the American secret services. AXE—never spelled out in acronymic form—probably just means EXECUTION. Its HQ is located at the sixth-floor offices of a building in DuPont Circle, Washington, D.C., under the Universal Exports–type cover name of Amalgamated Press and Wire Service. There are several departments with specific espionage-related functions. Nick Carter has the alpha-numerical code designation N3 on the 24-strong list of AXE-men. Of the four fully licensed to kill (with discretion) Killmasters, N3 is the most senior. In some novels, he is called the third Killmaster to work for AXE, with both his predecessors having been killed in action. Another-rank example is Z4—Zeke—who works in the AXE Psycho Lab.

Run, Spy, Run kicked off the new series. It was published by Award Books, the paperback division of Universal Publishing and Distributing Company (part of Conde Nast Publications, Inc.) in February 1964 (#A101F). The blurb blared: "A NEW YOUNG NICK CARTER IS HERE ... a suave, super-secret intelligence agent who is 'the American answer to Ian Fleming's James Bond'" (attributed to *The Third Degree Magazine*). Their publication would, in time, be taken over by Ace and—finally—Jove. The "real" authors will be cited from now on. It was co-written by Michael Avallone[7] and Valerie Moolman (October 24, 1927–). Apart from coauthoring four more "Killmaster" novels (see below) and editing many of the novels, Moolman worked on *Nick Carter, Master Detective* (2002), an audio-cassette compilation of stories from the 1943–1955 radio series, which starred Lon Clark (1911–1998). However, Avallone could have boasted a much stronger track record in the pulp-fiction field, where he considered himself to be "King of the Paperbacks" and "The Fastest Typewriter in the East" (New Jersey). With some justice. His bibliography runs to some 250 books and perhaps 1,000 items altogether.

Michael (Angelo, Jr.) Avallone was born in the Lower East Side of Manhattan, the son of a sculptor, then brought up in the Bronx with sixteen brothers and sisters. He served as a battle-star winner sergeant with the U.S. Army during and immediately after (European Army of Occupation) the Second World War (1943–46). While working at his bread-and-butter job as a stationery salesman (1946–55), Avallone "wrote his arm off" trying to break into the then fast-disintegrating pulp-magazine market. After five years and uncountable rejection slips, the short story "Aw, Let the Kid Hit!" was taken for the Fall 1951 issue of *Baseball Stories*. Several more short-form sales followed in the next few years, e.g., "The Man Who Walked on Air" (*Weird Tales*, July 1953).

Avallone's big break came with the hardcover publication of *The Tall Dolores*,[8] the first novel in a 30+ series to feature Ed Noon, his NYC-based PI. Steinbrunner and Penzler: "Autobiographical fragments appear in the unlikeliest places in the saga of Ed Noon. The early chapters of *The February Doll Murders* (1966) are based on Avallone's memories of combat in World War Two; *Little Miss Murder* (1971) reflects his love affair with the New York Mets; the spy's shipboard diary in *London, Bloody London* (1972) re-creates some of the incidents that occurred during his cruise to Europe aboard the *Queen Elizabeth II*." But the "Nooniverse" (as it came to be called) inexorably became obsessed with old Hollywood movies. "Hi, Noon!" was a standard film fan's referential greeting. Not to mention emphatic female sex characteristics. From *The Case of the Violent Virgin*[9]: "Her hips were beautifully arched and her breasts were like proud flags waving triumphantly. She carried them high and mighty" (cited in Bill Pronzini's *Gun in Cheek*[10]).

The Spitting Image (1953) and *Dead Game* (1954) would be the last Ed Noon novels to be published in American hardcover editions. After that came a long string of paperback originals, notably umpteen film (e.g., *Shock Corridor*: 1963) and TV (e.g., *Hawaii Five-O*: 1968) tie-in novelizations.

The title of *Run, Spy, Run* might well be a jesting by-blow at the elementary school primer. In any case, Nick Carter is a spy who does a lot of running. But the important thing is that it got the franchise off to a fine hell-for-leather start. Killmaster Carter has just closed a case in Jamaica, Bond's familiar stomping ground. Carter receives an anonymous letter asking him to return home on a flight where he will be contacted personally. Jump cut. Carter—and agentess Julia Baron—are sent to London, England, where they must protect the life of Lyle Harcourt, the staunchly anti–Communist U.S. ambassador to the United Nations. Nick and Julia tangle with Mr. Judas (see below), an international terrorist with no particular political affiliations, and his sadistic sex-maniac assistant, Braille. They duly save the ambassador—and the democratic day.

Killmaster Carter is credited with having served in the U.S. Army and the OSS during the Second World War. It can be assumed that he joined AXE sometime in the late 1940s or early 1950s. That's about it, biography-wise. His Wikipedia entry provides a composite physical description, slightly edited here: "Carter is tall (over six feet), lean and handsome with a classic profile and magnificently muscled body. He has wide-set steel gray eyes that are icy, cruel and dangerous. He is hard-faced, with a firm straight mouth, laugh-lines around the eyes, and a 'Kirk Douglas' cleft chin. His hair is thick and dark. Carter also has a knife scar on the shoulder and a shrapnel scar on the right thigh." A small blue-axe tattoo can be found on his left arm. It is the "ultimate ID" for an agent of AXE. Not to mention a dead giveaway. From *Istanbul* (1965), by Manning Lee Stokes (1911–1976):

> At the word AXE one of the little Chinese said something to his companion. They whispered for a moment, then one of them spoke to the Basque.
> "AXE? This man is of that organization? The American murder society?"
> "Right. Watch. I'll prove it."
> The Basque came around his desk and rolled up Nick's sleeve. He grunted in satisfaction and pointed to the tiny AXE symbol tattooed on the left arm just below the elbow. "You see," said the Basque in triumph. "I have seen that mark before. Once before. I killed that sonofabitch!"
> N3 did not flicker an eyelash. But he filed it away. That might be Matthews, he thought, who had never come back from a mission in Iran.[11]

Run, Spy, Run introduces David Hawk, Nick Carter's very own M—N1, rather—who is the head of AXE and N3's immediate superior. There was an N2 agent, but he was killed off in *The Red Guard* (1967: also by Manning Lee Stokes) and apparently never replaced. Hawk has been said to bear an uncanny resemblance to Uncle Sam. A more exact description is provided in *Seven Against Greece* (1967): "His gray hair was somewhat wispy now but his stride and bearing had the athletic ease of a man twenty years younger. He wore tweeds which looked as if they had been cut in London. His eyes, which could twinkle with ancient humour or remain as cold as a vivisectionist's, were merely thoughtful as he entered his private office, a large room, expensively furnished but almost as sparse and stripped for action as its owner. The old man walked directly to his heavy oak desk, nodding a greeting to the man who was already in the room and who appeared to be concentrating on blowing a perfect smoke ring."[12]

Of the three other main AXE-characters, Della Stokes—Hawk's personable personal secretary—is a sister-under-the-skin of M's Miss Moneypenny. Ginger Bateman takes her flirty-but-efficient place in later novels. The AXE equivalent to Q, Geoffrey Poindexter, commands the high-tech Special Effects and Editing Department.

N3 is a great deal more multilingual than 007. Apart from English (naturally), he is fluent in Cantonese (+ Mandarian), French, German, Greek, Hungarian, Italian, Portuguese, Russian, Sanskrit, Spanish, and Vietnamese. He can also get by in Arabic, Hindustani, Japanese, Korean, Romansch, Swahili, and Turkish. His weaponry makes the Beretta and/or Walther PPK of James Bond look dangerously inadequate. To start with, "Wilhelmina" is a stripped-down Luger, which he took from a Nazi officer during one of his wartime missions. It has been upgraded many times over the years, but each replacement keeps the same feminine nickname. "Hugo" is a pearl-handled 400-year-old stiletto, ostensibly handcrafted by Benvenuto Cellini (1500–1571). The blade retracts into the handle—like a modern flick knife—and it's worn in a special quick-release wrist sheath.

Nick Carter's archenemy is the aforementioned Mr. Judas—at least in a few of the earlier novels. He primarily works for CLAW, the SMERSH-like Red Chinese Special Branch in charge of sowing hatred, murder, and the seeds of war. From *Danger Key* (1966): "Judas, believed by some to actually be Martin Bormann [Hitler's deputy], was a 'Prussian Ox'—bullet-headed, broad-shouldered, barrel-chested."[13] And, from *The Judas Spy* (1968): "As he fed bits of banana to the pet chimpanzee attached to his chair by a chain, he looked like a genial veteran of half-forgotten wars, a scarred bulldog still good for the pit in a pinch. Those who knew more about him could correct this opinion. Judas was blessed with a brilliant brain and the psyche of a rabid weasel. His monumental ego was a selfishness so pure that to Judas there was only one person in the world—himself. His tenderness to the chimpanzee would last only as long as he felt self-satisfaction. When the animal ceased to please him he would toss it overboard or cut it in two—and explain his actions with warped logic. His attitude with human beings was the same. Even Muller and Geltsch and Nife did not know the real depths of his evil. They survived because they served."[14]

Nick Carter in fight-scene action, from *The Kremlin File* (1973): "The little weapon spun out of his hand and I fired a second time. The front of his white shirt bloomed red. He slammed back against the door and hung as if he were nailed there, his mouth dropping open for a scream that did not come. Then his knees gave and he crumpled. The door jarred against him but his body kept it from opening. I had moved as soon as I fired. Behind me a woman yelled. Hysteria was building all around."[15]

Nick Carter in sex-scene action, from *The Death Strain* (1970): "I moved close to [Rita Kenmore] and my lips pressed on hers, opening her mouth and I found her tongue with mine. She quivered and clung to me, welcoming me with an eagerness that permeated every movement of her body. I thrust my hand up beneath the sweater…. My hand closed around soft firmness and she gasped. I grasped the sweater and pulled it over her head. She was against me instantly, clinging, and I pressed her back upon the bed. Her breasts pointed up at me and I kissed them, tenderly first, then gently nibbling at each protruding tip. Her head strained backwards and she gasped again and again, her hands clutching at my back. Slowly, the nipples began to rise and harden. I pulled gently on them with my lips and Rita half-screamed."[16]

The Death Strain is worthy of a retroactive Bad Sex in Fiction Award, which has been established by Rhoda Keoenig, a literary critic, and Auberon Waugh, at that time editor of the *Literary Review* (literaryreview.co.uk/bad-sex-in-fiction-award). As, indeed, can be said about the "naughty bits" in most of the other Killmaster novels. Ditto this oft-quoted encomium from *The New York Times*: "Nick Carter loves women. He doesn't just *love* sex, he *enjoys* it enormously; but he really loves women.

He prefers to like the ones he goes to bed with … and he does not keep eager women waiting."

The Killmaster series didn't go in much for the spy-fi side of things. However, *Operation Moon Rocket* (1968) is a then-state-of-the-art exception. Four American astronauts have been killed, with their murderers found dead just a few hours later. ChiComs are the prime suspects, but who is masterminding the outfit? "Dr. Joy Sun, the beautiful NASA scientist, with a voracious sexual appetite. Alex Simian, the multi-millionaire, with the strange 'friends' in China. Major Sollitz, the career officer, with luxurious tastes his meagre salary couldn't satisfy. Candy Sweet, the sensuous playgirl, with a lust for bizarre kicks. Reno tree, the crippled hood, with ambitions to take over a Mafia empire. One of them was in the pay of Red China. But which one? Nick Carter could only wait—with himself as the bait" (blurb).

Real-life military and political figures are seldom up for lengthy discussion, although *Operation Ché Guevara* (1969) deals with the Argentinian-born (1928) physician who served as Fidel Castro's chief lieutenant during the Cuban Revolution (1959). He met a violent death while fighting in Bolivia (1967). But AXE has reason to believe that Ché is still very much alive and kicking under the *nom de guerre* of El Garfio—"The Hook." Nick Carter investigates, guidebook at the ready: "The flight was uneventful, and I was happy to see the lights of La Paz in the early evening darkness as we approached the runway of El Alto Airport. The airport lay outside the city on the other side of the mountains, on the *altiplano* or high tableland. Nestled under the Andes, La Paz is the highest capital city in the world…."[17]

The last-published Killmaster novel was *Dragon Slay* (1990), by Jack Canon (1934–2004). By that time, however, the once fail-safe formula had lost much of its effectiveness—a familiar fate for all long-drawn-out formula fiction.

But the editorial policy of using multiple journeyman writers ensured a basic level of competence that kept the concept from going stale too quickly. Lionel White (1905–1985) wrote the classic *noir* caper-novel *Clean Break* (1955), filmed as *The Killing* (1956) by Stanley Kubrick. Martin Cruz Smith (1942–), prior to his *Gorky Park* (1981) fame, wrote three Killmasters: *Inca Death Squad* (1972); *Code Name: Werewolf* (1972); *The Devil's Dozen* (1973). Smith proceeded to write (as Simon Quinn) six novels in his own "Inquisitor" series, featuring Francis Xavier Killy—a secret agent who spies for by the Vatican. Robert J. Randisi (1951–), the prolific mystery and western writer, racked up six Killmasters inside three years: *Pleasure Island* (1981); *Chessmaster* (1982); *The Mendoza Manuscript* (1982); *The Greek Summit* (1983); *The Decoy Hit* (1983); *Caribbean Coup* (1984).

Lyle Kenyon Engel had "previous"—as a Scotland Yard detective might say—experience when it came to reviving old pulp-magazine heroes in paperback form. He struck a deal with Conde Nast and Belmont Books in early 1963 to publish what became nine new paperback-original novels about the Shadow. *Return of the Shadow* (September 1963) was written by the character's original chronicler, Walter B. Gibson—under his own name, not the more familiar Maxwell Grant pseudonym.

Gibson remained faithful to the "Kent Allard" incarnation of the character and his regular helpmates (Margo Lane, Clyde Burke, Harry Vincent, etc.). The other eight Belmont novels were all written by Dennis Lynds,[18] as by Maxwell Grant.

Dennis Lynds was born in St. Louis, Missouri. He served with the U.S. Army Infantry during the Second World War (1943–46). Collins left his assistant chemist post at Charles Pfizer & Company (1942–43 and 1946) to take up editorial work with several technical magazines. At the same time, he sold stories to *Hudson Review, New World Writing, Mike Shayne's Mystery Magazine*, and *Alfred Hitchcock's Mystery Magazine*. Two novels appeared during the early 1960s: the autobiographical *Combat Soldier* (1962) and *Uptown Downtown*. (1963).

Lynds had a positive mania for using pseudonyms. As William Arden, he wrote five novels about the counter-industrial espionage operative Kane Jackson. The six cases of P.I. Paul Shaw were authored by Mark Sadler. "John Crowe" created a six-novel series based upon the Sheriff's Department in the fictitious Californian county of Buena Costa. But Lynds achieved his greatest anonymous fame with the "Dan Fortune" books, writing as Michael Collins, naming himself after the Irish Republican Army general (1890–1922). Dan Fortune (né Fortunowski) is a one-armed Chelsea district of New York–based private eye who appeared in twenty novels, from *Act of Fear* (1967) to *The Cadillac Cowboy*. (1995). *Act of Fear* was awarded an Edgar by the Mystery Writers of America as the best first novel of its year. Lynds/Collins also turned his hand to science fiction, with *Lukan War* (1969) and *The Planets of Death* (1970).

Beginning with *The Shadow Strikes* (October 1964), Dennis Lynds/Maxwell Grant followed the way-out radio series interpretation of the Shadow rather than the (comparatively) more prosaic pulp-magazine template laid down by Walter B. Gibson. This descriptive passage from *Shadow—Go Mad!* (September 1966) will serve to put across the general idea: "The man now in the back of the black Mercedes was Lamont Cranston, wealthy socialite and businessman, close friend of Police Commissioner Ralph Weston of New York City, well-known amateur criminologist—and the major alter-ego The Shadow assumed to hide his true identity. There were few in the world who knew the power that hid beneath the passive surface of Lamont Cranston. Only two people had ever known the real man—The Shadow himself, and his master Chen T'a Tze. The Master had been dead many years now, his powers passed on to The Shadow, and it no longer mattered who The Shadow had been so many years before he became The Shadow. That man was gone, and only The Shadow now existed...."[19]

Supplemental: "As Cranston, he had all the secret powers of The Shadow, except one. Cranston possessed the super hearing, the ability to see farther than most men by day or night, the muscular control that permitted his trained body to do anything his mind asked of it. [But] the power to cloud men's minds, to render them unable to resist, was a power only The Shadow could employ. The Shadow as The Shadow. [It was] a power possessed by only one man in each generation, and it had been passed to The Shadow by the dying hand of Chen T'a Tze."[20]

Espionage plays the occasional walk-on part in *Shadow Beware* (January 1965), *Cry Shadow!* (April 1965), *The Shadow's Revenge* (October 1965), *Mark of the Shadow* (May 1966), and *The Night of the Shadow* (November 1966). But the Shadow often finds himself at odds with the SPECTRE- and CLAW-like CYPHER. What the acronym—if it *is* an acronym—stands for has never been deciphered. If the Shadow knows, he isn't telling. But the organization exists only to help anyone who needed murder, robbery, and even a small army for criminal purposes. *Shadow—Go Mad!* revisited: "Cranston remembered CYPHER, and CYPHER remembered Cranston. Where he lay on the table, strapped down, he watched and listened. The men who worked in the room all wore the slim black coverall uniform of CYPHER, with the white circle insignia on the breast. Men with the faces of many nations, the insignia of many nations on their black uniforms. For CYPHER was composed of the dissatisfied and the disgruntled of many nations, the misfits and the killers from all countries; the soldiers who had turned their backs on their countries, but who were proud of their skills as soldiers."[21]

As the (slightly edited) blurb explains: "X-2 + humanity = minus one world. The Shadow discovered this negative answer to an evil-inspired equation, but could even *he* fight this ultimate weapon? X-2 could make a good man kill, influence a man's mind, control his brain, his very actions. X-2 could supply an army of fearless, undefeatable maddened killers instantaneously. X-2 could robotize the masses. X-2 could even make the Shadow go mad!"

Belmont saved their most spy-fi Shadow novel until the very end, with *Destination: Moon* (March 1967). From the back-cover blurb: "Three times the great rocket was prepared to go to the moon, and three times there was only failure. But this time THE SHADOW watched. As Lamont Cranston, he and Margo began a careful investigation … could it be the Russians? The Chinese? Or was it some group far more sinister, a private organization of men who wanted to reach the moon first, using their conquest of it to rule the world?" The sinister "private organization" is, of course, CYPHER. But the weed of even astronautical crime bears bitter fruit: "The Shadow fired a short burst from his sub-machinegun and then another. The three [CYPHER] guards went down as if poleaxed by the deadly accurate fire of the Avenger. His sub-machinegun blazing he moved steadily through the bright room toward the larger room he saw just ahead through a heavy glass partition. Four more CYPHER men fell under the hail of bullets from his blazing gun."[22]

Lynds had also found time in his busy schedule to ghost-write several Killmaster novels: *The N3 Conspiracy* (1974); *Green Wolf Connection* (1976); *Triple Cross* (1976); *The Execution Exchange* (1985); *Mercenary Mountain* (1986); *The Cyclops Conspiracy* (1986); *The Samurai Kill* (1986); *The Master Assassin* (1986); *Blood of the Falcon* (1987). Lynds's wife, Gayle (1945–) has been credited as the author of five Killmaster novels: *Day of the Mahdi* (1984); *The Mayan Connection* (1984); *Pursuit of the Eagle* (1985); *White Death* (1985); *The Execution Exchange* (1985).

Lancer Books (New York: 1962–71) was a major-minor paperback imprint that could sometimes punch above its lightweight division. They hit the spy-fiction Big Time with a nine-book series about the American super spy Steve Victor, written by Ted Mark. *The Man from O.R.G.Y.* (Organization for the Rational Guidance of Youth) ran up six large printings between May 1965 and May 1966. Opening paragraph: "My name is Steve Victor and sex is my profession. I have a Ph.D. from a bona fide U.S. college that labels me an expert in the field. I also have a juicy research grant from one of those dollar-dripping American foundations. This means that I can play Kinsey, and they'll pick up the tab." Closing paragraph: "It was good to be back on the job again." Subtlety, always subtlety. Dr. Alfred Kinsey (1894–1954) was an American behavioral scientist, most widely known for his books *Sexual Behaviour in the Human Male* (1948) and *Sexual Behaviour in the Human Female* (1953). He founded the Institute for Sex Research at the University of Indiana in 1942.

Theodore Mark Gottfried,[23] to give the author his full name, was born in the Bronx, New York City, the only son of Russian immigrants. After just one year of college, he worked as an office boy in the Warner Brothers publicity department. During the 1950s, Gottfried became a regular contributor to the sub–*Playboy* men's magazine *Scamp*. *The Midway at Midnight* (by "Leslie Behan"), his first of more than 100 books, was published by Lancer in 1964. As Kathleen Fuller, he would later write five novels in the well-received "Riverview" series for Ballantine/Ivy Books. Ted Gottlieb's many nonfiction books included *Alan Turing: The Architect of the Computer Age* (1997) and *The Quest for Peace: A History of the Anti-War Movements in America* (2000).

Lancer published seven more O.R.G.Y. novels: *The Nine Month Caper* (1965); *The Real Gone Girls* (1966); *A Hard Day's Knight* (1966); *My Son, the Double Agent* (1966); *Dr. Nyet* (1966); *The Unhatched Egghead* (1966); *Room at the Topless* (1967). Plus *The Ted Mark Reader* (1966), a collection of 18 short stories. The best of this mixed bag is arguably *Dr. Nyet*. She does not work for SMERSH, as one might expect, but for S.M.U.T, i.e., the Society for Moral Uplift Today. As explained to Steve Victor by someone calling himself Charles Putnam, who seemingly works for some unofficial and carefully unnamed British government department:

> "[S.M.U.T.] started in the New York area as an organization dedicated to stamping out what they considered to be pornographic literature and photographs and movies. However, today it is their announced intention to stamp out all so-called illicit sexuality. And their concept of what is illicit includes everything from bra ads to ballet costumes. They have struck out against such things as men wearing Bermuda shorts, urinals which are not fenced off from one another, comedians who tell slightly off-colour jokes, the display of Botticelli nudes in the Metropolitan Museum of Art, the Washington Monument which they claim is phallic, sightseeing expeditions to the Grand Canyon because they think it's blatantly ovarian, automotive designs which include headlights which they consider mammalian, and many other things."[24]

And there's more:

> "Dr. Nyet [the Russian word for No] is a 24-year-old Russian female. She is described as slender but voluptuous, with a large bosom, a small waist and ample hips. Her hair is

long and black and she was in the habit of wearing it very simply—loose and parted in the middle. High cheekbones, an oval face, small straight nose and deep-set blue eyes. At twenty-three the government provided her with a research laboratory of her own, complete with staff and latest equipment. A year later she had made an important discovery. And we are reasonably sure that she has joined forces with [S.M.U.T.]."[25]

Dr. Nyet seemed to be shaping up nicely as perhaps the most exotic villainess in all spy-fiction history—in more ways than one. But Mark missed the mark, here, keeping her off-page for way too much of the novel. She does make a memorable, if unidentified Dr. Da ("Yes!") appearance in some sleazy S.M.U.T.-run bordello. Which probably never happened to James Bond, and certainly not in *Dr. No*. She falls to a messy death on the penultimate page, clutching the fornication-formula in her hot little hand. An accidental death. Steve Victor is a reluctant spy who prefers to make love, not personal-combat war. There would be no Dr. Dasvidaniya, sad to say.

My Son, the Double Agent (1966), by Ted (That Man!) Mark, opens with an italicized letter from Steve Victor to his possibly Jewish mother. Edited highlights:

> *Dear Mom:*
>
> *Think back over the years to when I was twins. Now, as you told me the story, we were twin baby infants and one of us drowned in the bathtub. Anyway, aside from the fact of whether it was my twin brother or me who drowned, what I wanted to ask was this: Are you sure the immersion was fatal? No, it's not my macabre sense of humour. Honest, Ma, I'm being serious. You see, lately, I've had reasons to doubt that it was.... So will you please write and tell me if you're absolutely sure he went all the way down the drain? Maybe then I'll be able to concentrate on S.M.U.T.*
>
> *What's S.M.U.T.? Read the book, Ma. And while you're doing that, think of your ever-loving son,*
>
> *Steve*

Aside: Steve Victor's creator himself spent almost twenty years in psychoanalysis.

Ted Mark wrote the screenplay for *The Man from O.R.G.Y.* (Release date: April 3, 1970), aka *The Real Gone Girls* (from book #3) in some markets. It was an ultra-low-budget film assembled by Cinemation Industries United Hemisphere-Delta (distributors: Cinemation Industries Prima Film). Producer: Sidney W. Pink (1916–2002). Director: James Hill (1919–1994), working as James A. Hill. Worldwide locations were actually in Puerto Rico and New York City. The plot more or less follows that of *The Real Gone Girls*. Steve Victor (played by the then too youthful-looking Robert Walker, Jr.: 1940–1969) is sent to find three prostitutes entitled to share in a $15,000,000 trust fund set up by their deceased "manager." But the "treasure map" that leads to this "inheritance" can only be found when the posteriors of this titillating trio are uncovered and joined together.

Lancer lost their O.R.G.Y. rights to the longer-established and better-paying Berkley Books, who published the next three novels: *Back Home at the O.R.G.Y.* (1968); *Come Be My O.R.G.Y.* (1968); *Here's Your O.R.G.Y.* (1969). Berkley first issued a non–O.R.G.Y. novel—*The Square Root of Sex* (1967)—that could easily have been an actual O.R.G.Y. novel. Ditto the more spy-fiction related *I Was a Teeny-Bopper for the CIA* (1967): "Lolly Popstick was the most sizzling teeny-bopper [Vance Powers] had ever seen…. Here is espionage as you have never known it before, where the only skill a spy needs is the ability to make love—in a hundred 'way-out' ways. A swinging novel about between-the-covers work by a new kind of undercover agent."

Square Root and *Teeny-Bopper* make interesting companion pieces to Lancer's near-mainstream *Circle of Sin* (1967). Lancer had already branched out with the Ted Mark Laugh Romp sequence. *The Girl from Pussycat* (1965) featured a female secret agent who might have been called Stephanie Victor but who instead answers to Penny Candle. *Pussycat, Pussycat* followed one year later. *The Nude Who Never* (1967) is Llona Mayper. She quickly reappeared in *The Nude Wore Black* (ditto), Mark's ditzy take on the classic 1940 *noir* novel by William Irish (alias Cornell Woolrich), *The Bride Wore Black*. From its equally ditzy *Private Eyeful* blurb: "Remember Llona Mayper—*The Nude Who Never*? Well, she's a little more experienced now. Call her *The Nude Who Hardly Ever*, perhaps?"

Dell published *Dial O for O.R.G.Y.*, *Around the World Is Not a Trip*, and *The Beauty and the Bug* (all 1973). Plus three non–Steve Victors: *Regina Blue* (1972); *A Stroke of Genius* (1982); *A Stroke of Lightning* (1982). However, it was Zebra Books that brought the Man from O.R.G.Y. series to a climax—in every sense of the word—with *Thy Neighbour's Orgy* and *The Tight End* (both 1981). Mark took another hand in the spy fiction game with *The Man from Charisma*.[26] This amnesiac "perfect man" materializes unscathed in the Arctic tundra immediately after a nuclear-bomb test. He names himself Jonathan Relevant; it just feels *right*, somehow. Relevant speaks English, but everybody else hears him in their own language. Is he a mutant, an alien, or a superman—and super-lustful spy—created in the clandestine laboratory code-named Charisma? Jason Bourne—squared. The plots would thicken even further in *Right on, Relevant!* (1971) and *Rip It Off, Relevant!* (1971, the pair). Spy-fi fiction at its most demented.

Gary Lovisi interviewed Gottfried for *Paperback Parade* (#56, July 2001): "*The Man from O.R.G.Y.* was the result of my being asked to do a book on the Kama Sutra [for Lancer Books]. Original title was *The Kama Sutra Spy*. As I was writing it, the idea seemed absurd to me so I turned it into a satire. I never read a James Bond book and at the time the movies had not yet come out. I always thought *The Man from U.N.C.L.E.* was a ripoff of O.R.G.Y. What I liked best about doing the O.R.G.Y. books was being able to poke fun at political targets like George Wallace, J. Edgar Hoover and the C.I.A."

It wasn't long, however, before a rival counterspy sexologist-cum-counterspy put up his shingle in direct competition with Steve Victor and O.R.G.Y. *The Coxeman Comes*,[27] by Troy Conway, made itself felt less than two years later. "Not since The Man from O.R.G.Y. has there been an adventurer like Rod Gray—the Coxeman" (blurb). The eponymous comer could have been called The Man from L.S.D. (League for Sexual Dynamics), but that never officially happened. *Pace* some otherwise reliable sources, the two series are not connected, although they did share the same publisher (Paperback Library) for the entire run of play.

According to spyguysandgals.com, Rod—for Roderick?—Damon is 6' tall and weighs 180 pounds. Born in Wisconsin, he earned a B.Sc. (Sociology) degree before serving a three-year hitch as an army intelligence officer. Then, as a post-graduate student, Rod found a way to out–Kinsey Dr. Kinsey. Upon finding several willing co-eds and a stack of vintage sex manuals, Damon set about determining the "emotional responses of contemporary collegians to practices of civilizations past." Three fun-packed months later, he published his doctoral thesis, which duly took the academic world by storm. It led to a hefty foundation research grant and the establishment of L.S.D. Damon took the suitably *double entendre* title Coxeman when he was press-ganged back into espionage work by the threat of criminal prosecution. A nubile co-ed with whom he shared the twenty positions of Saluka, Goddess of Love, turned out to be only 13 years old. The Thaddeus X. Coxe Foundation (hence Coxeman) is a cover organization for an ultra-secret American security agency that is not even known to the CIA. However, Damon took every roving-commission opportunity to augment his knowledge of the only thing in life that really matters to him—sex. And, to avoid the accumulation of accidental offspring, he underwent a vasectomy operation in his mid-twenties.

Ted Mark spoke with a single authorial voice in his Steve Victor books, ensuring an evenness of tone throughout the series. But the 34 "Troy Conway" novels were the result of piecework by little-known writers like Johannes L. Bouma and Paul Gilbert. The better-known mystery/science fiction author Charles E. Fritch (1927–2012) ghosted three Coxemans, each of them in collaboration with Gilbert: *It's Getting Harder All the Time* (1968); *Last Licks* (1969); *The Sex Machine* (1970). More substantially, Michael Avallone's son, David, has identified the following 11 books as being the work of his father: *Come One, Come All* (1968); *The Man-Eater* (1968); *Had Any Lately?* (1969); *A Good Peace* (1969); *I'd Rather Fight Than Swish* (1969); *The Big Broad Jump* (1969); *The Blow-Your-Mind Job* (1970); *The Cunning Linguist* (1970); *All Screwed Up* (1970); *The Penetrator* (1971); *A Stiff Proposition* (1971). Another Killmaster alumnus, Gardner F. Fox[28]—*Night of the Condor* (1967)—contributed *The Best Laid Plans* (1969) and *Up and Coming* (1972).

A lawyer by first profession, the Brooklyn-born Gardner Francis Fox attended St. John's University, New York (B.A., 1932: LL.B., 1935). He wrote fantasy novels, science fiction, historical swashbucklers, romance, westerns, soft pornography, and just about everything else. In comics, he helped create, develop, or revive many superheroes, including Batman, the Flash, Green Lantern, the Atom, Zatara, Hawkman, the Spectre, and the Justice Society—later the Justice League—of America. Recommended reading: *Forgotten All-Star: A Biography of Gardner F. Fox*,[29] by Jennifer DeRoss. Fox lets it all hang out in the first chapter of *Up and Coming*: "My name is Rod Damon. I am a sexologist of world renown, being the founder of the League for Sexual Dynamics. Moreover, thanks to a generous Nature, I am extremely well endowed with what every man wants. I possess a hair-trigger response to anything sexually.... I am afflicted with satyriasis. This means that no matter how well

I perform the copulative act, or how often, I am always ready for another go at the hairy horseshoe. The fact has saved my life on my Coxeman missions more than once."

There follows a long tit-for-tat Socratic dialogue concerning the sexual politics of that time, which Rod Damon has been set up to win, just like Ben-Hur in his fixed chariot race. He knows all there is to know about the likes of WITCH (Women's International Terrorist Conspiracy from Hell), the Redstockings of WLM (Women's Liberation Movement), and Betty (*The Feminine Mystique*) Friedan (1921–2006).

Avallone introduces new readers to his unnamed front-man boss in *I'd Rather Fight Than Swish*: "The upper left hand corner [of the envelope] bore the printed title of THE THADDEUS X. COXE FOUNDATION. Which meant Walrus-moustache, which meant trouble. Every time I heard from him by word or deed, my peaceful, Utopian existence was shattered forever. A day later I could wind up in some God-forsaken place like Outer Mongolia. They have women there too, believe it or not. It isn't all yaks. The Coxemen pretend to be a dizzy, right-wing outfit in the U.S.A., as a cover-up for their real excuse for being. It is one of the greatest espionage organizations in the country. And so help me, every now and then, Rod Damon is their number one agent *provocateur*. I have done so much *provocateuring* for them in the past that it provokes the hell out of me."[30]

The happy-go-lucky Steve Victor always wore his hard-won erudition lightly. But Rod Damon was a right Clever Dick, to put it politely. From *The Wham! Bam! Thank You, Ma'am Affair*:

> I touched two dimples just above [Deborah Trent's] buttocks. They were round and deep. "These are the sacral dimples, my dear. Only about twenty percent of all women have them, but they're deemed absolutely essential in perfect feminine beauty."
> I let my forefinger run in a straight line between the dimples and then down to the beginning cleft of her buttocks and up again to the left dimple, forming a triangle. "This is the lozenge of Michaelis, my love. As you can see, it matches the public [*sic*] triangle in the front."
> "Alciphron spoke of it during the beauty contest between Myrrhine and Thryallis. Or read Rufinus' account of the judgment of Paris, which resulted in the Trojan War."[31]

Plot outlines for most, if not all, of the Coxeman books were provided by Hy Steirman (1921–), then a senior editor at Paperback Library. Titles like *The Wham! Bam! Thank You, Ma'am Affair* or *The Harder You Try, the Harder It Gets* (1971) might have been randomly generated, but they always bore a generic relationship to the one-sex-scene-after-another narrative arcs. Michael Avallone supplied a plotline of his own, *Hell's Belles*, which doesn't seem to have been used—under that title, at any rate.

Spy-fi is best represented by *Keep It Up, Rod!* (1968), where the Red Chinese create an artificial Abominable Snowman/Yeti/*Methohkangmi*, the "large, hairy, manlike creature who, according to legend, inhabits the Himalayas, bringing disaster to anyone who, for whatever reason, dares offend him." Ditto the 34th and last

Coxe-file, *A Hard Man Is Good to Find* (1973: attributed to Johannes L. Bouma). It has
very little in the way of action, despite having a female League for Sexual Dynamics
operative named Lisa Lithesome. "THE EXTRA SEXUAL POWER. Rod Damon must
crack a corrupt combine that intends to enslave mankind through an E.S.P. machine
that does more than show X-rated pictures …" (blurb). Flannery O'Connor (1925–
1964) did not live to see what Paperback Library had done to the title of her most
famous short story, which is probably just as well.

The distaff "sexpionage" side of the story was told by Gardner F. Fox, in his Eve
Drum, Agent Oh Sex: The Lady from L.U.S.T. series. L.U.S.T. = League of Undercover Terrorists. They were issued under the house name of Rod Gray. Fox had either
been fired or retired from DC comics in 1968, after—it would seem—an unresolved
dispute over health benefits. This led him to step up the production of science fiction
and historical novels. Under his own name, he created two virtually interchangeable
sword-and-sorcery heroes—Kothar (five books: 1969–70) and Kyrik (1975–76). But it
was the Eve Drum series that really took off, beginning with—what else?—*The Lady
from L.U.S.T.*[32] Recommended reading: "Kill My Assassin" (*The Paperback Fanatic
#23*, August 2012), by Andreas Decker: "That Lady from L.U.S.T." (*Paperback Parade
#86*, June 2014), by Gary Lovisi.

Typical Eve (38–24–35 brunette) Drum self-description: "With a Beretta in my
bra I'm an up-dated Fanny Hill, a tastier brand of Candy, a lethal Lolita. My crazy
life is just filled with bloodshed, bedrooms and belly laughs." Also, from an equally
typical blurb: "Not for nothing does she hold a Sixth Dan belt in judo. She didn't get
to be L.U.S.T.'s most highly prized operative on looks alone … she got in on—well,
find out for yourself!" Eve explains: "The league had been begun some years before,
as a result of the cold war and the spy activities of foreign countries carried on inside
the United States. L.U.S.T. had no official status. It was a by-blow out of the State
Department by way of the Central Intelligence Agency. Only a limited few knew of
its existence at all. Members of L.U.S.T. were given assignments which were criminal in nature."[33]

The T. for Terrorists made for a neat sexploitative anagram, but it also cut the
high moral ground out from L.U.S.T. *vis-à-vis* H.A.T.E. (Humanitarian Alliance for
Total Espionage): "In a sense [H.A.T.E.] corresponded with our own L.U.S.T. We
were natural enemies. When we met in the field, it was always a battle to the death."[34]

Six of one, half a dozen of the other. Eve does not profess herself to be a research
"sexologist" *ooh la* Steve Victor and Rod Gray. But she is a "student and mistress of
Eros" (*passim*), who uses her formidable feminine charms in the service of L.U.S.T.
Deadly Weapons, indeed, as per the mightily mammalian (73–32–36) Polish-born
stripper/actress Chesty Morgan (1937–), in the feature film of that title.

The plots of the Lady from L.U.S.T. novels are even more simplistic than most of
their Coxeman contemporaries—no mean feat, in itself. Andreas Decker: "Eve gets
her assignment, goes undercover, has a lot of torrid sessions with both sexes, gets
caught and tortured sadistically by the villain, escapes and kills the bad guys." No

useful purpose would be served by any blow-by-blow outlines, but Decker (spoiler alert) sums up the denouement of *Kiss My Assassin* (1968) as follows: "…the [third] Nazi had a sex-change and is now a woman who was lounging at the villa pool all the time and whose lover Eve already used as a stud. In a climactic shoot-out in a cemetery Eve dispatches him/her. Case closed." The titles are usually worth reading, at any rate. For example: *The 69 Pleasures* (1967); *To Russia with L.U.S.T.* (1968); *The Poisoned Pussy* (1970: aka *Sock It to Me*).

With the aptly titled *Laid in the Future* (1970), Fox took a more familiar, to him, science fiction/fantasy route; his first all-reading short story, "The Weirds of the Woodcarver," had appeared in the September 1944 issue of *Weird Tales*. And the blurb also did not lie: "Without a stitch in Time. Eve Drum takes an erotic trip to the year 3693 [don't ask how]. Eve thought it would be a drag to be the only real female in the weird, unisex world of the future, but it turns out to be a ball and a half! In a society where men and women have forgotten how to make love, Eve's curves and crevices start quite a revolution …" (blurb). Fox might have made something thoughtful out of this unusual spy-fi situation had he been sufficiently interested. But the interest—and/or the time—wasn't there, so he didn't. In 1975, Belmont/Tower published seven new novels in a "New Lady from L.U.S.T." series. Fox might or might not have been a contributing writer, but Decker has identified Jim Conaway as the author of *Go for Broke*, *Target for Tonight*, and *The Maracaibo Affair* (all 1975).

Fox had a hand in creating the "Cherry Delight" novels (as by Glen Chase), beginning with *The Italian Connection*.[35] Gary Lovisi took "A Look at the Cherry Delight Books" in *Paperback Parade* #105, October 2019. Issue #27 (January 1992) had featured "Gardner Fox in Paperback," by Roy G. James. The following overview has been gleaned from the Spy Gals and Gals website.

Cherry Delight (real name: Cherise Dellissio) is a beautiful female agent working for N.Y.M.P.H.O. (the New York Mafia Prosecution and Harassment Organization). Although based in NYC, doubtless to facilitate the acronymic logo, N.Y.M.P.H.O. fights organized crime—and not just the Mafia—on a national and international basis. Delight is an enthusiastic new recruit, with the job description of "call girl and killer, spy girl and seductress" (it says here, there, and everywhere). Her nickname indicates that she is a "glorious" natural redhead—cherry-red, in fact. Hence Cherry Delight, as per the *dellissio* dessert. She is also called the "Sexecutioner," using her sexuality, marksmanship, judo skills, and former medical-student knowledge to "remove" all proven enemies to Truth, Justice, and the Free World Way. Cherry does not have a regular boyfriend.

Fox wrote 24 out of the 29 Cherry Delight novels that were eventually published. Espionage *per se* plays an even smaller part than in the L.U.S.T. series, although *Silverfinger* (1973) has a nice Bondian-title ring to it. But the blurb puts paid to any such hopes: "The deadliest don in the Mafia gets a taste of Cherry, the sexiest crime fighter in the world." *Lights! Action! Murder!* (1975) sees Cherry infiltrating a blackmail ring in Hollywood as "skin-flick superstar" Coco Madrid. There was a biennial gap between Fox's final (#24) entry, *Roman Candle* (1975) and *The Devil to Pay* (1977), which high-kicked off the "All New Cherry Delight" series (also from Leisure Books). In the first significant change, Cherry is now working for D.U.E. (the Department for Unusual Events)—an organization dedicated to fighting Satanists, not mafiosi. Cherry's first occult-busting mission takes her to Paris, taking on devil worshippers who use rape and torture for their pleasure and profit. She has also lost the "Sexecutioner" job title, whilst retaining her libido-in-the-line-of-duty *modus operandi*. *The Devil to Pay* was written by Rochelle Larkin, as were *Greek Fire* (1977), *The Moorland Monster* (1977), and *The Man Who Was God* (1978). Leonard Levison wrote the remaining novel, *Where the Action Is* (1977).

Lyle Kenyon Engel came up with a "Killmistress" heroine to hopefully match the success of his ongoing Killmaster series. The Baroness made her first curtsy in *The Ecstasy Connection*,[36] followed in quick succession by *Diamonds Are for Dying*, *Death Is a Ruby Light*, *Hard-Core Murder*, *Operation Doomsday*, *Flicker of Doom*, *Sonic Slave* (all 1974), and *Black Gold* (1975). They were attributed to Paul Kenyon—actually a house name belonging to Engel's Book Creation, Inc. But the "real" Paul Kenyon was Boston-born journeyman author Donald Moffitt (1931–2014), who would later make a well-respected own name for himself writing science fiction and historical-mystery novels.

Brief-lives biography. Penelope Worthington was born into a wealthy Philadelphia banking family and completed her formal education at Miss Frothingham's Finishing School. At some unspecified early age, Penny married John Stanton Marlowe, an older "man of mystery" who is killed while flying his Gulfstream jet. Penny—blessed with jade-green eyes, raven-black hair, and "explicit cheekbones"— takes up lucrative employment as a model for *Elle* and *Vogue*. Then she marries Baron Reynaldo St. John Orsini, an Italian-British international playboy who drives to his death racing in the Monaco Grand Prix three years later. The widowed-again Baroness Orsini is recruited into American intelligence work by Caleb Hewitt, a friend of her counterspy first husband. Penelope receives training in weaponry and martial arts. But she soon decides to form an agency of her own. From *Diamonds Are for Dying*: "She knew, from things John Marlowe had let slip in the final months of his life, of the interagency rivalry between CIA and DIA and FBI and the rest of the alphabet soup. Wouldn't it be useful to have a small, reliable organization that only a handful of discreet people knew about—one that wouldn't be vulnerable to interagency security leaks?"[37] And so it came to pass, under the legitimate-business cover of International Models, Inc. There was a touch of Modesty Blaise (q.v.) about the Baroness, right down to costume, unarmed combat, and the frequent use of bow and arrows.

A few more "Man from … clone-series are worthy of mention, if not close critical attention. Not to be confused with *The Man …* and *Girl … from U.N.C.L.E.* novelizations" (q.v.).

Trevor Anderson began his priapic super-spy-assassin career in *Our Man from*

Sadisto,[38] by Clyde Allison. "Meet secret agent 0008, the most talented and irresistible killer in the Free World. Follow him as he embarks on the most dangerous mission of his career—to ravish his way through hundreds of pretty girls at the lair of a madman" (blurb). That extra "0" might have dissuaded the Ian Fleming Estate from suing Ember Library—or perhaps they just couldn't be bothered. Nineteen other novels followed, with such quirky titles as *Nautipuss* (1965), *Sadisto Royale* (1966), *The Merciless Mermaids* (ditto), and *Platypussy* (1968). Clyde Allison was a pseudonym for William Henley Knowles, who has been credited with writing a book almost every month during the 1960s, usually in the soft-porn genre. He committed suicide at the age of 46. His last agent, Richard Curtis, wrote: "[Bill] was a wonderful writer—he was too good for the books he wrote. All that talent wasted on worthless books." Ironically, the "worthless" 0008 books can now fetch three-figure sums in the collectable-paperback market.

One might think that Award's The Man from T.O.M.C.A.T. (Tactical Operations Master Counterintelligence Assault Team) series belongs in the same sexpionage league as O.R.G.Y., L.U.S.T. or N.Y.M.P.H.O., but one would be wrong. The nine novels, which run from *The Dozen Deadly Dragons of Joy* (1967) to *The Bra-Burners' Brigade* (1970), will tease more than please fans of Steve Victor, Eve Drum, and Cherry Delight. Credited to one Mallory T. Knight, they chronicle the Bondian exploits of Timothy ("Tim") O'Shane, an ex-captain in the U.S. Marine Corps who now works as a double agent for T.O.M.C.A.T. and BLINTS (Bureau of Liquidation, Intelligence, and Security)—SMERSH, in all but name. His M-figure is Colonel MacSwiver, who is usually described as an 81-year-old Scottish rake and lecher. Acronyms abound: GASH (Global Air Services Home); BELLS (Beam Activator Longrange Laser System); MUDSCS (Microwave Universal Dental Satellite Communications System); GHOST (George Henry Oak Security Trust); SOBees (Sons of the Bonny Blue Flag); FOG (Field Operations Group—London).

Veteran pulpster Norman Daniels (1905–1995) wrote eight neo–Bond novels about John Keith, aka The Man from A.P.E. (American Policy Executive): *Overkill* (Pyramid, 1964); *The Hunt Club* (1964); *Spy Ghost* (1965); *Operation K* (ditto); *Operation N* (1966); *Operation VC* (1967); *Operation T* (ditto); *Operation SL* (1971). Keith is a tall (6' 1") man in his early thirties, dresses well, fights better, and is fluent in several languages (particularly Russian). He ostensibly works for the Skinner, Maywell & Finch public relations firm, based in NYC's "mad men" Madison Avenue. A.P.E. is even more of a cover operation than Universal Exports. From *Operation T*: "We do not even know exactly whom we work for. We're recruited and trained by men we don't know and never see again. Most of us have been installed in posts over the world, where we are known and trusted. Our operatives range all the way from a dirty-necked, shoe-shine kid in Rome, to a statesman in Bonn."[39] Daniels wrote two not-dissimilar novels about bank president–counterspy Bruce Baron, for Lancer Books: *The Baron of Hong Kong* and *A Killing in the Market* (both 1967).

Will B. Day's Steven Flagg—the Man from M.O.D. (code-named David)—was an interesting variation on Donald Hamilton's Matt Helm (code-named Eric). Flagg appeared in *Bravo 9* and *The Man from M.O.D.* (1967 and 1968). No relation to the British Ministry of Defence (formerly the War Office) or *The Mod Squad* TV series (1968–73). He is one of the 19 agents who make up E Department of the CIA, headed by Edward Charles (more often called the "Old Man"). The entrance to its Washington, D.C., headquarters can only be entered through a fake florist shop, à la *The Man from U.N.C.L.E.* From the back-cover blurb of Book Two: "E Group, sometimes known as the 'MINISTRY OF DEATH' was no vengeance outfit, striking out as the commies do for purposes of terror or retaliation. Any bounce made by E Group was because that individual was a genuine threat to our side. There was only one exception: any individual responsible for the death of an E Division agent was automatically marked for the kill." E presumably equals Elimination (Department/Group/Division/whatever).

Yet again for Lancer Books, F.W. Paul (alias science fiction writer Paul W. [Warren] Fairman: 1909–1977), wrote ten novels about Bret Steele, from *3 for an Orgy* (1968) to *King on Queen* (1971). Steele is the Man from S.T.U.D., which stands for the Special Territories and Unique Developments Division of the Unlimited Insurance Co. (Ltd.). He is more of an insurance agent than G-man spy, although circumstances may dictate otherwise. *The Orgy at Madame Dracula's* (1968) is set in Transylvania: "A term policy has matured and you're to deliver the policy to the holder. A large policy—one million dollars [and] it's imperative that you deliver it as soon as possible. The policy holder's name is Bram Stoker."[40]

And now for something even more completely different—*The Man from Avon*,[41] by Michael Avallone. However, this one-book wonder doesn't work for the famous "Avon calling …" door-to-door cosmetics company. "He's a paperback salesman [for Avon Books] on the road of scorching adventure. He's Larry McKnight and even UFOs can't stop him" (front-cover blurb). *Ding-dong!*

CHAPTER TEN

Heavy Hitters

Although the O.R.G.Y.- and L.U.S.T.-type novels enjoyed high sales for 10–15 years, they represent only a strip sideshow in the main spy-fiction carnival. It was, moreover, a predominantly American phenomenon. The nearest British-born equivalent was created by (Frederick) Adam Diment (1943–), who burst upon the publishing world with *The Dolly Spy*.[1] "[Diment] is twenty-three; his hero, Philip McAlpine, is based on himself. That is to say he's tall, good-looking, with a taste for fast cars, planes, girls [Veronica Lom, in *Dolly Dolly*] and pot …" (Atticus: *The Sunday Times*). Diment wrote three more equally well-received McAlpine novels: *The Great Spy Race* (1968); *The Bang Birds* (ditto); *Think, Inc.* (1971). And then the suddenly publicity-shy Diment vanished into thin air—or at least to Zurich, Switzerland.

Espionage fiction things became even more frantic on the other side of the Atlantic during the 1960s. Fawcett had already cornered the market with their Sam Durell and Matt Helm Gold Medal paperback-original novels. Then senior editor Knox Burger decided to keep three more spy novelists on the go: Philip Atlee, Lawrence Block, and Dan J. Marlowe.

James Atlee Phillips could have been mistaken for a lead character in one of his own thrillers—and not just figuratively, perhaps. Biographical material about him is hard to come by; most of the following facts were gratefully gleaned from the what-when-how.com/pulp-fiction-writers website. Born in Fort Worth, Texas (no exact date found). Educated at Texas State University and University of Texas. Learned to fly a plane. Self-published two volumes of poetry. First novel: *The Inheritors* (1940). *The Case of the Shivering Chorus Girls* (1942). Airline pilot (Far East). Attached to "Flying Tigers" fighter squadron in China. Joined U.S. Marine Corps (1943). Travelled widely after the war: Mexico, the Caribbean, Tahiti, and the Canary Islands. *Suitable for Framing* (1949). *Pagoda* (1951). Down on his luck American Joe Gall teams up with a fellow-citizen friend in Burma, who turns out to be anything but friendly. Uncredited rewrite work on John Wayne's rabidly anti–Communist film *Big Jim McLain* (1952). *The Deadly Mermaids* (Dell First Edition No. 26, 1954). Never-named American secret agent tries to prevent a Communist revolution in Haiti. Shared writing credit for *Thunder Road* (1958), starring Robert Mitchum. Alcohol and narcotics abuse led to him being treated in a veterans' hospital. The rehabilitated Phillips moved to Arkansas, where he married for the third time and took up writing spy fiction again.

Philip Atlee opened fire for Fawcett with *The Green Wound* (1963). It was first-person narrated by Joe Gall, a relation in name only to the earlier Joe Gall of *Pagoda*. Joe Gall Release 2.0 had served as a U.S. Marine in the Pacific during World War II, where he suffered many serious combat wounds. After the war, he ran a car wash and studied law, but he finally found more challenging employment as a counterspy with the "Agency" (i.e., the CIA). Gall fell out with his politically motivated superiors over the botched Bay of Pigs operation, in which he participated. Atlee (from now on) could draw upon his own experiences and those of his younger brother, David Atlee Phillips (1922–1988), who spent twenty-five years as a CIA officer (receiving a Career Intelligence Medal). David became the CIA's Chief of Operations for the Western Hemisphere, personally serving in Latin America—Cuba, Mexico, the Dominican Republic, et cetera.

The Green Wound doesn't read like a typical Gold Medal spy novel, and it might even have been meant as a one-off. Gall is persuaded by someone he trusts, Carleton (Carl) Terhune Wiley, to undertake a freelance assignment on behalf of his former employers. (His former Agency boss, Howard Shale, had been killed in a helicopter crash in South Vietnam.) He is sent to defuse a volatile racial situation in Texas, as per this understated front-cover blurb: "It was a hell of a path Joe Gall had chosen to travel—paved with black magic, white slavery, race riots, narcotics, and good intentions." Knox Burger liked the character, however, and he called for a series. *The Silken Baroness* (1964) came out a year later, in which we learn that Gall is thirty-eight years old and was born in Dallas, Texas, the scion of a wealthy family who preferred the Marine Corps to college. He fought at Iwo Jima, among many other places. Both novels were later republished with the suffix *Contract*, for the same commercial reason that the Sam Durell novels had been given the *Assignment* prefix. Joe Gall—contractor—in his own words, from *The Kiwi Contract* (1972):

My real name, which never appears on the passports I carry, is Joseph Liam Gall. I am a counterintelligence agent, working only on individual contracts for a large U.S. agency.

I was a Marine Corps captain in the Second War to End All and a major in the Korean conflict. When I was recruited by the agency, I still had limited motion in [my wounded] left ankle but was otherwise fit. I worked all around the world and got on well enough until I told some august planners that the proposed Bay of Pigs invasion was bound to be a disaster.

When it turned out to be just that, the high brass and the civilians playing superspook went looking for a whipping boy. I was available and, for my temerity in being right, got my ass fired.[2]

Like his creator, Gall chose to live in deepest Arkansas.

The first official "Contract" novel was *The Death Bird Contract* (1966). Echoing *The Green Wound*, Gall himself becomes a heroin addict—on purpose—as part of an undercover operation. Apart from parts of *The Green Wound* (*Contract*), the early Joe Gall novels are neither ultra-violent nor salaciously sexy. Like James Bond, Gall has a yen for wine and women, though perhaps not for song. But he doesn't bang on about it in the over-emphatic fashion often employed by Fleming. Guns, cars, and gadgets are tools of his trade, only mentioned in passing. However, Gall is more Matt Helm than Sam Durell, eschewing the "soft intelligence racket." From *The Irish Beauty Contract* (1966): "I admit to being an assassin and to having dispatched eleven men since Howard Shale [his original spymaster] hired me. The thought does not trouble me at night. And before you construct some kind of Freudian night-mare around the fact, I invite you to consider that as a Marine officer in some rough Pacific and Korean campaigns, I killed several hundreds of people without having time to think about it...."[3]

Gall was first nicknamed the Nullifer in *Irish*. He is working undercover as the chief of security at a U.S. base in New Granada, another one of those mythical Latin American countries where the CIA writ runs without let or hindrance. The titular colleen is Kathleen Cullen, who—for financial reasons—must provide her husband with a male heir. And who—for other reasons—wants Gall to play his part in the begetting process:

> "Kathleen, Kathleen!" I sighed, dragging her back down into the embrace by her
> ash-blonde hair. "You really must learn to keep a civil tongue in my head."
> And after I had rapped her sharply a couple of times, she did.[4]

Joe Gall meets another Irish beauty called Kathleen—surnamed O'Connell—in Ireland, this time. *The Shankill Road Contract* (1973), to be geographically precise. He has been sent to Belfast, the capital city of Northern Ireland, where the British Army was then caught up in a civil war between Nationalists (Catholics wanting a united Ireland) and Loyalists (Protestants wanting to remain part of the United Kingdom). That particular phase of the conflict is succinctly dealt with in *Northern Ireland: The Troubles*,[5] by Charles Messenger. Quentin Elgin, the son of U.S. pres-ident Howard Elgin, has come under suspicion for several random murders and "punishment beatings" that have taken place there. Gall must either clear Quen-tin's name or "nullify" him. The background details are street-map skimpy, but Atlee should be given credit for tackling a controversial subject that his fellow Gold Med-allers left well enough alone. Atlee was on firmer ground when describing some-where like New Zealand, one of his own familiar South Pacific stomping grounds, in *The Kiwi Contract* (1972).

As an ex-officer and a natural gentleman, Joe Gall does not explicit-sex-scene and tell (much). Nor does he revel in excessive violence; just enough and no more, while not always avoiding collateral damage of innocent civilians. But he's *tough*, as demonstrated by this quote from *The Death Bird Contract*: "I didn't favour the [injured] arm, change my breathing, or even deign to notice the pain. I was on a los-ing assignment, and rage and outrage were slamming around in my head. McGuire strung up in that locked roost with the mad picador; Loco Sautto kicked to death and thrown to the bone-cleaning fish that had been specially imported from Brazil. Saun-ders, the wan agent now working in agency headquarters in Washington; a sharp man with two college degrees who was now not even a trustworthy filing clerk."[6]

Along the way, Gall acquired what could be called a surrogate family, giving him something more personal to think about than the next Big Job. Kelly Wu, the Canadian-Chinese heroine of *The White Wolverine Contract* (1971) and *The Kowloon Contract* (1974) became his common-law wife and the *de facto* concierge of his "clapboard castle" in the Ozarks. He also "adopted" Padraig (Paddy) O'Connell, the autistic and strife-shocked son of the fatally wounded Kathleen, immediately after fulfilling the "Shankill Road" contract.

Most of the Joe Gall novels have well-worked-out plots, as with these previously unmentioned early novels: *The Paper Pistol Contract* (1966); *The Star Ruby Contract* (1967); *The Skeleton Coast Contract* (1968); *The Rockabye Contract* (ditto). But they could take leave of their senses, every now and then. *The Trembling Earth Contract* (1969), for example. Gall's mission here is to infiltrate a Black militant organization calling itself the Republic of New Africa (based in rural Georgia, of all unlikely places). He goes undercover, after being chemically "turned into" a Black man, with an Afro wig hopefully adding credence to his (reversible) cunning disguise. It's like something out of a Black and White Minstrel Show. And surely the CIA must have had at least a few equally competent Black agents on its payroll, even back then. *The Fer de Lance Contract* (1970) is a semi-sequel, with the same archvillain doing an Ernst Stavro Blofeld–type repeat performance.

As intimated above, Joe Gall became more anti–Establishment and empathetic in his views. But he could never have been called "radical" or even mildly left wing (irrationally reserving a special place in Hell for "hippies"). It didn't happen immediately. Casual sexism runs rampant in *The Canadian Bomber Contract* (1971), in which Gall compliments Dr. Noelle on her "beautiful ass" (she leaps into bed with the big lug anyway, of course). He has a right old rant at "feminists" in *The Judah Lion Contract* (1972). But his progressive change of mind and heart runs through all these later novels: *The Spice Route Contract* (1973); *The Underground Cities Contract* (1974); *The Black Venus Contract* (1975); *The Last Domino Contract* (1976); *The Makassar Strait Contract* (ditto). Jeff Banks (in *Twentieth-Century Crime and Mystery Writers*): "…while the first half dozen books, with their exotic villains and extravagant gimmickry, remind the reader of Ian Fleming, the last half dozen are more comparable to Deighton and Le Carré. Yet Gall is as convincing and compelling at the end as he was at the beginning."

James Atlee Phillips died in his sleep from respiratory failure. As Philip Atlee, he was one of the Big Three spy-fiction writers published by Gold Medal, even if something of a "poor relation" to Aarons and Hamilton. But he did receive this ringing endorsement from Raymond Chandler: "I admire Philip Atlee's writing tremendously, the hard economy of style, the characterization, and the interesting and varied backgrounds." Knox Burger signed up some other proficient practitioners, who would make up in quality for what they lacked in relative quantity. Dan J. Marlowe was the earliest and most prolific of these backup espionage novelists, the creator of a super criminal turned reluctant super spy who answered to the name Earl Drake. Whenever it suited him….

Daniel James Marlowe[7] was born in Lowell, Massachusetts. Most potted biographies blandly state that he went on to have a career in accounting, insurance, and public relations, which is fair enough. The whole truth is much more complicated, however, as revealed in *Gunshots in Another Room: The Forgotten Life of Dan J. Marlowe*,[8] by Charles Kelly. Marlowe created the quirky lone-wolf New York detective Johnny Killain in *Doorway to Death*.[9] The "J" was dropped from Marlowe's early byline. His first stand-alone novel, *Backfire* (1961), concerned Marty Donovan, a policeman who falls in love with Lenore, his partner's wife. It reads like a collaboration between Georges Simenon and James M. Cain.

But Dan ("J") Marlowe really came to prominence with *The Name of the Game Is Death* (Gold Medal, 1962), which introduced an ultra-*ultra*-violent bank robber whose real name might or might not have been Chet Arnold but who is currently calling himself Roy Martin. In the very first chapter, this psychopath's psychopath has robbed a bank in Phoenix, Arizona, with his partner Bunny, killed three men, and been wounded in the arm. They split up, the plan being that Bunny will mail Roy's half of the $178,000 take from his faraway hometown. When the installment-plan scheme peters out, and Bunny fails to contact him, our essentially nameless anti-hero goes on a rampage to reclaim the money that is not rightfully his. Anthony Boucher wrote, in his review for *The New York Times*: "This is the story of a completely callous and amoral criminal, told in his own self-justified and casual terms, tensely plotted, forcefully written, and extraordinarily effective in its presentation of a viewpoint quite outside humanity's expected patterns."

"I'll be leaving one of these days, and the day I do they'll never forget it," vows Chet Arnold/Roy Martin at the end of *Game*. And who can blame him, after his face has been burnt off in a fire? But he is born again, Phoenix-like, during the painful course of *One Endless Hour* (1969). "I have a new face [plastic surgery], a new name [Earl Drake], and I had buried the past." Earl Drake would be his default persona from then on, sometimes ruefully referring to himself as "the man with nobody's face" (a tag which adorned many a front-cover blurb). The past isn't buried all that deeply, however, and Drake soon hits the vengeance trail.

Operation Fireball (1969) bridges that awkward gap between Earl Drake the vicious professional criminal and Earl Drake the equally vicious but accredited government agent. For one thing, he has found the love of a good and beautiful and wealthy six-foot redheaded woman called Hazel Andrews. For another thing, he is no longer a homeless hoodlum (Hazel owns a ranch in Nevada). But he is personally broke—and bored. Then old partner-in-crime Sterling hoves into view, recruiting him for a $2,000,000 heist—in Cuba!—masterminded by mysterious mobster Karl Erikson. It turns out that Erickson isn't a member of the Mob but an operative of the U.S. Treasury tasked with retrieving money sent to an anti–Castro politician just before Fidel took over. Hazel knew this all along. She wanted to have Earl's criminal record expunged and him gainfully employed as a secret agent. And so it comes to pass.

The seven-year gap between *Game* and *One Endless Hour* was filled with seven other Gold Medal books. *The Raven Is a Blood Red Bird* (1967) was written in collaboration with William Odell, who wrote several Nick Carter/Killmaster novels, e.g., *The Nowhere Weapon* (Charter, 1979). *Raven*'s back cover blurb: "She was no ordinary gypsy. Passionate, hot-tempered, treacherous—but that's where the resemblance ended. An ordinary gypsy girl doesn't know how to operate a secret radio transmitter to the Kremlin, and usually isn't a triple-agent for whatever espionage network will pay the most money—in American dollars. But the gypsy called Raven would dare anything...."

Earl Drake was one of the first two major crime-fiction "heroes" who killed policemen, bank guards, fellow crooks, and even innocent bystanders without breaking into an ethical sweat. All in the day's work, nothing personal, and you should have kept out of their way. The other single-minded sociopathic career criminal was Parker (no first name), created by Donald E. Westlake (1933–2008), using his Richard Stark persona.

The "growing pains" of *One Endless Hour* and *Operation Fireball* had been ironed out by the time of *Flashpoint* (1970). Earl Drake was well on his way to becoming a firmly established spy-fiction character. But Gold Medal still felt the need to add some potted background material to their back-cover blurb, for the benefit of new readers: "I had lived so long on the wrong side of the law I felt out of place as a special undercover agent for Uncle Sam. But I had no choice. One of the top brass in U.S. Intelligence [Karl Erickon] had my number. So we made a deal—his silence for my services in tracking down and infiltrating a gang of Mid-East terrorists. Besides, I had a personal interest in this job. They had stolen $75,000 from me."

Flashpoint won the 1970 Edgar Award from the Mystery Writers of America for Best Paperback Original novel. A title change to *Operation Flashpoint* came into effect two years later, on both sides of the Atlantic. *The Name of the Game Is Death* was rewritten to bring it into line with the new-look Earl Drake and reprinted as *Operation Overkill* (1973). Gold Medal had made *Operation* the tag *mot juste* for their latest spy-fiction brand.

The next two Earl Drake exploits—*Operation Breakthrough* (1971) and *Operation Drumfire* (1972)—were an uneasy amalgam of crime and spy fiction, as though Marlowe had some leftover plots that he wanted to use up. Unlike Aarons, Atlee, and Hamilton (the American spy-fiction "supergroup" of the 1970s), Marlowe left knotty geopolitical entanglements pretty much alone. But *Operation Checkmate* (1972) finds Earl Drake (and Hazel Andrews) involved with a Far Eastern flare-up that might be a prelude to World War Three.

Marlowe dutifully ticked the "chick" box on the spy-fiction writer's checklist. But these young ladies of quality can take better care of themselves than the average complaisant Bond girl. Chen Yi, for example, in both *Drumfire* and *Checkmate*: "No one who hadn't witnessed the tall [6' 4"] Chinese girl in action could believe the havoc she could wreak." When it comes to hot one-on-one sex action, however,

Drake can't tear himself away from Hazel Andrews, who is obviously the woman of his—and Marlowe's, it has been alleged—fetish-driven dreams. The following extract, from *Operation Hammerlock* (1974), is by no means an isolated case: "She giggled musically and reached beneath herself to take hold of the staff of life. After that nobody said anything for a long time. She agitated me expertly with every loving little trick she knew turned me on. We played, and then I settled her down. It was like floating down a mountain river: deep-feeling and languorously easeful until the explosively ride-the-rapids surge at its end."[10]

"DRAKE [ran the back-cover blurb] wasn't a good man; he wasn't a bad man; but his name was Earl Drake—and that was the difference." Which begs the question—just how different *was* the new "reformed" Drake? At best, he acts like a half-tamed polecat, working under the constant threat of being handed over to the proper authorities for his past crimes. Hazel had "enlisted" in the agency just to keep him sensible, if not honest. But it doesn't take much to set off the old inexorable blood-lust. From *Operation Deathmaker* (1974):

> "You can't kill me!" Stan Kirkman screamed. "YOU CAN'T KILL—"
>
> The slug hit him right in the center of his fast-moving mouth. His teeth, or his palate, changed its direction, because it burst from the top of the left-hand side of his skull. Part of his brain was splashed on the wall behind him before he slammed back into it, bounced off, and pitched forward onto his belly.
>
> I rounded the desk and went over to him, shoved a foot under a shoulder, and flipped him onto his back. With the lifesaving techniques available to the medical profession these days, if a man doesn't die at once from a gunshot wound he might not die at all.
>
> There was no medical technique available that was going to be of any assistance to Stan Kirkman. Instead, there was going to be a considerable problem identifying him.[11]

As time wore on, Marlowe tended to go over his carbons and recycle old plot-lines. In *Operation Stranglehold* (1973), for example, Karl Erickson is captured—again! Drake has to rescue him—again! From a Spanish prison, this time. To be fair, though, he did something refreshingly different in *Operation Whiplash* (also 1973). It is a straightforward mystery novel. No agency assignment, no foreign—or even just national—intrigue. *Operation Counterpunch* (1976) brought the twelve-book series to an end. Marlowe died of a stroke the following year, aged 69. It was not generally known that he collaborated with bank robber Alfred Frederick Nussbaum (1934–1996), who had been impressed by *The Name of the Game Is Death*.

The Earl Drake books never became Matt Helm–like bestsellers, but they did make the Fawcett publishing company more than a little bit richer. Dan J. Marlowe still has many admirers, including Stephen King (1947–), who dedicated *The Colorado Kid* (2005) to his memory ("hardest of the hardboiled"). *It Takes a Thief*, an ABC TV series that ran from January 9, 1968, until September 14, 1970, starred Robert Wagner as a gentleman criminal named Alexander (Al) Mundy who had been co-opted as a spy for one of those fictional clandestine government agencies. Gil Brewer (1922–1983) wrote three tie-in novelizations, based on teleplays, all for Ace Books: *The Devil in Davos* (1969); *Mediterranean Caper* (ditto); *Appointment in Cairo*

(1970). They were set in Switzerland, France, and Egypt, respectively. Al Mundy was, in effect, a more peripatetic doppelgänger of Earl Drake.

Lawrence Block (1938–) placed his first two "official" novels with Gold Medal in 1961: *Death Pulls a Double Cross* (reprinted as *Coward's Kiss* by Foul Play Press, New York, 1987) and *Mona*. Belmont published the TV tie-in novel *Markham: The Case of the Pornographic Photos* later that same year (British edition: Consul, London, 1965).[12] The CBS series itself, which starred Ray Milland as a hard-hitting Manhattan private eye, ran from May 2, 1959, until September 22, 1960. Then it was eventually back to Gold Medal for *The Case of the Long Green Heart* (1965). Bibliographical Note: *Fidel Castro Assassinated*, as by Lee Duncan, had been published on January 1, 1961 (Monarch Americana edition: paperback original). Hard Case Crime reprinted it under the title *Killing Castro* in 2009, using the author's now world-famous byline.

Block was born in Buffalo, New York State, and educated at Antioch College, Yellow Springs, Ohio (1955–59). His breakthrough Gold Medal novel, *The Thief Who Couldn't Sleep* (1966), introduced part-time secret agent and permanent insomniac Evan Tanner. He has been wide-awake since a piece of shrapnel destroyed the sleep center in his brain during the Korean War, at the age of 18 or 19. For the next 16 years, Tanner spent a sleepless life in constant study, relieved only by a daily 20-minute yoga regime. We first meet Evan (Michael) Tanner in a *Midnight Express*–lite Turkish prison. After further sojourns in Ireland, Spain, and Bulgaria, he is pitchforked into a secret agency that is neither the CIA nor the FBI (but loathed by both of them) by someone known only as The Chief: "[He] was a round-faced man, bald on top, with fleshy hands that remained in perfect repose on the desk in front of him. The desk was empty of papers. There was a box labelled IN and another labelled OUT. Both were empty. There was a globe on the desk and a map of the world on the wall behind him."[13]

Evan Tanner, the thief—and spy—who couldn't sleep, came back in *The Canceled Czech* (1966). Whoever wrote the back-cover blurb summarized the nutty plot in a nutshell: "The man-with-no-name headed an undercover agency so secret that even *it* didn't have a name. And all they wanted me to do was slip unnoticed into the middle of Czechoslovakia, smack into the clutches of a nearly mad blonde, an absolutely mad cataleptic, and a band of frenzied Israeli patriots—and right under all their noses I was to engineer the most outrageously impossible kidnapping of the century." More specifically, Tanner must rescue Janos Kotacek, a former Slovakian Nazi war criminal now living in Lisbon who has been abducted by the Czech police and brought back home for a fair trial and certain execution. The Chief explains the importance of Kotacek in words that resonate even today:

> We've known of Kotacek's whereabouts almost from the day he turned up in Lisbon. And we've been very careful to leave him alone. Kotacek has been one of the key figures in the global neo–Nazi movement … the orientation of Nazism has changed slightly since Hitler's death. Germans remain at the helm, but the *idée fixe* has shifted from Aryan

supremacy to general white supremacy. Anti-Semitism is still a chief tenet, but anti–Negro and anti–Oriental policies have come to the fore; integration and the Yellow Peril are evidently more potent scapegoats.[14]

The "nearly mad blonde" (see above) woman is Greta Neumann, the nymphomaniacal daughter of "little" Karl Neumann, a Teutonic Czech neo–Nazi activist. But Tanner will find Greta to be much more prepossessing—and predatory:

> My fingers drew swastikas upon her breasts. She giggled, and her hands reached and found. "Just like the poor old Slovak," she said. "Just like the Jews. Ah, what have I done!"
> "You have performed miracles."
> I held her and kissed her. Our flesh met. Perhaps I ought to take her along, I thought. Even smuggle her all the way back to America. Keep her around the apartment. How fine she was, and how soft and firm and warm, and how she moved, and what sounds she made....[15]

Tanner's Twelve Swingers (1967), in which Tanner made a drunken promise to rescue a beautiful gymnast from behind the Iron Curtain, was published by Coronet (1968). But the next three novels—*Two for Tanner* (1967: aka *The Scoreless Thai*: Subterranean Press, New York, 2001), *Here Comes a Hero* (1968: aka *Tanner's Virgin*: ditto, 1975), and *Tanner's Tiger* (ditto both)—also didn't make it across the Atlantic. In *Tanner's Tiger*, the Chief sends Tanner to the Montreal Expo to investigate suspicious goings-on at the Cuban pavilion there. Not only does Tanner tangle with cantankerous Cubans but he runs afoul of querulous Quebecois *and* foils an assassination attempt on Queen Elizabeth II of England. The appropriately titled *Me Tanner, You Jane* (1970) was published in hardcover by Macmillan (New York and London), with a subsequent paperback edition from Gold Medal. Jane is the daughter of American missionaries who changed her name to Sheena—as in "Queen of the Jungle" fame.

Evan Tanner took an unauthorized two-decade leave of absence from not just the agency but the whole human race as well (see below). Meanwhile, Block had diversified his literary interests by creating two non-espionage characters who lifted him out of the paperback-original rut for good. Although alcoholic ex-policeman turned part-time private investigator Matthew Scudder was originally a paperback hero, starting with *In the Midst of Death* (1976), the fourth novel, *A Stab in the Dark* (1981), and the fifteen (so far) successors have all been first-edition hardcovers. Master thief Bernie Rhodenbarr appeared in eleven bestselling novels, from *Burglars Can't Be Choosers* (1977) to *The Burglar Who Counted the Spoons* (2013). *The Burglar Who Liked to Quote Kipling* (1979) won the 1980 Edgar award for Best Novel presented by the Mystery Writers of America.

Evan Tanner made a belated comeback in *Tanner on Ice* (1998). He had been missing for twenty-five years after Harold Engstrom, a fanatical agent of SKOAL (an organization dedicated to restoring lost areas of Sweden and Norway to Danish control) spiked his brandy and then imprisoned him in a suspended-animation chamber. As one does. Then the Spy Who Slept Too Long becomes the Spy Who Came in from the Cold—literally:

"I was born in 1933," I said, "so if it's really 1997, I ought to be sixty-four years old. Do I look sixty-four years old?"

"No," he said without hesitation. "You look about thirty-nine."

"I *am* about thirty-nine. And it's 1972, isn't it?"

"No, it's 1997."

"It's 1997 and I'm thirty-nine."

"According to the calendar, you're sixty-four. But yes, I'm going to agree with your last statement. It is indeed 1997, and you are indeed thirty-nine years old."

I looked at him. He looked at me. I said, "I give up. How can that be possible?"

"Mr. Tanner," he said. "Have you ever heard of cryonics?"[16]

The Chief, who is the same only different, brings Tanner up to spy-story speed.

Financial necessity forces the sleepless knight of unorthodox espionage back on the payroll. Tanner no longer works for Uncle Sam, however indirectly, but Rufus Crombie, a billionaire freelance spymaster. Crombie gives him the covert assignment of destabilizing the government of Myanmar—a country formerly known to him as Burma. Most people still call it Burma, in fact. "Not an easy task, considering that once he arrives he's hounded by the local police [plus a subversive agency known as SLORC]; discovers a corpse in his hotel room; befriends a cool beauty with an agenda all her own; and receives an anonymous warning: *Get out of Burma or you die*. Putting all the pieces together is going to take Tanner's every waking moment" (blurb). Which—as we know—is *every* moment. Tanner succeeds, of course, but the Man Who Cannot Sleep has not been heard from since. He might just not be inclined to work for the dodgy Rufus Crombie again. As the Chief said: "I think he was sincere enough at the beginning, wanting to do some good in the world. But how could he avoid wanting to do himself some good at the same time?"[17]

"It's hard for me to tell how kindly Time has dealt with Tanner. The world has certainly changed. When I wrote these books, the Soviet Union with its Eastern Bloc allies was a monolith. That it should ever break up into pebbles was inconceivable. Tanner, a supporter of all lost causes, splinter groups, irredentists and separatist movements, might have been the only person on the planet unastonished by the events of the last decade" (introduction to the 1994 edition).

Richard S. (for Scott) Prather (1921–2007) was the first Fawcett Gold Medal "discovery" to strike it rich, and he helped make paperback originals a real paying proposition for many another writer who followed his lead. Shell Scott, Prather's "happy-go-looky" Hollywood P.I., debuted in *Case of the Vanishing Beauty* (1950), which was also his first published novel. The 6' 2" and 250-pound Scott is an ex–Marine with short-cropped white hair and steely gray eyes. He remains thirty years of age throughout his long career. Shell Scott's "birth" in 1950 coincided with the nascent Cold War/Warm Peace and the concomitant Red Menace; 20/20 hindsight reveals that most of the boring from within—pun intended—was done by HUAC (House Un-American Activities Committee), J. Edgar Hoover, and what President Eisenhower would later call the military-industrial complex. Back then, however, the *perceived* threat came from Fifth Columnists financed by Moscow and/

or Peking Gold. Commie-bashing quickly took the place of Nazi- and Jap-bashing in popular fiction.

In *Pattern for Panic* (1954), Shell Scott utters this diatribe against World Communism: "Shaping public opinion, whether it's in international relations or home-grown subversion is like the public relations business. Control enough of the words reaching people and you can make most of them believe damn near anything."[18] It is no accident that the ultra-violent *Panic* goes against the grain of Prather's generally easy-going and often downright hilarious work. Communist infiltration of labor unions is highlighted in *Darling, It's Death* (1952): "It's common knowledge, except among idiots, that a large number of union bosses are waiting only for the word from Moscow, and all the rest of it will begin."[19] However, the most overtly political novel is *The Trojan Hearse* (1964): "The welfare-state philosophy. Socialism. Or in another word: collectivism. Some would call it Creeping Communism."[20] By the late 1960s, Prather had toned down his polemics against Marxist-Leninist "moles," and he declared a moratorium on this increasingly played-out subject. Although Shell Scott generally works alone, he once worked with Chester Drum, the Washington-D.C.-based "international detective" created by fellow Gold Medaller Stephen Marlowe (1928–2008), in *Double in Trouble* (1959).

Stephen Marlowe's birth name was Milton Lesser. The MIT Science Fiction Society's *Index to the SF Magazines, 1951–1965* (compiled by Erwin S. Strauss in 1966), show that over ninety science fiction short stories by Milton Lesser (and several pseudonyms) appeared during that hectic period. After a Raymond Chandler *hommage* name change to Stephen Marlowe (which became his legal identity), he produced a quick succession of mystery novels, including *Catch the Brass Ring* (1954). *The Second Longest Night* (1955) was the first of twenty books about Chester Drum. Nicknamed "Chet" by the favored few, Drum is an erstwhile FBI agent, only somewhat less dour than Fox Mulder of *The X-Files*. But he's usually got a lot to be dour about, not least the fact that he operates in Washington, D.C., even then an unsavory location. "The sign on the pebbled glass of the door said Chester Drum, Confidential Investigations. Confidential. That was more necessary in Washington than elsewhere. The office was on F Street, where such offices are in Washington."[21] However, much of the action takes place in exotic Venezuela.

Given where he lives and works, Chester Drum frequently finds himself embroiled with cases that involve foreign intrigue and a hefty amount of foreign travel. *Mecca for Murder* (1956) takes him all the way to Saudi Arabia, on both private and State Department business. *Terror Is My Trade* (1958) followed much the same pattern, but set in London. Two of the most espionage-related novels are *Death Is My Comrade* (1960) and *Drum Beat—Berlin* (1964). Marlowe's last Chester Drum novel, *Drum Beat—Marianne*—appeared in 1968. However, he had already written *The Search for Bruno Heidler* (1966), a "high-speed chase across Europe ends in the most explosive confrontation between hunter and hunted in all of suspense fiction" (blurb). *Heidler* was followed by three even more substantial political thrillers: *The Summit* (1970); *The Man with No Shadow* (1976); *The Valkyrie Encounter* (1978).

Ironically, John D. (for Dann) MacDonald (1916–1986), the Fawcett author who had been most closely associated with real Intelligence work (the OSS, during the Second World War), wrote next to nothing that could be construed as being spy fiction.

Unlike JDM (for short), E. Howard Hunt[22] was a former American secret agent who did not prove backward in coming forward when it came to making fictional use of his "spooky" experiences. Like JDM, he started publishing crime-thriller paperback originals with Fawcett Gold Medal in the early 1950s: *The Violent Ones* (1950); *Dark Encounter* (ditto); *The Judas Hour* (1951); *Whisper Her Name* (1952); *Lovers Are Losers* (1953). William DeAndrea: "For a time, [Hunt] was the most famous mystery writer in the world. Of course, when he was convicted of six counts of conspiracy in association with the Watergate break-in [June 17, 1972] and related crimes, his (part-time and largely pseudonymous) career was the least famous thing about him. However, the notoriety was enough to get [publishers] to reissue some of the books [which are] better-than-competent 1950s and 1960s thrillers of the private eye and spy variety" (*Encyclopedia Mysteriosa*).

Everette Evan Hunt, Jr., was born in Hamburg, upstate New York, where his father was a prominent Republican Party official. He served as a commissioned officer, aboard a destroyer, in the United States Naval Reserve (1940–42) and then transferred to the United States Army Air Force (first lieutenant: 1943–46). A medical discharge led to him joining the OSS. He spent the last few months of World War II in China helping guerrilla forces fight the Japanese. After two peace-time years as a screenwriter, Hunt was recruited by the U.S. State Department. He would be based in Washington, D.C., and many foreign capital cities, including Paris, Vienna, Tokyo, and Montevideo. These assignments frequently involved cover stories for his actual job, with the CIA, and he established the agency's first office in Mexico (1949). In 1970, Hunt became a civilian "consultant" security expert. The following year he was appointed to the White House Special Investigative Group, better known as the "plumbers" because they tracked down leaks from the Nixon administration. The rest is black-ops history.

Of Hunt's stand-alone novels, *The Berlin Ending*[23] was given the most positive critical and popular reception: "Tense, brutal, action-packed ... the narrative has a fine pace and the writing is vivid and intelligent" (*The New York Post*). The blurb-writer for the Berkley paperback edition (May 1974) milked the ongoing Watergate controversy of all the publicity value it was then worth:

A NOVEL TORN FROM TOMORROW'S HEADLINES

About "Agents of influence"—not spies but "high government officials capable of altering the attitudes of an entire country," Howard Hunt's novel has the ring of total authenticity. Based on fact, THE BERLIN ENDING takes the reader behind the scenes to crime at the highest level, in Washinton, France, Holland, Scandinavia, and finally Berlin.

The step-daughter of West Germany's Foreign Minister, a Nobel Prize nominee, knows the dark secret of his bond with the Soviet. Her flight from Europe to Washington sets in train a chase and a sequence of events that threatens not only individual lives but the destiny of nations. The best book ever by America's master agent.

It wasn't until the mid–1960s that Hunt created Peter Ward, a *bona fide* super-spy series character. He used the penname David St. John, taken from the forenames of his two sons. *On Hazardous Duty*[24] was published as a paperback original by New American Library. NAL/Signet was still making a not-so-small fortune with the James Bond books, but the death of Ian Fleming in 1964 meant that no new "007 product" would be forthcoming. Apart from *Octopussy, and The Living Daylights,*[25] a slim two-story volume, they now had to rely mostly upon film tie-in editions. As a proven professional, Hunt was the first espionage-fiction writer called in to help fill the fiscal gap.

Ward and Hunt are both graduates of Brown, patriotic CIA employees, no strangers to the D.C. social whirl, and Hunt has described Ward as "the secret agent with the taste and the talent for fine living." Their backstories diverge significantly, however. Ward and his sister, Anne, were orphaned at an early age. They have been left enough of a fortune to see them both through the rest of their lives. But not nearly enough money for Peter, who combined a yen for action-packed adventure with the driving ambition to make his mark on the world. He satisfied the one by joining the OSS (later CIA) and the other by becoming a high-powered lawyer in Washington, D.C. The latter becomes a cover for the former, as Ward jets around the world on simultaneous overt and covert missions. He maintains an apartment in Georgetown but is almost never there. At the time of *On Hazardous Duty*, Ward has been a spy for over twenty years. Ward is assigned to Operation Omega by his boss, Hopwood, generally described as a tall man, fiftyish, with tousled graying hair. The mission entails contacting Soviet thermonuclear scientist Pavel Borisov, whose claim to being a potential defector might or might not be genuine.

This bullet-point description comprised the back-cover blurb for the 1967 British Four Square paperback (as *Hazardous Duty*):

MOST SECRET MOST SECRET
FOR RANKS G.2. AND ABOVE ONLY
Name: Peter Ward
Age: 35
Marital Status: Single
Cover: Professional playboy/gambler/connoisseur
Has substantial funds of his own
Occupation: Special Agent C.I.A. (Grading 3D)
Clearance: All to Most Secret
Cover No: 327—ZZ—537X
Description: Height 6' 0½" Weight 164 pounds
Expert Assassin.
Grade 2A car driver
Recommended assignment: International agencies
Current assignment: Paris

N.B. A close look at the front cover will reveal that the male model portraying Peter Ward is none other than George Lazenby (1939–), who replaced Sean Connery as James Bond in *On Her Majesty's Secret Service* (1969). Lazenby "is OK, but incredible action sequences take first chair; some 007 fans consider this the best of the series" (Maltin). But he turned out to be just a one-off 007, replaced by Connery in *Diamonds Are Forever* (1971).

Peter Ward's second adventure, *Return from Vorkuta* (1965), is considered by Marvin Lachman to be the best of the nine-book series: "A Royalist [the Conde de Prados] who may be a Russian spy is returned to Spain from Siberia, where he has been a prisoner since the Spanish Civil War. He claims the throne, and the CIA is worried about the U.S. NATO bases in Spain" (*Twentieth-Century Crime and Mystery Writers*). Lachman also special-mentions *The Venus Probe* (1966), a borderline spy-fi novel in which Ward investigates the disappearance, over several years, of seven Western scientists who together have the knowledge to launch successful deep-space rockets.

Hunt took another crack at creating a popular action hero with Jack Novak, in *Cozumel*.[26] Novack is more of an undercover policeman than a spy, working undercover for the DEA (Drug Enforcement Agency). Very *deep* undercover. He poses as the half-owner of a charter fishing boat based at the titular Cozumel (an island in the Caribbean Sea off the eastern coast of the Yucatan Peninsula, opposite Playa del Carmen). The author knew this part of Mexico very well, from past professional experience. Novack also owns a "vintage" seaplane that he flies for fun and contraband profit, helping to cement his hard-won reputation as a modern-day Harry (*To Have and Have Not*) Morgan. As a curtain-raiser to the series, Novack is hired to find a lost aircraft. His employers come to a sticky end and so he must find their killers or face arraignment as the prime suspect.

Guadalajara (1986) and *Mazatalan* (1987), from the same hardcover publisher, are of minimal espionage interest—if any. Although Novack has left the DEA in *Ixtapa* (1993), he rallies round the Old Firm by impersonating a drugs smuggler. We get closer to spy-stuff with *Islamorada* (1995) and *Izmir* (1996), where (a) Novack helps a former colleague fight against foreign rebels training in the Florida Everglades and (b) he is asked (on his honeymoon!) to find another former colleague who has vanished while working a case in Turkey. *Sonora* (2000), the last Jack Novack novel, takes him back to his Agency roots, preceding *Cozumel* by five years. E. Howard Hunt died of a stroke at his home in Miami. Autobiographical reading: *Give Us This Day: The Inside Story of the CIA and the Bay of Pigs Invasion—by One of the Key Organizers* (1973) and *American Spy: My Secret History in the CIA, Watergate, and Beyond* (2007), ghost-written by Greg Anapa.

NAL/Signet had also signed up another seasoned professional writer, Bill S. Ballinger,[27] who contributed a series of five novels about another CIA agent—Joachim Hawks. William Sanborn Ballinger was born in Oskaloosa, Iowa. After advertising and radio (81 scripts) work in Chicago and New York City, Ballinger relocated permanently to Southern California, where he took part in the booming television industry (150 scripts, from *Mr. Black* in 1949 to *Kolchak: The Night Stalker* in 1974–75). Apart from the occasional story credit, Ballinger also scripted three films: *Unsolved* (1960); *The Strangler* (1964); *Operation C.I.A.* (1965: co-written with Peter J. Oppenheimer). Ballinger's first novel, *The Body in the Bed*,[28] concerned a typically hardboiled Chicago P.I. named Barr Breed, as did *The Body Beautiful* (1949).

Signet had already published the aptly titled *Formula for Mystery* (1958), with a conventional "brainbox" sleuth by the name of Van Mars. But Joachim Hawks, starting with *The Spy in the Jungle* (May 1965), turned out to be something way-out-else again. From the back-cover blurb: "Graduate of a prominent American college. Speaks several languages like a native. Knows how to love a woman and kill a man. Son of a Nez Percé chieftain and a Spanish gentlewoman. TOP UNDER-COVER AGENT FOR THE C.I.A." Ballinger didn't dwell on Hawk's Native American-European background as much as Edward S. Aarons spent on the Cajun-born Sam Durell (see Chapter Twelve). He had only an average of 128 pages to tell his tangled tales, after all. For one (edited) example: "A shaman was a priest-magician who could send his own soul into Heaven or Hell. While in these regions, he could consult spirit-ghosts concerning cures, casting spells, foretelling the future, consigning the dead to their places, and manipulating weather—for good or ill. The shaman had a sacred drum, called 'the whip.' Beating it helped to whip, or drive, the soul of the shaman on his dangerous journeys."[29]

The ever-opportunistic Lyle Kenyon Engel would later create "John Eagle Expediter," a Joachim Hawks clone, for Pyramid Books. Fourteen novels made up this mass-produced series, from *Needles of Death* (1973) to *Silverskull* (1975). Paul Edwards was the house name foisted upon Manning Lee Stokes (who wrote several Killmaster novels: see above), Robert Lory (1936–), and Paul Eiden (?). John Eagle works for yet another anonymous American intelligence agency, with a boss known only as Merlin (probably "M," for short). He was born on an Apache reservation, south of the Gila River, which flows through New Mexico and Arizona. His mother died during childbirth and his grief-stricken father was killed in a construction accident soon after, leaving him to be brought up in the ways of hunting by a friendly Apache boy. Useful skills for a future secret agent.

But what really sets Joachim Hawks apart from other contemporary spy-fiction heroes is that the novels have all been set in a Southeast Asia far removed from the 1930s heyday of Hugh North and Mr. Moto. The old European colonial powers were now in full retreat from the area, although the British had successfully rid Malaya (now Malaysia) of Communist insurgents. Meanwhile, the Vietnam War (1954–75) in the former French Indochina was heating up, with American forces—both overt and covert—getting ever more closely involved. Graham Greene had predicted as much in his novel, *The Quiet American* (1955).

The Spy in the Jungle reveals Joachim (M.) Hawks to have been an integral part of that clandestine expansion program. "ASSIGNMENT [runs the "casefile" blurb]:

Vietnam and Laos. MISSION: Track an unknown adversary from the intrigue rid-den city of Saigon [capital of South Vietnam] to the treacherous jungles of northern Laos. OBJECTIVE: Find out what secret force deep in that Red Chinese strong-hold can ensure the failure of U.S. missiles launched half a world away." Hawks is an unseen but potent presence in the prologue. Howard Berke, CIA Director of Opera-tions, Los Angeles, and Roger Orth, a recognized Agency expert on Southeast Asian affairs, bring each other—and the reader—up to date on his personnel file: "Well.... I could say he's available—which he is. Hawks is on a vacation, the first he's had in three years. But that's not the important reason. I think he's the best man I've got for this particular job. It's easy to lose sight of his scholastic record in college because of what he did in athletics. He's a whiz in languages. As a kid, he grew up on that Lapwai Reservation. Up in Idaho. Trilingual—Nez Perce, Spanish, and English. He speaks French, German—and just about anything else he can hear. Picks 'em up like a sailor picks up girls on shore leave."[30]

We first meet Hawks, in chapter 1, enjoying a picnic lunch with the beautiful Linda Homes: "Her titian hair fell loosely onto the grass. A brief swimming suit clung to her body.... She nodded soberly, answering his look. Then he kissed her lips. They kissed for a long time; the girl slowly placed the cup on the ground beside her, and folded her arms around Hawks's neck. She sank back against the earth, pulling Hawks down with her, massaging his back with her fingertips."[31] But that's as far as it goes. Joachim and Linda are interrupted by the arrival of Trotting Pony (English name: Henry Long). Vacation over. Despite being code-named Swinger—a word that would acquire sleazy connotations in the late 1960s and beyond—Hawks refrained from getting "on the job" while he was on the job. Except, of course, in the line of duty.

Ballinger could not be accused of over-describing Joachim Hawks, but there are enough details to put together a thumbnail sketch. Hawk's mixed parentage has given him a Doc Savage–Man of Bronze complexion. His high-bridged "hawk-like" nose, lean face, and coal-black hair make it easy for him to pass for many people of different nationalities and ethnic backgrounds. Ditto his facility with learning for-eign languages. In-between assignments, he runs a one-man travel agency in Los Angeles, organizing group tours all over Latin and South America.

The Chinese Mask (June 1965) takes Joachim Hawks deep into spy-fi—and even *Octopussy*—territory. Sensor is the hottest weapon in the Cold War (sayeth the blurb). As Berke explains: "It's called psychosensory nerve blocking. What it does is depress the nervous system in such a way that anyone getting enough if it just gives up. No will left to think, or object, or fight. The gas doesn't kill anyone, but it sure as hell leaves them useless. Like a zombie. Try thinking what would happen to an army that was gassed with it. Every last soldier—private to general—would just throw down his arms and quit."[32] The next three novels reverted to *The Spy in …* title format. In *Bangkok* (1965) Hawks must prevent stolen nuclear missiles being sold to the Red Chinese. In *The Spy at* (for a change) *Angkor Wat* (1966), a deposed

Cambodian prince faces imprisonment or death unless Hawks can mount one of his patented impossible-rescue missions. *Java Sea* (1966) involves a crippled U.S. submarine, lost on the bottom of that titular sea. (Java is the most populated island of formerly Dutch Indonesia, situated between Sumatra and Bali.) Hawks's most difficult operation to date entails stopping the fully armed sub from falling into hostile hands. The ChiComs have their own "catalogue of persuasion—from *A* for Agents: caressing, provocative, seductive ... to *Z* for Zealots: persuasive, ingenious, deadly" (blurb).

It is no exaggeration to say that the Joachim Hawks novels were several cuts above most of the other Bondwagon books that oversaturated the 1960s spy-fiction market. But NAL/Signet pulled the plug on them after *The Spy in the Java Sea*, perhaps because they got lost in the super-fast shuffle. Or it might be that the Southeast Asian locale and the increasingly unpopular brush-fire wars being fought there alienated American readers in search of escapist entertainment. Ballinger wrote two more Signet paperback originals: *The Source of Fear* (1968) and *Heist Me Higher* (1969). He also novelized *The Law* (TV play) and *The Ultimate Warrior* (feature film) in 1975, both for Warner Books.

As the fickle Fates would have it, Hunt/St. John and Ballinger were both outperformed by James Dark, an Australian writer, and his all–American spy creation— Mark Hood. NAL/Signet had already reprinted over fifty non-espionage mystery novels by Carter Brown that were © Horwitz Publications Inc. Pty. Ltd., Sydney, Australia—and at least fifty more would follow (between 1958 and 1972). "Carter Brown"—sometimes "Peter Carter Brown"—was a house name mainly used by the London-born expatriate Alan Geoffrey Yates (1923–1985). Horowitz published 300+ of these pseudo–American potboilers, from 1951 until 1984. Background reading: *The Australian Vintage Paperback Guide*,[33] compiled by Graeme Flanagan. NAL/Signet hoped to replicate the high sales of Carter Brown books: "A new thriller by the international sensation whose books have sold over 25,000,000 copies throughout the world" (*The Wayward Wahine*, 1960). Signet used the pseudonym James Dark instead of the author's real name, J.E. MacDonnell, which had appeared on the Australian first editions.

James ("Jim") Edmond MacDonnell (1917–2002) was born in Mackay, Queensland, Australia, and raised in Toowoomba (ditto). MacDonnell joined the navy in 1934 and saw combat during the Second World War. He became best known as a prolific purveyor of sea-war tales, in which he made convincing use of his own hard-won nautical expertise. Flanagan lists 147 of these action-packed novels. MacDonnell had written several "James Dark" books for Horwitz, and NAL/Signet might have felt that was a more spy-fiction sounding name than the already quite familiar splice-the-mainbrace J.E. MacDonnell. *Come Die with Me* (July 1965) came out almost simultaneously from Horwitz and Signet, whose blurbs read: "Introducing an explosive new series of espionage thrillers starring MARK HOOD, the audacious secret agent from Intertrust" (front cover) and "COME DIE WITH ME is

a grand-slam of the sinister and sensational, delivered by JAMES DARK, new champion of the spy-cological thriller" (back cover). The interior blurb was a pithy plot
teaser:

> *GAUSS IS HIS NAME*
>
> He's stolen three torpedo boats equipped with top-secret nuclear devices, right from
> under the nose of the United States Navy. He's built a Führer-like aerie in the Brazilian
> mountains where he perfects plans for the resurgence of Nazi Germany. He's comman-
> deered the services of a lovely and talented scientist. The theft of the torpedoes is just a
> beginning. Gauss's real weapon is too monstrous to be imagined. But it works.
>
> He's a madman, of course. Like another madman who almost made it before....

Mark Hood makes a dramatic first entrance at the very start of chapter 2. He is
given a workout by Murimoto, his Japanese karate instructor, in the basement gym-
nasium of the International Club, Geneva: "Thirty-five tiles this time. We will make
a black belt second dan of you yet." Murimoto checks the layer of cement tiles held in
the wooden frame atop two concrete blocks, then he gives Hood the go-ahead signal
nod. "[Mark Hood] was a large man, something over six feet, and viewed from the
side he was perfectly in proportion; from front to back, there was a slouched, bearish
look about his heavy shoulders under the loose white karate blouse. His face, like his
voice, was genial. It was the type of face you might meet behind your bank counter,
good-looking in a rough way, and kindly; except for the hard closed look that came
upon it sometimes—as now, while he looked at the rack of tiles—and the remote,
almost glazed expression in his eyes. But this last was rare; you might be unlucky if
you saw it."[34]

Mark Hood is an Oxford graduate, of large private means, who has assumed
the hedonistic roles of Jet Set playboy and international sportsman. He enjoys motor
racing, karate (see above), and sailboat fishing, and his cricketing prowess is fully
the equal of E.W. Hornung's A.J. Raffles. Hood's age is never mentioned, but—since
he had served in the U.S. Navy during the Korean War (1950–53)—that would place
him somewhere between 35 and 40 in the mid–1960s. But what makes Hood stand
out from the secret-agent crowd is the fact that he is quite far from being a *secret*
agent: "[Hood] was thinking that his cover was no cover at all, really. And that was
why it worked. No elaborate subterfuge to be built up and maintained; he could act
quite naturally, with only his work for Intertrust, his real purpose, to be kept secret.
Almost all his assignments took him to cities, where there was often some sporting
fixture to explain his presence, whether it was cricket or skiing or car racing."[35]

But Hood goes over all 007 efficiency where mission preparation and firearms
are concerned: "Into an inside jacket pocket he thrust his international driving
license and British racing license. He checked his American passport, and into a
long, specially made fob pocket in his trousers he slipped a clip of ammunition, noting that the other two spares were in the bag. Lastly he took up the .32 Colt automatic, the ugly blue-black lump fitting snugly in his big hand. He withdrew the bolt
slightly, checking the shell in the chamber, pressed the safety catch, even though it

was on, and then let the weapon fall into the flat holster which depended from his belt down his spine. Twice, very quickly, he drew, and then buttoned his jacket and took up the bag."[36]

Despite having the air of a gentle giant, Hood's unmitigated fury can put Bull-dog Drummond to shame:

> Slowly Hood stood up. His face … not the sort you might meet behind your bank counter. A glazed look in his eyes, he struck, quite without science, with atavistic savagery at Lott's abdomen.
> It was lucky for Lott that Hood's hand had closed into a fist. Instead of the organ-rupturing smash of a karate blow he received a forceful punch. He jackknifed up in the bed and both Hood's hands, gripped together, crashed down with berserk force on the bridge of his nose. Bone broke and blood spurted. Lott screamed. He slammed back on the pillow, and again and again the dreadful hands pounded.
> The look was still in Hood's eyes when they came in and dragged him off the unconscious body.[37]

Hood is not averse to romantic female companionship, but he never lets it interfere with the main job of work in hand: "Women can be excited by different things—alcohol, of course, even violence, can sometimes produce passion. But Hood was not thinking of motives at all; the whole gamut of his intelligence concentrated into simple and galvanic feeling."[38]

Mark Hood's character and background were economically set in *Come Die with Me*. Intertrust remains a secretive autonomous agency established by the then four nuclear powers—the United States, United Kingdom, France, and the Soviet Union—to protect themselves from any "maverick" nuclear-weapon attacks. Money is no apparent object. From the "entrance" piece to *The Bamboo Bomb* (1965): "Intertrust was known to very few people. The purposes of Hood and the other three representative agents of Intertrust were not known even to the Secret Services of their countries—so that Hood could be what he was [see above]. Mostly he found this very pleasant. Not always." Hood has been sent to the Malay Archipelago. He must prevent a rogue nuclear-bomb test from taking place—yes, but exactly *where*? The third Mark Hood novel was entitled *Assignment Hong Kong* by Horwitz and *Hong Kong Incident* (both 1966) by Gold Medal, nimbly avoiding any potential confusion with Aaron's "Assignment" series.

Signet changed *Operation MissSat* (Horwitz) to *Assignment Tokyo* (both 1966). From the Horwitz blurb, for a change: "*It is only a normal precautionary operation,* they instructed [Hood] at Intertrust. *Go to Tokyo. Take* [Tommy] *Tremayne* [a fellow agent]. *Check on the safety of Oba.* Oba was the heavily-guarded base for the awesome missile satellite—MissSat—which whirred around the earth carrying its load of nuclear destruction. Under the guise of re-establishing the Samurai customs and culture, the brilliant mind of Sato-san conceived a plan so fantastical as to make the mind reel. Around him gathered the Knights of Heaven, a group of fanatical followers whose Tsuki training enabled them to perform feats that bordered on the supernatural." Hood's hand-to-hand combat skills are tested to possible destruction—*his* destruction.

The relatively conventional *Spy from the Deep* and *Caribbean Striker* (Horwitz)/ *Operation Scuba* (Signet) followed in 1966 and 1967, respectively. However, *Black Napoleon/Throne of Saturn* (1967) takes Mark Hood far into spy-fi territory, with a super villain who could knock the spots off Ernst Stavro Blofeld. From the Signet back-cover blurb: "Dominat is his name. He's the prince of an infernal scientific kingdom situated miles deep inside the walls of a volcanic crater on the [nonexistent] West Indian island of Dominica. He possesses an ultimate weapon geared to destroy the world's armies and navies. After which event, Dominat will crown himself Emperor [a Black Napoleon]. Hood has to get into Dominat's electronic torture-palace. Tommy Tremayne is already there and about as safe as an icicle in hell. Hood figures out a way to accomplish his mission: woo a singularly treacherous beauty [Mona Gillespie], and play her unusual night games!"

The Sword of Genghis Khan (1967) is an even headier phantasmagorical brew, in which an Outer Mongolian warlord armed with a secret weapon puts himself forward as a lineal descendant of the mighty empire builder (1167?-1227). Dr. Fu Manchu, Shiwan (*The Shadow*) Khan, and Greenmantle—all rolled into one. From then on, MacDonnell/Dark became one of the few spy-fiction writers who tried to out–Fleming Fleming and sometimes succeeded. *Spying Blind* (1968): Hood v. the attempted hijackers of a returning Russian Moon rocket. *Operation Octopus* (1968): Hood vs. the half-man/half-fish ruler of an undersea city who wants to rule the surface world as well. *Operation Ice Cap* (1969): Hood vs. the wielders of a weapon that can melt nuclear submarines. *The Invisibles* (1969): Hood vs. voodoo priests bent upon world domination who are buying up nuclear weapons for use in conjunction with their diabolical arts.

Things fall apart after that, MacDonnell/Dark bibliography-wise. Signet passed on *The Reluctant Assassin* (Horwitz, 1970), making it something of a collector's item. More Helm than Hood—reluctant or not. *Sea Scrape* (1970) marked the end of Hood's career, just as he was hitting his public and secret-agent stride. "A satanic genius has a plan to wipe out the world from underwater—and Intertrust agent Mark Hood may already be too late." He isn't, of course.

From 1948 through the 1950s and for a good few decades more, NAL/Signet enjoyed the financial rewards of publishing the Mike Hammer mystery novels written by Mickey Spillane.[39] At one time, Spillane novels held seven out of the top ten spots among bestsellers in American literary history—and not just in the mystery genre. Frank Morrison Spillane was born in Brooklyn and raised in Elizabethville, New Jersey, just across the Hudson River from New York City. Spillane soon tried his luck at fiction writing. See *Primal Spillane. The Early Stories: 1941-1942*,[40] edited and with an introduction by Max Allan Collins and Lynn F. Myers, Jr. As a freelance comic-book writer, Spillane helped to develop those iconic superhero Captains— America and Marvel. During the Second World War, he trained fighter pilots for the U.S. Army Air Force (enlisting the day after Pearl Harbor).

The American comic-book industry had fallen into a slump during the late

1940s, and Spillane found that his former markets had either cut back production or folded altogether. He tried to sell his own strip, about a tough New York private eye called Mike Danger, but it went nowhere fast. Then, some time in 1946, inspiration struck. He changed Mike's last name to Hammer and turned the strip into a novel entitled *I, the Jury*[41]—in three weeks flat. In *One Lonely Knight: Mickey Spillane's Mike Hammer* (1984), Max Allan Collins and James L. Traylor wrote *I, the Jury* had sold more than eight million copies in its paperbound edition, a tally that does not include the many translations and the hardbound editions.[42] Mike Hammer makes even the Continental Op of Hammett's ultra-violent *Red Harvest* look like Dudley Do-Right. Ogden Nash: "The Marquis de Sade/Wasn't always mad/What addled his brain/Was Mickey Spillane."

One Lonely Night (1951) was Spillane's only full-out Commie-bashing novel. Mike Hammer is back on more familiar territory with *Kiss Me, Deadly* (1952). The classic 1955 film version (minus the title comma) downplayed the Mob angle and introduced a non-canonical spy ring. Directed by Robert Aldrich (1918–1983), it starred a perfectly cast Ralph Meeker (1920–1985) as a ham-fisted Hammer and Maxine Cooper (1924–2009) as Velda. Mike and Velda are seemingly doomed to die from radiation sickness in the final scene, just as Mike faces a fiery death in the novel: "I looked, looked away. The door was closed and maybe I had enough left to make it."

Spillane left Mike Hammer hanging fire, as it were, for seven book-time years and ten real-time years. However, *The Girl Hunters* (1962) turned out to have been well-worth the wait, and it even had some relevant espionage interest. During the war, Hammer is told, Velda had been young, beautiful, intelligent, a perfect agent to use against men. She was in the O.S.S., the O.S.I, and another highly secretive group. All of which explains how she was able to become a licensed P.I. in New York City, with evidently no police experience. Recalled to duty, she has spent the last seven years behind the Iron Curtain as a particularly provocative *agent provocateur*. But now she's back in the United States, the uneasy prey of a KGB assassin code-named the Dragon.

The two "girl hunters" beat seven bells out of each other in the final chapter, with Hammer literally ball-peen hammering Comrade Gorlin (alias the Dragon) to the floor of a farmhouse. Luckily for the Dragon, he was unconscious at the time. Mike Hammer has closed another case—but Velda remains among the missing. She comes back in *The Snake* (1964), however, remarkably still a virgin and saving herself for the Big Lug love of her life. *The Snake* has no espionage interest whatsoever and Velda seems to have given up moonlighting as a sultry spy. "It took seven years to learn a man's secret and escape Communist Europe with information that will keep us equal or better than they are"[43] is about all she's got to say on the subject. But Spillane hadn't given up the secret-agent ghost. Collina and Traynor:

> Tiger Mann, Spillane's American "answer" to British James Bond, is essentially Mike Hammer, secret agent. [He] works for a super-secret organization supplying him with the

money and technology beyond Hammer's reach. Tiger's boss is ultra-rightwing billion-aire Martin Grady, whose "Group" is his own privately-financed espionage organization, working for apparently altruistic, patriotic purposes (though, to paraphrase Al Capp, what's good for Martin Grady is good for the U.S.A.). Tiger, Grady's top agent, has been involved in many successful missions and, while still extremely active and virile, is reluctantly approaching middle age.[44]

Tiger Mann entered the spy-fiction lists in *Day of the Guns*.[45] The inevitable Signet paperback edition carried this giving-the-game-away encomium: "Mickey Spillane moves from the private eye field into the realm of the international agent. His latest character, Tiger Mann, slugs, shoots and beds in true Spillane style and vies for attention with such established greats as James Bond" (*Boston Herald*).

But Spillane did more in *Day of the Guns* than simply change Mike Hammer's name to Tiger Mann and turn him from a private detective into a non-governmental counterspy. He cleverly subverted the plot of *I, the Jury*, in which Hammer had avenged the murder by gut shooting of Jack Williams—an old army buddy who had saved his life during the war. The murderer turns out to be (spoiler alert) Dr. Charlotte Manning, a beautiful blonde psychiatrist to whom Hammer had become engaged. Which does not stop him from shooting her dead. In the stomach. Tiger Mann, however, had been gut-shot by an O.S.S. colleague and Nazi double agent named Rondine Lund, who left him for dead in Hamburg. Now, twenty years later, she has returned, lovelier than ever and calling herself Edith Caine. The twist being that Edith is actually the late and unlamented Rondine's younger sister. In a romantic reversal of the original story, she kills the real *femme fatale* (Gretchen Lark) and then makes mad passionate (virginal!) love with the temporarily tamed Tiger.

"It was Saturday and I was going to get married," begins the first paragraph of *Bloody Sunrise* (1965).

Tiger Mann intends to make a married woman of Edith Caine, whom he Freudian-slip persists in calling Rondine. It might as well have been Velda, come to think of it. "Mentally I had already composed the letter of resignation Martin Grady would get. He wouldn't like it. He'd do his damndest to stop it but his damndest wouldn't be good enough. The day of the guns was past." But: "The phone beside me let out a sharp, discordant note …" and the wedding plans are put on hold. Indefinitely, as it would transpire (ditto Mike and Velda). Tiger and Rondine take on a Russian espionage outfit known as the Group. *Bloody Sunrise* ends with a veritable bloody sunrise: "The sun was just coming up in the east, the crescent tip of it a brilliant orange, reaching out to light the earth with fiery fingertips of a new day. Sonia [Dutko: a beautiful Russian skier-cum-spy] was still there with me, but she wasn't watching the sunrise. In essence, she was almost a part of it, a sparkling wet, red splash on the grey rubble of the building that reflected the glow of a fresh day and a job that was all over."

In *The Death Dealers* (1965), Tiger Mann is called upon to act as a thoroughly unofficial protector of Teish El Abin, the king of the Middle Eastern kingdom

Selachin, now visiting the United States. Once a barren desert, oil had been discovered there by one of Martin Grady's subsidiary companies. The American government is courting Teish for the oil concession, but the Russians prefer to kill him and grab it all for themselves. *The By-Pass Control* (1966) is the longest and the most spy-fi of the Tiger Mann novels. Explanatory dialogue between Tiger and General Charlie Corbinet (one of his wartime commanding officers): "One man installed the system, or was responsible for it, at least. Supposing that somewhere along the line his thinking got screwed up and he didn't want to see all that power and control go into the hands of someone who in his opinion shouldn't have that control. Supposing that one man [Louis Agrounsky], to satisfy his own desires and warped judgment, installed a system that could by-pass the original pushbutton device and could activate the ICBM system any time he chose to."[46]

By-Pass also marked the end of Tiger Mann's rampage through the espionage jungle. He failed to catch on with the great reading public, who saw through the molecular-thin membrane that separated him from Mike Hammer and averted their gaze. Collins and Traylor: "[Tiger Mann] is largely confined to Mike Hammer's New York; this works against the larger, wider-ranging concerns of Tiger Mann's assignments, as does the lone passionate avenger role, which comes awkwardly to a secret agent, who is traditionally cold and machine-like."[47] Like Hammer, Mann is a semi-tamed lone wolf who resents even the relatively free-rein authority of Martin Grady.

An even more drastic example of how not to treat a popular fictional character is the ABC TV series *Burke's Law* (September 20, 1963, to May 5, 1965). It starred Gene Barry (1919–2009) as multi-millionaire Amos Burke, who—as Captain Burke—lent his master-detective talents to the LAPD. The first two seasons mixed murder and mirth in episodes with titles which always began "Who Killed ...?" Then all that changed. Richard Meyers: "In 1965, the heyday of James Bond and other cinematic secret agents, someone got the bright idea of making Burke a super-undercover operative. At the beginning of the series' third season, the title and concept was changed to *Amos Burke—Secret Agent*. Gone were the LAPD people and the single murders. Gone was Amos Burke's habit of spouting Chan-like aphorisms and dubbing them 'Burke's Law.' In their stead was an unseen government boss called 'The Man' who gave an uncomfortable Burke his new globetrotting assignments."[48]

Gene Barry later played another secret agent in the ITV Entertainment series, *The Adventurer* (September 29, 1972, to March 30, 1973). This time he posed as a wealthy film star named Gene Bradley. It was another one-season wonder. Before that, he had played Simon Grant, a more orthodox counterspy, in *Maroc 7* (1967), produced by the Rank Organization and co-starring Elsa Martinelli (1935–2017), Cyd Charisse (1922–2008), and Leslie Phillips (1924–). "Slow robbery-murder tale of secret agent out to catch split personality thief" (Maltin). The novelization[49] was written by Martin Sands (alias John Burke: 1922–2011), based upon the original story and screenplay by David Osborn (1923–).

Mickey Spillane's other significant espionage-related character was Morgan the Raider—so-called because his audacity equals that of Sir Henry Morgan (1635–1688), the Welsh pirate who made good as the Governor of Jamaica. In *The Delta Factor*,[50] Morgan stands convicted of having stolen $40,000,000—no small-time crook, he! His jail-breaking expertise leads some unidentified government agency to offer him a reduced sentence. If he breaks into an escape-proof Latin American prison known as the Rose Castle and frees another of those indispensable rocket scientists (or whatever). Kim Stacy, a beautiful female secret agent, is assigned to partner—and watch—Morgan.

The Delta Factor was filmed in 1970, written and directed by Tay Garnett (1894–1977), starring Christopher George (1931–1983) as Morgan and Yvette Mimieux (1942–) as Kim Stacy. Spillane co-wrote the script with Garnett, but he received no screen credit. Signet published a tie-in edition early the following year. A sequel novel remained unfinished until 2011. As the eventual coauthor, Max Allan Collins, explained: "[*The Delta Factor*] enjoyed considerable critical and commercial success. After a disappointing experience producing a *Factor* film, however, the frustrated Spillane set aside the already-announced second Morgan novel, *The Consummata*. Twenty years ago, he entrusted the incomplete manuscript to me, saying, 'Maybe someday we can do something with this.' Thanks to Charles Ardai of Hard Case Crime, that day is here. The story is set in the late '60s, when Mickey began it."

Along with *The Consummata*, Spillane gave Collins two incomplete Mike Hammer novels, under the same "maybe someday we can do something" condition. Collins duly finished the work that "the Mick" had set aside. *The Big Bang* (2010) had everything to do with drug traffickers and nothing whatever to do with espionage. In *Complex 90*,[51] however, Hammer "accompanies a conservative politician [Senator Allen Jasper] to Moscow on a fact-finding mission. While there, he is arrested on a bogus charge, and imprisoned, but he quickly escapes, creating an international incident by [killing forty-five] Russian agents" (back-cover blurb). From the posthumous coauthor's prefatory note: "The setting is 1964 and the novel is, in part, a sequel to the Mike Hammer comeback novel of 1961, *The Girl Hunters*."

Thirteen of the 38 Ed Noon novels by Michael Avallone have their New York–based P.I. hero involved with quasi-official counterspying; but he bears no relation to the dour Organization Man character that Avallone ghost-wrote about in the Nick Carter/Killmaster franchise. The first four Ed Noon novels were as conventional as any Ed Noon novels could ever be. Then, in *The Alarming Clock* (1957), Noon is mailed a strange alarm clock and an even stranger message, which leads him into conflict with fanatical ex–Nazis who are plotting to sabotage the testing of the latest super-duper American atomic bomb. It also initiates Noon's first contact with *The Espionage Establishment*[52] and the White House itself—but emphatically not his last. *The Living Bomb* (1963) took place four months before Kennedy's assassination on November 22, 1963:

They can't set off Hydrogen bombs without Conroy. Everything that blows up nuclear-wise in the good old U.S.A. needs Conroy to press the starting button. And worse, far worse, or maybe just more important, Conroy holds the key to the Cobalt Bomb. The big-gest firecracker of them all. When that goes off it isn't going to leave anybody around to wonder about radioactive fallouts. So on Wednesday, July 3, Homer Conroy, age thirty-nine, and the biggest brain in nuclear research, disappeared and set the whole country on its civilized ears.[53]

Three pages later, Ed Noon is kidnapped by an FBI agent calling himself "John Smith" and taken to the White House for an interview with the President Who Is Never Named (in any administration). "Ed," the President explains. "I'm going to step through that door on your right in exactly two minutes. Urgent appointment with my Cabinet. You will not see me again. You will be ushered out of this build-ing and that will be an end to our association. We will not be helping you or work-ing with you. In that manuscript I gave you is a complete bio on Homer Conroy. That's all I can say now. I have to leave. One thing I can guarantee you—and that alone—when you have found him, if you ever do, and on that condition alone—dial Sunflower 111 and ask for the Rocker and we'll know it is you. We've made special arrangements with the phone company. You'll get straight to me. Sunflower 111—ask for the Rocker. Is that clear?"[54]

Noon nods. "Sunflower 111. The Rocker."

The next Spy Noon novel was *The February Doll Murders* (1966), the first of four to be published in paperback by NAL/Signet. This new case begins when Kyle Crosby, one of ex–Sergeant Noon's many old army buddies, calls him about the dollar bill that Noon made his whole squad sign during the Second World War. "It helped my trip down Memory Lane. 'Bing' Crosby, not the Hollywood one, was coming calling, and bringing with him Camp Dix, overseas service, Munich, battle scars, and com-bat fatigue." But Crosby is killed before they can meet and the dollar bill has gone missing (plus Mrs. Crosby). Believe it or not, Noon is then pestered by three talking (actual) dolls arrived in his mailbox *and* becomes mixed up in a conspiracy to sabo-tage the United Nations. In *Assassins Don't Die in Bed* (1968), the seemingly eternal President requests Noon to bodyguard the distinguished diplomat Henry Hallmark as he crosses the Atlantic on the S.S. *Francesca*.

The Doomsday Bag (1969; UK title: *Killer's Highway*, 1971) was front-cover billed by NAL/Signet as "A NEW SPY TO MR. PRESIDENT THRILLER." It is also the most realistic and low-tech spy-fi of all the Ed Noon espionage-slanted novels. When Lyndon B. Johnson (1908–1973) stood down as the POTUS in 1969, he expressed relief at how marvelous it was "not to be followed by that man with the bag!" It was only then that Americans became publicly aware about the existence of an agent who carried a satchel containing the vital nuclear attack codes. "The Bagman had been a strong factor in the Kennedy Administration," muses Noon. "The four hours it had taken in Truman's time to set in motion any counteroffensive should aerial enemies fly toward Washington had been whittled down to a supercharged, technologically swift fifteen minutes. So the Bagman was as constant with any American president as his own shadow. [Nobody] ever called the Bagman by his Christian name or surname. And for the bag itself, euphemism was the first order of the day. It was known, variously, as *the black bag*, the *Doomsday Bag*, and the *football*."[55]

And now the Bagman had gone missing, and so had the Doomsday Bag itself. Noon's mission is blindingly obvious; get the "fatal football" back—with or without its human carrier.

CHAPTER ELEVEN

Agents in the Outfield

Fawcett Gold Medal and NAL/Signet had cornered the quality paperback-original market on American spy fiction for most of the mid–twentieth century. The more conservative Bantam Books had published only the most "literary" espionage paperbacks, e.g., the Mr. Moto books and the "entertainments" of Graham Greene. *Our Man in Havana* (q.v.) proved to be a runaway bestseller for them (January 1960 + innumerable reprints). Then, perhaps inspired by that success, they commissioned Robert Sheckley[1] to write a spy-fiction series about "international detective" Stephen Dain.

Robert Sheckley was born in New York City, the son of David Sheckley and Rae Helen Sheckley (née Feinberg). *Untouched by Human Hands* (1954) was the first of his many short-story collections. *Immortality Delivered* (retitled *Immortality, Inc.),* his first of comparatively not-so-many novels, followed four years later. Damon Knight praised his "unique touch with a wacky civilization, a clean, compact style, and a satirical wit that is dry without being bitter." Recommended reading: *Comic Inferno: The Satirical World of Robert Sheckley,*[2] by Gregory Stephenson. Bantam had already published three original Robert Sheckley story collections before *Calibre.50* (1961), the first Stephen Dain novel, went to press: *Pilgrimage to Earth* (1957); *Store of Infinity* (1960); *Notions: Unlimited* (ditto). Extracted from his wistful "Bring Back Stephen Dain!" reminiscence:[3]

> More years ago than I care to remember, I wrote five novels around an international American operative named Stephen Dain. He was my attempt to break into the James Bond craze then sweeping the country.
>
> I called Dain a secret agent. I don't remember affiliating him with any specific organization. I made him a sombre, somewhat cynical man, who did what his superiors asked him to do in various foreign countries. Dain had no morality except the idea that in a dirty world, we're cleaner than they are.
>
> To tell the truth, Dain's character eluded me from the start. I wanted to make him highly idiosyncratic, with a list of characteristics that would rival Sherlock Holmes. What came out was a sort of faceless guy who resembled, if anyone, my own father [an insurance broker].

Bantam's burbling-blurb introduction had all the subtlety of a sawn-off shotgun: "Meet Stephen Dain!—unique, ruthless, infallible—his assignments: anything too hot for regular U.S. agents to handle! Meet Stephen Dain—the world is his beat!

Like a hurricane on the horizon, trouble hung over the Caribbean." The word from the State Department was, "Call Stephen Dain!" It makes his first appearance seem a bit on the anticlimactic side: "Dain appeared to be in his late thirties. Although Thornton's first impression had been of unusual height, he could see now that Dain was not over six feet tall. His tanned leanness made him look taller. He was polite, reserved, low-voiced, and self-contained. There was not much of the gunman visible now; just a little. Enough so that Thornton could sense a detached and cynical toughness in Dain, a go-to-hell quality that was accentuated by his politeness. Thornton thought that he would not like to be an enemy of Mr. Dain; and even a friend might have to be careful."[4]

As for his official employment status: "Like hell we're both in the Treasury Department," Beader said bitterly. "What are you trying to sell me? You're in any department you like working from. Today it's Treasury, tomorrow you'll be in the Navy, and the day after you'll be back with your buddies in the FBI. Don't give me any of that team-spirit stuff."[5] Dain's mission is to prevent smuggled arms and ammunition from reaching Coruna, a "small [mythical] Central American republic sandwiched between Nicaragua, Honduras, and El Salvador."

During an enforced lull in the slim but hectic 120-page second novel, *Dead Run* (1961)—which fairly zips through London, Amsterdam, Paris, and Venice—Dain uses the time for a spot of soul-searching reflection: "During the years between OSS and the present, Dain had become a political man, inevitably, and to his regret. He had viewed his own evolution with the deepest suspicion. He felt that too much of human importance had become merely accessory to him. He suspected a lessening of himself in the very act of trying to serve Humanity rather than humans. It was suspect, like trying to serve God or Nature, it hinted at a barrenness that could only partially be explained by natural austerity, a coldness that no political necessity could obliterate. He felt that he was less than he should be, and that his choice of work masked a man who had failed as a human."[6]

If *Calibre .50* and *Dead Run* can be called "entertainments" à la Graham Greene, then *Live Gold* (1962) is a full-on foray into darkest Greeneland. Instead of gunrunners or stolen secret documents, Sheckley has Stephen Dain contend with modern-day slavery in North Africa and Arabia. Well, not quite *modern*-day. Chapter 1 takes place on November 23, 1951, in Mecca, Saudi Arabia, which—as the birthplace of Mohammed—is the holiest city of the Islamic world. A Nigerian boy named Auda avoids capture by Mustapha ibn Harith, the fake preacher and authentic slave trader (who deals in "live gold"). Auda vows vengeance, but the wise counsel of his rescuer, Zeid Mohammed Mijbil, prevails. "It was a difficult decision to make, but Auda decided—for a time—that he would hold his hand. He would tell the police the full story of Mustapha ibn Harith. Then he would see what happened."[7]

Chapter 2 is datelined May 10, 1952—EL GEZIRA. "It was a routine sort of report, and Colonel Frank Parris would normally have read no further than the title: PRACTICE OF SLAVERY IN NORTH AND NORTH-CENTRAL AFRICAN AREAS.

Having seen that it did not pertain to him, he would have put it away with a thousand other documents sent to Parris's bomber base at El Gezira in Libya. This time, however, Parris did not file and forget the report. Quite suddenly he could see how slavery might be of considerable interest to him. He read the entire bulky document with care."[8]

Colonel Parris providentially believed that he could give "aid and assistance" in the case of Mustapha ibn Harith. He was currently playing host to a civilian employee of Military Intelligence, a young man named Stephen Dain. It seemed both reasonable and desirable to him that this highly trained cloak-and-dagger operative should be off chasing a notorious slave trader instead of hanging around an unimportant little bomber base inspecting the sales of surplus and obsolete equipment. "In the Sahara, where new equipment broke down and had to be discarded monthly, who was going to care about the fate of a dozen or so World War Two trucks and weapons carriers? Who was going to find fault in the disappearance of a few hundred out-of-date Springfield rifles and some badly worn Garands? Who was going to question a few thousand rounds of ammunition unaccounted for?"[9]

Unfortunately for Parris, however, an "economy drive" at the Finance Section of Bomber Command in Tripoli had led to a "routine check" on such (to him) inconsiderable trifles. He had "stretched the happy freewheeling" postwar days about five years longer than anyone else, to "the point where a narrow-minded man might consider some of his practices to be nothing more than downright theft." It should have all been buried in the dead past. But this eager-beaver Dain might well turn up something, and it would be much pleasanter if he were off somewhere on a slave-trader hunt....

Dain's manhunting mission finally takes him to Dauqa, Saudi Arabia (August 22, 1952), with a few stopovers along the way. Fort Lamy, for instance (August 3, 1952), the former name of N'djamena, the capital of Chad (independent from France since 1960). After many undercover machinations, Dain brings Mustapha ibn Harith to justice in his own quiet, efficient, largely nonviolent, and inexorable way. Following Oscar Wilde, in *The Importance of Being Earnest*: "The good ended happily and the bad unhappily" (Act 2, Section 2). Or as near as dammit. The last chapter is headed "August 23, 1952, to July 1, 1953—SOME TEMPORARY DISPOSITIONS."

It is only fitting that *Live Gold* should have ended up with closure between Auda and Mustapha ibn Harith (on the pearling island of Dhorai):

> Auda stared at his old enemy. Harith's features were unchanged. But other things about him had changed.
> Harith no longer wore rich robes. Instead, he had on nothing but a loincloth. His head was shaven, and he looked very thin. He wore something around his neck. At first, Auda thought it was an amulet. Then he realized it was a nose-plug.
> He understood then that Mustapha ibn Harith was a pearl diver, and that he sat among other pearl divers. And finally he understood that Harith the enslaver was himself a slave.[10]

Like Marquand's original, non-movie Mr. Moto, the mysterious Stephen Dain flits in and out of his "own" novel—mostly out. The action is driven forward by subsidiary characters like Rasim Nicholai Prokopulous (Greek merchant), Tim McCue (American civil engineer), Major Harkness (British army officer), Charles Ott (Rhodesian diamond smuggler), Leslie Hastings (acting Chief of Police in El Fasher, Sudan), and El Tikheimi (slave trader). Above all, however, Sheckley used *Live Gold* to point a stiff little moral that might have pleased Graham Greene, had he ever read it. Stephenson: "This instance of poetic justice or divine retribution [the enslavement of arch-slaver Harith] serves to offset the general atmosphere of corruption in the novel. [It] reprehends the selfishness and viciousness to which humanity is so often inclined, while affirming the power of choice and the capacity for right action possessed by each human being."[11]

"D stands for Death, Danger and DAIN—Stephen Dain! World-famous international detective who tackles his toughest assignment in the ferocious mountains and deadly deserts of Iran, where heroin for the export trade is manufactured from the fine, black opium of Baluchistan," blares the back-cover blurb for *White Death* (1963). D could also stand for Disinformation. Far from being "world famous," Dain is even further removed from the wider world and the reader in this novel than he was in *Live Gold*. The story is told in the first person by an Iranian citizen who renders Dain invaluable assistance: "My name is Achmed Abotal el Din, and I was born here in Isfahan, the most glorious of the great cities of Iran. My father is of an old Teheran landholding family, come upon evil times since the fall of Reza Shah. My mother is of Bokhara nobility, much reduced since the death of the last Emir. She gave me the Mongol name of Abotal, and she instructed me in her language and lineage, which she claimed went back to Uzbek Khan."[12]

After playing cameo roles for much of *Live Gold* and *White Death*, Stephen Dain was prominently onstage throughout *Time Limit* (1967). An inattentive reader might even have mistaken him for Sam Durell—though not James Bond or Matt Helm. There is, however, a certain world-weariness about him now, evident in some "existential espionage" passages that can rank with anything written by Graham Greene and John le Carré. For example: "Since spying can be classified as a profession, it necessarily has many features in common with other, more mundane professions. It is a way of life with its own jargon, discontents, internal rivalries, and intramural jokes. It is a line of work which combines a high degree of danger with an even higher degree of boredom. Out of this insatiable and explosive compound a spy's typical moments are made."[13]

This unfortunate lack of belief in causes generally deemed worth fighting for comes to a head at the end of *Time Limit* (a title with more than one meaning). Stephen Dain not only closes the Rakkan (Rakka being a nonexistent Arab state) case but also puts a hold on his career as a Military Intelligence operative—or "international detective," as the Bantam blurb team would have it. Mr. Manley—then Dain's immediate superior—realized that "the man *was* tired, and clearly in need of a rest.

A few weeks in London or Paris would do Dain a world of good, and he would return to work in fighting trim." There was a revolution brewing in Haiti, a clear-cut case of Good versus Evil, which had a superb chance of success with Dain on the undercover job. But: "Dain didn't see it that way. He was planning to take an indefinite leave of absence rather than a few weeks' rest; and rather than spend his time in America or one of the European capitals, Dain was planning to go to a small and rather primitive island in the Pacific. He wouldn't tell Mr. Manley what the island was called. But he did mention that the place received newspapers only about once a year, had no television, and that short-wave reception was sporadic and exceedingly poor."[14]

As Stephenson muses in *Comic Inferno*: "There he may recover his sense of purpose and emerge again to resume his struggle against the forces and agencies of corruption, or perhaps like Joenes and Lum in *Journey Beyond Tomorrow* [1962], Dain will remain there, recognizing and embracing a mode of life that is as close to true civilization as mankind is ever likely to approach."[15] Sheckley might have taken the hint. From his reminiscence (see above): "Let Dain ride again. He's got a job to be done [killing Osama bin Laden]. Let others argue the morality and ethics of it. Dain already knows he's damned if he does what they want."

In between *White Death* and *Time Limit*, Sheckley had written *The Game of X*,[16] a standalone novel that was one of the earliest and still one of best spy-fiction spoofs. William P. Nye, down-and-out young American in Paris, is offered a one-off espionage job by an old high school friend called George. A piece of cake. No danger, no guns—and, unfortunately, no mysterious *femme fatales*. Nye considered his (lack of) qualifications for the supposedly adventurous life of a secret agent: "I knew that George was serious, and even feeling a little grim about the whole thing; but I just couldn't get into an appropriate mood. I had always heard that Europe was filled with secret agents of all nationalities, sexes, sizes, shapes and colours; but the thought of George or me in that kind of work seemed ludicrous."[17] Just *how* ludicrous becomes clear not long after Nye accepts an assignment from George's "autonomous organization," which "cooperates" with the CIA. Critical reactions to *Game of X* were mostly positive: "A hilariously funny send-up of every spy story you care to name from *Our Man in Havana* to *Goldfinger*" (Peter [*Dr. Strangelove*] George). "Combines ironic wit with suspense to remarkable effect" (John le Carré). If Sheckley ever intended to turn William P. Nye into a series character, he never followed through.

But the world was to hear from *Game of X* and William P. Nye again; obliquely, and with only the most vigilant Sheckley fan picking up on it. Walt Disney Productions released *Condorman* in 1981—"inspired," as they said, by Sheckley's novel. Director: Charles Jarrott (1927–2011). It starred Michael Crawford (Woodrow "Woody" Wilkins), Oliver Reed (Krokov), and Barbara Carrera (Natalia Rambova). Not one but two novelizations were based upon the screenplay (Marc Sturdivant, Glenn Caron, and Mickey Rose), by (a) Joe Claro and (b) Heather Simon.[18] "**Cartoonist Crawford is transformed into Condorman, a comic-book superhero who assists Carrera in her efforts to defect. Silly Disney film for only the most undiscriminating" (Maltin).

Belmont's not inconsiderable success with the souped-up "Shadow" series (see Chapter Fourteen) inspired them to create a pulp-fiction hero of their very own. The result was Gregory Hiller—*The Spy Who Loved America* (1964)—written by Jack Laflin. Introductory back-cover blurb: "Here is an uproarious new spy thriller by an uproarious new writer who is as prolific as Mickey Spillane (he finished his second novel before this one was at the printer's) and who has the imagination of an American Ian Fleming. He's a Princeton graduate sportscaster in real life, if that's what you want to call it after reading this book." According to his obituary in the *Hartford Courant* (February 4, 2012), Jack Carlock Laflin[19] was born in Brooklyn, New York City. Laflin graduated from Polytechnic Preparatory Country Day School, Brooklyn, and Princeton University (*cum laude*) class of 1943, serving as alumni secretary for 27 years. He was a longtime sports editor for Channel 18 and a fervent fan of the Yankees and the Giants. Laflin sold short stories to *Mike Shayne's Mystery Magazine* ("O'Kane Was Able": January 1966) and *Shell Scott Mystery Magazine* ("Cry Wolf," February 1966). His first published novel was *The Flaw* (Belmont, 1964).

We are first introduced to the Spy Who Loved Russia: "Piotyr Grigorovitch Ilyushin, opening his eyes on the seventh post-operative day in Moscow's Plastic Surgery Institute, knew immediately, on two counts, that whatever the reason for his presence there it was something of transcendental importance."[20] General Vassikovsky recites data from Ilyushin's dossier in order to (a) refresh his memory and (b) pass on biographical information to the reader: "Born at Kiev [capital city of Ukraine; independent since 1996] May 17th, 1928. Placed in a state school 1935, after which your parents moved to Stalingrad, where they were killed in the German bombardment of that city 1944. Member of Komsomol, Communist party, Red Army two years. Politically reliable. No adverse marks on your record. Unmarried. And you speak English, do you not?" Ilyushin replies: "Yes, Comrade General, I do. Somewhat accented, of course, but passable. I was able to improve it greatly during my assignment in London."[21] The General had previously shown Ilyushin a photograph of his new visage:

> He was looking at himself as in a mirror! The same close-cropped hair, deep-set eyes, slightly protruding ears, cleft chin. In only two features did the faces differ, and then only in an extremely minor degree. The man in the snap-shot had at some time suffered a broken nose that had healed improperly…. In addition, at the left-hand corner of the mouth there was a thin scar running diagonally toward the chin and disappearing beneath it. Colonel Glazov had selected him, first of all, because of his uncanny resemblance to the stranger whose picture he was staring at. That was a point of departure at least, and would explain his presence in the Plastic Surgery Institute.[22]

The man whose likeness has been surgically stamped upon the face of Ilyushin is Major Anderson Jeffers, an American weapons and armor expert. Laflin devotes the rest of chapter 1 (ten and a half pages) to Jeffers's personal history (e.g., he was born in Columbus, Ohio) and how the substitution will be made. Salient points: Jeffers was, until recently, stationed at the U.S. Army Proving Grounds at Aberdeen, Maryland. He had worked as an aide to General Hottelet, who heads a super-secret military project known only by the code name "Seashell." They are developing an ultrasonic ray that disintegrates all organic matter, plus a protective shield to protect its operators from self-inflicted harm.

The opening chapter of *The Spy Who Loved America* is one long (15-page) narrative hook. It also sets the general tone, tells the reader when and where the action is taking place, and what is happening to whom and why. But a lot of development had to be packed into the next 100-odd pages, and Belmont's 50,000-word straitjacket made Laflin cut too many narrative corners. Although understandably making up for the enforced need to remain celibate (or nearly so) and frugal, Ilyushin/Jeffers's rapid conversion to capitalistic hedonism and conspicuous consumption does not quite ring true. "His was a grim, important mission that involved a honeymoon at the Waldorf with another man's wife [Karen Jeffers] and gallons of champagne—all paid for by the wrong government" (front-cover blurb). And all in less than a fortnight—give or take a few days.

General Vassikovsky and Colonel Glazov had thought of everything—well, *almost* everything. As Steve Burman of the Central Intelligence Agency explains to Ilyushin/Jeffers, at the climactic moment: "They fixed your face. They fixed your teeth. They sharpened up your English. They provided you with all the facts you'd possibly need. But one thing those meticulous experts of yours didn't do ... some badly-needed plastic surgery on your—ah—sex organ. It was that, and that alone, which betrayed you. If it's any consolation to you, everything you did was perfect, so perfect I still can't believe it. Had it not been necessary to make love to Karen Jeffers, you'd be hopping a plane tomorrow for Washington and reporting to 'Seashell' Monday. You see, the one tiny flaw was this: *Anderson Jeffers was circumcised, and you are not.*"[23]

The denouement is a conversational coda that stretches over the final seven pages, in which federal agent Steve Burman does most of the talking. Edited transcript:

"Within the next forty-eight hours you will be taken secretly by night to an undisclosed location somewhere in the Middle West, where you will be kept under around-the-clock surveillance in the unlikely event there has been a leak and someone displays undue curiosity in the shy and retiring Mr. Gregory Hiller. Oh yes, I almost forgot. That's the new name we decided on for you.

"As soon as we can have the arrangements completed, we will undertake to give you a new set of features, moulded for you both through the medium of plastic surgery and the newly developed science of molecular reconstruction. If we could change your fingerprints we'd do that also, but unfortunately our technology hasn't advanced that far. Surgery will be performed on your vocal cords so that even your voice assumes an entirely different timbre and quality."[24]

But the final words belong to Piotr [Anatol?] Grigorivich Ilyushin/Anderson Jeffers/Gregory Hiller:

He had won, then lost, now had won again; the fruits of this final victory, if wielded judiciously and with common sense, would far outweigh anything he had gained previously while working for the Soviet Union. The grim spectres of death, prison or deportation were vanished; in their stead extended a long and useful horizon, a lifetime dedicated to the frustration and harassment of a former employer who had lied to him and used him. His gratitude and relief knew no bounds; all he could do was look up at Burman and say very simply, in an emotion-choked voice:

"Thanks, Steve, I'll give it all I've got."

Silently, savouringly, as if tasting a delicious new dish for the first time, he ran the words around his tongue.

Gregory Hiller, American.

It had a nice ring to it.

"Ingenious" is how Anthony Boucher described *The Spy Who Loved America*, in his *New York Times* book review column. Laflin carried this ingenuity over into *A Silent Kind of War* (1965), where Gregory Hiller, American, begins by recalling "the nightmare of two hundred forty-three days of captivity thinly cloaked in the guise of freedom, while his politico-ideological reliability was determined, and he felt trapped, entombed, cut off from mankind. More specifically, from womankind."[25] Then "Janus" (Burman) had called "Longfellow" (Hiller) and the former Russian undercover agent was soon off on his first official assignment for the United States government. Burman/Janus explained to Hiller/Longfellow that CIA trouble-spot evaluation experts were concerned about possibly orchestrated racial unrest breaking out in Hawaii. Hiller sees it all safely through, and Burman gives him an off-the-record pat on the back.

"WHO NEEDS JAMES BOND, WHEN YOU HAVE GREGORY HILLER?": burbling blurb for *The Spy in White Gloves* (1965). The front-cover blurb for *The Spy Who Didn't* (1966) was obviously influenced by the then current and high-camp *Batman* TV series: "Explosive! Pow! Wild! Bam! Action! Terror! Excitement!! Thrills!! Power! Intrigue!" Hiller speaks for himself in its back-cover counterpart: "SO HERE I AM, ABOUT TO DIE AGAIN, in, of all places, Shady Knoll Sanitarium. I still don't know exactly how I wound up a prisoner here, but as I watch Erica Von Eckhardt, the gorgeous nymphomaniacal wife of the resident psychiatrist preen herself, I suspect something unusual is about to happen. I mean, I've been in lots of trouble before, but what a way to go.... HERE COMES GREGORY HILLER AGAIN!"

Laflin came close to losing the edginess that made Gregory Hiller such an attractively different and dissolute defector in the first place. He almost became interchangeable with Sam Durell and Joe Gall, if not James Bond or Matt Helm. Interesting idea, badly set out. But *The Reluctant Spy* (1966)[26] would change all that, for the better. "NOW! GREGORY HILLER returns to the hell of the Russia he left as a counter spy" (front-cover blurb). Even with his surgically re-re-altered face, Hiller runs the constant risk of being recognized as Piotr Grigorivich Ilyushin and facing a firing squad—if that tender mercy is granted him.

It was, however, a case of too little too late and Belmont sanctioned the "spy who loved America" with extreme prejudice. A larger paperback publisher like Fawcett Gold Medal might have made a better editorial and marketing fist of it, exploiting Gregory Hiller's quirky potential to the full. But even the mighty Fawcett Gold Medal machine could slip out of gear every so often. Case in point: Peter Rabe and Manny deWitt.

Peter Rabe was born Peter Rabinowitsch to Michael Rabinovitch (a Russian Jew) and Elisabeth Margarete Beer, in Halle, Saxony-Anhalt, Germany. The family soon moved to Hanover, where Michael worked as a physician and surgeon. After the Nazi takeover in 1933, Dr. Rabinovitch came under suspicion and his medical license was revoked. The family left Germany for the United States in mid–1938, sponsored by Michael's brother Robert Rubin, who lived in Detroit, Michigan. Their surname was changed to "Rabe," combining "Ra" from Rabinovitch with "Be" from Margrete's maiden name. Michael Rabe took up practice as an obstetrician in New Bremen, Ohio, a German-American town. His son, Peter, graduated from Ohio State University before serving in the U.S. Army. He then attended Western Reserve University, Cleveland, earning a master's degree and a Ph.D. in psychology.

Rabe did some work as an experimental psychologist and tried to establish himself as a therapist before finding more congenial employment in advertising. His first book, *From Here to Maternity*[27] (which he also illustrated) had appeared as "Who's Having This Baby?" in *McCall's Magazine* for September 1954. It was a light-hearted look at the birth of their first son, Jonathan (April 5, 1953). A long string of crime-fiction novels followed for Fawcett Gold Medal, beginning in 1955 with *Benny Muscles In*, *A Shroud for Jesso*, and *Stop This Man!* Quick on the authorial draw, Rabe had seen eighteen of his books in print from 1955 through 1961. He used the pen-name Marco Maloponte for two soft-core porn novels: *Her High School Lover* (Beacon Books, 1962) and *New Man in the House* (ditto).

Jack Jesso, in *A Shroud for Jesso* is a Syndicate fixer who can find himself on the fringes of international intrigue. But the standalone *Blood on the Desert*[28] is fully steeped in espionage derring-do and foreign-parts intrigue. American freelance secret agent Anthony Wheeler is recruited by Major Pitt, a British intelligence officer, and sent to Kaden (another North African equivalent of Never Land). He must find out why three incessantly feuding Arab chieftains have suddenly become the best of friends. Seven years later, Rabe would take a crack at creating his own idiosyncratic spy-fiction series hero. *The Girl in a Big Brass Bed*[29] introduced Manny deWitt—a high-powered lawyer who is all-too-often forced to act more like James Bond than Perry Mason. His first recorded case involves retrieving *The Girl*, a painting by Jan Vermeer (1632–75) which had once been stolen by Hermann Goering (1893–1946) and has now come back on the Old Master black market. "Intrigue, forgery, kidnapping, sudden death and [of course] a girl in a big brass bed" (blurb).

Manny (short for Manford) deWitt has been hired, fired, hired again and again by Hans Lobbe, the eccentric entrepreneurial head of Manhattan-based Lobbe Industriel. He resembles a cross between Ernst Stavro Blofeld and Fat Tony, head of the Legitimate Businessman's Association in *The Simpsons*, with a dash of Nero Wolfe thrown in for seasoning. From chapter 1 of *The Spy Who Was 3 Feet Tall* (1966):

> [Hans Lobbe] was short and round, like something drawn in slow motion. His thin hair was half yellow and half white, and his gentle, deceptive eyes, with their white lashes, were looking at me.
>
> Lobbe, of course, was Dutch. As is the case with all Dutchmen who want to be understood in this world, he had to know some other languages. Lobbe not only knew a dozen of them, but often used them interchangeably. I have seen him speak Malay to an uncomprehending American and then apologize in German. Entirely as a matter of mood, he can stick to English quite flawlessly, and when that happens he is usually serious to a dangerous degree. So far, with schnapps in hand, he seemed unaccountably friendly.[30]

Rabe's first-person narration means that we only know Manny deWitt from whatever he chooses to tell us about himself—not very much—and how he interacts with other people. He often comes across as being a bit slow on the uptake and not quite "all there," which annoys the hell out of his friends and foes alike. Hans Lobbe, especially.

Manny deWitt (FYI: a Flemish family name meaning white) is duly dispatched to the former French West African colony of Motana, where he meets Inge (Lobbe's niece) and Prince Plozzi. Also Yum Lee, leader of the "Chinese Cultural Mission" that rivals Hans Lobbe Industriel for the road-building project—among other, infinitely more profitable things. Rabe was years ahead of his time, where the exploitation of Africa by China is concerned. Manny scans the airport terminal building at Villeblanche, Motana's capital city. It was "white stucco inside and out. Inside it looked as if someone were in the process of moving in but with little conviction of staying. Three rows of wooden benches were unevenly aligned. The ticket agent's counter held a litter of papers and also cups, glasses, and plates. Besides handling reservations, the counter dispensed coffee, wine, and French rolls. A brown telephone booth stood at an angle, and there was a three-foot space between it and the wall. A half-naked baby was yanking on the cable that connected the booth to a junction box."[31]

The "half-naked baby" turns out to be the titular spy who was three feet tall, a thirty-year-old Motanese pygmy who has "moled" his way into the Red Chinese headquarters. Manny employs Baby (as he so condescendingly calls him) as a chauffeur and general factotum. Mijnheer Hans Lobbe has the last words, as per usual. When deWitt yells that he had completely forgotten to pay Baby, he replies: "I know that, Manny. I took care of it." Then he looked at me over his shoulder. "You did not know he was a Lobbe?"

Code Name Gadget (1967) is the generic spy-fiction title of the third and most generic Manny deWitt spy-fiction novel. It opens with Manny in his lawyerly capacity for Lobbe Industriel: "I was in Honduras renegotiating the lobster-bed rights which Grandfather Gaenserich Lobbe had acquired in 1888. How Gaenserich had managed that little deal in the midst of a bloody revolution is a tale to curdle the blood of any ordinary robber baron." But no sooner does Manny arrive back in New York than he is packed off to London, England, with orders to buy the Gadget: "What I knew about the Gadget undoubtedly did not do the invention justice, though for me it was a sufficient yardstick of the importance that Mijnheer Lobbe had been trying to buy it for a number of years. So had DuPont, whose name, in Lobbenese, was *Dreck*." As the back-cover blurb intimates, however: "FIND IT—FIND *THE GADGET*. But how could deWitt even know for sure he'd found it, when nobody *really* knew what it looked like? One 'reliable' source insisted The Gadget would look like four telephone booths stacked on end. Another 'expert' told deWitt it would fill a medium-sized factory. Manny deWitt embarks on a tortuous and shadowy trail of espionage and counter-espionage in a chilling race against time as the Doom Machine ticks on...."

If Fawcett Gold Medal had any intention of starting a Code Name series, nothing ever came of it, and *Gadget* was the last Manny deWitt novel. Rabe then wrote two episodes of the *Batman* TV series: "The Joker's Last Laugh" (February 15, 1967) and "The Joker's Epitaph" (February 16, 1967). Also, the film tie-in novelization for *Tobruk*.[32] After that, he gave up full-time writing to become a psychology teacher at California Polytechnic State University. He lived in Atascadero, California, until his death from lung cancer on May 20, 1990. Rabe had mixed feelings about his three Manny deWitt lawyer/spy novels. George Tuttle ("A Conversation with Peter Rabe"): Why did you venture into spy fiction? "I just thought it was fun. I think it was sort of a curiosity to deal with, like a man like [John] le Carré who deals with the subject in considerable depth, or [Len] Deighton. I very much like his work. I just picked it as another area in which to write. [But] what really makes them fall short from my point of view is that they are sort of arched, and I don't really care for that kind of story" (www.mysteryfile.com). N.B. Stark House Press published an omnibus volume in 2017.

What follows is an A–Z checklist of also-ran authors and their ephemeral spy-fiction creations.

AGNEIL, Lucien (1919–1988). Agneil worked for the *Charlotte News*, the U.S. Information Agency, Radio Free Europe, and *U.S. News and World Report*. *Code Name: Icy* (Paperback Library, 1970). "Fred Sherman of the CIA wants 'ICY'—alive. Sherman believes that 'Icy,' an East German secret agent, is really Eric Hendricks, an American soldier presumed to have been killed during World War II" (blurb). *Pressure Point* (Paperback Library, 1970). Superspy: Lt. Commander Dan Devlin. Set in Red China and Taiwan. *Zeppelin* (Paperback Library, 1971). Film tie-in novelization.

BOND, Walter. Pseudonym of George Wolk (1941–1980). Aka Norman Gant, Heinrich Graat, Janet Kidde, Barney Parrish, and Sebastian Watt. *The Kill Squad* (Lancer, 1968). "Murder and torture were routine for members of the X Agency. But Twig Grey wouldn't join—until death came so close that he had no choice ..." (blurb). Crossroads Press edition published in 2016, as by George Wolk.

BRANDNER, Gary (1930–2013). *The Aardvark Affair* (Zebra, New York, 1975). No. 1 in "The Big Brain" series. "*Special Agent with X-Ray Intelligence!* Colin Garrett a Super Hero with Super I.Q. Powers. A mind instantly capable of separating complex truth from compound lies, spotting disaster and crime still in the making. America's highest level spy operation, Agency Zero, thrust him into the Aardvark case—a top secret project which has turned three Agency people into mental vegetables. Garrett's vast intelligence and lightning reaction is needed to break up a formidable international threat to the peace of the world ..." (blurb). Sequels: *The Beelzebub Business* (1975) and *Energy Zero* (1976).

CRANE, Robert. Pseudonym of British-born writer Bernard Glemser (1908–1990), who served as a Royal Air Force intelligence officer during the Second World War, after which he settled in the USA. His hero, Ben Corbin, started fictional life as an American soldier based in Korea: *Sergeant Corbin's War* (Pyramid, 1963) and *The Sergeant and the Queen* (ditto, 1964). Corbin became a CIA agent in *Operation Vengeance* (Pyramid, 1965: updated as *Time Running Out* in 1974). Ditto *The Paradise Trap* (Pyramid, 1967). "BEN CORBIN. Two-fisted swinger—the agent they called 'The Butcher'—rougher than Bond, harder than Hammer. Hot after a ring of brutal murder merchants, Peiping stooges profiteering an insidious brand of death" (from back-cover blurb to *Tongue of Treason*: Pyramid, 1967).

CROSSEN, Kendall Foster (1910–1981) was a New York–born science fiction writer. He achieved his greatest fame, however, with the 21-volume "Milo March" series, as by M.E. Chaber. Although March is primarily a freelance insurance investigator (retained by the International Insurance company), his OSS and CIA background leads to him working for one government intelligence agency or another. From *Hangman's Harvest* (Henry Holt, 1952: as *Don't Get Caught*: Popular Library, 1953) to *Born to Be Hanged* (Holt, Rinehart, 1973).

CURTIS, Wade. Pseudonym for science fiction writer Jerry Pournelle (1933–2017). *Red Heroin* (Berkley, 1969). Paul Crane is a 28-year-old divorced consulting engineer who lives in Seattle, Washington. His security clearance and yachtsman's knowledge of the local waters make him temporarily useful to the CIA. Crane becomes the bait in a trap set for an organization smuggling heroin into the United States from Red China. "The most convincing and realistic counterespionage story I've read in a long, long time—and besides that, a hell of a good yarn" (Robert A. Heinlein). Sequel: *Red Dragon* (Berkley, 1971).

DAGMAR (no forename). Pseudonym for Lou Cameron (1924–2010). Regina (no surname) is a freelance spy code-named the Blue Queen who sells her special services to the highest Free World bidder. "Blue Queen"—it says here—is an extra queen placed upon a chessboard that can be used by both players.

She adopts the secret identity of a popular globe-trotting cabaret singer. Novels: *The Spy with the Blue Kazoo* (Lancer, 1967); *The Spy Who Came in from the Copa* (ditto). "Dagmar writes again! TV's Top-Most Entertainer Returns ... with a mixed-up melange of espionage in high (above the clouds) and low (under the bed) places that makes any other spy book you've read look like a script for Lassie" (back-cover blurb for *Copa*).

KERN, Gregory. Pseudonym of British science fiction writer E.C. Tubb (1914–2010). Cap Kennedy is a wealthy "Secret Agent of the Spaceways" who flits about the Milky Way in his private starship, the *Mordain*. DAW Books published seventeen Kern novels, from *Galaxy of the Lost* (1973) to *The Galactiad* (1983). He works for FATE, headed by Elias Weyburn, who "sat like a spider at the centre of a web, directing his agents, the Free Acting Terran Envoys, dedicated men [and women] of whom Kennedy was the foremost. Men who could work in the dark, bribing, manipulating, killing if the need arose. The agents of FATE, each their own judge, jury and executioner. The hidden claws of the tiger that was Earth. But, in the vastness of space, in the empty dark of unknown regions, could lurk other forms of life. Entities which had not followed a normal pattern of evolution. Creatures of incredible power against whom the race of man would be as ants to a sweeping fire" (from *The Galactiad*, pp. 18–19).

KIRK, Philip (?). Butler—yet another one-name secret agent—has been fired from the CIA and he is now employed by something called the Barclay Institute. Thirteen novels, from *The Hydra Conspiracy* (Leisure Books, 1979) to *The Midas Kill* (ditto, 1984). Back-cover blurb to *Chinese Roulette* (1979): "THE DEADLIEST MISSILE! During a routine customs search, vials of Bubonic Plague serum and guided missile components were found on a Chinese junk in Hong Kong harbour. Only Butler could be trusted to ferret out the significance of the deadly cargo. But there were powerful forces at work, whose main objective was to make sure the renegade superspy didn't live to discover the truth!"

KURLAND, Michael (1938–). Peter Carthage is The Man from W.A.R. (Weapons Analysis and Research). Back-cover blurb for *Mission: Third Force* (Pyramid, 1967): "Are you a little country with BIG trouble? WAR, INC. will develop your weapons, train your troops, plan your strategy, and even fight your wars! Peter Carthage of WAR, Inc. races to Asia on a crash-priority mission—find a way to stop a guerrilla army terrorizing a tiny, independent kingdom. But there's a joker in the contract—a hidden party to the conflict—and Carthage and his WAR, Inc. team are in the fight of their lives against the mysterious, deadly THIRD FORCE." Sequels: *Mission: Tank War* (1968); *Mission: Police Action* (1969); *A Plague of Spies* (1969).

MADDOCK, Larry. Pseudonym of Jack Owen Jardine (1931–2009). Ace Books published the Agent of T.E.R.R.A. futuristic spy-fi series, starting with *The Flying Saucer Gambit* (1966). "Hannibal Fortune had been one of the first wave of T.E.R.R.A. recruits. In a sense, Temporal Entropy Restructure and Repair was still a young organization, having been created by secret vote of the Galactic Federation Security Council in 2558. Its base-time now was the year 2572, which made T.E.R.R.A. only fourteen years old. Fortune had been with it for twelve of those fourteen years. He'd never heard of Gregor Malik and the sinister organization called Empire until after T.E.R.R.A. had recruited him. But now, thanks to the illegal [since 2554] temporal transporter which T.E.R.R.A.'s scientists were continually perfecting, he'd logged some sixty years' experience fighting Empire." His closest ally is a small, 15-pound alien named Webley who can shape-change at will. Sequels: *The Golden Goddess Gambit* (1967); *The Emerald Elephant Gambit* (1967); *The Time-Trap Gambit* (1968).

MAIR, George B. (1914-?). Like Philip McCutchan (see above), Mair was a Briton who found a niche in the American spy-fiction market. And his counterspy hero, Dr. David Grant, had an American mother. After being invalided out of RAF Bomber Command during the Second World War, he earned his M.D. and eventually became a secret agent for NATO. Grant's SPECTRE-like bugbear is SATAN (Society for the Activation of Terror, Anarchy, and Nihilism). He appears in ten novels, from *Death's Foot Forward* (Jarrolds, London, 1963) to *Paradise Spells Danger* (ditto, 1973). From the back-cover blurb to the 1968 Berkley paperback edition of *Live, Love and Cry* (Jarrolds, 1965): "A weapon more terrifying than 'The Bomb' causes the birth rate [in major Western cities] to drop suddenly and sharply. And David Grant, passionately involved with a famous scientist's blonde and beautiful daughter, must take the fate of millions firmly in his hands…." Mair scored a standalone success with *The Day Khrushchev Panicked* (Cassell, London, 1961).

MANSON, Will (?). © Howard LeRoy. Black is the only-name hero of *A Man Called Black* (Flagship Books, 1967). He is a secret agent for an unnamed secret agency, run by the secretive Colonel Tompkins (who "christened" him Black). From *The Chinese Conundrum* (1967): "That Black had endured was a credit to a number of his characteristics, among them careful thinking, alertness, physical strength, a high tolerance of pain and total immersion in and dedication to his work. He was a big man and if you did not know differently you might take him for an experienced running back on a professional football team. His face had a battered appearance, his nose had been broken and poorly reset, there was a scar on his chin and a faint red line at his hairline where the hair refused to grow. Black was unobtrusive, his manner was reserved and he seldom spoke unless it was essential for him to say something." The other "Black" novels are *The Dangerous Ones* (1968) and *A Very Black Deed* (ditto).

SEWARD, Jack. Pseudonym of Jack Seaward (1924–2010). Seaward was a World War II Military Intelligence officer later assigned to Japan because he knew the language. Curt Stone, his private-eye spy, is also based there, employed by Far Eastern Investigations. Five novels, from *The Cave of the Chinese Skeletons* (Tower, 1964) to *Assignment: Find Cherry* (ditto, 1969). Back-cover blurb to *The Frogman Assassination* (1968): "Tokyo's toughest private eye was right there when political fanatics tried to kill the Emperor of Japan—and blame the assassination on the United States. Unless Stone got to the mysterious frogman in time, the Far East would blow sky-high. The only thing he had to go on was a savage killer called The Porcupine whose only weakness was beautiful blondes. And while the fuse burned shorter, Stone knew the only people he could really count on were his flip-talking assistant Gus Makano and his sexy secretary Jeanne Auber." Remaining "Stone's the Name" novels: *Eurasian Virgins* (1968) and *Chinese Pleasure Girl* (1969).

SMITH, Don. Pseudonym of Donald Taylor Smith (1909–1978). Smith was born in Port Colborne, Ontario, Canada. From 1934 until 1939 he was a foreign correspondent for the *Toronto Star* in Peking. He became an RAF fighter pilot during the Second World War (earning a DFC for his part in the 1944 Dieppe raid). He later wrote 21 upmarket spy novels for Award Books, which were unfortunately packaged to resemble the Nick Carter Killmaster (q.v.) series. They were all prefixed *Secret Mission*, from *Peking* (1968) to *The Strausser Transfer* (1978). Phil Sherman is a tall (6' 2"), middle-aged (World War II veteran) American businessman and part-time spy based in Paris who then becomes a full-time CIA agent. He had previously appeared in the paperback original novel *Red Curtain* (Beacon Books, 1959), as by Duncan Tyler. In *The Libyan Contract* (1974), Sherman has to prevent an American hitman from assassinating Colonel Khaffafi and sparking off a Middle East conflagration.

SOMERS, Bart. Pseudonymn of Gardner F. Fox (q.v.) p. 191. Commander John Craig is a Special Agent for the elite Investigation Corps, United Worlds Space Fleets, who introduced himself in *Beyond the Black Enigma* (Paperback Library, 1965). Back-cover blurb: "Suave, handsome John Craig did not relish the assignment to conquer The Black Enigma. He would have preferred to continue romancing the beautiful Elva Marlowe—or any other of his many women. But when Alert Command informed him that two space fleets had been consumed by the Enigma, and that the menacing blob was swelling steadily, Craig couldn't resist the challenge. Armed with three protective inventions, Craig set forth eagerly. But he soon found out that getting BEYOND THE BLACK ENIGMA was not going to be just another heroic stunt. If he failed in his mission, it could end his life and Planet Earth!" Sequel: *Abandon Galaxy!* (Paperback Library, 1967).

TABORI, Paul (1908–1974). Tabori was born in Budapest, Hungary. His father died in the Auschwitz concentration camp. He escaped with his mother to England, continuing his career as a journalist and fiction writer. Three of Tabori's novels concerned a do-gooding group known as The Hunters. They were first published in the USA by Pyramid Books: *The Doomsday Brain* (1967); *The Invisible Eye* (1967); *The Torture Machine* (1968). Back-cover blurb for *Torture*: "THE HUNTERS. Two men and a woman dedicated to vengeance against those the law will not touch. Endowed with physical powers so precise and finely tuned that they border on the psychic. Total professionals schooled in the delicate and deadly art of the chase—to track, to trap … and to kill. THE PREY. Gia. A man of intense personal magnetism and strange lusts. A man who rose from the position of Castro's Chief Executioner to become the most brilliant revolutionary hero since Lenin. A man with a perfect plan for world anarchy, an ultimate machine of torture—and all the money necessary to make his raging vision a reality."

TRALINS, Bob. Transparent pseudonym used by Robert Tralins (1926–2010). "Robert Tralins wrote banned and bordello books, as well as stories that inspired 'Beyond Belief' [TV series: 1997–2000]" (Andrew Meachem, *Tampa Bay Times*: April 2, 2015). Lee Crosley is *The Miss from S.I.S.* (Belmont, 1966). S.I.S. = Society of International Security, an organization comprised of notable professional women (doctors, lawyers, etc.) whose aim is setting the male-dominated world to rights. *Miss from S.I.S.* involves them—and especially Ms. Crosley—with a POTUS who plots to make himself an absolute monarch. The front-cover blurb for *The Chic Chick Spy* (1966) says it all, really: "This is the most absurd book you will read this year. Absolutely nothing in it is true, realistic or possible but for sheer fun, excitement, intrigue, you couldn't spend a better 50 ¢." Memorably entitled third and last novel: *The Ring-a-Ding UFOs* (1967). N.B. Not to be confused with the nymphomaniacal Lady from L.U.S.T. (q.v.) or the much sleazier British equivalent, the Girl (Virginia Box) from H.A.R.D. (Hemisphere Administration for Regional Defence), written by James Moffatt (1922–1992). Three novels: *The Girl from H.A.R.D.* (New English Library, 1974); *Virginia Box and the Unsatisfied* (ditto, 1975); *Perfect Assignment* (ditto both).

VON ELSNER, Don (1909–1997). Von Elsner was a master bridge player. Ditto his fictional alter ego, Jake Winkman, who combined Grand Slams with espionage in six books: *The Jake of Diamonds* (Award, 1963: aka *How to Succeed at Murder Without Really Trying*) to *The Best of Jake Winkman* (M. Hardy, 1981: short-story collection). Back-cover blurb to *The Ace of Spies* (Award, 1966): "Washington sweltered in a mid–August heat wave; tempers flared all over Capitol Hill—especially among the internationally renowned bridge luminaries competing in the Nationals Tournament. With customary coolness and finesse, Jake Winkman concentrated on racking up points, oblivious to rising temperatures and temperaments. But when somebody selected Jake's bed to die in, the FBI moved in on surveillance. In the hotel's labyrinthine corridors, the CIA conducted its own investigation, while sinister forces awaited the signal to close in on Winkman for the double cross they thought he had pulled. Jake Winkman had never been the target of such diversified interest … and when the wheels of the *foreign* operatives began bearing down on him, the heat was *really* on!"

WINSTON, Peter. An Award Books house name used by Jack Laflin (see above). It was also the name used for the hero of five "Peter Winston" novels: *Assignment to Bahrein* (1966: Paul Eiden); *The ABC Affair* (1967: Paul Eiden); *Doomsday Vendetta* (1968: Jim Bowser); *The Glass Cipher* (1968: Jim Bowser); *The Temple at Humquh* (1969: Jack Laflin). Back-cover blurb for *Bahrein*: "Eight years ago, Peter Winston walked into a subway fight with a bunch of knife-wielding thugs—a melee from which he emerged a bloodied, scarred 'hero-for-a-day.' But from that demonstration of seemingly pointless courage came his job in the International Adjustments Department of White, Whittle, Limited [the world's largest construction company]. Gradually, Winston had learned of THE ADJUSTERS, a privately financed supranational organization. PURPOSE: The preservation of world peace. FUNCTION: To make 'adjustments' as needed in the temperamental machinery of governments the world over. From that vantage point as head of a company with world-wide engineering projects, Edgar White Whittle was uniquely able to take preventive or corrective measures to adjust any international crisis."

CHAPTER TWELVE

Multimedia Master Spies

"Television in America has taken over radio's duties of providing drama and comedy and has consistently failed to provide entertainment with either the quality of the more serious radio plays or the magic appeal of radio's great thrillers and fun shows," wrote Jim Harmon. "Today's radio happily abdicates providing drama for even a minority audience. Radio proudly proclaims that it is making more money than ever through the playing of phonograph records with up to twenty-five minutes per hour taken up with commercials…. Some radio stations experimented briefly with old transcriptions of *The Shadow, The Lone Ranger*, and others. Some of the language and stories had dated. Some had serious technical difficulties, scratches and clicks that obliterated words. They were not a fair test of the basic appeal of radio drama."[1]

The situation was radically different in the United Kingdom, where "at least one network [the BBC] is operated in the public interest and not for profit, radio drama and comedy still retain an important share of the general audience, some radio shows competing successfully with TV."[2] Further reading: *The Radio Companion*,[3] by Paul Donovan. Cue the BBC's first daily radio serial produced along American lines—*Dick Barton—Special Agent*. "Captain Richard Barton, late of the Commandos, was fearless, straight as a die and a natural leader of men. With his trusty sidekicks Snowey White and Jock Anderson, sergeants both but decent enough chaps all the same, he thrilled a grey and tired nation with cliffhanging, crimebusting adventures from 1946 to 1951, injecting breathless escapism into the long grey years of rationing and austerity" (Donovan). Episode 1 concerned the theft of a secret weapon that could fire bubonic plague rays and shoot through walls.

As told before, the British-made *Danger Man* TV series had introduced the mature and thoughtful American super spy John Drake to American audiences. Three years later, Patrick McGoohan reprised the role in a new one-hour format. *Danger Man* 2.0 racked up 45 monochrome and 2 color episodes from October 13, 1964, until January 12, 1968. John Drake had been re-imagined as a true-blue *British* "Special Security Agent" working for a based-somewhere-in-London government department called M9. McGoohan's American-Irish-English background and subsequent "transatlantic" accent made for an effortless transition between nationalities. But nothing much else about John Drake had changed. From *Danger Man and*

The Prisoner,[4] by Dave Rogers: "It is true that [Drake] was (slightly) less clinical in his investigative approach, but *perfection* was still a byword in the agent's dictionary."[5] The revamped *Danger Man* was unimaginatively renamed *Secret Agent* for its return to the CBS network (April 3, 1965, to September 10, 1966), perhaps to distinguish it from the original program, then running in syndication.

"Colony Three" (UK season 2, episode 10: October 27, 1964) led to McGoohan's creation of *The Prisoner.* A recently ex–British secret agent (who might or might not have been John Drake) is abducted and taken to a place known only as the Village, where suave-but-sadistic interrogators from we-never-know-where try to find out why he resigned. The Prisoner was designated Number Six, which also refers back to Colony Three: "They've given you a number, and they've taken away your name." To which McGoohan here gave this invariable response: "I am not a number, I am a free man." *The Prisoner* lasted for only 17 52-color episodes, from "Arrival" (September 29, 1967) to "Fall Out" (February 2, 1968). American CBS broadcasts: June 1 to September 21, 1968. However, it would turn conventional TV spy-fiction upside down and inside out, taking in espionage, neuropsychology, and surrealism.

The 47 hour-long color episodes of that other successful British import, *The Saint,* were syndicated by NBC from May 1, 1967, to September 12, 1969 (after its three-year monochrome run). But the full-color Simon Templar was now acting more like John Drake, almost becoming a *Secret Agent* himself. For example: *The Fiction Makers* was a feature-film compilation of two episodes (December 8 and 15, where Roger Moore spoofed 007 five years before he got to play him "for real" in *Live and Let Die*). Plot: S.W.O.R.D. (Secret World Organization for Retribution and Destruction), its leader Warlock and special agent Charles Lake were merely figments of Amos Klein's hyperactive imagination until a copycat Warlock turned fiction into fact. When Ian Ogilvy (September 30, 1943–) inherited the heroic halo from Roger Moore in *Return of the Saint,* Simon Templar became more like a freelance James Bond than ever. Co-produced by ITC Entertainment and the Italian broadcaster RAI, it became an international success story. But only twenty-four episodes were made, from "The Judas Game" (September 10, 1978) to "The Diplomat's Daughter" (March 11, 1979). Sir Lew Grade had decided to close down his TV drama unit in favor of filmmaking—a big mistake on his part, as it would transpire.

ITC had the habit of hiring American actors to play the leads in otherwise very British TV series. For example: Richard Bradford (1934–2010) in *Man in a Suitcase* (1967–1968), as McGill, a drummed-out CIA agent and London-based private detective; Stuart Damon (1937–2021) in *The Champions* (1968–1969), as an agent of Nemesis; Joel Fabiani (1936–), of *Department S* (1969–1970) fame; Tony Curtis (1925–2010) in *The Persuaders* (1971–1972), as New York-born "persuader" Danny Wilde (co-starring Roger Moore as Lord Brett Sinclair). Even John Creasey's John Mannering—*The Baron* (1966)—became a Texas oil baron counterspy in the person of real-life Texan Steve Forrest (1925–2013).

The Avengers took both the UK and the USA by video storm in the mid- to late

1960s; this time not thanks to ITC but Associated British Cinemas: later Corporation (Television) Ltd. It had been developed from *Police Surgeon*, a half-hour forensic series broadcast from September 10, 1960, to December 3, 1960. Complete details can be found in *The Complete Avengers*,[6] by Dave Rogers. Cutting a too-long story short, Patrick Macnee[7] played a dapper secret agent called John Steed in the new series. Macnee was soon joined by Honor Blackman (1925–2020) as anthropologist and judo-expert Catherine Gale. Dr. Gayle was no standard-issue Bond Girl and Honor Blackman would be the first atypical Bond Woman when she played Pussy Galore in the 1964 film version of *Goldfinger*, treating 007 more like a Galore Man. Neither the 1962 nor the 1963–64 seasons of *The Avengers* were sold to an American network, and a proposed feature-film version foundered when Blackman did not return after making *Goldfinger*.

More than sixty hopefuls were auditioned for the role of Steed's new partner, Mrs. Emma Peel, before it was given to the young Shakespearean actress Diana Rigg.[8] As the Contessa Teresa di Vicenzo (Tracy, for short), in *On Her Majesty's Secret Service*, Rigg would become the lawfully wedded wife of James Bond—if only for a little while. Her departure led to the casting of Canadian-born Linda Thorson (1947–) as Tara King. ABC America prime-time broadcast *The Avengers* from March 28, 1966, until September 15, 1969, the last two seasons being in color. But it was canceled after being put up against the insanely popular *Rowan and Martin's Laugh-In* (NBC: 1968–1973). *The New Avengers* ran for 26 episodes: UK (October 22, 1976, to December 17, 1977); USA (CBS: September 5, 1978, to March 23, 1979). Joanna Lumley (1946–) played the high-kicking, sharp-shooting Purdey (named after the famous make of sporting shotguns). She reversed the usual process by appearing in a Bond film (*OHMSS*, as "The English Girl") before becoming an *Avengers* lady.

The Avengers anticipated, even if it did not directly influence, American tongue-in-cheek spy series like *The Man from U.N.C.L.E.* and *Mission: Impossible* (see both below). It also paved the way for many more proactive TV spy-fi heroines (ditto), though the nearest antecedent to the future *Avengers* superwomen would be Honey West, created by G.G. Fickling; a joint pseudonym used by the writing team of Forrest Ellison Fickling (1925–1998) and his wife Gloria Gautraud (her maiden name) Fickling (1925–).

Forrest—nicknamed "Skip"—was born in Long Beach, Southern California, and grew up in Lynwood, Los Angeles County. He served as a U.S. Army Air Corps gunner in the Second World War, receiving many military honors (including the British Air Gunner award and the American Air Medal with three oak-leaf clusters). Forrest and Gloria were married in May 1949. The Ficklings moved to Laguna Beach in 1950, where they worked in advertising and journalism (Skip as a sports broadcaster). Gloria Gautraud Fickling was born in Brooklyn, spending her early years in St. Albans, Long Island. After her graduation from high school, she went to Los Angeles, eventually becoming a fashion journalist for *Look* and *Women's Wear Daily* magazines. Gloria supported Skip while he tried to break into fiction writing—with a signal lack of success. But things looked up when their friend and Laguna Beach neighbor Richard S. Prather (q.v.) pointed out that nobody had created a successful female private eye along the lines of his own tough but tenderhearted (at least to "gorgeous tomatoes") Shell Scott.

To think was to act, and the Ficklings had come up with the basic "Honey West" concept before the year was out. "I first thought of Marilyn Monroe, and then I thought of Mike Hammer and decided to put the two together," Skip told *The Los Angeles Times* in 1986. As for the character's name: "We [Skip and Gloria] thought the most used name for someone you really like is Honey. And she lives in the West, so there was her name."[9] Gloria has generally been given coauthor credit for the Honey West novels, but she has always claimed that Skip did most—if not all—of the actual writing. From the *World Biographical Encyclopedia*: "As Gloria would later describe it, Skip had the inspiration but not the organization, so Gloria used her talents as an editor to pull the books together with plot devices and a sure fashion sense" (cited in *The Los Angeles Times* for April 11, 1998).

This Girl for Hire (1957) was the first of eleven Honey West novels to be published by Pyramid Books. The back-cover blurb might have been written by Skip and Gloria themselves. It describes Honey West as "the nerviest curviest private eye in LA, with the sleuthmanship of Mike Hammer and the measurements of Marilyn Monroe" (see above). Whoever wrote the Mayflower-Dell blurb (London, 1966) got a bit carried away: "NAKED EYE. With a deadly .32 and a lively 38–22–36, HONEY WEST is on the prowl for a murderer. From peeling down to rescue a 'drowning' man, to playing strip poker with four murder suspects, Honey's hunting a killer—and she doesn't mind hunting bare! Her technique is lethal, her statistics are vital, and she can't say NO—except in an emergency." Honey had a close-but-fraught relationship with Lieutenant Mark Storm of the LAPD Homicide Squad. Pyramid published eight more Honey West novels, in reasonably quick succession: *A Gun for Honey* (1958); *Girl on the Loose* (1958); *Honey in the Flesh* (1959); *Girl on the Prowl* (1959); *Kiss for a Killer* (1960); *Dig a Dead Doll* (1960); *Blood and Honey* (1961); *Bombshell* (1964). Honey's virtue is frequently set at risk—but never violated, with even Lt. Mark Storm behaving like a perfect gentleman throughout. Espionage interest is virtually nonexistent, however, save for the resurgent-Nazis-stealing-an-atomic-submarine plot in *Bombshell*. This torture scene demonstrates both Honey's vulnerability and her ability to fight back.

Unlike Richard S. Prather's Shell Scott, who had been her literary godfather— *The Cockeyed Corpse* (1964) dedication read: "For SKIP and GLORIA FICKLING"— Honey West looped the lucrative loop from printed page to cathode-ray tube. Skip was approached by Dick Powell of the Four Star International production company in 1964. A year later, the character was "piloted" in an episode of *Burke's Law* (q.v.). In "Who Killed the Jackpot?" (April 21, 1965), Anne Francis (1930–2011) played a goody-goody Honey, with John Ericson (1926–2020) as her hi-tech and ruggedly handsome partner, Sam Bolt (replacing Lt. Mark Storm). *Honey West* (ABC/Four

Star) ran for 30 × 25m b & w episodes (September 17, 1965, to April 8, 1966). It was developed for television by screenwriter Gwen Bagni (1913–2001), Skip Fickling taking the "Executive Advisor" title. Richard Meyers:

> When Honey got into a fix she couldn't kick or shoot her way out of, Bolt would bolt from here to there to save his partner's sexy skin. The show had a ludicrous number of gimmicks. Honey had a four-wheeled electronic detective lab in a van marked H.W. Bolt & Co., TV Service. She had a pet ocelot called Bruce. She had an annoying and non-canonical aunt played by Irene Hervey [1909–1998].
> Honey was loaded down with gadgets that never helped when the going got tough. Besides the .38 in her handbag and the derringer tucked elsewhere, Honey had a compact which exploded, a garter-belt gas mask, tear-gas earrings, and a lipstick microphone. Anne Francis played Honey as best she could given the circumstances, but it is doubtful if even Raquel Welch could have saved this show.[10]

Honor Blackman was actually the first actress considered to play Honey West, but she decided against it, probably to avoid typecasting. In the event, Anne Francis made the part very much her own, a kind of grown-up Nancy Drew with attitude. She won a Golden Globe (Best TV Star—Female). John Ericson, on the other hand, played Sam Bolt like either Frank or Joe Hardy. Francis had taken lessons in Okinawa Te from Sensei Gordon Doversola, so Honey West, Cathy Gale, and Emma Peel had at least martial-arts proficiency in common. Only two episodes can be said to have any real espionage interest: "Invitation to Limbo" (December 17, 1965: industrial spy leaking company secrets) and "Rockabye the Hard Way" (December 24, 1965: stolen guided-missile parts). The novels kept on selling steadily, even after the TV series had folded, which enabled Skip and Gloria to live in "The House That Honey Built" (as they gleefully called it).

Seven years after the publication of *Bombshell*, Pyramid revived Honey West—as a female super spy to rival the lubricious likes of Eve Drum and Cherry Delight (see Chapter Fourteen). Blurb for *Stiff as a Broad* (1971): "Honey's hard on her feet, soft on her back, a karate-chopping spy-queen who always gets her man—one way or another. This time Honey's after a woman. Madame Fong, dragon-lady of the Chinese Commies, has plans to send all of Frisco on a no-return trip via an annihilating dose of lethal nerve gas. So Honey has to get Madame Fong. But first she has to sidetrack three watchdog studs, challenging their talents in bed and out. That's how the Commies found out that when Honey West does a job, she gives it all she's got." *Honey on Her Tail* (also 1971) was the only sequel. "How to catch the world's sexiest spy?" asked the blurb, answering: "When it comes to undercover work, Honey is at her best." Dell/Gold Key published a one-shot TV tie-in *Honey West* comic book in 1966, with two stories written by Paul S. Newman: "The Underwater Raiders" and "The Fall Guy" (illustrated by Jack Sparling).

It just so happens that the closest female equivalent to James Bond—Modesty Blaise—sprang from a comic strip created by an Englishman named Peter O'Donnell.[11] He was born in Lewisham, South London, the son of journalist Bernard O'Donnell, employed by the *Empire News* (a now long-gone British Sunday newspaper). During the Second World War, Peter saw active service with the Eighth Army in Persia (Iran), Syria, Egypt and the Western Desert, Italy, and Greece. After the war, he worked as an editor for Clarke and Cochran (1946–51) before establishing himself as a newspaper comic-strip writer: *Garth* (1953–56) and *Romeo Brown* (1956–62) for the *Daily Mirror*; *The Affairs of Eve* (1953–55) and *Tug Transom* (1954–68) for the *Daily Sketch*.

O'Donnell adapted *Dr. No* for its comic-strip serialization in the *Daily Express* (May 23, 1960, to October 1, 1960). Two years later, Beaverbrook Newspapers commissioned him to create an original comic strip. From "Peter O'Donnell's *Modesty Blaise*,"[12] by Michael Richardson and Neil & Sue Alsop: "O'Donnell wanted [this strip] to reflect the changing role of women in society, and over the following months he came up with [Modesty Blaise], a heroine who was to inspire a radical re-evaluation of female characters in adventure fiction. When asked who he would like to draw the strip, he had no hesitation in recommending his friend, Jim Holdaway (1927–1970), with whom he had worked on *Romeo Brown*. The first story quickly established the characters of Modesty [and her Cockney sidekick, Willie Garvin]: both strong and resourceful, but subject to strong human emotions and by no means certain to triumph over evil. [The strip] was immediately syndicated out to a number of other newspapers."

Modesty Blaise's family background is not so much obscure as nonexistent. Her nationality is also a matter of some dispute, despite being long domiciled in the United Kingdom: Near the end of World War II, an amnesiac orphan girl escapes from a German prison camp in Greece. She endures a lone fight to survive in refugee camps all over Turkey and Persia. In one camp, she saves the life of an old man known as the "Professor," who becomes her mentor in exchange for pilfered food. He names her "Modesty"—ironically, considering her total lack of inhibitions. Studies in Arthurian legend lead her to adopt the surname Blaise (who was the tutor of Merlin). By the age of twenty, Modesty has built up a large criminal organization, the Network, but her inordinately high moral standards precludes any dealing in drugs and vice. Modesty meets Willie Garvin during a kickboxing contest in Saigon, and later bails him out of jail. Garvin becomes a loyal second-in-command to the woman he gratefully calls "Princess." Six years later, they have made themselves rich for life, disbanded the Network, and retired to London. Modesty ensconces herself in a penthouse while Garvin opens a riverside pub. However, the quiet life palls and they are soon back in action, often at the behest of Sir Gerald Tarrant, head of the British Secret Service (without pay and taking no official orders). If there is a romantic relationship between Modesty Blaise and Willie Garvin, it is never consummated on-page.

The *Modesty Blaise* strip first ran in the London *Evening Standard* (later just *The Standard*) from May 13, 1963, until April 11, 2001. But its American circulation, primarily in the *Detroit Free Press*, was spotty at best, owing to the occasional (and censored) nude scenes. "Modesty" often distracted male—and some female—villains by suddenly appearing topless—an invariably effective tactic she called the "Nailer." However, the fact that she had been raped as a child rules out the use of casual sexploitation scenes: Modesty might have nothing in common with Nancy Drew, but she is also no Lady from L.U.S.T.

A *Modesty Blaise* feature film was released by Twentieth Century–Fox on May 5, 1966. Its director, Joseph Losey (1909–1984), had stepped well outside his cinematic comfort zone. O'Donnell had spent months crafting a screenplay, and then it was rewritten by at least six different people, including Harold Pinter (uncredited). Only one line of his original screenplay made it into the finished film. The Italian producer, Joseph Janni (1916–1994), cast the blonde Italian actress Monica Vitti (1931–) as the famously brunette Modesty Blaise. Box-office draw Terence Stamp (1938–) played himself playing Willie Garvin, while Harry Andrews (1911–1989) was the perfect choice for Sir Gerald Tarrant. Dirk Bogarde (1921–1999)—a Losey regular—pulled out all the stops as the over-the-top villain of the piece, Gabriel. Staked out in the desert, he is heard to moan: "Champagne! Champagne!" He also wears an outlandish blonde wig, à la Andy Warhol. "Director Losey ate watermelon, pickles, and ice cream, went to sleep, woke up, and made this adaptation of the comic strip about a sexy female spy. Filmed at the height of the pop-art craze, it tries to be a spoof at times, doesn't know what it's supposed to be at other moments" (Maltin).

With a "major motion picture" in the pre-production offing, several British publishers wanted to add Modesty Blaise to their lists. O'Donnell signed a deal with the independent Souvenir Press, with Pan Books issuing the paperback editions one or two years later. He had an original novel in mind, but the film producers wanted a novelization of something close to the final shooting script. The book O'Donnell delivered was actually based on the very *first* script, which meant that it bore only a fleeting resemblance to the released film.[13] Pan published the UK tie-in edition. O'Donnell kindly provided this pen-portrait of Modesty Blaise, via Sir Gerald Tarrant: "The voice held a mellow timbre with a slight foreign inflexion. The intonation was cool but not unfriendly. The face was smooth and calm, with high cheekbones under dark, contemplative eyes. She would be five foot six, Tarrant thought, but with the black hair drawn up into a chignon on the crown of her head she appeared taller. Her skin held a soft, matte tan that would have made a fortune for any man who could get it into a bottle."[14]

The "novelization" of the film based upon the initial screenplay of the film concerned an attempt to hijack a consignment of diamonds that Her Majesty's Government is using to pay for an oil concession in a conveniently fictional Middle Eastern country. Tarrant sends Modesty and Garvin to prevent the robbery—but only after she has saved her impetuous partner from being hanged. Gabriel is the criminal mastermind, of course (who had first appeared in the third comic-strip adventure, "The Gabriel Set-Up"). O'Donnell fleshed out the character of McWhirter, Gabriel's dour Scottish right-hand man, played in the film by Clive Revill (1930–).

Modesty Blaise would become an even bigger bestseller in book form than she was in the rather problematical comic strip. O'Donnell put her peacefully through ten more novels (Souvenir Press and Pan Books): *Sabre-Tooth* (1966/1967); *I, Lucifer* (1967/1969); *A Taste for Death* (1969/1971); *The Impossible Virgin* (1971/1973); *The Silver Mistress* (1973/1975); *Last Day in Limbo* (1976/1977); *Dragon's Claw* (1978/1979); *The Xanadu Talisman* (1981/1982); *The Night of Morningstar* (1982/1984); *Dead Man's Handle* (1985/1986). Also, two short story collections. (1) *Pieces of Modesty* (Pan paperback original, 1972: first hardcover edition: The Mysterious Press, New York, 1986); (2) *Cobra Trap* (Souvenir Press, 1996: no paperback edition). The early strips were reprinted by Star Books, London, in two standard-format paperbacks: *In the Beginning*; *The Black Pearl and The Vikings* (both 1978). Titan Books then published eight large-format volumes, from *The Gabriel Set-Up* (1984) to *Uncle Happy* (1990).

Kingsley Amis might have written *The Modesty Blaise Dossier* as a companion piece to his famous file on James Bond. From his review of *Last Day in Limbo*, in the *Evening Standard*: "Peter O'Donnell's *Modesty Blaise* thrillers are peppered with ingenious ideas…. The other ingredients are a sharply twisting story line, varied locations, a really formidable criminal project to be foiled, lots of healthy violence, nasty villains, well-sketched minor characters, expert grading of tension, and above all the bond of faith and respect between Modesty and Willie Garvin, her lieutenant. Theirs is one of the great partnerships in crime fiction, bearing comparison with (though necessarily different from) that of Sherlock Holmes and Dr. Watson."

Anne Francis never really looked like becoming America's answer to Modesty Blaise, but Raquel Welch (1940–) made it all the way as Fathom Harvill in *Fathom*, a feature film released by Twentieth Century–Fox (October 1, 1967). Producer: John Kohn (1925–2002). Director: Leslie H. Martinson (1915–2016). It was written by Lorenzo Semple, Jr. (1923–2014), based upon the novel *A Girl Called Fathom*,[15] by Larry Forrester (1924–1979). Tony (*Matt Helm*) Franciosa co-starred as insurance agent Peter Merriwether, and Clive Revill played the full-of-vim villain, Serapkin. "Fast-paced, tongue-in-cheek spy caper with sky-diver Welch getting mixed up with dubious good-guy Franciosa. Great fun, with Revill's performance as eccentric millionaire stealing the show" (Maltin). Fathom Harvill might have gone several films better than Modesty Blaise, but *Fathom* remained a one-off film, with no discernible cult following.

And so the Bond-driven cinematic bandwagon rolled unstoppably on. It is now time to take stock of their too-often overlooked small-screen equivalents. Apart from the ephemeral half-hour *Danger Man* (see above), early 1960s American television represented a cultural desert so far as actual spy series were concerned. To be fair, private-eye shows like *77 Sunset Strip* (October 10, 1958, to September 9, 1964) and *Hawaiian Eye* (October 7, 1959, to September 10, 1963) did feature some espionage-related episodes, though not all that often. Then Ian Fleming, who was no stranger to the making—or not making—of media deals (see Introduction) took a small but eventually significant hand in the game.

Fleming had lunch in London with Norman Felton (1913–2012), an American (but London-born) producer, who had recently scored a massive hit with *Dr. Kildare* (NBC: September 28, 1961, to August 30, 1966). They met again in New York, but Fleming's most viable suggestion was the name "Napoleon Solo" for the title character. By that time his health was failing, and he also worried about how a Fleming-based TV series might affect the Bond film franchise. He sent a formal letter to Felton at the MGM studios in Culver City, California: "This will serve as my assignment to you of all my rights and interest in any material written or contributed by me in connection with an original television series featuring a character named Napoleon Solo. I assign to you all rights of every kind to the use of this character and material…. I hereby acknowledge the receipt of the sum of One Pound (£1) in consideration of this assignment."[16]

Felton pressed on with the production of *Solo*—only to hit an unexpected snag. Eon Productions not only dissuaded Fleming from involving himself with the series, but they also objected to its putative title: Solo had been a "Unione Sicilione" villain in *Goldfinger* (then in the process of being filmed). Cue lawsuit. Nothing daunted, Felton hired writer-producer Sam Rolfe to turn Fleming's vague concept into a firm and unique fictional reality. Rolfe had produced the offbeat western series *Have Gun—Will Travel* (CBS: September 14, 1957, to September 21, 1963), starring Richard Boone as a moody mercenary one-named Paladin. He turned the lone-wolfish Napoleon Solo into a team player for the supra-national security organization called U.N.C.L.E. (United Network Command for Law and Enforcement).

The Man from U.N.C.L.E. (NBC/MGM/Arena Productions) premiered on Tuesday, September 22, 1964. Episode One, "The Vulcan Affair," was an edited version of the color *Solo* pilot, first broadcast in black-and-white to match the other 28 first-season episodes. Director: Don Medford (1917–2012). Sam Rolfe wrote the Fleming-derived script. It also introduced the SPECTRE-like organization THRUSH, which stood for nothing at first but later became the Technological Hierarchy for the Removal of Undesirables and the Subjugation of Humanity. "Vulcan" was later re-edited into the first *Man from U.N.C.L.E.* feature film, *To Trap a Spy* (February 22, 1965), with "The Four Steps Affair" (February 22, 1965). Luciana Paluzzi (1937–) who played the female assassin Fione Volpe in *Thunderball*, took the role of Angela. Another James Bond connection is Richard Kiel (1939–2014: Jaws in *The Spy Who Loved Me* and *Moonraker*), as a guard (uncredited).

The Man from U.N.C.L.E. Book: The Behind-the Scenes Story of a Television Classic,[17] by Jon Heitland, is exactly that, and it makes for a comprehensive one-volume guide. Some pertinent background details follow. U.N.C.L.E. HQ was located in the East Forties district of New York City. Entrance to the complex was gained through Del Floria's tailor shop, after which agents would receive their triangular badges with the distinctive U.N.C.L.E. insignia (stylized globe, stylized armed-man figure). Eight operational sections, in descending order: Policy and Operations; Operations and Enforcement; Enforcement and Intelligence; Intelligence and Communications; Communications and Security; Security and Personnel; Propaganda and Finance; Camouflage and Deception. Every U.N.C.L.E. agent was issued with a custom-made .38 automatic pistol, c/w mounted telescopic sight, long magazine extension, silenced-barrel ditto, shoulder stock, and muzzle break. It could also fire tranquilizer charges.

The plum role of urbane philosophy major, Korean War veteran, and lady's man Napoleon Solo was offered to the New York–born actor, Robert Vaughn,[18] himself a Ph.D. (University of Southern California, 1970). He had followed in the footsteps of his theatrical family, becoming a familiar face on prime-time TV series (including *The Rifleman* and *87th Precinct*). Vaughn's first, if inauspicious, film-star part was playing "The Symbol Maker's Teenage Son" in *Teenage Cave Man* (Roger Corman: 1958), now a cult classic of its B-movie kind. But the next year he received a Best Supporting Actor Oscar nomination for *The Young Philadelphians*; and the year after *that* came his career-boosting turn as one of *The Magnificent Seven*.

However, *the* Man from U.N.C.L.E., Napoleon Solo, was rapidly overtaken in popularity by a fellow agent, the Russian Illya Kuryakin, who had been given just four lines in "The Vulcan Affair." Kuyakin was personified by David McCallum,[19] a young and then little-known (in America, where he had only just arrived) Scottish-born actor. McCallum's blond boyish good looks formed a cool contrast to the dark and masterful Vaughn. There was also the matter of fashion sense. Richard Meyers: "Illya had a habit of wearing turtlenecks instead of a shirt and tie [unlike the conservative Solo]. What started as a character trait soon blossomed into a fad and then a sartorial staple. A poster depicting Illya in his turtleneck and pointing the U.N.CL.E. gun became one of the sixties' best-sellers."[20] On a more "geopolitical" level, Kuryakin's Russian nationality helped *The Man from U.N.C.L.E.* rise above or at least sideline the Cold War and catch the more "positive-wavey" mood of the time.

The U.N.C.L.E. equivalent of M was the droll and tweedy Englishman Alexander Waverley, played by the droll and tweedy English actor Leo G. (for George) Carroll.[21] Alias "The Professor" spymaster in Hitchcock's *North by Northwest* (1959), Carroll was a Hitchcock stalwart who had already gained a measure of TV fame as [Cosmo] *Topper* (1953–55: 78 episodes). He was the center of gravitas in what could sometimes descend into a farrago of nonsense. His only complaint, cited by Richard Meyers: "I'm stuck behind a table all the time! All I do once a week is press a couple of buttons to send the agents on their way." But there is no such thing as a small part, only small-minded actors, and Carroll did not play down Mr. Waverley. "Classy and charming" (*TV Guide*).

Robert Vaughn explained the basic *Man from U.N.C.L.E.* setup in his autobiography, *A Fortunate Life*[22]: "There would be an opening scene or two to serve as a teaser, often involving an ambush or attack by [T.H.R.U.S.H]. Then Illya and I would be shown strolling into a nondescript tailor shop [Del Floria's] on a side street near the United Nations building. The mustachioed Italian tailor would tap twice on the handle of his pressing machine, opening up the back wall of the shop and revealing the hidden entrance to U.N.C.L.E. headquarters."[23] Vaughn also told how Solo and Karyakin would contact Mr. Waverly by activating their "Open Channel D" pen phones. And just about every episode ended with an elaborate, gadget-ridden chase scene (often in an "exotic" studio-backlot city).

It would be impractical—and unnecessary—to provide plot summaries of all 105 episodes, which are available online (IMDb) and in *The Man from U.N.C.L.E. Book*. As Robert Vaughn explained, all the scripts were constructed to a basic formula that allowed for only the occasional random variable. *U.N.C.L.E.* was, essentially, a triumph of insouciant style over a solidly built substance. "The Project Strigas Affair" (November 24, 1964) is particularly memorable for marking the first appearance together of William Shatner (1931–: Michael Donfield) and Leonard Nimoy (1931–2015: Vladek) before *Star Trek* (NBC: September 8, 1966, to September 2, 1969). MGM and Arena were aware that *The Man from U.N.C.L.E.* could be profitably transferred from the small screen to the big screen. However, tight schedules precluded simultaneous production, so they cobbled together feature-film versions of mainly two-part episodes, with additional footage to reach the necessary running time (130 + minutes). Including *To Trap a Spy* (see above), eight such films were made for both the home and foreign markets. All of them did respectable box-office business and also looked good against some more expensive competitors, e.g., the "Matt Helm" franchise. Sam Rolfe received a "developer" writing credit (as per usual).

The Spy with My Face (UK release date: August 16, 1965). Adapted from "The Double Affair": (November 17, 1964). Director: John Newland (1917–2000). Writers: Joseph Calvelli (1920–1983); Clyde Ware (1930: 2010). Supporting cast: Senta Berger: Serena; Michael Evans (1920–2007: Darius Two); Sharon Farrell (1940–: Sandy Wister); Harold Gould (1923–2010: Doctor).

One Spy Too Many (U.S. release date: February 28, 1966). Adapted from "The Alexander the Great Affair" (September 17, 1965, and September 24, 1965). Director: Joseph Sargent. Writer: Dean Hargrove (1938–). Supporting cast: Rip Torn (1931–2019: Alexander); Dorothy Provine (1935–2010: Tracey Alexander); Yvonne Craig (1937–2015: Maude Waverley: Alexander's daughter).

One of Our Spies Is Missing (U.S. release date: July 29, 1966). Adapted from "The Bridge of Lions Affair" (February 4, 1966, and February 11, 1966). Director: E. Darrell Hallenbeck (1922–1987). Writers: Howard Rodman (1920–1985); Henry Slesar (1927–2002: story). Supporting cast: Maurice Evans (1901–1989: Sir Norman Swickert); Vera Miles (1929– : Madame Raine De Sala); Bernard Fox (1927–2016: Jordin).

The Spy in the Green Hat (U.S. release date: February 3, 1967). Adapted from "The Concrete Overcoat Affair" (November 25, 1966, and December 2, 1966). Director: Joseph Sargent. Writers: Peter Allan Fields (1935–2019); David Victor (1910–1989: story). Supporting cast: Jack Palance (1919–2006: Louis Strago); Janet Leigh (1927–2004: Miss Diketon); Eduardo Ciannelli (1889–1969: Arturo "Fingers" Stilletto); Allen Jenkins (1900–1974: Enzo "Pretty" Stilletto); Jack La Rue (1902–1984: Frederico "Feet" Stilletto); Joan Blondell (1906–1979: Mrs. "Fingers" Stilletto).

The Karate Killers (Japanese release date: July 22, 1967). Adapted from "The Five Daughters Affair" (March 31, 1967, and April 7, 1967). Director: Barry Shear (1923–1979). Writers: Norman Hudis; Boris Ingster (1903–1978). Supporting cast: Joan Crawford (1904–1977: Amanda True); Curd (Curt) Jurgens (1915–1982: Carl Von Kesser): Herbert Lom (Randolph); Telly Savalas (1922–1994: Count Valeriano De Fanzini); Terry-Thomas (1911–1990: Constable); Jill Ireland (1936–1990: Imogen Smythe); Kim Darby (1947– : Sandy True); Philip Ahn (Sazami Kyushu).

How to Steal the World (U.S. release date: March 7, 1968). Adapted from: "The Seven Wonders of the World Affair" (January 8, 1968, and January 15, 1968). Director: Sutton Roley (1922–2007). Writer: Norman Hudis. Supporting cast: Barry Sullivan (1912–1994: Dr. Robert Kingsley); Eleanor Parker (1922–2013: Margitta Kingsley); Leslie Nielsen (1926–2010: General Maximillian Harmon); Tony Bill (1940–: Steven Garrow); Peter Mark Richman (1927–2021: Mr. Webb); Albert Paulsen (1925–2004: Dr. Kurt Erikson); Hugh Marlowe (1911–1982: Grant); Dan O'Herlihy (1919–2005: Professor David Garrow); Ruth Warrick (1916–2005: Alice Garrow).

The Helicopter Spies (U.S. release date: June 21, 1968). Adapted from "The Prince of Darkness Affair" (October 2, 1967, and October 9, 1967). Director: Boris Sagal (1923–1981). Writer: Dean Hargrove. Supporting cast: Carol Lynley (1942–2019: Annie); Bradford Dillman (1930–2018: Luther Sebastian); Lola Albright (1924–2017: Azalea); John Dehner (1915–1992: Dr; Parviz Kharmusi); John Carradine (Third-Way Priest); Julie London (1926–2000: Laurie Sebastian); H.M. Wynant (1927– : The Aksoy Brothers).

Terry Carr (1937–1987), a science fiction writer and senior editor at Ace Books, approached Michael Avallone (q.v.) in late 1964 with the idea of writing a *Man from U.N.C.L.E.* tie-in novelization. The series hadn't really taken off at this point and Avallone was offered only a $1,000 flat fee to write the book—which he did, in a single December day! Ace had paid MGM/Arena $6,000 for the rights to what they saw as a one-shot production. However, *The Man from U.N.C.L.E.* (1965: to be reprinted as #1: *The Thousand Coffins Affair*) eventually sold several million copies at home and in sixty foreign-language editions. It was Avallone's first TV—rather than movie-based—novelization, and although receiving no royalties for any of those sales, he went on to write a whole lot more over the years. Avallone had hopefully written a follow-up *U.N.C.L.E.* novel, entitled *The THRUSH and the Eagles Affair*, which he abandoned when Ace contracted with other writers instead (but see below). The British edition of *The Man from U.N.C.L.E.* (also *sans* the *Thousand Coffins* tag-title) was published simultaneously in hardcover by Souvenir Press and in paperback by The New English Library/Four Square Books (September 1965).

U.N.C.L.E. #1 led to a complicated chain reaction. From Kurt Peer's *TV Tie-Ins: A Bibliography of American TV Tie-In Paperbacks*[24]: "A shared arrangement allowed each publisher to sign writers from its own country for the first printings, and to buy the reprint rights for the existing books from the other publisher. Thus, Souvenir Press signed Britons Peter Leslie [q.v.], John T. Phillifent [1916–1976], John Oram

[1906–1992], and Joel Bernard [no relation to the present-day American author of the same name], and bought from Ace the reprint rights for the American books by veteran Harry Whittington [1915–1989], newcomer David McDaniel [q.v.], and Avallone. Of the 16 Souvenir Press books, 11 were originals and five were reprints of American editions. Of the 23 Ace books, 12 were originals, and 11 were reprints of the British editions."[25] For example: Phillifent, a British science fiction author who often used the pseudonym John Rackham, wrote *The Mad Scientist Affair* (1966), *The Corfu Affair* (1967), and *The Power Cube Affair* (1968).

The first three American and British titles were published in the same order: Avallone's *The Man from U.N.C.L.E.*; *The Doomsday Affair* (1965), by Harry Whittington; *The Copenhagen Affair* (1965). As a matter of bibliographical interest, the Four Square edition of *Copenhagen* went through eight printings between January and March. Then the international sequences diverge. One example will be enough. USA #4 = *The Dagger Affair* (1965), by David McDaniel; UK #4 = *The Stone Cold Dead in the Market Affair* (1966), by John Oram, published as #22 (1969) in the USA. Seven American titles—numbers 10 to 15 and 17—did not see UK publication at that time. McDaniel coined the acronym for THRUSH (see above) in *The Dagger Affair*. In *Masters of Adventure: James Bond and His Rivals*,[26] Don D'Ammassa reported that *The Final Affair* (McDaniel, again) was circulated around U.N.C.L.E. fandom, but never officially published. Also: "*The Malthusian Affair* appeared more recently in an undated edition with no author or publisher listed, not even a copyright notice. It is said to be the novelization of the screenplay by Sam Rolfe for a proposed 1979 reunion movie that was never made."[27]

The *Men* from U.N.C.L.E. (including equal-partner Ilya Kuryakin) books are not "novelizations" in the formal sense of that term, but original novels bearing no relation to any broadcast teleplays. They run the gamut from prosaic espionage to the most flamboyant spy-fi, often in the very same volume! Avallone had set the template with *Thousand Coffins*. He also created a Fleming-type villain named Golgotha, otherwise known as The Man with the Skull: "It was exactly one hour since he had recovered in the dungeon room to find himself shamed and disgraced. By the reckoning of the account from the guards, the man Solo and his lady confederate [Geraldine Terry: "Jerry Terry"] had escaped in the MIG, sometime in that elapsed period of sixty minutes. Even the intricate system of alarm bells had been fruitless. Obviously, this Solo was a resourceful man."[28]

U.N.C.L.E. also spun off other significant publications. *The Man from U.N.C.L.E. Magazine* was conceived by Leo Margulies (q.v.). Philip Sherman: "A license agreement between Metro-Goldwyn-Mayer, Inc. (MGM) and Leo Margulies Corporation (LMC) was signed on October 1, 1965. It concerned *The Man from U.N.C.L.E.* television series, scheduled for broadcast in the 1967–1968 season. The license granted LMC the right to publish a monthly 'pocket-sized soft-cover fiction magazine,' using '*The Man from U.N.C.L.E.*' as its name. The agreement required the stories be approved by the legal department of MGM, to avoid infringement with stories by Ian Fleming, the originator of *The Man from U.N.C.L.E.* The outline of each story needed MGM's prior approval. In some cases, authors would send outlines to the company."[29] The 24 issues featured a "NEW FULL LENGTH U.N.C.L.E. NOVEL" by Robert Hart Davis—actually a house name used by several writers. Margulies might or might not have been trying to set up a subliminal link with the distinguished British publisher Rupert Hart-Davis (1907–1999), who had helped establish Ray Bradbury's literary reputation in the UK. They ran from February 1966 (*The Howling Teenagers Affair*, by Dennis Lynds) to January 1968 (*The Million Monsters Affair*, by I.G. Edmonds).

Whitman published three *Man from U.N.C.L.E.* titles in their venerable Big Little Book "juvenile" series: *The Affair of the Gentle Saboteur* (1966) and *The Affair of the Gunrunners' Gold* (1967), both by Brandon Keith (?), and *The Calcutta Affair* (1966), by George S. Elrick (1921–1997). Walter B. (*The Shadow*) Gibson wrote *The Coin of Diablo Affair*,[30] an oversized (8" × 11") 48-page chapbook, with a photographic front cover and interior line drawings by I.H. Guyer. Gold Key Comics acquired the rights to *Man from U.N.CL.E.*, publishing 22 titles between 1965 and 1969. Michael Richardson dealt with the UK side of things in "The Man from U.N.C.L.E. Spin-Offs" (*Book and Magazine Collector* No. 59, February 1989). WDL (World Distributors, Ltd.) issued their first Christmas "annual"—an old British yuletide tradition—in 1966. Other annuals followed, in 1968 and 1969.

The Man from U.N.C.L.E. ended on a high note with "The Seven Wonders of the World Affair": Part Two (see above). In general, however, the series had become the parodic opposite of its original hard-edged but essentially soft-hearted self. The obligatory gadgets went from the sublime—radio transponder pens (plausible enough)—to the ridiculous—ice-lollipop grenades (in "The Suburbia Affair": January 6, 1967). Solo and Kuryakin drove an AMT Piranha sports coupé that rivaled 007's Aston Martin DB5 for super-duper optional extras. Farewell fadeout. But *U.N.C.L.E.* did not go gently into that good night of reruns and syndication....

Return of the Man from U.N.C.L.E., a 96-minute TV movie, was first broadcast by CBS on April 5, 1983. Leo G. Carroll having passed away nine years before, the new Number One of Section I, Sir John Raleigh (perhaps a lineal descendant of Sir Walter), was played by another English-gentlemanly actor—Patrick (John Steed) Macnee. Mr. Waverley's photograph is, however, on prominent display here and there. Section II (Enforcement and Intelligence) has also undergone some drastic personnel changes, with the early retirement into civilian life of its onetime key agents Napoleon Solo and Illya Kuryakin. Solo has since become a "Napoleon" of the computer industry, while Kuryakin—who left U.N.C.L.E. with a professional "black mark" against him—is now an internationally famous fashion designer! THRUSH had been much stricken in the preceding fifteen years. Now one of its many splinter groups has decided to mount a comeback in the grand old style—possibly having seen a re-release of *Thunderball*. They have stolen a powerful new thermonuclear bomb (code-named H957) and demanded $350,000,000 for its safe return—to be delivered by none other than Napoleon Solo. Sir John presses Napoleon—and the even more reluctant Ilya—back into the service of their ever-loving U.N.C.L.E. George Lazenby makes an effective cameo appearance as a white-tuxedoed and Aston Martin–driving character called "J.B.": *On Her Majesty's Secret Service*, revisited.

Halfway through the second season, MGM/Arena decided to produce a spin-off series—*The Girl from U.N.C.L.E.* Women in the "mainline" series were either eye-candy secretaries, fatal THRUSH females, or innocent broads abroad—never *ever* fully operational agents. Norman Felton took the name "April Dancer" from Ian Fleming's original concept of a "Miss Moneypenny" for the M-type character in his aborted *Solo* proposal. An installment of the parent show, "The Moonglow Affair" (Season 2, Episode 23: February 25, 1966), served as the pilot episode. April Dancer—a "girl" aged 24—was initially played by Mary Ann Mobley (1937–2014), a former Miss America from Biloxi, Mississippi. Norman Fell (1924–1998) took the role of her older-and-wiser partner, Mark Slate.

The plot—such as it is—opens with Napoleon and Ilya rendered *hors de combat* by a "quartzite radiation projector" while investigating a THRUSH plot to sabotage the American space program. Mr. Waverley assigns April Dancer, the first trainee U.N.CL.E. Enforcement Agent to the case, with the help of Mark Slate, who is apparently past the 40-year retirement age for field work. It would seem that Slate had also "mentored" Napoleon Solo, back in the day. For some good and sufficient reason, April turns fashion model to infiltrate the cosmetics firm run by Arthur Caresse (played by Kevin McCarthy: 1914–2010), but her cover is blown by his smarter sister, Jean Caresse (Mary Carver: 1924–2013). Against all odds, however, Dancer and Slate find the antidote, foil the foul scheme, and—of course—rescue Solo and Kuryakin. Suitably impressed, Mr. Waverley teams them up on a regular basis—but not before ordering Slate to correct the "typographical error" in the age box of his U.N.C.L.E. personnel file. N.B. "Moonglow" is the name of a Caresse lipstick that glows in the dark.

On the insistence of NBC, however, the part of April Dancer was recast for the actual *Girl from U.N.C.LE.* TV series, with Stefanie Powers[31] playing the role as a more confident and experienced agent. Kathleen Crighton: "With her long red hair and slender build, Powers typified the hip, trendy look that was coming into fashion. [She] wore bright-coloured miniskirts, go-go boots, and berets" (*Epi-Log Journal* #13, February 1994). Mark Slate, in his turn, was redefined as a much younger and "swinging" Englishman, played by Noel Harrison (1934–2013)—the son of Rex (*My Fair Lady*) Harrison (1908–1990). "Harrison was British—it was very trendy to be British in the heyday of the Beatles—and had a singing career. His Slate adopted a Carnaby Street look, wearing such popular fashions as corduroy suits, turtlenecks, and jaunty hats" (*ibid.*).

The effectively second pilot episode of *Girl from U.N.C.L.E.*, "The Dog-Gone Affair," was telecast on September 13, 1966. Sam Rolfe received his "developer" credit throughout the 29-episode run. Abandon common sense, all ye who enter here. THRUSH operative Apollo Zakinthius (Kurt Kasznar) plans to test Apathane—a drug that causes people to move in slow-motion mode—on a Greek island. April Dancer and Mark Slate are sent to stop him—along with a dachshund called Putzi whose fleas carry the antidote. Mark strikes up a professional acquaintance with the beautiful Tuesday Hajadakis, played by Luciana Paluzzi. Meantime, April loses Putzi. She is duly captured and hung over a pit full of piranhas that THRUSH has provided for just such a purpose. But sometimes nothing succeeds like excess, and that is certainly the case with "The Mother Muffin Affair" (September 27, 1966). Mark Slate being otherwise engaged somewhere, April is partnered by Napoleon Solo for this assignment in London. Guest star Boris Karloff hams it up in drag as the eccentrically evil Agnes Tewksbury, aka Mother Muffin, assisted by Rodney Babcock (fellow Hollywood Englishman Bernard Fox). Emulating Vincent Price in *House of Wax* (1953), Mother also wants to make "real" waxwork figures of the pesky U.N.C.L.E. agents.

Noel Harrison followed in his father's musical-theater footsteps as Mark Slate, doing a "Henry Higgins" impression in "The Galatea Affair" (September 30, 1966). April Dancer being busy elsewhere, Slate teams up with Illya Kuryakin, Napoleon Solo having caught pneumonia from an impromptu dip in a Venetian canal. Slate's part of the assignment is to transform Rosy Shlagenheimer (born in Brooklyn: "father a butcher, mother a lady wrestler"), whom we first meet performing her specialty "Lady Godiva" routine, into the Baroness Bibi De Chasseur. Don't ask why. Rosy/Barbara is impeccably overplayed by Joan (*Dynasty*) Collins. Napoleon Solo recovers quickly enough to make a last-minute cameo appearance.

Kathleen Crighton, hitting the nail right on the head: "In reality (but then, this show bore no resemblance to reality), you had to wonder how a bimbo like the April Dancer we saw in the show ever got through her basic training with U.N.C.L.E., much less kept her job. Camp was all the rage, and [*Girl*] was camp to the hilt." *The Girl from U.N.C.L.E.* bowed out with "The Kooky Spook Affair" (April 11, 1967), an enjoyably whimsical piece about Mark Slate inheriting a haunted castle in England and having to fend off disgruntled relatives. Meanwhile April Dancer hunts for a THRUSH assassin who is lurking about the ancestral pile. The ever-delightful Estelle Winwood (1883–1984) is played Lady Bramwich. Stefanie Powers would go on to much more substantial TV success with *Hart to Hart* (1979–84), while Noel Harrison resumed his musical career.

In paperback-book terms, *Girl* followed the example of its male counterpart, but for Signet, this time, and on a much smaller scale. Appropriately enough, as New American Library had long been Ian Fleming's mass-market publisher in the USA. Michael Avallone's rejected *Man from U.N.C.L.E.* novel, *The THRUSH and the Eagles Affair* (see above) was rushed into print as the first *Girl* tie-in, retitled *The Birds of a Feather Affair* (September 1966). From the very much of its time back-cover blurb: "She moves with trained-to-kill reflexes, clicks with an IBM brain.

She's cool, ingenious, and sexy as all get-out. She's a pro from the top of her beautiful head to the tip of her chemically painted toenails. She's Mr. Waverly's right-hand girl and her heart belongs to U.N.C.L.E. Watch her infiltrate the ranks of THRUSH as she tries to reach kidnapped Mark Slate, an U.N.C.L.E. agent who's being held for ransom that's too high to pay. See her in action—5 ft. 5 inches … 108 lbs. of dynamite…. U.N.C.L.E.'s newest weapon…. APRIL DANCER." Chapter 1, "What the Girl Is," concludes:

> In the morning, she'd check out of the hotel, having no further need of her cover as Agnes Malloy, dress buyer from Chicago, Illinois. She could return to her own little apartment downtown and resume her identity as Miss April Dancer.
> U.N.C.L.E. needed women agents, too. If a female enemy agent walked into the powder room, April Dancer could follow her.
> Not even her working partner Mark Slate could do that.

The Blazing Affair (#2), also by Avallone, followed in October 1966. He then wrote *The Devil Down Under Affair,* but Signet had decided to publish no more tie-in titles for a visibly sinking TV series. Avallone did contribute a possibly linked series of espionage stories to *The Saint Magazine,* featuring David Seven, The Man from INTREX (International Trade Experts—perhaps an affiliate of Universal Exports): "Seven of INTREX" (September 1966); "Send a Man from INTREX" (January 1967); "Seven Miles from INTREX" (May 1967); "Address: INTREX, Saigon" (October 1967). Three other *Girl from U.N.C.L.E.* tie-ins were published by Souvenir Press/ Four Square in the UK, where the program had struck a more sympathetic chord. *Birds of a Feather* was relegated to second place in the running order, behind *The Global Globules Affair* (1967), a very "British" novel by Simon Latter. They passed on *The Blazing Affair,* for whatever reason—its trite neo–Nazi storyline, perhaps. The remaining two novels followed the lead of *Global Globules,* with April Dancer and Mark Slate coming to bear a closer and increasingly unflattering resemblance to Modesty Blaise and Willy Garvin. Simon Latter returned for *The Golden Boats of Taradata Affair* and Peter Leslie wrote *The Cornish Pixie Affair* (ditto).

Leo Margulies had another go with *The Girl from U.N.CL.E. Magazine,* but it was only an anemic clone of its parent periodical. Once again, all of the seven "new complete book-length" novels were attributed to Robert Hart Davis, from December 1966 (*The Sheik of Araby Affair,* by Richard Deming) to December 1967 (*The Sinister Satellite Affair,* by I.G. Edmonds). Gold Key produced five *Girl from U.N.C.L.E.* comic books, from February 1967 ("The Fatal Accidents Affair") to October 1967 ("The Harem-Scarem Affair"). World Distributors, Ltd., published the first of their three *Girl from U.N.C.L.E.* annuals in time for Christmas. It included some useful articles for the female readership, e.g., "Pretty Long" (hairstyling) and "The Way to Mark's Heart" (cookery). Of more general interest is the CONFIDENTIAL FILE ON U.N.C.L.E. AGENTS (#17337/225).

The Man from U.N.C.L.E's ABC of Espionage is a nonfiction book published in 1966 by Ace (October) and Souvenir Press/Four Square (November). John Hill

(?) received an author credit on the Ace edition's front cover, but only a copyright notice (John Hill Productions, Ltd.) in the British editions. The "unreal life" Napoleon and Ilya contributed an autographed foreword, which ends, "When you read these facts—and they are all *true facts*, not fiction—you will be studying details that are also recorded in the files of the CIA, MI5, and Deuxième Bureau." Neither one of the U.N.C.L.E. TV series held anywhere near firm to those lofty ideals—especially *Girl*, which—unlike *Man*—had been deliberately modeled after the "high camp" *Batman* TV series (January 12, 1966, to March 14, 1968). The great original *Man from U.N.C.L.E.* was canceled after only sixteen episodes of the third season, in December 1967. But the series has left an indelible mark upon the wide, wild world of popular culture.

Midway through the *U.N.C.L.E.* run, Robert Vaughn had starred in the MGM film version of Helen (Clark) MacInnes's bestselling novel *The Venetian Affair*,[32] by Helen MacInnes (1934–2013). Producer-director: Jerry Thorpe (1926–2018). MacInnes co-wrote the screenplay, with E. Jack Neuman (1921–1998). Vaughn plays an ex–CIA agent, Bill Fenner, who is now an embittered freelance journalist. Boris Karloff steals the film as Dr. Pierre Vaugiroud. *Venetian* had nothing to fear from at least the minor "entertainments" of Graham Greene; it should have justified the hoary old "major motion picture" hype-work. But it was made as a TV movie, indifferently directed, and most of the long novel's intricate storyline and subtle characterization could not be squeezed into just 89 minutes running time. The very title might have misled some cinemagoers into expecting another Napoleon and Ilya mini-epic. It doesn't rate even a passing reference in Vaughn's otherwise thorough autobiography.

Four years after *U.N.C.L.E.* folded, Vaughn signed up to play the part of security agent "Harry Rule" in a British half-hour TV series called *The Protectors* (52 episodes: September 29, 1972, to March 15, 1974). It was produced for Lew Grade's ITC by Gerry Anderson (1929–2012), who made such "Supermarionation" puppet series as *Joe 90* (1968–69) and *The Secret Service* (1969: partly live-action), which are of some espionage interest. Harry Rule worked with regular cast members Nyree Dawn Porter (1936–2001: Contessa Caroline di Contini) and Tony Anholt (1941–2002: Paul Buchet). Novelization: *The Protectors*,[33] written by Robert Miall, actually John Burke (q.v.). Robert Sellers: "Vaughn was under no illusion as to why he'd been cast in *The Protectors*. 'I didn't see Harry Rule as anything other than a variation of *The Man from U.N.C.L.E.*'s Napoleon Solo.' Nor was he enamored of the scripts. 'I couldn't understand them when I read them. I couldn't understand them when I did them. I never understood them when I saw them on the air.'"[34]

The Protectors represented one more desperate attempt by Lew Grade to produce an ITC series that could rival the international success of ATV's *The Avengers*. But at least he still had *The Saint* and *Danger Man/Secret Agent* to fall back on.

David McCallum starred in the 1970 spy-fi TV movie *Hauser's Memory*, based upon the 1968 novel by Curt Siodmak (1902–2000). It was a thematic sequel to the author's classic *Donovan's Brain* (1943), but without its central character, Dr. Patrick

Cory. Director: Boris Sagal. Writer: Adrian Spies (1920–1998). CIA agent Joseph Slaughter (Leslie Nielsen) persuades biochemist Hillel Mondoro (McCallum) to inject himself with the cerebrospinal fluid extracted from Karl Hauser, a dying East German scientist who has defected to the West. This fluid contains RNA—ribonucleic acid—in which memory is (supposedly) stored. Hauser knows all about a new Russian anti-missile missile system. But it is not only Hauser's *scientific* memory that will be transferred.

McCallum also starred in the short-lived (thirteen episodes) 1975–76 American make-over of *The Invisible Man*, as immaterial scientist Dr. Daniel Westin. From *The Encyclopedia of TV Science Fiction*,[35] by Roger Fulton: "In the pilot TV film [May 6, 1975], Westin discovers how to make himself invisible and must then try to keep the secret from unscrupulous agents who want to use it as a means of achieving world power. He has a friend Nick Maggio [Henry Darrow: 1933–2021] who makes a lookalike mask for him to wear so that he can appear in public (and we can get to see the star once in a while). In the series, Westin and his visible wife Kate [Melinda Fee: 1942–2020] take on various assignments for the government such as testing out a security system ['The Fine Art of Diplomacy': December 15, 1975]."

The Invisible Man faded out with "An Attempt to Save Face" (January 26, 1976). Michael Jahn (1943–) novelized the pilot episode for Gold Medal. A quasi-remake, *Gemini Man*, starring Ben Murphy (1942–) took its place—but not for long (September 23, 1976, to October 28, 1976). In more recent years, McCallum has played pathologist Donald ("Ducky") Mallard in *NCIS* (Naval Criminal Investigation Service), the CBS TV series, from 2001 until the time of writing.

Man + Girl from U.N.C.L.E. inspired two rival espionage-related TV series—*I Spy* and *Mission: Impossible*. There had been a 39-episode anthology series entitled *I Spy* (1955–56), hosted by Raymond Massey (1898–1983) as Anton, the Spymaster. But the new *I Spy* (NBC/Sheldon Leonard/Desilu Productions) was a case of "and now for something completely different" (to purloin a *Monty Python* catchphrase). Working title: *Danny Doyle*. It ran for 82 hour-long episodes, from September 15, 1965 ("So Long Patrick Henry") to April 15, 1968 ("Pinwheel").

Robert Culp[36] played Kelly Robinson, a Princeton law graduate turned SSA (Special Services Agency) operative who worked undercover as a peripatetic tennis pro. His fellow agent/trainer-coach, Alexander Scott (Rhodes scholarship alumnus and expert linguist), was played by Bill Cosby.[37] They shared the code name Domino. By that time, Culp was a TV veteran, having starred in the western series *Trackdown* (CBS/Four Star: 1957–58), as Texas Ranger Hobey Gilman, and appeared in several live-drama productions. Cosby was then best-known as a stand-up comedian and recording artist. More controversially, however, he had become the first Afro-American actor to star in an American prime-time dramatic series. A risky move, considering that *The Nat King Cole Show* was dropped in 1958 because it had failed to find a sponsor. Jon E. Lewis and Penny Stempel: "Solutions to the delicate points of black/white relations were overcome in many ways. Culp's Kelly tended to be in command (as Don Johnson would be in *Miami Vice* some twenty years later when working with black actor Philip Michael Thomas); the series [mostly] took place not in the States but [usually] in foreign lands; and Cosby's Scott was well dressed, well spoken and assimilated. He was also presented as less sexual and less of a ladies' man than Culp although he did appear opposite black women such as Cicely Tyson, Nancy Wilson and Gloria Foster."[38]

Lewis and Stempel (continued) : "Cosby won three Emmys for his role. Arriving during an era of intense racial turmoil, *I Spy* projected a vision of black and white harmony. It set a precedent for televisual inter-racial male bonding." Culp and Cosby became fast friends; apart from delivering the carefully scripted lines, they kept up an informal flow of flummery that—like Napoleon Solo and Ilya Kuryakin— helped them rise above the usual robotic "G-man at work" level. Typical quote:

> COSBY: "Has anyone told you how good you look in that?"
> CULP: "Why, no...."
> COSBY: "Well, if they do, smack 'em in the face real fast, because they're not your
> friend."

I Spy scored heavily over *Man* and *Girl from U.N.C.L.E.* in its extensive location shooting, not relying overmuch upon familiar studio backlots. For example: "Bridge of Spies" (September 11, 1966). Director: Alf Kjellin (1920–1988). Writer: Stephen Kandel (1927–). Location: Italy. Plot: "A beautiful tour guide, a handsome tennis pro and the romantic city of Venice would make for an intimate friendship if the tour guide didn't like to slip knives between men's ribs" (IMDb). Culp himself wrote the first episode (see above), plus: "The Loser" (October 10, 1965); "The Court of the Lion" (February 2, 1966), also directed; "The Tiger" (May 1, 1966); "The War Lord" (January 2, 1967); "Magic Mirror" (March 15, 1967); "Home to Judgment" (August 8, 1968), for which he received an Outstanding Writing Achievement Emmy Award nomination. Like its avuncular counterpart, *I Spy* was converted into a series of paperback tie-in novels (from Popular Library) unrelated to any existing teleplays. Unlike *U.N.C.L.E.*, however, they were all written by one person—Walter Wager, under his personal pseudonym of Walter Wager. *I Spy. Masterstroke, Superkill, Wipeout, Countertrap,* and *Doomdate* appeared in 1967; *Death-Twist* followed in 1968.

Walter Herman Wager (1924–2004) was born in the Bronx, New York City. Educated at Columbia College, graduating in 1944, he earned a Harvard Law School degree three years later. Wager passed the bar exams but chose not to practice, instead taking a master's degree in aviation law from Northwestern University, Chicago. He was then awarded a Fulbright fellowship and spent a year at the Sorbonne (the University of Paris). It wasn't long before Wager developed a freelance writing career with *Playbill* and *Show* magazines. His first novel, *Death Hits the Jackpot* (1954) was a paperback original, under the John Tiger pseudonym. Its plot concerned money stolen from an OSS courier killed in Madrid during the Second World War, with the money surfacing at a Chicago casino in 1953. The now–CIA is quickly on the case. Wager also contributed scripts to the TV series *America after Dark* (1957). Kurt Peer: "Wager was already a fan of [*I Spy*] when he was contacted by former college chum James A. Bryans, Editor-in-Chief at Popular Library, who asked him to do [a tie-in] book. It worked, and the six sequels followed."[39]

Wager's tie-in work for *I Spy* went above and beyond the usual novelization call of duty. He fleshed out the characterizations and beefed up the technical detail. David Spencer, cited in *TV Tie-Ins*: "Such deliberate changes enhanced and made TV tie-ins unique unto their own right in very special cases, as with Walter Wager's *I Spy* books. Creating detailed backstory for the leads, identifying their employer as the CIA (the series never did; in one episode they answered to the 'State Department' and in the 1994 reunion TV-movie Kelly had become head of an unidentified government espionage branch that was pointedly *not* the CIA); giving them a boss, the pudgy, square-but-not-stupid Carolinian Donald Mars; codenaming them 'Domino,' etc. added richness, depth, and a lore that, because it was so evocative, occasionally seems missing from the episodes when they're watched anew."

I Spy the novel posits a polyglot group called Force I with the aim to scramble the minds of key personnel in the Pentagon. Force I—now renamed Force One— make a world-domination comeback in *Superkill*. A mad scientist who has invented a Great Whatsit that can destroy all life on Earth in *Wipeout*; the Domino duo are also up against an equally megalomaniacal Caribbean dictator. ODESSA, the Nazi Old Boy Network, makes malevolent in *Doomdate*. The recipe for *Death-Twist* consists of a "deluxe suspense kit containing 1 master-villain, 1 South American mini-nation, 1 lethal maxi-plot, 2 supergirls—and the high-test team from *I SPY*" (blurb).

But they were all put in the shade by *I Spy #2: Masterstroke*. It really *could* have been page-by-page and word-for-word filmed. Wager's prefatory note is a harbinger of the jaunty style to come: "Everything and everybody in this book is pure fiction. There is no such place as Red China, no such thing as a hydrogen bomb and no U.S. government branch called the Central Intelligence Agency. Every word, character and event herein is pure fantasy—except for those a trifle impure, for which the author apologizes." Back-cover blurb: "A brilliant madman has invented a foolproof, detection-proof scheme to bring America and its allies to their knees with one press of a button. He calls it: MASTERSTROKE. The only men with a faint chance of stopping MASTERSTROKE are Kelly Robinson, whose ne'er-do-well charm hides a nerve of steel, and Alexander Scott, the quipster with a computer mind—the I SPY team. Their one slim—but well-rounded clue—a redheaded Chinese beauty, recent companion of the enemy mastermind, who shows a suspicious yen for Kelly.... Meantime, the hand moves toward the button that activated MASTERSTROKE." From chapter 1:

> His name was Kelly Robinson. He had formerly been an international champion on both clay and grass courts, and now he travelled around the world as a charming, sophisticated "tennis bum." He was actually more than that, although few people knew it. He was one half of something called "Domino."

The other American male with him on the cruiser was a husky crew-cut Negro from Philadelphia, an ex–All Eastern football player and former Rhodes Scholar who could speak eleven languages. His name was Alexander Scott, and for nearly six years he'd been winging and swinging around the globe as Kelly Robinson's trainer and companion. Scott was the other half of "Domino," which was the codename for this secret "operation team" of the Central Intelligence Agency. Playing at tournaments in Tokyo and Cairo and Paris was merely a convenient cover for their espionage missions.[40]

Enter Wager's very own M: " [Donald] Mars, a stocky smooth-faced civil servant with a pleasant South Carolina accent, had a genuine talent for names. He had chosen 'Domino' for this team, and he had picked the pseudonym 'Mars' for himself. As a senior executive in the Central Intelligence Agency, he was allowed to indulge in such imaginative sports. He was a tidy, dedicated, cheerfully compulsive man who'd been in the cloak-and-dagger business since 1942."[41]

Kelly Robinson *does* take a leaf or three out of 007's playbook in chapter 10:

He took her in his arms, and he kissed her full on her moving hungry lips for at least thirty seconds. Then he kissed her again, and Dolly Chan pressed as tightly against his chest as she could. She felt the flickering begin somewhere deep inside her as her womanly wanting challenged her rational controls.

"You have plied me with kindness and liquor, you charming rat," she accused as she stroked his jaw.

"Spooks play dirty," Robinson confessed. His hand was moving down her back; she shivered.

"You are an unethical, unspeakable, handsome...." She paused, groping for a word.

"Try 'civil servant.' I'm very civil and completely at your service," the intelligence agent replied—groping, but not for a word.[42]

Walter Wager "graduated" to writing such bestselling thrillers as *Viper Three* (1972), later filmed as *Twilight's Last Gleaming* (1977); *58 Minutes* (1987), transformed into the Bruce Willis (1955–) airport buster *Die Hard 2* (1990); *Telefon* (1975), suspensefully filmed under that same title in 1977.

I Spy didn't spawn a digest magazine à la the U.N.C.L.E.s. But there was a Whitman mini-hardback—*Message from Moscow* (1966), by Brandon Keith—which, sad to say, fell far beneath even their usual low literary and artistic bar. Gold Key issued six *I Spy* comic books. A "Special Racial Issue" of *Mad* magazine (#111, June 1967) featured a parody entitled "Why Spy?—Hang-Up in Hong Kong," taken from the "Caustic Agents Dept." Killy (Robert Culp) and Scout (Bill Cosby) search Hong Kong for a kidnapped atomic scientist who also happens to be a part-time swimsuit model. It was written by Stan Hart (1928–2017) and illustrated by Mort Drucker (1929–2020). Sample panel:

CHIEF: "Killy.... Scout ... as Secret Agents you are the only men who can handle this assignment."
KILLY: "What's that, Chief?"
CHIEF: "To make an hour show out of ten minutes worth of plot."

Culp and Cosby made a Robinson and Scott comeback in *I Spy Returns* (Citadel Entertainment/SAH Productions/Sheldon Leonard Enterprises: February 3,

1994). Director: Jerry London (1947–). Writers: Morton Fine; David Friedkin; Michael Norell (1937–). The 26-year time difference made it unfeasible for the agents to return in their original active-service capacities (as with Napoleon and Ilya). Kelly Robinson has long since given up international tennis-bumming to become a middle-rank administrator in the SSA. Alexander Scott is now a distinguished college professor. But when Bennett Robinson (George Newbern: 1964–) and Nicole Scott (Salli Richardson [-Whitfield]: 1967–) follow in their fathers' footsteps, the old warhorses decide to play a paternal role in their first field mission (looking after some endangered Russian scientists).

The third and longest-lasting of the "Big Three" American espionage-related TV series from the 1960s was *Mission: Impossible* (CBS: September 17, 1966, to September 8, 1973). It was created by Bruce Geller (1930–1978) for Desilu Productions (see *I Spy* above), which had been founded in 1951 by Desi Arnaz (1917–1986) and Lucille Ball (1911–1989) to produce their hit comedy show *I Love Lucy* (1951–57). Patrick J. White goes into the "how, when, what and why" of the IMF (Impossible Mission Force) in *The Complete Mission: Impossible Dossier*,[43] from which the foregoing citations have been taken. But Richard Meyers had already written a cut-to-the-chase overview:

> "Good morning, Mr. Briggs." Those four words were first spoken on September 17, 1966. For the first year the leader of [the IMF: Impossible Mission Force] was Dan (short for Daniel) Briggs, a quiet, dark-haired brain played by Steven Hill [1922–1996]. "This tape will self-destruct in five seconds" (classic climax line). Briggs would [then] select the agents needed for the assignment. [Usually]: Barney Collier, an electronics and engineering whizz (played by Greg Morris: 1933–1996). The role was originally conceived for a white man and Morris [jokingly] said he was cast because he was tall … and good. Willy Armitage was played by strongman Peter Lupus [1932–]. Cinnamon Carter [a fashion model] was Barbara Bain [1933–1996]. Man-of-disguise Rollin Hand, played by Bain's real-life husband, Martin Landau [1928–2017], initially was reserved for a few "special guest star" appearances.[44]

Indeed, *Mission: Impossible* seldom used brute force to help implement its elaborate con tricks, especially after the first season. Patrick J. White: "When [violence] was unavoidable, the IMF preferred to use a quick chop to the neck or a small 'slap needle' which, when applied, 'zapped' their opponents to sleep. The villain's demise (usually at the hands of his own people via IMF instigation) was generally performed off-camera, the sound of a gunshot telling us that our heroes had maneuvered the enemy into killing their own man." [However, the IMF frequently took what could be seen as the low moral ground.] "In *Mission: Impossible*, the end always justified the means. If they couldn't nail [someone] for something he did, they'd see to it that he was punished for something he didn't do, or something they made him do."[45]

The untitled pilot episode (unusually for that time, none of the *Mission: Impossible* episodes were ever given on-screen titles) opened as follows: "Good morning, Mr. Briggs. General Rio Dominguez, the dictator of Santa Costa, makes his headquarters in the Hotel Nationale. We've learned that two nuclear warheads furnished to Santa Costa by an enemy power [carefully unnamed] are contained in the hotel vault. Their use is imminent. Mr. Briggs, your mission, should you decide to accept it, would be to remove both nuclear devices from Santa Costa. As always, you have carte blanche [see above] as to method and personnel, but of course should you or any other member of your IM Force be caught or killed, the Secretary will disavow any knowledge of your actions. As usual, this recording will decompose one minute after the breaking of the seal. I hope it's welcome back, Dan. It's been a while."

The pilot episode also introduced Lalo Schifrin's once-heard-never-forgotten theme music. Boris Claude "Lalo" Schifrin was born in Buenos Aires, Argentina, on June 23, 1932. At the age of six, he began taking piano lessons from Enrique Barenboim, the father of renowned concert pianist and conductor Daniel Barenboim. Bruce Geller and Jack Hunsaker (1923–2018), the music supervisor at Desilu, both knew that music would be crucial in a dialogue-light TV series like *Mission: Impossible*—but even they were pleasantly surprised at the positive impact of Schifrin's aural contribution. Hunsaker (cited by Patrick J. White): *Mission*'s theme became one of television's most popular pieces of music, launched two soundtrack LPs, and set the tone for the entire series. One subtheme became almost as famous as the main title. The *Mission* March, with its snare drum and precise military tempo, "was used when we wanted to identify the *Mission* team,"[46]

The tape scene segued into another obligatory *Mission: Impossible* set piece—the team-selection process. Dan Briggs was next seen in his functional black-and-white apartment, where he perused a hefty "Impossible Missions Force" portfolio. Several photo-illustrated files are strewn over the coffee-table top, one by thoughtful one. White: "It was via this dossier scene that we learned all we would ever know about the operatives. A magazine clipping showed Willy Armitage lifting an enormous barbell; Barney Coller's dossier was a brochure for Collier Electronics and a close-up of its president; Cinnamon Carter graced the cover of *Elite* magazine, where she reigned as model of the year; Rollin Hand (originally Martin Land) was seen on a theatrical flyer. To keep things fresh over the years, the photos would change. The dossiers Dan rejected were usually pictures of crewmen and their wives...."[47]

Then came the dress-rehearsal apartment scene, in which the IMFers cryptically discuss their impending mission, presenting intriguing bits and pieces of their plan and demonstrating devices to be used later in the show. The regular team members are comparatively relaxed—even seen cheating at penny-a-point poker! "Rollin is flamboyant, Cinnamon mock-narcissistic, Barney self-assured, and Willy virtually mute (since he is squeezed into a suit through most of the show), his physique does his talking for him."[48] But it was Martin Landau who suffered the most for his art: "For the role of [General Rio] Dominguez, Landau endured a bald cap, receding hair wig, upper and lower eye bags, chin wadding, mustache, false teeth, and rubber grease, *plus* four foam-rubber appliances for his forehead, nose, chin, and cheekbones. The actor was unrecognizable in the disguise, and Geller, Kowalski, and Solow liked what they saw."[49]

But it was all too much time-consuming and therefore expensive hard work for an episodic TV action series. White: "Then Bob Dawn: [1921–1983] had assistants take actual face moulds of the actors who were to be impersonated by Landau. It was an arduous, three-day long process, but the result worked realistic wonders." As White explained: "The masks were used for the 'peel-off,' a famous bit of business in which the guest villain—supposedly Rollin in disguise—reaches for his neck (covering his face with his arm in the process). After a cutaway to whoever is watching him, the scene resumes, this time with *Landau*, in clothing identical to the guests', already peeling off the latex mask and hairpiece."[50]

Without further ado, the IMF troupe swung into synchronized action, in what resembled nothing so much as a classic "heist" film. Bruce Geller (cited in *Dossier*): "I have always admired movies such as *Rififi* [1954: directed by Jules Dassin], *Topkapi* [1964: also directed by Dassin, based upon Eric Ambler's 1962 novel, *The Light of Day*] , and [*The*] *League of Gentlemen* [1960: directed by Basil Deardon, based upon John Boland's 1958 novel]." Indeed, the *Mission: Impossible* pilot episode features many scenes without dialogue (à la *Rififi*), and a scene where a safecracker's hands are broken (lifted straight from *Topkapi*).

Richard Meyers: "Much of the camaraderie and questions of morality disappeared the following year, when Peter Graves,[51] a brother of James [Marshal Matt Dillon of *Gunsmoke*: 1955–75] Arness took over the Force's leadership as Jim [never James] Phelps. He was a craggy-faced, white-haired, all-business hunk of a leading man. With him as head of the group, *Mission: Impossible* settled onto the course it would follow for many years. Each week he would be told he had 'a mission, should you decide to accept it,' and every week, without refusal, he would deliver the goods with the help of his team and an outrageously timed plan which depended on split-second timing and ridiculous coincidences to work."[52] Steven Hill was undoubtedly a well-trained and well-respected exponent of "Method" acting, as per Lee Strasberg (1901–1982) and the Actors Studio. In the cited (*Dossier*) words of Martin Landau: "When I first became an actor, there were two young actors in New York: Marlon Brando and Steven Hill. He was legendary. Nuts, volatile, mad, and his work was exciting." However, Albert Paulsen (1925–2004) claimed that "there were always problems. Steve is a terrific guy, but he intensifies problems that are always there for actors. But you work it out, you don't stop everything. He stops and ruminates and changes things. It's not a vicious thing, it's just a problem with how he sees the truth and what it means to him" (*Dossier*). His replacement as leading man on *Mission: Impossible* could not have been more different, either in acting experience, temperament, or work ethic.

Peter Duesler Aurness (originally Aursness) was born in Minneapolis, Minnesota, of Norwegian, German, and English ancestry (he would take the stage surname Graves from the maternal side of his family). Graves—to simplify matters—graduated from South West High School (1944). He served in the U.S. Army Air Force during what was left of the Second World War, leaving as a corporal. Further personal data can be found in *James Arness: An Autobiography*,[53] co-written by his elder brother, James King Aurness (1923–2011), and James E. Wise, Jr. Graves became a B-movie leading man in several cult sci-fi flicks, e.g., *Red Planet Mars* (1952) and *It Conquered the World* (1956). Also, a bigger-name star on the smaller screen: *Fury* (NBC: October 15, 1955, to September 3, 1966); *Whiplash* (7 Network [Australia]/ATV [UK]: September 10, 1960, to June 10, 1961); *Court Martial* (ITC [UK]: December 16, 1965, to September 22, 1966). *Dossier*: "His impact upon the show was so profound that some find it unimaginable to think of one without the other, and many people are not aware that *Mission: Impossible* ever existed without him. To this day, *Mission*'s first season is not rerun as often as the later shows in some markets, presumably because Graves is not in it."[54]

The proactive approach and general likability of Peter Graves as Jim Phelps got season two off to a flying start. *Mission: Impossible* also went into warp-speed mode, with few—if any—wasted words or actions. As for characterization, the get-it-done-*fast* scripts made *Dragnet* look like something adapted from a Jane Austen novel. Not for nothing did the show become known as the Director Killer.

"I love it when a plan comes together" might have been a line spoken by Jim Phelps rather than Hannibal Smith (George Peppard) of *The A-Team* (1983–1987). "The ventilating system of any building is the perfect hiding place; no one will ever think of finding you in it and you can travel to any other part of the building undetected": #6 on William Goldman's list of TEN THINGS WE'D NEVER KNOW WITHOUT THE MOVIES. It was usually Barney Collier who made his unerring way through such conveniently wide ventilator shafts, loaded down with all sorts of essential equipment. "Should you want to pass yourself off as a German officer, it will not be necessary to speak the language—a German accent will do" (#8 ditto). But, since many *Mission: Impossible* episodes were set in mythical Eastern European states, an ersatz language called "Gellerese" came into being. For example: *machina werke* (machine repair) and *zöna restrik* (restricted area). Rollin Hand's uncannily convincing life masks and bodysuits fooled even close associates of the impersonated personnel, and he seldom suffered a costume emergency. We are left to guess how the IMF team made their way in and out of those unfriendly countries, fully equipped and driving an *A-Team* SUV.

It would be both right *and* wrong to say that if you've seen one *Mission: Impossible* episode you've seen them all. The scripts *were* written to a formula, but it was a flexible formula that allowed for the occasional spanner that would *almost* gum up the works. Patrick J. White published full plot summaries in *Dossier*, and they can also be found online. But the Season Five episode "Submarine" (January 16, 1970) is worthy of examination as the IMF caper *par excellence*.

Preamble: "Good morning, Mr. Phelps. You are looking at Kruger Schielman, who is due to be released in three days from a prison in the East European Republic, after serving a twenty-five-year stretch for war crimes. Schielman is the only man alive who knows the whereabouts of the funds stolen by the SS from the countries occupied by the Nazis in World War II. This enormous sum is intended to finance a neo–Nazi coup in Europe, which is to trigger as soon as they get the money. Your mission, Jim, should you decide to accept it, is to learn where this vast horde of cash is hidden before the neo–Nazis do. As always, should you or any of your IM Force be caught or killed…." Kruger Schielman (Stephen McNally: 1911–1994) is drugged by the IMF team and placed aboard a fake submarine that is ostensibly bound for SS headquarters, somewhere in Scandinavia:

> The "sub" is set upon by an "enemy destroyer" whose "depth charges" force the sub to the "ocean floor." When heavy damage is suffered, Phelps drowns the crew and jettisons a screaming Paris [Leonard Nimoy: see below] through the escape hatch. "There is only one form of evidence a destroyer commander will accept," he tells an admiring Schielman. Jim and Schielman don buoyancy jackets and masks to leave the sub. Schielman, afraid he won't survive the trip to the surface, insists on giving Phelps the account number of the stolen loot to relay to headquarters. "Take the account number," he begs, "prove to them I never cracked!" But regular navy Phelps doesn't care. He crawls into the escape hatch and vanishes as Schielman screams the account number at him.[55]

N.B. "Submarine" is such a typical *Mission: Impossible* episode that CBS included excerpts from it as part of the gala special, *On the Air: A Celebration of 50 Years* (1978).

Desilu Productions became Paramount Television in July 1967, after Lucille Ball had sold her independent studio for about $17 million; the walls between their adjoining lots were torn down. Although Bruce Geller stayed the whole course as Executive Producer, many other management changes would impact upon *Mission: Impossible* from then on (see White's *Dossier* for the full behind-the-scenes story). The general viewing public noticed nothing untoward until Season Four (October 12, 1969, to March 29, 1970), when both Martin Landau and Barbara Bain were conspicuous by their absence or even mention. They quit the series after pay talks with Paramount broke down. Landau and Bain wouldn't act together on episodic television until they co-starred in the syndicated British sci-fi series *Space: 1999* (1975–77).

Landau was replaced by Leonard Nimoy, who had just come off *Star Trek* (see above), on a $7,000 per episode par with Peter Graves. Ironically, he'd been working right next door to *Mission: Impossible* for the previous three years, playing Mr. Spock—the star-making role that Landau had turned down back in 1964. Nimoy played the Great Paris—another consummately professional actor—in 49 episodes, from "The Code" (September 28, 1969) to "The Merchant" (March 17, 1971).

White: "Paramount quickly learned that Barbara Bain would not be so easy to replace as her husband. There was no telling when or if Bain would legally be forced to return and fulfil her contract, so another actress could not be hired on a permanent basis."[56] Bruce Geller chose (sequentially): Lee ("Catwoman") Meriwether (1935–), who had guest-starred in "The Bunker" (February 3 and 9, 1969), as Anna Rojak and "Tracey," in "Submarine"; Dina Merrill (1923–2017), as "Meredyth" in the Season Four opening double episode: "The Controllers" (October 12 and 17, 1969);

Leslie (Ann) Warren (1946–), as Dana Lambert; Lynda Day George (1944–), as Lisa Casey; Barbara Anderson (1945–), as Mimi Davis.

Sam Elliott (1944–) temporarily "stood in" for the absent Peter Lupus/Willy Armitage. He played IMF physician Dr. Doug Robert in 13 episodes, from "The Innocent"' (March 10, 1970) to "Encore" (September 25, 1971).

Four tie-in novelizations were published by Popular Library. The first, *Mission: Impossible* (1967), and *Mission: Impossible #4: Code Name: Little Ivan* (1969), were written by John Tiger (Walter Wager: see above). Max Walker (?) bylined #2, *Code Name: Judas*, and #3, *Code Name: Rapier* (both 1968).

Whitman published two "Young Adult" volumes, by Talmage Powell: *The Priceless Particle* (1969) and *The Money Explosion* (1970). The books are true to their source material and reflect its changing cast list.

Kurt Peer: "Dan Briggs is gone after the first book, replaced by Jim Phelps for the balance. Rollin and Cinnamon are gone after the third Popular Library book and the first Whitman. The fourth [Leipzig-based] Popular Library and the second Whitman were written with Rollin and Cinnamon originally, but were rewritten for the new characters. Rollin was replaced by Paris in both books, while Cinnamon was replaced by 'Annabele Drue' (a character not in the show) in *Code Name: Little Ivan* (the book, hastily re-written by the editorial staff, still mentions Cinnamon's name on the back cover) and by Tracey in *The Money Explosion* (author Talmage Powell was paid a bonus to rewrite the book). Barney Collier and Willy Armitage are featured throughout the books."[57]

Dell/Gold Key published four *Mission: Impossible* comic books, using this regular "IMF" team. World Distributors, Ltd. (UK), published their *Mission: Impossible Annual 1972* (© 1971). During 1973, Polystyle Publications (also UK) printed several original *Mission* comic strips in *TV Action* magazine. Back in the USA, *Mad* magazine published two *Mission* parodies (reprinted in *Dossier*). "Mission Ridiculous" (#118, April 1968) featured Mr. Phelts, Blarney, Billy, and Barbara Bain as Synonym. "A TV Scene We'd Like to See" (#134, April 1970) had a surprise ending worthy of the great O. Henry himself.

Unlike the lowercase liberal *Man from U.N.C.L.E.* and *I Spy*, the IMF team looked as if they were recruiting-poster boys and girls for the CIA (or even the wartime OSS). "OUR SECRET SERVICE, ALWAYS IN THE RIGHT!" sort of thing. By the late 1960s, however, the sometimes-unsavory truth about American—and British or French, for that matter—covert operations around the world had begun making its way into the public domain. White: "Spearheaded by the youth movement of the late sixties, public antipathy towards American involvement in the Vietnam War had at last reached entertainment executives, whose livelihoods depend on keeping the American public edified. This season [1970–71] the IMF would spend less time in foreign countries and more time in the USA ... Phelps and company concentrated almost all their attention on a battle with organized crime, most commonly referred to as 'the Syndicate.'"[58]

Jim Phelps and the Impossible Mission Force super-secret agents began to look more like Eliot Ness and *The Untouchables* (ABC: October 15, 1959, to September 10, 1963)—extraordinary Federal cops taking on the modern equivalent of Al Capone and his organized-criminal kind. The enemies weren't even dignified with a cool acronym like SPECTRE or THRUSH. This "domestication" process had, in fact, been presaged some years before, by a two-part episode entitled "The Council" (November 19 and 26, 1967). If the many other Syndicate-related episodes had matched "The Council" for pace and ingenuity, the *Mission: Impossible* viewership would have been in clover. Director: Paul Stanley (1922: Directors Guild nomination). Writers: Allan Balter (1925–1981) and William Reed Woodfield (1928–2001). But they didn't. In 1968–69, Paramount emulated MGM and *The Man from U.N.C.L.E.* by turning "The Council" into a feature film for non–American markets: *Mission: Impossible Versus the Mob*. The two parts were simply integrated with no additional footage, giving it an acceptable running time of 110 minutes. *Mob* made a healthy profit, but the studio decided against "featurizing" any more two-part episodes.

Mission: Impossible made it to 168 episodes before being canceled after its seventh season. A made-for-TV *Mission: Impossible* "reunion" film was planned in 1978, which would also serve as a pilot for another series, but it came to nothing. Bruce Geller had been killed in a plane crash on Sunday, May 28, of that year, aged just forty-seven. The idea did not go away, however, resulting in such abortive projects as *Mission: Impossible 1980*, *Mission: Impossible 1981*, and *Good Morning, Mr. Phelps* (*Mission: Impossible: The Movie*). Then, in 1988, a 150-day Hollywood Writers Guild strike led to the production of a "blackleg" series filmed in Australia. It lasted for 35 episodes, from "The Killer" (October 23, 1988) to "The Sands of Seth" (February 24, 1990). White:

> By mid–July, Peter Graves was signed to return as Jim Phelps. A quick but exhaustive search brought together an attractive new cast. Thaao Penghis [1945–], an Australian actor of Greek descent and a popular daytime television performer [*Days of Our Lives, General Hospital*] was cast as Rollin Hand. The role of Barney Collier went to Greg Morris' son, Phil [1959–], who also made a splash in daytime television [*The Young and the Restless*] and had series roles in [*Mr. Merlin* and *Marblehead Manor*]. Pegged for Willy Armitage was English-born, Australian-raised Tony Hamilton [1952–], another daytime drama vet [*One Life to Live, The Guiding Light*], best known for his role in the short-lived spy series *Cover Up* [1984–85]. The role of Cinnamon Carter went to Terry Markwell, an [Arizona-born] actress-model-designer living in Australia.[59]

Greg Morris guest-starred as Barney Collier in "The Condemned" (November 20, 1988) and "The Golden Serpent" (September 21 and 28, 1989). Ditto Lynda Day George as Lisa Casey in "Reprisal" (April 15, 1989). Jane Badler (1953–), best-known for *V* (NBC: 1983–85), replaced Terry Markwell halfway through the first of two seasons, as Shannon Reid. The revived series dealt with some "real world" espionage-related issues, including Northern Irish sectarian conflict: "Banshee" (November 30, 1989). "Target Earth" (November 9, 1989), written by Stephen Kandel, zoomed into spy-fi territory. White: "The IMF foil a terrorist takeover of a space launch, but not before Shannon, posing as the shuttle pilot, is launched into orbit, space-walks to repair a laser, and is set adrift before she can re-enter the ship."[60] It makes a lot more dramatic and scientific sense than the 1979 film version of *Moonraker*—which wasn't all that difficult, come to think of it. The revamped *Mission: Impossible* did not return for a third season, with the dismal ratings putting paid to any other projected TV movie. Perhaps, as Patrick J. White has suggested, it "could never have succeeded again, no matter how well done. The uniqueness which helped make the original show a hit has been eroded by twenty years' worth of imitations; and in this age of sound bites and MTV, a series that requires an audience's attention may itself be an impossible mission."[61]

The Man (and *Girl*) *from U.N.C.L.E.*, *I Spy*, and *Mission: Impossible* could pass themselves off as straight TV spy dramas with variant levels of self-parody. But *Get Smart* (NBC/CBS: September 18, 1965, to September 11, 1970) was unabashedly nonsensical for the whole of its long-running time. *Get Smart* was co-created by Mel Brooks (1926–) and Buck Henry (1930–2020). Brooks had written for *Your Show of Shows* (1950–54) and *Sid Caesar Invites You* (1958). Henry had written for *The Steve Allen Show* (1963–64) and created a short-lived (15 episodes) TV series about a nerdy "super hero" called *Captain Nice* (NBC: 1967). Jon E. Lewis and Penny Stempel: "*Smart* was the tale of Maxwell Smart, enthusiastic but incompetent Agent 86 for Washington-based international intelligence agency C.O.N.T.R.O.L .Headed by 'The Chief,' with headquarters in a music hall, C.O.N.T.R.O.L. waged war against the evil agents of K.A.O.S., led by mastermind Siegfried and his assistant Starker. Max (catchphrases: 'Sorry about that, Chief' … and 'Would you believe …') went undercover as a greetings card salesman and his equipment included a telephone in one of his shoes which rarely worked. He was aided by Agent K13, a dog named Fang, genius robot Hymie and beautiful and brilliant partner Agent 99. In the 1968–69 season love blossomed between the mismatched agents and they married. When NBC cancelled the show in 1969, CBS picked it up for an additional season [138 episodes in total]."[62]

Maxwell Smart, who made Inspector Jacques Clouseau seem like Maigret crossed with James Bond, was immortalized by ex–U.S. Marine and stand-up comic Don Adams (1923–2005). As the rigid and buttoned-up Agent 86, even his hair had a "clenched" look about it. The never-named and comparatively super-competent Agent 99 was played by ex-model Barbara Feldon (1933–). According to Feldon, her character had originally been named Agent 100 ("because she was one hundred per cent"), but Buck Henry deemed 99 to be more feminine! Edward ("Ed") Platt (1916–1974) personified Thaddeus, their understandably nervous-wreck Chief. "I'm a foil. A frustration symbol who borders on the psychotic" (cited in *TV Detectives*). The large ensemble cast would come to include Bernie Kopell (1933– : Conrad Siegfried McTavish); Robert Karvelas (1921–1991: Larrabee): David Ketchum (1928–: Agent 13); Stacy Keach, Sr. (1914–2003: Carlson); King Moody (1929–2001: Starker); Dick

Gautier (1931–2017: Hymie, the C.O.N.T.R.O.L. robot); Victor French (1934–1989: Agent 44); Jane Dulo (1912–1994: 99's mother).

Episode One ("Mr. Big") contains this typically sardonic dialogue scene between Maxwell Smart and the titular villain (played by the diminutive actor Michael Dunn: 1934–1973), which takes place on board a boat at sea:

> MAX (FOR SHORT): "Would you believe that seven Coast Guard cutters are converging on us at this very moment?"
> MR. BIG: "I find that hard to believe."
> MAX: "Would you believe six?"
> MR. BIG: "I don't think so."
> MAX: "How about two cops in a rowboat?"

C.O.N.T.R.O.L.H.Q. could easily be found at 123 Main Street, Washington, D.C.—it might well have been listed in the local telephone directory. There wasn't even a fake shopfront, as per the U.N.C.L.E. building. Access to the Chief's inner sanctum came only after a tortuous route: two elevator doors opened on to a stairway that led down to a corridor intersected by several sliding and/or swinging doors which ended in a phone booth, the floor of which fell out when Max inserted a coin and dialed some secret number. William Schallert (1922–2016) occasionally guest-starred as former chief Admiral Harold Harmon Hargrade (Rtd.)—an increasingly senile simulacrum of M. Agent 13 (see above) invariably turned up hiding in sofas, cigarette machines, bookcases, grandfather clocks, cupboards, and any other disguise contraptions invented by whoever headed *Get Smart*'s Q Branch. As for Bondian super-scientific gadgetry, great play was often made with the Cone of Silence—an anti-bugging device that rendered just about everything said within its influence unintelligible to everyone concerned. Max had several protective devices in his apartment, including an "invisible wall" that would never fail to incapacitate the wrong person whenever activated.

William Johnston (1924–2010) wrote nine tongue-through-cheek novelizations for Tempo Books, New York, starting with *Get Smart!* (1965). Burbling blurb: "In this original story about the super-sleuth, Max is, as usual, determined to eradicate evil. His adversary is FLAG, the freelance organization of spies whose highest devotion is to Money. His assignment: keep Fred, the eye-revolving robot programmed with all the knowledge of Western man, out of the hands of the Bad Guys. Entanglements with a Southern tourist with a suspiciously Russian accent, Fred's beautiful but over-eager inventor, poetry-loving beatniks, and other far-out characters, put all of Max's deadly skills (or whatever it is he has) to the test. Does Good triumph over Evil? Read this hilarious spoof of international intrigue—and you'll still wonder!" The remaining eight novels are *Get Smart: Sorry, Chief …* (1966); *Get Smart Once Again!* (1966); *Max Smart and the Poisonous Pellets* (1966); *Missed It by That Much!* (1967); *And Loving It!* (1967); *Max Smart—The Spy Who Went Out to the Cold* (1968); *Max Smart Loses Control* (1968); *Max Smart and the Ghastly Ghost Affair* (1969).

Associational reading: *Get Smart: Would you Believe?*,[63] by Don Adams and

Bill Dana. Dell (*sans* the Gold Key logo) published eight *Get Smart* tie-in comic books, from June 1966 to September 1967 (reprint of the first issue). *Get Smart* has been called the most successful parody series in American TV history; it won seven Emmies, including three consecutive Best Actor awards (1967–69) for Don Adams. The relationship between Max and 99 changed radically with season 4, during which they married and almost—but thankfully not quite—became more like characters in a domestic sitcom (à la *Bewitched*). After a change of networks (see above), the final *Get Smart* episode aired on May 15, 1970. "I Am Curiously Yellow" spoofed the 1967 Swedish "art house" movie *I Am Curious (Yellow)*.

But you can't keep a good, bad, or indifferent spy down for long. Ten years later, Don Adams reappeared as Agent 86 in a feature film that was to be entitled *The Return of Maxwell Smart*, but which was actually released as *The Nude Bomb* (Universal Pictures: May 9, 1980). Director: Clive Donner (1926–2010). Mel Brooks and Buck Henry having busied themselves elsewhere, the writing credits read: Bill Dana (1924–2017); Arne Sultan (1925–1986); Leonard Stern (1922–2011). Lalo (*Mission: Impossible*) Schifrin worked his musical magic on the score. Apart from Adams, the only other original cast member was Robert ("Larrabee") Karvelas. Dana Elcar (1924–2017) took over as the Chief from Edward Platt, who had since passed away. Agent 99's irreplaceable place was taken by Andrea Howard (1947), as Agent 22, and Pamela Hensley (1950–) as Agent 36; Barbara Feldon later claimed that she hadn't been invited back. Even C.O.N.T.R.O.L. had become the P.I.T.S. ("Provisional Intelligence Tactical Service").

The story is even dafter than they usually come. Max Smart is called out of retirement to help stop K.A.O.S. from exploding a bomb that does not kill but destroys all forms of clothing. K.A.O.S. would then monopolize the entire international "rag trade" market. Vittorio Gassman (1922–2000) plays Norman Saint-Sauvage (né Nino Salvatore Sebastiani), the Blofeld winnable and chief fashion designer for K.A.O.S.; the entrance to his mountain lair is through a gigantic zipper! Although it is now something of a cult classic, *The Nude Bomb* grossed only $14.7 million on a budget of $15 million. "[Agent 86] returns in a feature length spoof ... co-scripter Bill Dana has a funny bit as fashion designer Jonathan Levinson Siegel. Agreeable time-filler" (Maltin). Telecast by NBC in 1982 as *The Return of Maxwell Smart*.

Get Smart, Again! was an "intentional" made-for-TV movie (ABC/IndieProd Productions/Phoenix Entertainment Group: February 26, 1989). It benefited from bringing back all the available original cast members—save one, unfortunately. Credit: "This movie is dedicated to the memory of Ed Platt, 'the Chief.'" Director: Gary Nelson (1934–). Writers: Leonard Stern; Mark Curtiss; Rod Ash. A revamped 1995 series of *Get Smart* on the Fox network lasted for only seven episodes. Max is now the Chief of C.O.N.T.R.O.L., routinely driven to distraction by his rookie-spy son, Zach (Andy Dick: 1965–), who is even more bumbling than Agent 86. Elaine Hendrix (1970) played his sexy sidekick, Agent 66. Meanwhile, Agent 99 has become a congresswoman with strict budgetary control over C.O.N.T.R.O.L.

Get Smart was born to spoofiness, while *The Man from U.N.C.L.E.* had spoofiness thrust upon it. *The Wild West* (CBS: September 17, 1965, to September 19, 1969. 104 episodes), however, has been mooted to be the most successful comedy-drama fusion, which—despite its seemingly generic title—was and was not just another TV western series of that time. *Wild* was created for Bruce Lansbury Productions by Michael Garrison (1922–1966), who had co-bought the screen rights to *Casino Royale* with Gregory Ratoff. He pitched the concept as "James Bond on horseback." In the 1870s (we must believe), President Ulysses S. Grant sends crack secret agents Captain James ("Jim") T. West (Robert Conrad: 1935–2010) and Artemus Gordon (Ross Martin: 1920–1981) on far-out missions to protect the far-flung Frontier. The two-fisted "wild" West and the master-of-disguise inventor Gordon have the use of a specially equipped locomotive that would make even Q turn green with envy. Richard Meyers:

> Their adversaries were very impressive, Lloyd Bochner [1924–2005] played Zachariah Skull in one episode ["The Night of the Puppeteer": February 22, 1966]. Victor Buono played Count Manzeppi, an evil Magician, in another ["The Night of the Feathered Fury": January 13, 1967]. But the most famous of the show's villains was Dr. Miguelito Loveless, played by Michael Dunn, an actor who was a dwarf. His size did not stop him from trying to take over the world time and time again [10 episodes, from "The Night the Wizard Shook the Earth," October 1, 1965, to "The Night of Miguelito's Revenge," December 13, 1965].[64]

Richard Wormser wrote the single solitary tie-in novel. Unfortunately, *The Wild Wild West*[65] was more of a routine western than "steampunk" (futuristic fiction set in Victorian times) spy-fi. The interior blurb reads: "Major James West dines on *escargots* in garlic butter, finishes up with demitasse and cognac, plays a hand of poker with his English butler (who cheats). [Paxton, not Tennyson.] His home is a luxuriously appointed railroad car; his job is to ferret out trouble along the borders and frontiers of the untamed West. Here West and his sidekick (a man of instant disguises) infiltrate the ranks of restless redskins as they hunt down a railroad saboteur. Along the way they pick up a cussing Irish beauty, a Dartmouth-educated Indian chief, a one-armed general, some wily Wall Street magnates, and finally, of course, the villain." In a nice touch, however, Wormser has West and President Grant keep in touch via Morse code and closed-circuit telegraph.

Jon E. Lewis and Penny Stempel: "Ultimately, though, *The Wild Wild West* was a success because it was a spoof. Not only of the genres it raided—western, sci-fi and, especially, spy—but, most cleverly of all, of itself. In 1969 the high-style series was canceled by the head of CBS, Dr. [Frank] Stanton, to appease a periodic moral panic by the US Congress concerning violence on TV."[66] Time passed, times changed....

The Wild Wild West Revisited TV movie was first shown by CBS Entertainment on May 9, 1979. It was directed by Burt (*Support Your Local Sheriff*) Kennedy (1922–2001), who would later write the autobiographical *Hollywood Trail Boss: Behind the Scenes of the Wild, Wild Western* (1997). Writer: William Bowers (1916–1987). By

1885, James West has retired to his Mexican hacienda and Artemus Ward is treading the boards as a peripatetic Shakespearean actor. President Grover Cleveland, in the person of Wilford (A.) Brimley (1934–2020), has recalled them to prevent Dr. Miguelito Loveless, Jr. (Paul Williams: 1940–), from dominating the world with android replicas of national leaders ("Six-hundred-dollar men"). Laughs considerably outweighed thrills, but positive audience reaction led to the Kennedy directed and Bowers-written *More Wild Wild West* (October 7, 1980). Any plans for a *Yet More Wild Wild West* had to be shelved after the untimely death of Ross Martin.

Dr. Miguelito's "Six-hundred dollar man" quip is an in-joke reference to *The Six Million Dollar Man* (ABC: October 20, 1973, to March 6, 1978). Lewis and Stempel: "Lee Majors [1923–], late of *The Big Valley* [1965–69] and *Men from Shiloh* [1971–71] played Colonel Steve Austin, a handsome NASA pilot who endured a near-fatal crash and was refurbished by Dr. Rudy Wells, at a cost of six million dollars, with atomic-powered legs, arms and left eye [complete with a zoom lens and built-in grid screen]. Thus 'bionically' equipped, Austin could perform incredible feats of strength and speed—usually filmed in slow motion—and sallied forth on behalf of the Office of Strategic Investigations [another offshoot from the OSS], headed by Oscar Goldman, to fight the usual array of megalomaniacs, criminals, and aliens which threaten the US of A."[67] (Bionics is the process of adapting biological systems to man-made electronic devices.)

USAF Colonel Steve Austin was the creation of noted aerospace writer and military historian Martin Caidin.[68] New Yorker Caidin had served in the merchant navy (1945) and as a sergeant in the United States Air Force (1947–1950). *Marooned*[69] became an international bestseller and, in 1969, a hit film directed by John Sturges (1910–1992). "This is the hair-raising story of three American astronauts trapped in a capsule orbiting 280 miles above the earth. With only 43 hours of oxygen left, they are doomed to death by asphyxiation … " (blurb for the specially revised Bantam tie-in edition). Apollo 13—well ahead of its time! If *Marooned* was an early "techno-thriller," then *Cyborg* (short for cybernetic organism)[70] featured one of the first techno-thriller serial-hero characters: "We all know Colonel Austin's background [Oscar Goldman]. Test pilot, astronaut, a man who's been to the moon [three times]. But there's more. There's an extraordinary rounding out of this particular individual. Physically an outstanding specimen. A great athlete. An advanced student of the military arts. At the same time, a man with no less than five degrees. Steve Austin breezed through his masters and his doctorate."[71]

Caidin would hold himself at a safe distance from the video incarnation of Steve Austin. Arbor House (USA) and W.H. Allen (UK) published three sequels in a short row: *Operation Nuke* (1972: 1974); *High Crystal* (1974: 1975); *Cyborg IV* (1975: 1977), which sends Austin back into space, where he links himself "symbionically" to a spacecraft and does battle with hostile Russian cosmonauts. Michael Jahn novelized several key episodes for Warner Books. *Wine, Women and War* (1975: first shown on October 20, 1973), which incorporated elements from *Operation Nuke* ;

The Solid Gold Kidnapping (1975: first shown on November 17, 1973), as by "Evan Richards." *The Rescue of Athena One* (1975: first shown on March 15, 1974). Included "Straight on 'Til Morning" (first shown on November 8, 1974). In between *Gold* and *Athena*, Jay Barbree (1943–2021) wrote *Pilot Error* (1975: first shown on September 27, 1974). Jahn then moved over to Berkley for two more books. *The Secret of Bigfoot Pass* (1976: first shown on February 1 and February 4, 1976). *International Incidents* (collection: 1977). Contents: "Double Trouble" (October 3, 1976); "The Deadly Test" (October 19, 1975); "Love Song for Tanya" (February 15, 1976).

Of general interest, Austin meets Andy Sheffield—"The Bionic Boy" (November 7, 1976), played by Vince (later Vincent) Van Patten (1957–). Of particular interest is Austin's childhood sweetheart, Jaime Sommers, played by Lindsay Wagner (1942–). Created by Kenneth Johnson (1942–), Jaime appeared in "The Bionic Woman" double episode of *The Six Million Dollar Man* (March 16 and March 23, 1975). Although killed off, Jaime was brought back by popular demand in another double episode: "The Return of the Bionic Woman" (September 14 and September 21, 1975). Dr. Rudy Wells explained that she had been put in suspended animation until full restorative bionic surgery became possible. "Welcome Home, Jaime" (January 14, 1976) was part 1 of the pilot episode for *The Bionic Woman* TV series (ABC/NBC: January 21, 1976–September 2, 1978). Eileen Lottman (1927–) wrote *The Bionic Woman: Welcome Back, Jaime* for Berkley Books (1976). The UK edition (same year) was retitled *Double Identity* and published under her "Maud Willis" pseudonym.

According to Wikipedia (no citation yet given), Lee Majors once claimed that Steve Austin "hates the whole idea of spying. He finds it repugnant, degrading. If he's James Bond, he's the most reluctant one we've ever had." True words, spoken or not. Austin only becomes a secret agent out of gratitude to Dr. Rudy Wells and the manipulative appeal to his patriotism made by Oscar Goldman, who didn't get where he was by being a totally nice guy. Roger Fulton: "Initially, Austin finds it hard to reconcile himself with being a 'freak' and tries to commit suicide—a touching display of human emotion that went down well with critics and public" (*The Encyclopedia of TV Science Fiction*). It invited comparison with the self-tormented Bond of Fleming's later novels (see below). But, when the series veered back to its techno-thriller roots, the personality of Steve Austin became more and more robotic—with Majors underplaying the character as unexpressively written and directed. Lindsay Wagner had a better "human interest" time of it as Jaime Sommers, especially in the empathic crossover episodes and TV movies alongside her bionic counterpart.

The same "robotic" quality pervaded other American spy-fi TV series of the 1970s; especially *Search* (NBC: September 13, 1972, to August 29, 1973), which was based upon a TV movie entitled *Probe* (February 21, 1972). It starred Hugh (*Wyatt Earp*: 1955–1961) O'Brian as Hugh Lockwood, who works for the Probe Division of World Securities Corporation. Lockwood is electronically connected to a computer system controlled by V.C.R. Cameron (Burgess Meredith: 1907–1997). When *Probe* became *Search*, for copyright reasons (there was a news program called *Probe*), its writer/creator Leslie Stevens (1924–1998) added Christopher R. Groves (Doug McClure: 1935–1995) and Nick Bianco (Tony Franciosa) to the duty roster. Richard Meyers:

> These men carried a miniature spy arsenal on their persons. They had transmitters in their ears, cameras on their rings and tiepins, and implanted monitors under their skin. All this stuff saved them from hiring legmen to check out their leads since the computer did it for them.
>
> That did not mean that the production house did not have to hire actors to play the assistants, however. Every time the scene switched back to Cameron, 10 extra actors were on camera occupying themselves by looking intently at their readouts and pressing buttons. And since the scriptwriters did not have to write long scenes with the detectives researching clues, they scrambled for other ways to waste time.
>
> *Search*, in short, was pretty much a joke, and not a very good one at that. The plug was pulled after a year.[72]

Robert Weverka (1926–2009) wrote two tie-in novelizations for Bantam: *Search* (1973) followed the TV movie; *Moonrock* (ditto) was based upon the episode of that title (October 4, 1972). Back-cover blurb: "In *Moonrock* [Hugh] Lockwood is caught up in a deadly puzzle that starts with a trip to the moon and carries him headlong into murder, a military coup, missing moonstones and mysterious and dangerous women!"

Big-screen spoofs "in the tradition" of *Our Man Flint* (q.v.) and *The Silencers* (ditto) include *The Spy with a Cold Nose* (1966), a British film co-starring Laurence Harvey and Daliah Lavi. It was based upon an original screenplay by Ray Galton (1930–2018) and Alan Simpson (1929–2017). Blurb to the Dell edition of their own novelization[73]: "What kind of secret agent chases sticks in the daytime and sleeps with the Russian Premier at night?" Answer: a "bugged" bulldog code-named Disraeli, presented as a gift to the Russian ambassador. There is also *The Man Called Flintstone* (1966): "[Directors] Joseph Barbera, William Hanna. Voices of Alan Reed, Mel Blanc, Jean Vander Pyl, June Foray. Feature-length cartoon based on TV series (*The Flintstones*: 1960–66) of Stone Age characters satirizes superspy films. Mainly for kids" (Maltin).

CHAPTER THIRTEEN

Up Until Today

Or: *Exit Ian Fleming.*

"Heroic" espionage fiction had held its poplit own during the 1950s: Edward S. Aarons and F. Van Wyck Mason in the USA; John Creasey and—of course—Ian Fleming in the UK. The smash-hit success of *Dr. No* (1962) led to the most durable single-character series in cinematic history. Films about Sherlock Holmes have long since reached treble figures, but they were made over a much longer period, and by several different production companies. As with Conan Doyle and his most famous creation, Ian Fleming will always be inextricably linked to the name of Bond—James Bond. However, more people today know 007 through the films than the original books—and much the same thing could be said about Doyle and Holmes. *Dr. No* and *From Russia with Love*, both directed by Terence Young, made and released before Fleming's passing in 1964, followed their source novels faithfully enough. See *The Bond Files*,[1] by Andy Lane and Paul Simpson. For one significant difference: Dr. No (Joseph Wiseman: 1918–2009) drowns in a water-cooled nuclear reactor, not smothered under a pile of bird dung, as in the novel.

The book and film versions of *Dr. No* and *Russia* were straightforward spy thrillers that could have been set in the 1930s. *Dr. No* can be seen as borderline spy-fi, but only in a one-tick-of-the-clock ahead kind of way. The Bond of the films, however, has a much more open and urbane personality than the Bond of the books, whom it is hard to imagine flirting with Miss Moneypenny or regaling fellow roisterers in a local hostelry with ribald remarks. On the other hand, Sean Connery became adept at delivering deadly deadpan quips like "That's a Smith and Wesson, and you've had your six" (*Dr. No*) and "I'd say one of their aircraft is missing" (*Russia*). None of which detracts from the violent business-at-hand, especially in *Russia*'s now iconic Orient Express fight scene between Connery and Robert Shaw. James Chapman has summed it up perfectly well:

> In this instance, snobbery is followed immediately by violence as Bond and Grant fight to the death in a confined train compartment. Unlike most movie fight sequences, which were often filmed in long takes, the Bond-Grant struggle is a montage of fast shots, with hand-held cameras used to cut into the screen space and sound effects emphasizing the violence.[2]

Goldfinger's cinematic adaptation (by Richard Maibaum and Paul Dehn) lent some much-needed verisimilitude to the far-fetched Fleming original. Director: Guy Hamilton (1922–2016). Bond also shows off his previously unsuspected talent for mental arithmetic: "Fifteen billion dollars in gold weighs 10,500 tons. Sixty men would take twelve days to load it into 200 trucks. Now, at the most, you're going to have two hours before the Army, Navy, Air Force and Marines make you put it back." But it was the ramped-up gadgetry that made *Goldfinger* the most fun-tastic Bond film so far. Main Exhibit: Bond's venerable Bentley Mark IV, replaced by an Aston Martin DB5, with these Q-added "optional extras" to the standard production model: revolving number plates; bulletproof front and rear windscreens/-shields; passenger-side ejector seat; tire shredders; variable lights; high-pressure water cannons; reinforced "ramming" bumpers, fore and aft; long-barreled Colt. 45 in hidden dashboard compartment; radar-screened "Homer" device; oil sprays; heat-seeking rockets; miscellaneous instrumentation. It's a wonder that this overloaded "sports" car could spin wheels at all, let alone speed along twisty-turny alpine roads. From then on, most fictional secret agents worth their salt were issued with a similar souped-up set of wheels. However, the Saint continued to make daredevil-do in an unmodified Volvo P1800, while John Steed kept his own vintage Bentley in fine, fighting fettle.

Bond film #4, *Thunderball* (Terence Young) has a comparatively simple but effective plot: "The letter [from SPECTRE] to Britain's Prime Minister amounts to monstrous blackmail—two high-jacked [*sic*] atomic bombs will be exploded in unspecified Western cities, failing payment of a fantastic ransom of £100 in gold bullion" (from the 1963 Pan edition blurb material). The book reads like a novelization, which was indeed the case: "…based on a Screen Treatment by K. McClory, J. Whittingham, and the author" (ditto). Kevin McClory (1926–2006) was an Irish-born film producer who had collaborated with Ian Fleming and scriptwriter Jack Whittingham (1910–1972) on converting a story idea by Ernest Cureo (1905–1998), a lawyer friend of Fleming's, into *Thunderball*. He won the remake rights, after a long and acrimonious court case. *Never Say Never Again* (1983) was the eventual result. See *The Battle for Bond: The Genesis of Cinema's Greatest Hero*,[3] by Robert Sellers. N.B. "[*Thunderball*] was taken from the expression used by US soldiers witnessing an atomic test to describe the mushroom cloud" (Henry Chancellor).

You Only Live Twice (June 12, 1967) threw plausibility and plain common sense to the spy-fi winds. Director: Lewis Gilbert (1924–1999). Like Fleming's novel, it is mostly set in Japan, but there only the most remote resemblance lies. "James Bond Will Return In…. *On Her Majesty's Secret Service*" had been the end-title teaser for *Thunderball*. It would have been appropriate to film *OHMSS* and *Live Twice* in sequence, considering Blofeld's killing of the briefly Mrs. James Bond, *née* Contessa Teresa (Tracy) di Vicenzo, in the former, and Bond's violent vengeance, in the latter. Scenarist Roald Dahl, with "additional story material" by Harold Jack Bloom (1924–1999), substituted a thrilling-wonder plot about SPECTRE sky-jacking American and Russian manned space capsules, with "pirate" spacecraft launched from their dormant-volcano base. Blofeld is still just plain Blofeld, seen full face for the first time, happily hammed up by actor Donald Pleasence (for the only time). Just before location shooting began in Tokyo (July 1966), Connery made it clear that *Live Twice* would be his last Bond film. He had long been unhappy with the unfavorable financial arrangements between himself and Eon Productions. From *Sean Connery: The Measure of a Man*,[4] by Christopher Bray: "Truth to tell, Connery would have had cause enough to resent such gimmickry even if he had been realising a profit from it. If the Bond of Thunderball had had little enough to do, the Bond of *You Only Live Twice* has almost nothing to do: here is Connery looking silly in a helmet and a helicopter not much bigger than a bicycle; here is Connery looking absurd in a fibre 'Japanese' wig and what look like sticking-plaster eyelids."[5]

Connery expressed concern that he might have been typecast in a film genre now past its peak and on the way down. Familiarity was starting to breed irreverence, if not contempt, as with the home-released *Carry on Spying* (July 29, 1964) and *The Intelligence Men* (April 13, 1965). *Spying* was the ninth in the series of slapstick "Carry On" films that lasted from 1958 (*... Sergeant*) until 1992 (*... Columbus*). A top-secret formula has been stolen by STENCH (Society for the Total Extinction of Non-Conforming Humans). The anonymous Chief of the British Secret Service (Eric Barker: 1912–1990) needs must send his only available agents bumbling into the field to somehow retrieve it, including Desmond Simpkins (Kenneth Williams: 1926–1988) and Daphne Honeybutt (Barbara Windsor: 1937–2020). *Intelligence* (*Spylarks* in the USA) marked the comparatively intelligent feature-film debut of English comedy duo Eric Morecambe (1926–1984) and Ernie Wise (1925–1999). Swinging London coffee-shop manager Eric Morecambe, as Eric Morecambe, accidentally makes contact with an agent of SCHLECHT (the German word for "bad"). With the problematical help of his MI5 (office boy) friend, Ernie Sage (Wise), he infiltrates SCHLECHT, impersonating the deceased Major Cavendish.

Bray: "In fact, the non-stop action of *On Her Majesty's Secret Service* and the comic delights of *Diamonds Are Forever* (1971) aside, Connery was quite correct. From here on in the Bond pictures, while still performing well enough, would take progressively less at the box office. [They] would descend into humourless travesties as Connery's scalding irony was substituted for Roger Moore's pantomime charm school, as Connery's lethal physicality was substituted for Moore's stiff-kneed waddle, as Connery Bond's smouldering cigarettes were substituted for Moore Bond's Freudianly effete cigars."[6] See also *Bond on Bond: The Ultimate Book on 50 Years of Bond Movies*,[7] by Roger Moore (with Gareth Owen).

Time to step back. It has been a long and many-forked road from Harvey Birch to Matt Helm, from Bulldog Drummond to James Bond, and from Dick Tracy to *Search*. By the early 1970s, the "Golden Age" of James Bond in the movies—with Sean Connery, and, to a much lesser extent, George Lazenby—had faded into the "Silver Age" of Roger Moore. The law of diminishing returns from pale imitations and lame parodies came into often deadly force at the box office. Apart from that, the influence of Ian Fleming himself was on the wane, with the films now taking public precedence over the books. Super-hero spies were also being challenged by anti- or even non-hero spies in the "realistic" novels by emerging writers like John le Carré and Len Deighton. Just as Eric Ambler and Graham Greene had done before them, and were still doing, e.g., *The Intercom Conspiracy* (1969) and *The Human Factor* (1978).

John le Carré[8] was the "square" (in French) pseudonym of David John Moore Cornwell. He was born in Poole, County Dorset. McCormick and Fletcher: "[Cornwell] joined the Foreign Office which we now know covered his intelligence activities [with both MI5 and MI6]. For five years, 1959 to 1964, [he] was directly involved in secret intelligence work." Cornwell began his literary career while still in Her Majesty's Secret Service, hence the need for an ambiguous *nom de plume*. *Call for the Dead* (1961) and *A Murder of Quality* (1962) introduced his best-known character, George Smiley, who acted more like a Scotland Yard detective than the wily spymaster he was cracked up to be. The unsmiling Smiley makes Ashenden look like Patrick Dawlish, if not Gregory Sallust or James Bond. He had a walk-on role in le Carré's breakthrough novel, *The Spy Who Came in from the Cold*,[9] but took center stage in *Tinker, Tailor, Soldier, Spy*[10] and held it evermore. Recommended reading: *Smiley's Circus: A Guide to the Secret Service of John le Carré*,[11] by David Monaghan. N.B. "Circus" is le Carré's nickname for MI Whatever, supposedly headquartered at Cambridge Circus, West Central London.

Le Carré had scant regard for the James Bond type of poster-boy spy, as evidenced by Alec Leamas, the actual *Spy Who Came in from the Cold*. Leamas was perceptively portrayed by Richard Burton (1925–1984) in the now-classic film, perceptively directed by Martin Ritt (1914–1990). From *John le Carré. The Biography*,[12] by Adam Sisman:

> "What the hell do you think spies are?" he asks his distressed girlfriend: "moral philosophers measuring everything they do against the word of God or Karl Marx? They're not! They're just a bunch of seedy, squalid bastards like me: little men, drunkards, queers, hen-pecked husbands, civil servants playing cowboys and Indians to brighten their rotten little lives." This was a very different depiction of spying from the one presented in Ian Fleming's bestselling novels.[13]

Len Deighton[14] has long been linked with John le Carré when it comes to "realistic" British spy fiction. McCormick and Fletcher: "Len Deighton was educated at Marylebone Grammar School, St. Martin's School of Art and the Royal College of Art in London. When he left school he began work as a railway clerk before doing his National Service in the R.A.F. ... For a while he also worked as an illustrator in New York and as an art director of an advertising agency in London. Then, deciding it was time to settle down, Deighton plunged into writing...."[15] Continued: "*The Ipcress File*[16] was an instant success. [It] introduced a ... working-class boy from Burnley suddenly precipitated into a strange new world of intrigue among people out of his class whom he did not trust. This background gave Deighton's hero an unusual appeal as well as an added feeling of identification."[17] The nameless Northerner of the novel became Londoner "Harry Palmer" in the film version (March 18, 1965), which starred Michael Caine.[18] Director: Sidney J. Furie (1933–). Producer: Harry Saltzman, moonlighting from the Bond movies. Sequels: *Funeral in Berlin* (February 24, 1967), directed by Guy (*Goldfinger*) Hamilton, and *Billion Dollar Brain* (January 14, 1968), dementedly directed by Ken (*Women in Love*) Russell (1927–2011).

"Harry Palmer" was at least nominally a spy-hero character. Deighton then changed tack by writing standalone espionage novels, of which *Spy Story* (1974) and *Twinkle, Twinkle, Little Star* (1976) are prime examples. Blurb (*Spy Story*): "From the secretive computerized college of war studies in London via a bleak, sinister Scottish redoubt to the Arctic ice cap where nuclear submarines prowl ominously beneath frozen wastes, a lethal web of violence and doublecross is woven." Blurb (*Twinkle, Twinkle*): "A Russian scientist defects, believing that in the West he will more easily realize his dream of contacting planets in outer space. But British Intelligence and the CIA have more worldly plans for him and move quickly." Deighton later created Bernard Samson, an older and even more cynical—if possible—incarnation of "Harry Palmer": *Berlin Game* (1983); *Mexico Set* (1984); *London Match* (1985).

See Mike Ripley's *Kiss, Bang: The Boom in British Thrillers from CASINO ROYALE to THE EAGLE HAS LANDED* [Jack Higgins].[19] Its sentence-case tagline: How Britain lost an empire but its secret agents saved the world. And the dedication reads: "For Len Deighton, who has a lot to answer for."

Meanwhile, American spy-fiction writers threw in the occasional wee thingy bit about CIA covert operations, but they seldom went far against the grain of generic assumptions. A radical exception being Richard Condon[20] and *The Manchurian Candidate*, published by McGraw Hill in 1959. U.S. Army Sergeant Raymond Shaw is a thoroughly unlikeable man who, along with his entire platoon, is captured in Korea, subjected to extreme psychological "conditioning," and—immediately upon his return home—decorated with the Congressional Medal of Honor for "saving" his platoon. He has, in reality, been programmed to assassinate Senator Johnny Iselin (channeling Joseph McCarthy), who is running for president, at an upcoming nomination ceremony. John Frankenheimer (1930–2002) directed the 1962 film version. Writer: George Axelrod (1922–2003). The unsympathetic Shaw was played sympathetically by Laurence Harvey (1928–1973), with Angela Lansbury (1925–) as his manically manipulative mother, Eleanor, the wife of Senator Iselin (James Gregory). Frank Sinatra (1915–1998) played Intelligence officer Major Bennett Marco, who—as Captain Marco—had led the doomed platoon. Sinatra caused the film to be withdrawn for thirty years after the assassination of JFK.

In the 1950s, it was still possible for the UK to see itself as being the proud possessor of an empire-cum-Commonwealth on which the sun never set. Twenty years later, the empire that had begun during the reign of Elizabeth I had been wound up during the reign of Elizabeth II, and the Commonwealth was soon to become little more than a talking shop. Recommended reading: *The British Empire*,[21] by Colin

Cross. Ian Fleming was acutely aware of this waning imperial power and how it affected what he called the British Secret Service, particularly in *You Only Live Twice* (1964). From *The Politics of James Bond: From Fleming's Novels to the Big Screen*,[22] by Jeremy Black: "M tells Bond that the Japanese have made major advances in deciphering, enabling them to discover Soviet secrets. However, although the Japanese provided the information to the CIA, the latter was no longer passing this on.... The American refusal to pass on information was attributed to their treatment of the Pacific as a 'private preserve,' but also to their concern about Britain as a security risk. [After the serial defections of Guy Burgess, George Blake, and Kim Philby.] It no longer seemed credible, as in *Thunderball* (1961), to suggest that Britain was still great, and that she and the United States were partners."[23]

The decline and fall of British Empire is reflected in the decline and (almost) fall of James Bond, who goes from the nave but effective counterspy of *Casino Royale*, through his brief physical-wreck phase in *Thunderball*, to the burnt-out case study at the end of *You Only Live Twice* and the beginning of *The Man with the Golden Gun*. From *The Bond Files: An Unofficial Guide to the World's Greatest Secret Agent*,[24] by Andy Lane and Paul Simpson:

> Kissy [Suzuki] finds Bond, who is suffering from amnesia. She gets the other islanders to conspire to hide him, and 007 is presumed dead, with his obituary appearing in *The Times*. Some months later, though, he finds the word Vladivostok on a piece of paper—which triggers his memory. Still not knowing he is an SIS agent, Bond sets off for Russia....
>
> James Bond returns to London, brainwashed by the KGB into attempting to kill M. The attempt is foiled, and Bond is restored to something approaching normality by electroshock therapy. Concerned over Bond's mental health, M sends him on a mission to assassinate a professional killer named Francisco Scaramanga.

Dr. No and *The Man with the Golden Gun*. Compare and contrast. Jeremy Black: "Britain is no longer the imperial power. Unlike at the close of *Dr. No*, the officials are no longer British and praise has now to be distributed at the behest of the independent government of Jamaica: independence had been granted in 1962. A judicial inquiry produces an account of Bond's operation that is misleading. The commissioner of police inaccurately reports that Bond, Nicholson and Leiter carried out their duties 'under the closest liaison and direction of the Jamaican CID.' The three men are awarded the Jamaican Police Medal for 'Services to the Independent State of Jamaica.' The empire had gone."[25]

As early as 1962, *The Harvard Lampoon* had parodied Bond, in *Alligator*,[26] by I*N FL*M*NG. "LACERTUS ALLIGATOR, TOOTH [The Organization Organized to Hate], OPERATION PARLAFLOAT ... these three—the man, the organization, the plan—secret agent J*mes B*nd must ferret out and crush. He has only one lead, one person who can help him, if she will. That person is Anagram, the beautiful, desirable, mysterious, fiery blonde who is Lacertus Alligator's constant companion" (blurb). Burbling biography: "I*N FL*M*NG is a spy. As a cover he pretends to work for The British Diplomatic Corps in Moscow. During World War II he hid in a large hole in the north of England and was not seen until 1951, at which time he emerged bearing several thousand sheets of pencilled manuscript."

Golden Gun having been left effectively unfinished at the time of Fleming's death, Kingsley (*The James Bond Dossier*) Amis took up the (uncredited) post of script doctor. He found Scaramanga to be a "thin" character, who showed poor judgement in hiring a total stranger like Bond for his personal security agent—perhaps blinded by a perverse sexual attraction. Three years later, Amis wrote *Colonel Sun*[27]; the first of many pastiche Bond novels (see below). A decidedly non–PC encomium ran: 007 is maneuvered by Kingsley Amis (writing as Robert Markham) into "a super-dooper spy story combining all the best elements of the genre: fast movement, exotic locale, beautiful Mata Haris, a slit-eyed Oriental sadist [Sun Liang-tan] who is cool, cool, cool when applying knife and skewer to quivering flesh!" (*National Review*). "Unlucky Jim" Bond.

It would be well over a decade before the next James Bond "sequel by another hand"—*Licence Renewed*,[28] by John (Edmund) Gardner (1926–2007). *The Liquidator* (1964) had been filmed in 1965 (release date: November 28, 1966), starring Rod Taylor (1930–2015) as Gardner's idiosyncratic spy anti-hero, Boysie Oakes, and Jill (*Diamonds Are Forever*) St. John (1940–). Director: Jack Cardiff (1914–2009). "Nice location photography and adequate acting add up to a rather limp Bondian imitation. Even Taylor can't save this one" (Maltin). Gardner wrote 15 more follow-on Bond novels, from *For Special Services* (1982) to *Cold* (1996: *Cold Fall* in the USA). *Licence to Kill* (1989) was a novelization of the first Timothy Dalton (1946–) Bond film. *GoldenEye* (1995) ditto, for the first Pierce Brosnan (1953–) Bond film. The American author Raymond Benson (1955–) took over to pen 11 original novels, from *Zero Minus Ten* (1997) to *The Man with the Red Tattoo* (2002). These books included a trilogy of novelizations: *Tomorrow Never Dies* (1997); *The World Is Not Enough* (1999); *Die Another Day* (2002). Also, three short stories: "Blast from the Past" (1997); "Midsummer Night's Doom" (1999); "Live at Five" (1999). Christopher Wood (1935–2015) novelized his own screenplays: *James Bond, The Spy Who Loved Me* (1977); *James Bond and Moonraker* (1977). His memoirs were entitled *James Bond, The Spy I Loved* (2006).

Mickey Spillane wasn't the only Big-Name American mystery writer who turned to the potentially more lucrative spy-fiction market. Manfred Lee, half of the Ellery Queen (q.v.) writing duo, approached Talmadge Powell (1920–2000) with the idea of writing a six-book series about Manhattan police chief Timothy ("Tim") Corrigan (Popular Library paperback originals). "It was more a collaboration than a ghosting assignment," as Powell later explained. Corrigan, a Korean War veteran who wears a piratical eyepatch, spent most of his time on normal police-procedural duties (à la *Where Is Bianca?*: 1966). But Powell's second EQ novel-for-hire, *Who Spies, Who Kills?* (1966) lived up to its epigraph: "He that spies is the one who kills" (alleged Irish proverb). The remaining four strictly non-spy Tim Corrigan novels were co-written by Lee and Richard Deming (1915–1983): *Why So Dead?* (1966); *How Goes the Murder?* (1967); *Which Way to Die* (1967); *What's in the Dark?* (1968: aka *When Fell the Night*). Fredric Dannay, the other "Queen" half, preferred to concentrate upon editing *Ellery Queen's Mystery Magazine* (founded in 1941 and still going strong today). Lee and Walt Sheldon (1917–1996) wrote the standalone spy novel, *Guess Who's Coming to Kill You* (Lancer, 1968). It features Pete Brook, an agent of FACE (Federation for Art and Cultural Exchange).

The Eiger Sanction[29] and *The Loo Sanction*,[30] by Trevanian, both featured a morally imbecilic secret hooligan named Jonathan Hemlock. They are riddled with mostly intentional black humor. "Trevanian" was a pseudonym of Dr. Rodney William Whitaker,[31] an associate professor at the University of Texas who also published fiction as Nicholas Seare (e.g., *Rude Tales and Glorious*: 1983) and nonfiction under his real-name variant Rod Whitaker (e.g., *The Language of Film*: 1970). He is also said to have written novels as by Beñat La Cagot and Edoard Moran. Born in Granville, New York. Hemlock is a mountaineer, art historian, collector of black-market paintings, and assassin-in-chief for an American Intelligence department called CII, which specializes in "sanctioning" enemy agents or anybody else who arouses their homicidal interest. The fact that Hemlock has absolutely no sense of personal guilt makes him the very man for this kind of wet-work job. Character sketch:

> Hemlock's popularity with students had several unrelated bases. For one, at thirty-seven he was the youngest full professor in the Art faculty. The students assumed therefore that he was a liberal. He was not a liberal, nor was he a conservative, a Tory, a wet, an isolationist, or a Fabian. He was interested only in art, and he was indifferent to and bored by such things as politics, student freedom, the war on poverty, the plight of the Negro, war in Indochina, and ecology. But he could not escape his reputation as a 'student's professor.' For example, when he met classes after an interruption caused by a student revolt, he openly ridiculed the administration for lacking the ability to crush so petty a demonstration. The students read this as a criticism of the establishment, and they admired him more than ever.[32]

Jonathan is duly ushered into the office of Mr. Dragon, CII's Big Boss, by the well-named Mrs. Cerberus: "His eyes adjusted to the dark, and Dragon's face became visible. The hair was white as silk thread, and kinky, like a sheep's. The features, floating in the retreating gloom, were arid alabaster. Dragon was one of nature's rarest genealogical phenomena: a total albino. This accounted for his sensitivity to light; his eyes and eyelids lacked protective pigment. He had also been born without the ability to produce white corpuscles in sufficient quantity. As a result, he had to be insulated from contact with people who might carry disease. It was also necessary that his blood be totally replaced by massive transfusions each six months. For the half century of his life, Dragon had lived in the dark, without people, and on the blood of others. This existence had not failed to affect his personality."[33]

Clint Eastwood (1930–) played Hemlock in his 1975 self-directed film version of *Eiger*, and Thayer David (1927–1978) was a perfect Mr. Dragon. Rod Whitaker received a writing credit, with Hal Dresner (1937–) and Warren Murphy (1933–

2015). "*½ Pseudo–James Bond misfire, often unintentionally funny. Thrilling mountain-climbing climax does not make up for film's many faults and ungodly length [128 minutes]. Jack Cassidy as gay, treacherous spy contributes the only creative acting" (Maltin). *Loo* references a nonexistent British counterspy unit, the Loo Organization, that is headquartered in a former lavatory (for which "loo" is an English euphemism). It could have been retitled *Carry on Spying at Your Convenience* (same again) for the UK market.

Seven years later, Eastwood produced, directed, and starred in the film version of Craig Thomas's innovative 1977 techno-thriller *Firefox*. David Craig Owen Thomas (1942–2011) was a Welshman who wrote a long-running series about MI6 spymaster Sir Kenneth Audley. Although Sir Kenneth kicks off *Firefox*, its main protagonist is veteran USAF fighter pilot Mitchell Gant. His joint CIA-MI6 mission is to steal one of the two prototype Soviet MiG-31 warplanes, which incorporate stealth technology, hypersonic flight, and—most importantly—a thought-guided weapons system. The spy-fi novel won widespread critical praise, unlike the film: "1½ Lamentably dull, slow-moving espionage yarn …" (Maltin). Gant would pop up once again, in *Firefox Down* (1983).

Trevanian's Jonathan Hemlock novels are among the last significant first-generation copies of James Bond. Another exceptional example is Blackford ("Blacky") Oakes, created by William F. Buckley, Jr. (1925–2008). Eleven novels, from *Saving the Queen*[34] to *Last Call for Blackwood Oakes*.[35] New York born William Francis Buckley served with the U.S. Army during the Second World War (1944–46). He was later attached to the CIA in Mexico for almost a year, under the command of E. Howard Hunt (q.v.). Most of the Oakes novels are set in the 1950s and 1960s, as with *Who's on First*.[36] Blurb to the 1980 penguin edition:

TIME: The Cold War
PLACE: Paris, Budapest, Washington, DC, Stockholm, Moscow
SECRET AGENT: Young irresistible Blackford Oakes of the CIA
ASSIGNMENT: Win the satellite space race with the Soviets
Enter master agent Rufus, CIA Director Allen Dulles, former Secretary of State Dean Acheson, and Tamara, a beautiful Hungarian freedom fighter. Blacky risks his neck—literally—to carry out his assignment. His mission is complicated by the President, the US Navy, a KGB area chief, and the alluring Sally, who loves him, hates his work.
The Buckley tension, wit, ingenuity and high drama shows why, in his class, he's first.

Nonfiction: *The Blackwood Oakes Reader* (1999).

In 1979, Fawcett published *The November Man*, by Bill Granger (1941–2012), the first novel in a 13-book series about a spy called Devereaux. But Granger/Devereaux would not be joining Aarons/Durell or Hamilton/Helm on the illustrious Gold Medal roster of fictional secret agents. *Schism* (1981) was published by Crown, as were the next four entries: *The Shattered Eye* (1982); *The British Cross* (1982); *The Zurich Numbers* (1984); *Hemingway's Notebook* (1986); *There Are No Spies* (1986). Bill Granger grew up in a working-class district on the South Side of Chicago and was educated at De Paul University (1959–63). He served two years in the U.S. Army

(1963–65), after which came a journalistic career with two Chicago newspapers: reporter, *Tribune* (1966–69); columnist, *Sun Times* (1969–78). He went freelance from 1980 until his retirement. Granger also wrote a series of articles on Northern Ireland for *Newsday*.

Peter (as he is first-named once, in *The November Man*, and never again) Devereaux works for R Section, a "ghost-squad" unit of the CIA. R Section was formed by President Kennedy after the botched Bay of Pigs operation, in order to provide an independent watchdog over the out-of-control Intelligence agencies. It is officially attached to the Department of Agriculture. *The Zurich Numbers* (1984) flashes back to Devereaux's childhood years in Chicago, living with his great-aunt Melvina. He calls M-figure Hanley an "asshole"; something that James Bond would never even dream of calling the real thing. Devereaux is code-named November Man, by the way.

On his first recorded mission, Devereaux investigates an IRA plot to murder prominent English politician Lord Slough. He is also up against a Russian secret agent and treachery from within the CIA itself. McCormick and Fletcher: "This novel gained national publicity when the IRA assassinated Lord Louis Mountbatten by planting a bomb on his boat on 27 August 1979. What horrified everyone was that the fictional plot was so close to predicting the motives and methods the IRA actually used…. Even though the book was finished by 1978, it was published two weeks before his murder" (*Spy Fiction: A Connoisseur's Guide*). From Granger's afterword to the 1986 edition: "The parallels between what in fact happened off the Irish coast to a cousin of the Queen and what happened in the pages of *The November Man* … were derived from the terrorism and sorrow of a radically divided Ireland. In one case, a real life ended; in my book, I wrote from knowledge of my own time spent reporting the story of death and terror in Northern Ireland."

Pierce (James Bond) Brosnan starred in *The November Man* (2014), which was based upon *There Are No Spies* (see above), the seventh Devereaux novel. "At one point Devereaux, who apparently quit the CIA out of slow-building revulsion, lectures his former pupil on the need for moral clarity, telling him that you can be a man or a killer of men, but not both, because one will eventually extinguish the other" (Matt Zoller Seitz).

The next big thing to come along was the techno-spy-thrillers of Clive Cussler and Tom Clancy.

Clive Eric Cussler[37] was born in Aurora, Illinois, growing up in Alhambra, Illinois. He studied at Pasadena City College (1949–51) before enlisting in the USAF during the Korean War (discharged as a sergeant and flight engineer). Cussler would later work for various advertising agencies, including his own company. He founded the Washington-based NUMA (National Underwater and Marine Agency), in 1978, of which he served as chairman. His main fictional character, Dirk (Eric) Pitt, is a tall (6 foot, 3 inch), two-fisted marine engineer with an equally fictional version of the NUMA oceanographic research organization (headed by Admiral James

Sandecker). *The Mediterranean Caper* (aka *Mayday!* Sphere, London, 1977)[38] was the first Dirk Pitt novel to be published, but it wasn't the first written. From the foreword to *Pacific Vortex!*[39]

> Not that it really matters, but this is the first Dirk Pitt story.
>
> When I mustered up the discipline to write a suspense/adventure series, I cast around for a hero who cut a different mould. One who wasn't a secret agent, police detective, or a private investigator. Someone with rough edges, yet a degree of style, who felt equally at ease entertaining a gorgeous woman in a gourmet restaurant or downing a beer with the boys at the local saloon. A congenial kind of guy with a tinge of mystery about him.
>
> Out of the fantasy, Dirk Pitt materialised.

Dirk Pitt would evolve into a cross between Doc Savage, James Bond, and perhaps even Aquaman, saving the world on a regular basis. *Iceberg*[40] marked a distinct improvement over *Mediterranean Affair/Mayday!* "The towering iceberg drifting in the North Atlantic was a floating tomb. Embedded in the great gleaming mass was a ship—sealed in so solidly that not even its mast protruded. Here was a sea mystery to rank with the Bermuda Triangle and the *Marie Celeste*. But for Major Dirk Pitt, top troubleshooter for [NUMA], it was also the first link in a fantastic chain of events that would lead him too close too often to violent death. And to the discovery of the most sinister and bizarre conspiracy of the century ..." (blurb to the 1976 Sphere paperback edition). But Cussler and Pitt really got going with novel number three— *Raise the Titanic!*[41] (as opposed to C.S. Forester's *Sink the Bismarck!*).

"*Raise the Titanic!* is a great adventure thriller, capable of riveting readers in same way *The Day of the Jackal* [Frederick Forsyth] did.... The fantastic, elaborate job of locating the wreck [which contains an incredible substance that could make the free world invulnerable to attack forever!], then preparing to raise it, is awesome, but Cussler has more in store—contemporary Russian and American spies, a plot spinning back into the past and involving a stalwart crew of Colorado miners in the early 1900s, and even, at a crucial moment, a most beautiful naked lady. Also a hurricane ready to strike just as the ship is being raised ..." (*Publishers Weekly*).

Sir Lew Grade (q.v.) chose *Raise the Titanic!* as the opening shot in his campaign to become a major movie mogul, with Richard Jordan (1937–) well playing Dirk Pitt. Director: Jerry Jameson (1934–). Release date: August 1, 1980. Big mistake. "*½ Long [112 minutes], dull adaptation of Clive Cussler's bestseller about intrigue leading to the biggest salvage job of all time. Silly plotting and laughable dialogue undermine excitement of climactic ship-raising" (Maltin). Unkind critics claimed that the money would have been better spent in lowering the Atlantic. The film version of *Sahara* (1992), directed by Breck Eisner (1970–), fared little better. Release date: April 4, 2005. "**½ Dirk Pitt [Matthew McConaughey] and his lifelong ex– Navy SEAL pal Al [Steve Zahn] set off in search of a Civil War ironclad that they believe made its way to the River Niger. [They are] joined by a World Health Organization doctor [Eve Rojas: played by Penelope Cruz] who's trying to contain a possible plague in the country of Mali, where all three discover they're facing formidable opposition. … [It] has lots of action but an inconsistent tone and too much plot" (Maltin).

"125,000,000 Clive Cussler novels in print" (brag line on the Pocket Star Books tie-in edition of *Sahara*). Cussler wrote seventeen "#" Dirk Pitt novels before entering into collaboration with his son Dirk (1961–), after whom Pitt was named, from *Black Wind* (2004) to date. Summer Pitt, Dirk's daughter, first appeared in *Trojan Odyssey* (1998). Autobiographical reading: *Clive Cussler and Dirk Pitt Revealed*.[42]

Though Cussler died in 2020, his bibliography remains very much a work in progress. The NUMA Files Adventure novels, co-written with Paul Kemprecos (1939–) currently run from *Serpent* (1999) to *Fast Ice* (2021). They main-feature Kurt Austin, head of the NUMA Special Projects Division. The *Oregon Files* focus upon a high-tech research ship owned by NUMA and helmed by Juan Cabrillo. Introduced in *Flood Tide* (1997): *Golden Buddha* (2003) to *Marauder* (2020). Alternating collaborators: Craig Dirgo (1959–); Jack Du Brul (1968–); Boyd Morrison (1967–). Sam and Remi Fargo, a husband-and-wife team of treasure hunters: *Spartan Gold* (2009) to *The Serpent's Eye* (2022). Alternating collaborators: Grant Blackwood (1964–); Thomas Perry (1947–); Russell Blake (1955–); Robin Burcell (1960–). Isaac Bell, investigator for the Van Dorn Detective Agency (set in the early 20th century): *The Chase* (2007) to *The Saboteurs* (2020). Collaborators (after *The Chase*): Justin Scott (1944–) and Jack Du Brul.

Thomas Leo Clancy, Jr.,[43] was born in Baltimore, Maryland. An Irish-American Roman Catholic, he was educated at St. Matthew School, Loyola High School, and Loyola College, where, in 1969, he obtained his BA in English Literature. After graduation, he entered the insurance business, initially with the Hartford Fire Insurance Company (the Hartford Group). Clancy lies outside my mid–1980s time limit, nor does he fit easily—if at all—into the "Ian Fleming" spy-fiction mold. Carol Simpson Stern: "Clancy's books … harness a vast array of highly technical detail and construct a gripping account of a chase, vividly capturing the geopolitical ramifications of the kernel incident which gives rise to the plot. Like Forsyth, Ludlum and le Carré, Clancy writes with immediacy, precision, and a wealth of information. His zeal to research his subject thoroughly enabled him to write a novel which brilliantly captures the reality of submarine warfare with such specificity that it won the admiration of the U.S. Naval Institute, making them his first publisher (*Twentieth-Century Crime and Mystery Writers*)."

The Hunt for Red October was, indeed, sold for $500 to the Naval Institute Press of Maryland (published on October 1, 1984). It received an early pat on the back from Casper Weinberger (1917–2006), then the U.S. Secretary of Defense: "Critics who take themselves seriously will no doubt fault the characterization as weak and unrealized, but none except the most jaded will be anything but enthralled by the swift and expertly built crescendo of narrative excitement, the intricacy of the plot, and the chilling but wholly believable series of tightly-knit episodes that build through many subclimaxes, to a most exciting and satisfying conclusion. There are many lessons here for those who want to keep the peace. This is emphatically not a work of propaganda. It is rather a splendid and riveting story that demands to be finished in one sitting" (*Times Literary Supplement*). The 1990 film version was a smash hit. Director: John McTiernan (1951–). "[Sean] Connery stars as a Soviet submarine captain who may or may not be planning to defect during the maiden voyage of a super-secret nuclear submarine. [Alec] Baldwin is the American intelligence ace who tries to anticipate his every move. Long, potentially confusing at times, but always manages to make a course correction in the nick of time … " (Maltin).

The "American intelligence ace" is Dr. John Patrick Ryan—Jack Ryan, for short. Like Tom Clancy, Ryan was born and raised in Baltimore, though he obtained his bachelor's degree from Boston College. After distinguished service as a Marine, he returned to college under the G.I. Bill of Rights, earning a doctorate in History. Ryan made it financially big as a stockbroker, then gave it up to teach History at the Naval Academy, where he was recruited by the CIA. Unlike most fictional spies, Ryan would enjoy super-fast promotion: from rookie to Chief Analyst to Deputy Director of Intelligence to National Security Advisor to Vice-President of the United States and finally the presidency itself. Apart from all that, he wrote a biography of Admiral William "Bull" Halsey, Jr. (1882–1959) *and* picked up an honorary British title (for "secret services rendered"). As they say in Ireland: "A right Clever Dick, if ever there was one." James Bond was eventually promoted from Commander to Captain in the Royal Navy, but his chances of becoming Prime Minister of the United Kingdom—or even just replacing M—were slim to beyond the vanishing point.

Jack Ryan would appear in fifteen more novels, from *Patriot Games*[44] to *Power and Empire* (2017), ghost-written by Marc Cameron (1961–). *Patriot Games* is actually a prequel, in which the young Jack Ryan, visiting London, becomes inadvertently concerned with the ULA (Ulster Liberation Army), a Maoist splinter group from the Provisional IRA; and if you believe *that*, you'll believe anything. It was filmed by director Philip Noyce (1950–) in 1992, with Harrison Ford as Jack Ryan and Anne Archer as his wife, Cathy. Ford and Archer (plus Noyce) returned for *Clear and Present Danger* (1994). *The Sum of All Fears* (2002) saw Ben Affleck in the main role. Chris Pine played Ryan as his younger CIA analyst self in *Jack Ryan: Shadow Recruit* (2013). Director: Kenneth Branagh (1960). There was an eight-episode *Jack Ryan* TV series (2018), with Carlton Case.

Tom Clancy did not create the techno-thriller genre. See, for instance Martin Caidin (q.v.) and Joe Poyer (1939–), the underrated author of *Operation Malacca* (1968) and *The Balkan Assignment* (1971). But he turned it into a more "realistic" version of spy-fi. Which could also more-or-less be said for the spin-off series that began with *Tom Clancy's Op-Center* (1995), created by Clancy and Steve Pieczenik (1943–). "[Op-Center] is a beating heart of defence, intelligence and crisis management technology. [When] a job is too dirty, or too dangerous, it is the only place the government can turn. But nothing can prepare Director Paul Hood and his team for what they are about to uncover—a very real, very frightening power play that could unleash new players in a new world order ..." (blurb). It was published concurrently with a two-part TV mini-series, which starred Harry (*Clash of the Titans*) Hamlin (1951–) as Paul Hood. Clancy also created and/or inspired *Ghost Recon*, *EndWar*, *Splinter Cell*, *Net Force*, *Power Plays*, *The Division*, *Elite Squad*, *X Defiant*, and many other collaborative novels and online game franchises, which have continued ever since his death from heart failure in 2013. Further reading: *The Tom Clancy Companion*,[45] edited by Martin H. Greenberg.

Stuart Woods (1938–2022) wrote *Deep Lie*,[46] which gives *Red October* a good run for its techno-thriller money. Blurb to the 1987 Pan edition: "Soviet submarines probe Sweden's defences. A top KGB official disappears to resurface as the head of the elite strike force SPETNAZ. An Italian computer expert is summoned to Moscow Centre. A US spy satellite discovers a top secret military base on the Latvian coast. And a young Russian naval lieutenant is given the chance of a lifetime.... In Washington, Kate Rule, head of the CIA's Soviet Office, patiently fits the jigsaw pieces of intelligence together and begins to smell a rat. Trouble is, no one else does. Or wants to." Except, that is, for William Lee, who takes a much stronger role in six other novels. His career trajectory runs from Georgia police chief to secret agent to senator and finally president of the United States. Lee might even have run against Jack Ryan!

The more character-driven work of Robert Ludlum[47] has proved itself to be just as commercially durable as that of Cussler and Clancy—if not more so. Ludlum was born in New York City, raised in Short Hills, New Jersey, and educated in Connecticut: Rectory School, Pomfret; Kent School; Cheshire Academy; Wesleyan University, Middletown (B.A. in Fine Arts). Although underaged, the 17-year-old Ludlum was accepted by the Marine Corps, serving from 1945 until 1947. He married Mary Ryducha, an aspiring actress, in 1951. Ludlum himself soon became a professional stage and TV actor: "I was always typecast as either a homicidal maniac or a lawyer. I thought there was a connection somehow." Ludlum also produced several plays at the North Jersey Playhouse, Fort Lee, New Jersey, and the Playhouse-on-the-Mall, Paramus, New Jersey (one of which was *The Owl and the Pussycat*, starring Alan Alda).

At the age of 40, the successful but discontented Ludlum put his actor-producer theatrical experience to good novelistic use. *The Scarlatti Inheritance*[48] concerns the search for a skeletons-in-the-cupboard file on the shady Scarlatti family. Roger Allen: "Competing for it are Matthew Cranfield, a Major in the U.S. Intelligence Service; ex–Nazi, Heinrich Kroeger; and Elizabeth Scarlatti, family matriarch and guardian of its secrets ... the main characters in this book are almost all rich and powerful, but that doesn't mean that they are treated uncritically. Ludlum has a healthy disrespect for American politics and the state of its society, and this adds a dimension to his writing that is absent from that of most of his rivals" (*Book and Magazine Collector* No. 110, May 1993). *Scarlatti* duly zoomed up all the bestseller lists and became a Book of the Month Club selection.

Ludlum's second novel, *The Osterman Weekend*,[49] was not only different from

Scarlatti, but *very* different from any other novel he would ever write. Apart from its protagonist, John Tanner, there are no sincerely sympathetic central characters. "John Tanner, network news director, is looking forward to a weekend party with his closest friends—the Ostermans, the Tremaynes and the Cardones. But then the CIA tell him that they are all suspected Soviet agents, fanatical, traitorous killers working for Omega, a massive Communist conspiracy. From this moment on, Tanner and his family are caught up in a nightmare whirlpool of terror, helpless isolation, violence and slaughter. Until the shattering climax, Tanner cannot know who are his friends, who are his implacable, deadly enemies …" (from blurb to the 1984 Granada paperback edition). The film version was released on November 4, 1983, starring Rutger Hauer (1944–2019) as Tanner. Director: Sam Peckinpah (1925–1984). "Consistently interesting but aloof and cold, despite a top-notch cast [Hauer, John Hurt, and Burt Lancaster]" (Maltin).

The Matlock Paper (1973) was followed by a string of article-adjective-noun entitled bestsellers: *The Rhinemann Exchange* (1974); *The Gemini Contenders* (1976); *The Chancellor Manuscript* (1977); *The Holcroft Covenant* (1978); *The Matarese Circle* (1979). Then came what is generally considered to be the high point of Ludlum's career. *The Bourne Identity*[50] introduced amnesiac spy-on-the-run Jason Bourne, who spent this novel and two sequels—*Supremacy* (1986) and *Ultimatum* (1990)—investigating his true past while trying not to get killed by seemingly every other secret agent in the world. Even American secret agents. *Especially* American secret agents. Argonaut Jason + "The undiscover'd country from whose bourn no traveller returns" (*Hamlet*: Act 3, Scene 1, Line 56") …?

Spoiler-alert synopsis: Before *Identity*, David Webb was an American Foreign Service officer in Phnom Penh, Cambodia, where he lived with his Thai wife, Dao, and their two children (Joshua and Alyssa). His family is killed in a friendly firebomb attack during the Vietnam War. Webb joins a secret assassination unit, Medusa, training in Saigon, and he is given the code name Delta. Jason Charles Bourne, an Australian-born member of Medusa, turns out to be a double agent (involved with slavery and drug smuggling). Delta/Webb executes Bourne, who—for certain security reasons—is listed as Missing in Action. Webb later joins Treadstone 71, a black-ops arm of the CIA. Jason Bourne is "reactivated" as Cain (i.e., David Webb), whose homicidal activities are meant to draw the real-life assassin, Ilich Ramirez Sànchez—alias Carlos the Jackal—into the open, by taking the credit for his kills. One such marked man was an African diplomat, Nykwana Wombosi, but Cain/Webb botches the job. He is shot several times, once in the head, and falls into the Mediterranean. The wounded Cold Warrior is picked up by a fishing boat, but the head injury has made him an amnesiac. By chapter 4, Webb has found an ally in Marie St. Jacques, employed by the Canadian government. He has also identified himself with an American called Jason Charles Bourne, the possessor of a Swiss bank account worth $4 million. And the deadly hunt begins….

The Bourne Identity was made into a two-part TV movie (ABC: May 8, 1988), directed by Roger Young (1942–) for Warner Brothers Television. The writer, Carol Sobieski (1939–1990), kept it close enough to the source novel for Ludlum's comfort. It starred Richard (*Dr. Kildare*) Chamberlain (1934) as Jason Bourne and Jaclyn (*Charlie's Angels*) Smith (1945) as Marie St. Jacques.

It is no coincidence that Jason Bourne equates to James Bond—if only by the initial letters of their names. Like Bond in *You Only Live Twice* and *The Man with the Golden Gun* (the book versions), Bourne is an amnesia victim who is being manipulated by malign forces beyond his control or even conscious knowledge. Unlike Bond, however, Bourne has no fatherly and all-forgiving M to welcome him back into the Secret Service fold. Ludlum did not share Fleming's essentially sentimental view of his fictional hero. The Bourne trilogy calls to mind a bestselling novel that also depicted "national security" agencies with a darker tone: *Six Days of the Condor*,[51] by James Grady (1949–), written just after the escalation in Vietnam and the aftermath of Watergate. McCormick and Fletcher: "[A CIA researcher] returns from lunch to discover that all his colleagues have been murdered in his absence. From that moment on Ronald Malcolm, code-named Condor, is on the run trying to escape the agency and the hired killers determined to find him" (*Spy Fiction*). Just *Three Days of the Condor* (September 24, 1975) starred Robert Redford (1936–) as Malcolm. Director: Sydney Pollack (1934–2008). Writer: Lorenzo Semple, Jr. (1923–2014). Malcolm reappeared in *Shadow of the Condor* (1976) and *Last Days of the Condor* (2015).

An even earlier novel of home-grown menace was *Seven Days in May*,[52] by Fletcher Knebel (1911–1993) and Charles W. Bailey II (1929–2012). The Joint Chiefs of Staff plot to depose an unpopular "peacenik" U.S. president (in 1974) and set up a military government. Epigraph: "…In the councils of government, we must guard against the acquisition of unwarranted influence, whether sought or unsought, by the military-industrial complex. The potential for the disastrous rise of misplaced power exists and will persist. We must never let the weight of this combination endanger our liberties or democratic processes—President Dwight D. Eisenhower, January 17, 1961." The film version (February 2, 1964) was directed by John (*Manchurian Candidate*) Frankenheimer and scripted by Rod (*Twilight Zone*) Serling (1924–1974). Cast list: Burt Lancaster (Air Force General James Mattoon Scott); Kirk Douglas (1916–2020: Colonel "Jiggs" Casey); Fredric March (1897–1975: President Jordan Lyman).

"THE GREATEST NEW NOVEL SINCE SEVEN DAYS IN MAY" was how Pyramid Books front-cover blurbed their paperback edition (October 1970) of *The Spy Who Spoke Porpoise*,[53] by Philip Wylie (1902–1971). More accurately: "The forbidden inner sanctum of CIA Headquarters in Virginia, where the fate of the nation was being decided by men free of all control … a top security project in Hawaii protected by high fences, armed men, and savage dogs … a mysterious linkup between American secret agents and top Russian operatives …" (internal blurb). In Ringling Wallender (R.W., for short) Grove, Wylie had the makings of a viable series-character counterspy. Former circus acrobat. Animal trainer. Magician. Ex-OSS officer. Multimillionaire. Semi-retired gentleman … until the body of a murdered CIA agent is found floating in Sea Life Park, Honolulu. Alas, it was not to be.

The aforementioned TV movie of *Identity* had toned down the violence to a family-audience acceptable level, which can't be said for the updated blockbuster-film version (June 6, 2002), starring Matt Damon (1970–) as Bourne and Franka Potente (1974–) as Marie (Kreutz—not St. Jacques). It out-bonded Bond both on screen and at the box office. "Kudos to [director Doug Liman] for keeping the action taut, the characters believable, and the excitement at a high pitch throughout" (Maltin). Both sequels were directed by Paul Greengrass (1955–): *Supremacy* (July 23, 2004). "When an assassin tracks down Jason Bourne and his girlfriend, who are living in exile in India, the CIA-trained killer is forced back into action to find out why he's being hunted. Filmed with nail-biting car chases and fight scenes, edited in a rat-tat-tat manner, but lacks the humour and sexual spark that made [*Identity*] so good. Brutal and cold-blooded, like its leading character; we're rooting for Bourne not because he's a hero but simply by default" (Maltin); *Ultimatum* (August 3, 2007). "Third chapter in Robert Ludlum's *Bourne* series has the CIA-trained operative traversing the world as he continues to search for his identity and how to settle old scores. All you could ask from an action film, with well-chosen international locales, an intelligently wrought cat-and-mouse narrative, and one breathless action set piece after another. Damon, again, is right on target as Bourne, but his character's virtual indestructability drains some of the humanity from the proceedings" (Maltin).

Eric Van Lustbader (1946–) has competently extended the Jason Bourne saga in eleven novels (to date), from *The Bourne Legacy* (2004) to *The Bourne Initiative* (2017). Jeremy Renner (1971) replaced Matt Damon in the film version of *Legacy* (August 10, 2012). "Renner has been genetically programmed by [Edward] Norton's deep-secret government agency to become a super-strong field operative. Then a possible security leak causes the organization to terminate all of its agents. Renner escapes just in time to help another victim of bureaucratic targeting: research doctor [Rachel] Weisz. Dense, action-packed screenplay works best when it keeps moving, but too much time is spent with Norton and his cold-blooded, espionage-speaking colleagues, which weighs down the film and bloats its length [135 minutes]. Still pretty exciting, and Renner hits a bull's-eye in the leading role. Eleventh-hour attempts by screenwriters Tony [also director] and Dan Gilroy to relate this to earlier [*Bourne*] movies are arbitrary and preposterous" (Maltin).

The Jason Bourne box-office set would have a lasting salutary effect upon spy films, especially the James Bond franchise, which had languished in the four-year Limbo between *Die Another Day* and the "authorized" remake of *Casino Royale* (November 14, 2006). Director: Martin Campbell (1924–). Daniel Craig[54] was even more grim-faced and laconic than Connery or Dalton, though both of them were not above cracking an off-color quip from time to time. The same goes double for Lazenby or Brosnan—and *triple* for Roger Moore. The film went back to basics, showing how Bond got his license to kill. "A bit overextended, but also refreshingly tough-minded, with some terrific set pieces … and a worthy love interest in [Eva] Green [as Vesper Lynd]. Craig makes for a lean, mean, surprisingly human Bond" (Maltin). Sequels: *Quantum of Solace* (2008); *Skyfall* (2012); *Spectre* (2015); *No Time to Die* (2021). N.B. *No Time to Die* was the title of a 1958 Warwick Films production (U.S. title: *Tank Force!*), co-produced by Irving Allen (1905–1987) and the pre–Bond Albert R. Broccoli. It starred Victor Mature (1913–1999) and Luciana (*Thunderball*) Paluzzi.

The John Drake of *Danger Man/Secret Agent* had a worthy All-American successor in the Angus MacGyver of *MacGyver* (ABC: September 29, 1985, to September 16, 1991). MacGyver was played to the hilt by Richard Dean Anderson (1950–), who had previously appeared as Dr. Jeff Webber in *General Hospital* (from 1975 until 1981) and as Naval Air Station officer Lt. Simon Adams, in *Emerald Point N.A.S.* (1983). Like Drake, MacGyver is averse to the use of firearms; in his case because a childhood friend had been accidentally killed by a revolver. Also like Drake, he can use ordinary objects—particularly a Swiss Army knife and duct tape—to create extraordinary effects, a knack which has entered the language as "MacGyvering" (or "to MacGyver"). These "MacGyverisms" have been spoofed time and again, most notably in the "A Star Is Burns" episode of *The Simpsons* (March 1995). After Mac-Gyver has saved a South American village from destruction:

"Thank you, Señor MacGyver!"
"Don't thank me. Thank the moon's gravitational pull."

Unlike John Drake, however, MacGyver was granted a fully filled-out backstory. He received his scientific education at Western Tech before serving in the U.S. Army Special Forces as a Bomb Team Technician/EOD (Explosive Ordnance Disposal). Then the MacGyver we know "shot trouble" for the Phoenix Foundation in Los Angeles and also worked as an agent of DXS (the equally fictional government Department of External Services). MacGyver's M is Pete Thornton (Dana Elcar: 1927–2005), an ex–DXS agent who became director of operations at the Phoenix Foundation. Jack Dalton (Bruce McGill: 1950–) played the obligatory comic sidekick, in much the same tradition of John Wayne and Gabby Hayes. The pre–*Lois & Clark* (1993–97: as Lois Lane) and *Tomorrow Never Dies* (1997: as Paris Carver) Teri Hatcher appeared in six episodes as Penny Parker, a ditzy secret agent who does whatever side she happens to be on more harm than good.

Anderson acted in, and executive-produced, two made-for-TV *MacGyver* movies. *MacGyver: Lost Treasure of Atlantis* (May 14, 1994) was directed by Michael Vejar (1943–). Writer: John Sheppard. The co-stars included Sophie Ward (Kelly Carson) and Brian Blessed (Atticus). *MacGyver: Trail to Doomsday* (September 25, 1995) was directed by Charles Correll (1944–2004). Writer: John Considine. Sophie Ward returned as Kelly Carson, with Peter Egan as Frederick Moran. Both films were made in Europe. In 2012, he also produced a few short films for Mercedes-Benz, promoting their new MPV Citan: MacGyver now operates a mobile repair service with his daughter Caitlin, but then duty calls again.... Image Comics published a five-issue run of *MacGyver* graphic novels, from October 2012 to February 2013, which were later collected in the trade paperback *MacGyver—Fugitive Gauntlet*. Tie-in novels: *MacGyver on Ice* (Armada, London, 1987), by Mark Daniel, and *MacGyver: Meltdown* (www.macgyveronline.com), by Lee David Zloloff and Eric Kelley.

CBS commissioned a reboot *MacGyver* pilot episode in October 2015, with Lucas Till (1990–) as MacGyver and George Eads (1967) as Lincoln. The series itself premiered on May 18, 2016, with Till and Eads (following a name change to Jack Dalton) heading the cast. Co-stars: Justin Hires (1985– : Wilt Bozer, MacGyver's roommate); Sandrine Holt (1972– : Patricia Thornton, director of operations for DXS); Tristan Mays (1990–): Riley Davis, a flighty female computer hacker). *MacGyver the Second* made it through 5 seasons, with 94 episodes, concluding on April 30, 2021.

*   *   *

Several attempts have been made to create new pulp-fiction super-spy characters, with a singular lack of lasting success. Agent 13: The Midnight Avenger, created by Flint Dille and David Marconi, did, however, make up this trilogy for TSR Books: *The Invisible Empire* (1986); *The Serpentine Assassin* (1986); *Acolytes of Darkness* (1988). "In 1907, a gifted child was kidnapped and taken to a place known as 'the Shrine,' the ultra-secret headquarters of the sinister 'Brotherhood.' The child's real name was erased, and he was given the number 13. As memories of his parents faded, he was trained in the arts of power. An exemplary student, he seemed destined to become a great agent of the Brotherhood. Instead, 13 learned the true nature of the Brotherhood, and fled. Thus began a deadly cat-and-mouse game between Agent 13 and the Brotherhood" (generic blurb). See also: *Agent 13 Sourcebook* (1988), by Roy Winninger.

Spy fiction "proper" faced increasingly fierce competition from sci fi (*Star Trek*, *Star Wars*, etc.), and a whole new genre created by Don Pendleton[55]: men's action-adventure fiction, featuring fast-trigger vigilante heroes. Donald Eugene Pendleton had served in the wartime U.S. Navy (1941–47), and he returned to active duty in 1952, during the Korean War.

George Kelley: "Pendleton's creation of Mack Bolan, a soldier who was a guerrilla warfare specialist and sniper in Vietnam, was inspired by the frustrations of the Vietnam War overseas and the lack of success of 'the war on crime' on the home front. Bolan returns home to the funeral of his parents and sister and learns they were killed by the Mafia. He then launches a one-man war on organized crime, battling the Mafia from city to city—and more recently, international terrorists—for over 200 books in the continuing Executioner series" (*Twentieth-Century Crime and Mystery Writers*). Pendleton wrote 37 Mack Bolan novels for Pinnacle Books, from *War on the Mafia* (1969) to *Satan's Sabbath* (1980), plus *The Executioner's War Book* (1977: a "technical manual" and series overview). After that, ghost writers have produced well over 200 more books, racking up sales of well over 200 million. Mack Bolan himself: "The world is full of avaricious men who would prey on the innocent and trusting. Humankind cannot allow this. *I* will not allow this."

Seismic Surge (Gold Eagle, Toronto, October 2012), ghost-written by Doug Wojtowicz, is volume 121 in Don Pendleton's Stony Man: America's Ultra-Covert Intelligence Agency series. "When the President hits the panic button, it's Stony Man that answers the call. An elite, covert group, Stony Man strikes before terror can gain a foothold. A plot orchestrated to destabilize the Western world has its roots in a mysterious business conglomerate with ties to Chinese conspirators. And the established battleground is a volcanic island off the coast of Spain. There, an army of multinational terrorists bound by hate and violence is about to trigger a tsunami that will wash hell across two continents. While Stony Man's cyber-crew runs real-time command and control, Phoenix Force and Able Team launch a multipronged ground assault on the corporation behind the planned tidal wave and its ruthless backers" (blurb).

Further reading: *Sticking It to the Man: Revolution and Counterculture in Pulp and Popular Fiction*,[56] edited by Andrew Nette and Iain McIntyre.

At the extreme outer limits of 1970s spy fiction were several novels and films exploiting the Kung Fu craze of that time. For best example: *Enter the Dragon* (1973), which starred Bruce Lee (1940–1973). The novelization was written by Mike Roote (Award, USA: Tandem, UK), from Michael Allin's original screenplay. "Every kind of evil is being planned in the secret lair of Mr. Han, international magnate of crime. Only Lee, indomitable student of the ancient Martial Arts of the Orient, can crack the defences of the mysterious island deep in the China Seas, and confront the renegade Han and his army of trained thugs" (blurb to the Tandem paperback edition). Of possible esoteric interest, Michael Avallone wrote three novels for Warner Paperback Library concerning Satan Sleuth Philip St. George ("Fighting for reason and right against the Devil and his disciples"): *Fallen Angel* (1974); *The Werewolf Walks Tonight* (1974); *Devil, Devil* (1976). James Bond only had mundane enemy agents and Ernest Stavro Blofeld to worry about....

Epilogue:
The Shape of Spies to Come?

As the saying goes: "I could tell you. But then I'd have to kill you." It *is* safe to say, however, that there will always be secrets, people who want to keep those secrets, and other people who want to find out those secrets.

"SPY AGENCIES SAY THE FUTURE IS BLEAK," headed a leading article in *The New York Times International Edition* (April 19, 1921). It reads, in part: "[The world] is rent by a changing climate, aging populations, disease [particularly Covid-19], financial crises and technologies that divide more than they unite. Politics within states are likely to grow more volatile and contentious, and no region, ideology, or governance system seems immune or to have the answers. At the international level, it will be a world increasingly shaped by China's challenge to the United States and Western-led international system, with a greater risk of conflict." Nonfiction upgrades: *The New Spymasters: Inside Espionage from the Cold War to Global Terror*,[1] by Stephen Grey; *Intercept: The Secret History of Computers and Spies*,[2] by Gordon Corera.

Spy fiction has been in a state of flux for the past twenty-odd years. The Jason Bourne mini-franchise looked good for a while, but it didn't turn out to be the "new" James Bond cultural phenomenon. Spoof film series like *Austin Powers* (1997–2002) and *Kingsman* (2014–2021) have proved to be more popular than the real thing. Even the "old" Bondian progression has long been a thing of fits and starts, with its post–Daniel Craig future now hanging in the box-office balance. Ian Fleming, whose books kicked the whole thing off, hardly gets a look-in anymore.

Filmmakers have looked to the past, concocting "reboots" of former hits, e.g., *Mission Impossible*, *The Man from U.N.C.L.E.*, *I Spy*, *The Saint*, *Get Smart*, and *The Wild Wild West*, of which only Tom Cruise's IMF Force team has really fired the popular imagination. On the other hand, U.S.-made TV series like *24* (2001–2010), *Alias* (2001–2006), *Nikita* (2010–2013), *Homeland* (2011–), and the UK-made *Spooks* (2002–2011) have racked up high audience figures. As for books, new British writers like Charles Cummings (1971–) and Mick Herron (1963–), plus their American counterparts Dale Brown (1956–) and Brad Thor (1969–) regularly hit the bestseller lists. The "Jack Reacher" novels of British-born writer Lee Child (1954–) enjoy a large transatlantic audience, unlike the film versions—so far. And Dan Brown's

Robert Langdon (*The Da Vinci Code*, etc.) is an "agent in the outfield," if ever there was one! Fiction upgrade: *Cold Warriors: Writers Who Waged the Literary Cold War*,[3] by Duncan White.

For me, the most enjoyable part about writing this book has been reading the novels and watching the films and TV series featuring fictional American secret agents. One thing is certain. Whatever the future of real-life espionage, the "special relationship" that pertains between James Bond and his American opposite numbers is likely to last a lot longer than the increasingly iffy one between their respective governments.

Chapter Notes

Introduction

1. August 25, 1930, to October 31, 2020. Films include *Darby O'Gill and the Little People* (1959); *Marnie* (1964); *The Man Who Would Be King* (1975).
2. Ian Fleming, *Casino Royale* (London: Jonathan Cape, 1954).
3. Nicholas Rankin, *Ian Fleming's Commandos: The Story of the Legendary 30* (Oxford: Oxford University Press, 2011).
4. Sheldon Lane, ed., *For Bond Lovers Only* (London: Panther, 1965, p. 13).
5. 1959 Pan paperback edition, London, p. 45.
6. May 31, 1907, to August 18, 1971. Noted for *Brazilian Adventure* (Alden Press, Oxford, 1933).
7. Clive Bloom, *Bestsellers: Popular Fiction Since 1900* (London: Palgrave Macmillan, 2002).
8. Karen Hinckley and Barbara Hinckley, *American Best Sellers* (Bloomington & Indianapolis: Indiana University Press, 1989).
9. Thomas L. Bonn, *UnderCover: An Illustrated History of American Mass Market Paperbacks* (New York: Penguin, 1982).
10. August 2, 1899–June 15, 1995. Bennett was an Alfred Hitchcock veteran, e.g., *Blackmail* (1929) and *The Thirty-Nine Steps* (1935).
11. June 26, 1904, to March 23, 1964. Né Lázló Lówenstein. Born in Rozsahezy, Austria-Hungary. Films include *M* (1931); *Beat the Devil* (1953); *The Raven* (1963).
12. Colin Wilson, *Dreaming to Some Purpose* (London: Century, 2004); 2005 Arrow paperback edition, pp. 247–8).
13. John F. Kennedy, *Profiles in Courage* (New York: Harper & Brothers, 1955).
14. Tony Bennett and Jane Woolacott, *Bond and Beyond: The Political Career of a Popular Hero* (London and New York: Macmillan, 1987).
15. Hinckley and Hinckley, *American Best Sellers*, p. 148.
16. John Pearson, *The Life of Ian Fleming* (London: Jonathan Cape, 1966).
17. John Pearson, *James Bond: The Authorized Biography of 007* (London: Granada, 1985).
18. Richard Gant, *Ian Fleming: The Man with the Golden Pen* (London: Mayflower-Dell paperback original, 1966).
19. O.F. Snelling, *007 James Bond: A Report* (London: Neville Spearman, 1964).
20. Kingsley Amis, *The James Bond Dossier* (London: Jonathan Cape, 1964).
21. Kingsley Amis, *The James Bond Dossier* (Pan paperback edition, London, 1966), p. 11.
22. *Ibid.* p. 12.
23. March 19, 1928, to January 13, 2009.
24. Titan Books, London, have issued the *Daily Express* Bond strips in book form, beginning with *The James Bond Omnibus Volume 001* (2009).
25. April 5, 1909, to June 27, 1996.
26. October 27, 1915, to September 28, 1994.
27. Stephen Jay Rubin, *The James Bond Films: A Behind the Scenes History* London: Talisman Books, 1981; plus revised editions.
28. James Chapman, *Licence to Thrill: A Cultural History of the James Bond Films* (London and New York: I.B. Taurus, 1999: second edition, 2007).
29. Arthur Marwick, *The Sixties: Cultural Revolution in Britain, France, Italy, and the United States c. 1958–1974* (London: Oxford University Press, 1998), p. 18.
30. Chapman, *License to Thrill*, p. 95.
31. Philip Knightley, *The Second Oldest Profession: Spies and Spying in the Twentieth Century* (London: André Deutsch, 1986).
32. Terry Crowdy, *The Enemy Within: A History of Espionage* (Oxford and New York: Osprey, 2006).
33. Donald McCormick and Katy Fletcher, *Spy Fiction: A Connoisseur's Guide* (New York and Oxford: Facts On File, 1990).

Chapter One

1. September 15, 1789, to September 14, 1851.
2. James Fenimore Cooper, *The Last of the Mohicans: A Narrative of 1757* (Philadelphia: Carey & Lea, 1826).
3. G.A. Henty, *With Wolfe in Canada* (Glasgow: Blackie, Glasgow, 1887).
4. Robert Middlekauff, *The Glorious Cause: The American Revolution, 1763–1789* (Oxford University Press, 1982).
5. John J. Bakeless, *Turncoats, Traitors and Heroes* (Philadelphia: J.P. Lippincott, 1959).
6. Howard Fast, *April Morning* (New York: Crown, 1961).
7. James Fenimore Cooper, *The Spy* (New York: Wiley & Halstead, 1821).

8. *The Leatherstocking Saga: Being parts of* THE DEERSLAYER, THE LAST OF THE MOHICANS, THE PATHFINDER, THE PIONEERS, *and* THE PRAIRIE (London: Collins, 1955) is a convenient one-volume abridgement.

9. *The Spy* (New York: Popular Library Student Edition, 1972), p. 343.

10. *Ibid.* p. 350.

11. It was privately printed by J & J Harper, New York, for the author, H.L. Barnum, who was previously best known for *The Farmer's Own Book* (1932) and other textbooks. Barnum's unreliable "biography" was undoubtedly written to cash in on the success of *The Spy*, and it did become a bestseller in both America and Britain.

12. Walter Lord, *The Dawn's Early Light* (New York: W.W. Norton, 1972).

13. J. Christopher Herold, *The Mind of Napoleon: A Selection from His Written and Spoken Words* (New York and London: Columbia University Press, 1955).

14. January 19, 1809, to October 7, 1849.

15. Peter Ackroyd, *Poe: A Life Cut Short* (London: Chatto & Windus, 2008).

16. *Graham's Lady's and Gentleman's Magazine*, April 20, 1841.

17. *The Gift: A Christmas, New Year and Birthday Present: 1845* (Philadelphia: Carey & Hunt, 1844).

18. *The Philadelphia Dollar Newspaper*, June 21 and 28 issues, 1843.

19. *Graham's Magazine*, July 1841.

20. Fletcher Pratt, *Ordeal by Fire: An Informal History of the Civil War* (New York: Harrison Smith & Robert Hass, 1935).

21. Susan Mary Grant, *The War for a Nation* (New York: Routledge, 2006).

22. *Ordeal by Fire* (New York: Pocket Books Cardinal paperback edition), p. xi.

23. Harnett T. Kane, *Spies for the Blue and Gray* (New York: Doubleday, 1954).

24. Ace Star paperback edition, 1961, pp. 7–8.

25. James Mackay, *Allan Pinkerton: The First Private Eye* (Edinburgh: Mainstream Publishing Company, 1996).

26. February 12, 1809, to April 15, 1865.

27. Kennedy was portrayed by Dick Powell (November 14, 1904, to January 2, 1963) in *The Tall Target*, a fanciful but close-to-the-facts 1951 film directed by Anthony Mann.

28. Edward S. Ellis, *The Forest Spy: A Tale of the War of 1812* (New York: G.W. Carleton, 1884).

29. J. Randolph Cox, *The Dime Novel Companion* (Westport, Connecticut: Greenwood, 2000).

30. D. Appleton & Co., New York, 1895, and William Heinemann, London, 1896; Macmillan, New York and London, 1936; Harper and Brothers, New York, and Frederick Muller, London, 1956; 1982, 1985, 1988; Random House, New York, and William Heinemann, London, 1984).

31. Peter Hopkirk, *The Great Game: On Secret Service in High Asia* (Oxford University Press, 1990: updated in 2005).

32. Ron Goulart, *Cheap Thrills: An Informal History of the Pulp Magazine* (New York: Arlington House, 1972).

33. *Ibid.* p. 31.

34. *Street & Smith's New York Weekly*, September 18, 1886.

35. *The Halfpenny Marvel*, no. 6, December 1893.

Chapter Two

1. 1 September 21, 1866, to August 13, 1946.

2. H.G. Wells, *The War That Will End War* (London: Frank & Cecil Palmer, 1914).

3. H.G. Wells, *Mr. Britling Sees It Through* (London: Cassell, 1916).

4. H.G. Wells, *The War of the Worlds* (London: William Heinemann, 1898).

5. Michael Foot, *H.G. The History of Mr. Wells* (London: Doubleday, 1995).

6. I.F. Clarke, *Voices Prophesying War 1763–1984* (London: Oxford University Press, 1966).

7. Panther paperback edition, London, 1970, p. 1.

8. Michael Moorcock (editor), *Before Armageddon: Anthology of Victorian and Edwardian Imaginative Fiction Published before 1914* (London: W.H. Allen, 1975); *England Invaded* (ditto, 1977).

9. William Le Queux, *The Great War in England in 1897* (London: Tower, 1894).

10. July 2, 1864, to October 13, 1927.

11. Moorcock, *Before Armageddon*, p. 12.

12. Hugh S. Johnson, "The Dam" (*The Red Book Magazine*, April 1911).

13. Sam Moskowitz (editor), *Science Fiction by Gaslight: A History and Anthology of Science Fiction in the Popular Magazines, 1891–1911* (Cleveland, Ohio: World Publishing Company, 1968).

14. Montgomery of Alamein, *A Concise History of Warfare* (London: William Collins, 1972), pp. 273–4.

15. May 22, 1859, to July 7, 1930.

16. Conan Doyle, *The War in South Africa* (London: Smith Elder, 1902).

17. Conan Doyle, *His Last Bow* (London: John Murray, London, 1917).

18. Erskine Childers, *The Riddle of the Sands: A Record of Secret Service Recently Achieved* (London: Smith Elder, 1903).

19. June 25, 1870, to November 24, 1922.

20. Tom Cox, *Damned Englishman: A Study of Erskine Childers* (Hicksville, New York: Exposition Press, 1975).

21. John Atkins, *The British Spy Novel: Styles in Treachery* (London: John Calder, 1984).

22. April 1, 1875, to February 10, 1932.

23. Edgar Wallace, *The Four Just Men* (London: Tallis Press, 1905).

24. Joseph Conrad, *The Secret Agent* (London and New York: Harper, 1907).

25. December 3, 1857, to August 3, 1924. Né Teodór Jósef Konrad Korzeniowski. Born in Berdychiv, Ukraine.

26. Joseph Conrad, *Under Western Eyes* (London and New York: Harper, 1911).

27. G.K. Chesterton, *The Man Who Was Thursday: A Nightmare* (Bristol: Arrowsmith, Bristol, 1908).

28. October 22, 1866, to February 3, 1946.

29. E. Phillips Oppenheim, *Mysterious Mr. Sabin* (London: Ward Lock, 1898).

30. E. Phillips Oppenheim, *The Yellow Crayon* (London: Ward Lock, 1903).

31. Robert Standish, *The Prince of Storytellers* (London: Peter Davies, 1957).

32. William Le Queux, *The Invasion of 1910–14* (London: Nash, 1905).

33. William Le Queux, *The Mystery of a Motor-Car* (London: Hodder & Stoughton, 1906).

34. William Le Queux, *Spies of the Kaiser* (London: Hurst & Blackett, 1909).

35. William Le Queux, *German Atrocities: A Record of Shameless Deeds* (London: Newnes, 1914); *Britain's Deadly Peril: Are We Told the Truth?* (London: Stanley Paul, 1915).

36. Chris Patrick and Stephen Baister, *William Le Queux: Master of Mystery* (self-published: January 2007).

37. A.J.P. Taylor, *The First World War: An Illustrated History* (London: Hamish Hamilton, 1963).

38. John Buchan, *The Thirty-Nine Steps* (Edinburgh: Blackwood, 1915). It had been serialized in *Blackwood's Magazine*, under the pseudonym H. de V, from August to September 1915.

39. August 26, 1875, to February 11, 1940.

40. John Buchan, *Memory Hold-the-Door* (London and New York: Hodder & Stoughton and Houghton Mifflin; published in the United States as *Pilgrim's War: An Essay in Recollection*).

41. Ursula Buchan, *Beyond the Thirty-Nine Steps: A Life of John Buchan* (London: Bloomsbury, 2019).

42. John Buchan, *The Power-House* (Edinburgh: Blackwood, 1916).

43. Robert A. Harris and Michael Lasky, *The Films of Alfred Hitchcock* (Secaucus, New Jersey: The Citadel Press, 1976).

44. Robert A. Harris and Michael Lasky, *The Films of Alfred Hitchcock* (Secaucus, New Jersey: The Citadel Press, 1976).

45. John Buchan, *Greenmantle* (London: Hodder & Stoughton, 1916).

46. Richard Usborne, *Clubland Heroes: A Nostalgic Study of Some Recurrent Characters in the Romantic Fiction of Dornford Yates, John Buchan and Sapper* (London: Constable, 1953; revised edition from Barrie & Jenkins, London, 1974).

47. Christopher Frayling, *The Yellow Peril: Dr. Fu Manchu and the Rise of Chinaphobia* (London: Thames & Hudson, 2014).

48. February 15, 1883, to June 1, 1959.

49. Pan paperback edition, London, 1960, p. 127.

50. Barbara Tuchman, *The Zimmermann Telegram* (New York: Viking Press, 1958).

51. Alan Moorehead, *The Russian Revolution* (London: William Collins and Hamish Hamilton, 1958).

52. *A Short History of the World*. From the 1965 William Collins edition, revised and brought up to date by Raymond Postgate and Professor G.P. Wells (the author's eldest son), p. 308.

53. Edgar Wallace, *The Adventures of Heine* (London: Ward Lock, 1919).

54. Neil Clark, *Stranger Than Fiction: The Life of Edgar Wallace, the Man Who Created KING KONG* (London: The History Press, 2014).

55. E. Phillips Oppenheim, *Up the Ladder of Gold* (London: Hodder & Stoughton, 1931).

56. Hodder & Stoughton paperback edition (undated), London, p. 105.

57. September 28, 1888, to August 14, 1937.

58. Sapper, *Bull-dog Drummond: The Adventures of a Demobilized Officer Who Found Peace Dull* (London: Hodder & Stoughton, 1920).

59. Cited by Jonathon Green in *Oxford Dictionary of National Biography* (London: Oxford University Press, 2004).

60. Sapper, *Bulldog Drummond: His Four Rounds with Carl Peterson* (London: Hodder & Stoughton, 1938).

61. August 7, 1885, to March 5, 1960.

62. A.J. Smithers, *Dornford Yates: A Biography* (London: Hodder & Stoughton, 1982).

63. Dornford Yates, *Blind Corner* (London: Hodder & Stoughton, 1927).

64. July 18, 1888, to October 27, 1954.

65. Sydney Horler, *The Curse of Doone* (London: Hodder & Stoughton, 1928).

66. Sydney Horler, *Tiger Standish* (London: Hodder & Stoughton, 1932).

67. *They Called Him Nighthawk* (London: Hodder & Stoughton, 1937).

68. May 12, 1907, to April 15, 1993.

69. Ian Dickerson, *A Saint I Ain't* (London: Chinbeard Books, 2019).

70. Burl Barer, *The Saint: A Complete History in Print, Film and Television of Leslie Charteris' Robin Hood of Modern Crime, Simon Templar, 1928–1992* (Jefferson, North Carolina: McFarland, 1992, + revised editions).

71. January 8, 1897 to November 10, 1977.

72. Dennis Wheatley, *The Young Man Said* (London: Hutchinson, 1977); *Officer and Temporary Gentleman* (ditto, 1978); *Drink and Ink* (ditto, 1979).

73. Phil Baker, *The Devil Is a Gentleman: The Life and Times of Dennis Wheatley* (London: Dedalus, 2009).

74. September 17, 1908, to June 9, 1973.

75. Armchair Detective Press, White Bear Lake, Minnesota, 1968. Revised edition, 1969.

76. John Creasey, *The Death Miser* (London: Andrew Melrose, 1933).

77. W. Somerset Maugham, *Ashenden: or, The British Agent* (London: William Heinemann, 1928).

78. January 25, 1874, to December 15, 1965.

79. Pan paperback edition, London, 1952, pp. 9–10.

80. Robert Calder, *Willie: The Life of Somerset Maugham* (London: William Heinemann, 1989).

81. Anthony Masters, *Literary Agents* (Oxford: Basil Blackwell, 1987).

Chapter Three

1. David Stuart Davies (editor), *The Casebook of Sexton Blake* (Ware, Herefordshire: Wordsworth Editions, 2009).

2. Frank Gruber, *The Pulp Jungle* (Los Angeles: Sherborne Press, 1967).

3. William F. Nolan, *The Black Mask Boys* (New York: William Morrow, 1985).

4. *Ibid.* p. 32.

5. *Cheap Thrills*, p. 85.

6. Philip Sherman, *Leo Margulies. Giant of the Pulps. His Thrilling, Exciting, and Popular Journey* (New York: Altus Press, 2017).

7. *Cheap Thrills*, p. 86.

8. Nick Carr, *America's Secret Service Ace: The Operator 5 Story* (Mercer Island, Washington: Starmont, 1985).

9. *Cheap Thrills*, p. 89.

10. Tom Johnson and Will Murray, *Secret Agent X: A History* (Oak Forest, Illinois: Robert Weinberg, 1980). Revised edition: Seymour, Texas: Fading Shadow, Inc., 1991).

11. *Ibid.* pp. 9–10 (1980 edition).

12. Nick Carr, *The Flying Spy: A History of G-8* (Chicago: Robert Weinberg, 1978).

13. *Ibid.* p. 87.

14. Donald E. Keyhoe, *The Flying Saucers Are Real* (Greenwich, Connecticut: Gold Medal paperback original, 1950). Expanded from an article in *True* magazine (January 1950).

15. Don Hutchinson, *The Great Pulp Heroes* (Oakville, Ontario, and Buffalo, New York: Mosaic Press, 1996).

16. *Ibid.* pp. 60–1.

17. Donald E. Keyhoe, *Captain Philip Strange: Strange War* (Silver Spring, Maryland: Age of Aces/Adventure House, 2011).

18. *The Great Pulp Heroes*, p. 189.

19. *Cheap Thrills*, pp. 91–2.

20. *The Great Pulp Heroes*, p. 201.

21. Jim Harmon, *The Great Radio Heroes* (New York: Doubleday, 1967). Revised edition from McFarland, Jefferson, North Carolina, 2002.

22. Ace paperback edition, New York, 1968, p. 49.

23. September 12, 1897, to December 6, 1985.

24. Walter B. Gibson, *Return of the Shadow* (New York: Belmont paperback original, 1963).

25. Walter B. Gibson and Litzka R. Gibson, *The Complete Illustrated Book of the Psychic Sciences* (New York: Doubleday, 1966).

26. Thomas J. Shimeld, *Walter B. Gibson and The Shadow* (Jefferson, North Carolina: McFarland, 2003).

27. Frank Eisberger, Jr., *Gangland's Doom* (Mercer Island, Washington: Starmont House, 1985).

28. *Ibid.* p. 42.

29. *The Great Pulp Heroes*, p. 34.

30. John L. Nanovic, *Doc Savage, Supreme Adventurer* (Melrose, Massachusetts: Odyssey Press, 1980).

31. October 4, 1904, to March 11, 1959.

32. Lester Dent, *Lady in Peril* (New York: Ace, 1959).

33. Lester Dent, *Honey in His Mouth* (New York: Hard Case Crime, 2011).

34. Kenneth Robeson, *The Mystic Mullah* (New York, Bantam, 1965).

35. Philip José Farmer, *Doc Savage: His Apocalyptic Life. [As the Archangel of Technopolis and Exotica. As the Golden-eyed Hero of 181 Supersagas. As the Bronze Knight of the Running Board. Including His Final Battle Against the Forces of Hell Itself.]* (New York: Doubleday, 1973). Revised edition: Panther paperback, London, 1975.

36. Robert Weinberg (editor), *The Man Behind Doc Savage* (Chicago: Weinberg, 1974).

37. Will Murray, *Doc Savage* (Melrose, Massachusetts: Odyssey Press, 1978) and *Secrets of Doc Savage* (Ditto, 1981).

38. Jim Harmon and Donald F. Glut, *The Great Movie Serials: Their Sound and Fury* (New York: Doubleday, 1972).

39. Robin Cross, *The Big Book of B Movies: Or, How Low Was My Budget* (London: Frederick Muller, 1981).

40. William K. Everson, *The Detective in Film* (Secaucus, New Jersey: The Citadel Press, 1972).

41. *The Detective in Film.* p. 123.

42. Stephen C. Earley, *An Introduction to American Movies* (New York: Mentor Books, 1978).

43. *Ibid.* pp. 177–8.

44. Ron Goulart, *Great History of Comic Books* (New York: Contemporary Books, 1986).

45. Allan Holtz, *American Newspaper Comics: An Encyclopedic Reference Guide* (Ann Arbor: University of Michigan Press, 2012).

46. Denis Gifford, *The History of the British Newspaper Comic Strip* (Oxford: Shire Publications, 1971).

47. Chris Steinbrunner and Otto Penzler, *Encyclopedia of Mystery and Detection* (New York: McGraw-Hill, 1976).

48. Harmon and Glut, *The Great Movie Serials*, p. 165.

49. *Ibid.* pp. 173–4.

50. Max Allan Collins, *Dick Tracy* (New York: Bantam paperback original, 1990). Based on the screenplay by Jim Cash and Jack Epps, Jr., and Bo Goldman and Warren Beatty. Walt Disney Productions.

51. May 27, 1894, to January, 1961.

52. October 2, 1909, to September 6, 1956.

53. Dashiell Hammett, *The Big Knockover*, edited by Lillian Hellman (New York: Random House, 1974).

54. William F. Nolan (1928–), *Dashiell Hammett. A Life at the Edge* (New York: Congdon & Weed, 1983).

55. *Ibid.* pp. 136–7.

56. Dashiell Hammett and Alex Raymond, *Dashiell Hammett's Secret Agent X-9* (Princeton, Wisconsin: Kitchen Sink Press, 1990).

57. Leslie Charteris and Charles Flanders, *The Phantom Plane* (Long Beach, California: Pacific Comics Club, 1980).

58. Tom Roberts, *Alex Raymond: His Life and Art* (Silver Spring, Maryland: Adventure House, 2007).

59. http://www.markcarlson-ghost.com/index.php/2017/06/10/secret-agent-x-9.

60. Charles Flanders, *Secret Agent X-9* (Racine, Wisconsin: Whitman, 1936).

61. Robert Storm, *Secret Agent X-9 and the Mad Assassin* (Racine, Wisconsin: Whitman, 1938).

62. Maxwell Grant, *The Shadow and the Ghost Makers* (Racine, Wisconsin: Whitman, 1942).

63. Ted Okuda, *The Monogram Checklist: The Films of Monogram Pictures Corporation* (Jefferson, North Carolina: McFarland, 1999).

64. *Leonard Maltin's Movie Guide. The Modern Era.*

65. James Luceno, *The Shadow* (New York: Ivy Books, 1994).

66. *The Great Pulp Heroes*, p. 73.

67. *Ibid.* pp. 73–74.

68. Cited by Martin Quigley, in *The Film Daily* (January 2, 1940).

69. Robert Sampson, *Spider* (Bowling Green, Ohio: Popular Press, 1987).

70. Philip José Farmer, *Tarzan Alive: A Definitive Biography of Lord Greystoke* (New York: Doubleday, 1972).

Chapter Four

1. November 11, 1901, to August 28, 1978.

2. *Cosmopolitan*, July 1948, pp. 101–102.

3. F. Van Wyck Mason, *The Branded Spy Murders* (New York: Doubleday, 1932).

4. Cited in *The New York Times* (June 6, 1940).

5. Aka *When the Guns Say—Die!* (*All-Story Western*, July 1950).

6. F. Van Wyck Mason, *Lysander* (New York, Pocket Books, 1956).

7. F. Van Wyck Mason, *The Barbarians* (New York, Pocket Books, 1954).

8. Harold Lamb, *Hannibal: One Man Against Rome* (New York: Doubleday, 1958).

9. George MacDonald Fraser, *The Hollywood History of the World* (London: Michael Joseph, 1988).

10. F. Van Wyck Mason, *Return of the Eagles* (New York: Pocket Books, 1959). Rewritten from *All Save One Shall Die* (*Adventure*, October-November-December 1939 and January 1940).

11. F. Van Wyck Mason, *Eagle in the Sky* (Philadelphia: J.P. Lippincott, 1948).

12. F. Van Wyck Mason, *Three Harbours* (Philadelphia: J.P. Lippincott, 1938).

13. Cited by Richard Dalby in *Book and Magazine Collector* (November 2009).

14. F. Van Wyck Mason (editor), *The Fighting American* (New York: Reynal & Hitchcock, 1943).

15. F. Van Wyck Mason, *Cutlass Empire* (New York: Doubleday, 1949).

16. F. Van Wyck Mason, *The Brimstone Club* (Boston: Little, Brown, 1971).

17. F. Van Wyck Mason, *Spider House* (New York: The Mystery League, 1932).

18. Geoffrey Coffin, *Murder in the Senate* (New York: Dodge, 1935).

19. F. Van Wyck Mason, *Seeds of Murder* (New York: Doubleday, 1930).

20. F. Van Wyck Mason, *The Vesper Service Murders* (New York: Doubleday, 1931).

21. F. Van Wyck Mason, *The Fort Terror Murders* (New York: Doubleday, 1931).

22. F. Van Wyck Mason, *The Three Arrow Murders* (New York: Doubleday, 1935).

23. Pocket Books paperback edition, New York, 1941, pp. 62–4.

24. *Ibid.* pp. 116–7.

25. *Ibid.* pp. 265–6.

26. *Ibid.* pp. 83–84.

27. *The Singapore Exile Murders*, p. 10.

28. James Hadley Chase, *Twelve Chinks and a Woman* (London: Jarrolds,). Revised edition: *Twelve Chinamen and a Woman* (Novel Library, London, 1940). Retitled *The Doll's Bad News* (Panther paperback edition, London, 1970).

29. *The Singapore Exile Murders*, pp. 43–4.

30. *Ibid.* pp. 163–4.

31. *Ibid.* p. 126.

32. F. Van Wyck Mason, *The Castle Island Case* (New York: Reynal & Hitchcock, 1937).

33. Interior blurb to 1948 Bantam paperback edition.

34. *Ibid.* p. 14.

35. *Ibid.* p. 24.

36. Pocket Books edition, pp. 15–6.

37. Ewen Montagu, *The Man Who Never Was* (London: Evans Brothers, 1953).

38. Mayflower-Dell edition, p. 65.

39. F. Van Wyck Mason, *The Multi-Million-Dollar Murders* (New York: Pocket Book Cardinal paperback, 1960).

40. Geoffrey Coffin, *The Forgotten Fleet Mystery* (New York: Dodge, 1936).

41. Arrow paperback edition (London, 1953, p. 9).

42. Jim Cox, *Radio Crime Fighters: More Than 300 Programs from the Golden Age* (Jefferson, North Carolina: McFarland, 2002).

43. *The New York Times* (October 4, 1958).

44. Obituary in *The Washington Post* (August 30, 1978): "F. Van Wyck Mason, Prolific Novelist," by J.Y. Smith.

45. F. Van Wyck Mason, *Roads to Liberty* (Boston: Little, Brown, 1972).

46. F. Van Wyck Mason, *Armoured Giants* (Boston: Little, Brown, 1980).

Chapter Five

1. November 10, 1893, to July 16, 1960.
2. John J. Gross, *John P. Marquand* (New York: Twayne, 1963).
3. John P. Marquand, *The Unspeakable Gentleman* (New York: Scribner, 1922). Magazine version: *Ladies' Home Journal* (February to May, 1922).
4. John P. Marquand, *Warning Hill* (Boston: Little, Brown, 1930).
5. John P. Marquand, *The Late George Apley* (Boston: Little, Brown, 1937).
6. John P. Marquand, *Ming Yellow* (Boston: Little, Brown, 1935). Magazine version: *The Saturday Evening Post* (December 8, 1934, to January 12, 1935).
7. Pocket Books (UK) edition, pp. 6–7.
8. August 26, 1884, to April 5, 1933. Born in Warren, Ohio. Non–Charlie Chan books include *Seven Keys to Paldpate* (1913) and *Fifty Candles* (1926).
9. John P. Marquand, *No Hero* (Boston: Little, Brown, 1935).
10. John P. Marquand, *Mr. Moto Takes a Hand* (London: Robert Hale, 1940).
11. David Zinman, *Saturday Night at the Bijou: A Nostalgic Look at Charlie Chan, Andy Hardy, and Other Movie Heroes We Have Known and Loved* (New York: Arlington House, 1973).
12. *The Enemy Within*, 214–5.
13. Earl Derr Biggers, *The House without a Key* (Indianapolis: Bobbs-Merrill, 1925).
14. *Ibid.* pp. 76–7.
15. Yunte Huang, *Charlie Chan: The Untold Story of the Honourable Detective and His Rendezvous with American History* (New York and London: W.W. Norton, 2010).
16. John P. Marquand, *Your Turn, Mr. Moto* (New York: Berkley paperback edition, 1963).
17. Souvenir Press, London, 1987, pp. 19–25.
18. *Ibid.* p. 8.
19. *Ibid.* p. 9.
20. *Ibid.* pp. 3–4.
21. *Ibid.* pp 6–7.
22. *Ibid.* pp. 31–2.
23. Cited in *Encyclopedia of Mystery and Detection*.
24. Little, Brown paperback edition, 1985, pp. 18–9.
25. Pocket Books paperback edition, 1940, pp. 94–5.
26. Consul paperback edition, London, 1964, p. 129.
27. Little, Brown paperback edition, 1986, p. 267.
28. Cited by Frederick C. Orthman, in *The Washington Post*, November 29, 1937 ("Lorre Learns How to Emote from Rasslers: Film Player Gets Points from Groan and Grunt Bouts on Coast").
29. *The Detective in Film*, p. 80.
30. *Encyclopedia of Mystery and Detection*.
31. May 17, 1905, to November 7, 1995. Best known for his stage play (1953) and screenplay (1956) adaptations of Vern Sneider's novel *The Teahouse of the August Moon* (1951).
32. November 17, 1905, to June 19, 1988. Other films include *Run Silent, Run Deep* (1958) and *You Only Live Twice* (1967).
33. John W. Vandercook, *Murder in Trinidad* (New York: Doubleday Crime Club, 1933).
34. Stephen D. Youngkin, Jones Bigwood, and Raymond Cabana, Jr., *The Films of Peter Lorre* (Secaucus, New Jersey: Citadel Press, 1982).
35. November 23, 1887, to February 2, 1969. Né William Henry Pratt. Born in London. Other films include *Frankenstein* (1931); *Charlie Chan at the Opera* (1936); *Targets* (1968).
36. Cited in *The New York Times* (January 20, 1957): "Welcome, Mr. Moto," by Anthony Boucher.
37. *Ibid.*
38. John P. Marquand, *Stopover: Tokyo* (Boston: Little, Brown, 1957).
39. Berkley paperback edition, New York, 1963.
40. Popular Library paperback edition, New York, 1977.
41. Williams Collins, London, pp. 66–7.
42. *Ibid.* p. 11.
43. *Ibid.* p. 33.
44. *Ibid.* p. 174.
45. *Ibid.* pp. 92–3.
46. *Ibid.* p. 175.
47. Ian Fleming, *Thrilling Cities* (London: Jonathan Cape, 1963).
48. John Brosnan, *James Bond in the Cinema* (London: The Tantivy Press, 1972), p. 93.
49. *Ibid.* p. 94.
50. John P. Marquand, *Women and Thomas Harrow* (Boston: Little, Brown, 1958). Magazine version: *Ladies' Home Journal* (July to November 1958).
51. John P. Marquand, Jr. *The Second Happiest Day* (New York: Harper & Bros., 1953).
52. Leslie Halliwell (with Philip Purser), *Halliwell's Television Companion: Third Edition* (London: Grafton Books, 1986).
53. E.V. Cunningham, *The Case of the One-Penny Orange* (New York: Holt Rinehart, 1977).
54. Stuart M. Kaminsky, *Think Fast, Mr. Peters* (New York: St. Martin's Press, 1988). Other novels include *He Done Her Wrong* (1993) and *Mildred Pierced* (2003).

Chapter Six

1. Max Hastings, *All Hell Let Loose: The World at War 1939–45* (London: Harper Press, 2011). Retitled *Inferno* for the Vintage Press trade paperback edition (New York, 2012).
2. Leslie Charteris, *Prelude for War* (London: H & S, 1938).
3. Pan paperback edition (as *The Saint Plays with Fire*), London, 1959, pp. 8–9.
4. June 20, 1909, to October 22, 1998. Novels include *Epitaph for a Spy* (1938); *Judgment on Deltchev* (1951); *The Light of Day* (1963).

5. October 2, 1904, to April 3, 1991.

6. Graham Greene, *A Sort of Life* (London: The Bodley Head, 1971).

7. Norman Sherry, *The Life of Graham Greene, Volume 1: 1904–1939* (London, Jonathan Cape, 1989); *Volume 2: 1939–1955* (ditto, 1994); *Volume 3: 1955–1991* (ditto, 1999).

8. Graham Greene, *A Gun for Sale* (London: William Heinemann, 1936).

9. Graham Greene, *The Ministry of Fear* (London: William Heinemann, 1943).

10. *Literary Agents*, p. 121.

11. Arrow paperback edition, London, 1955, p. 208.

12. *Ibid.* pp. 215–6.

13. Arrow paperback edition, London, 1960, p. 16.

14. Peter Cheyney, *This Man Is Dangerous* (London: William Collins, 1936).

15. Peter Cheyney, *Sinister Errand* (London: William Collins, 1945). As *Sinister Murders* (Avon paperback edition, New York, 1957).

16. Cited in *Spy Fiction. A Connoisseur's Guide* (Oxford and New York: Facts On File, 1990), by Donald McCormick and Katy Fletcher.

17. Michael Harrison, *Peter Cheyney, Prince of Hokum* (London: Neville Spearman, 1954).

18. Leonard Rubenstein, *The Great Spy Films* (Secaucus, New Jersey: The Citadel Press, 1979).

19. Clyde Jeavons, *A Pictorial History of War Films* (London: Hamlyn, 1974).

20. Bradford W. Wright, *Comic Book Nation: The Transformation of Youth Culture in America* (Baltimore, Maryland: The Johns Hopkins University Press, 2001).

21. *Ibid.* pp. xiii–xiv.

22. *Ibid.* p. 30.

23. Roy Thomas, *Superman. The War Years 1939–1945* (New York: Chartwell Books, 2015). Companion volumes: *Batman* and *Wonder Woman*.

24. *Ibid.* p. 12.

25. *The Encyclopedia of American Comics*, p. 344.

26. Joan Schenkar, *The Talented Miss Highsmith: The Secret Life and Serious Art of Patricia Highsmith* (New York: St. Martin's Press, 2009.

27. *The Great Movie Serials*, pp. 244–5.

28. Eric Stedman, *The Adventures of Spy Smasher in the Comics and the Movies* (Southampton, Pennsylvania: The Serial Squadron, 2019).

29. Leslie Charteris, *The Saint in Miami* (New York: Doubleday, 1940).

30. *The Saint Steps In* (Pan paperback edition, London, 1958, pp. 176–7).

31. *The Saint on Guard* (Hodder paperback edition, London, 1963, p. 121).

32. *Ibid.* p. 108.

33. Raymond Chandler, *The Lady in the Lake* (New York: Alfred Knopf, 1943).

34. Pan paperback edition, London, 1979, p. 26.

35. Brett Halliday, *Dividend on Death* (New York: Henry Holt, 1939).

36. Brett Halliday, *The Corpse Came Calling* (New York: Dodd Mead, 1942).

37. Brett Halliday, *Blood on the Black Market* (New York: Dodd Mead, 1943). Retitled *Heads You Lose* (Dell paperback edition, New York, 1958).

38. *Ibid.* p. 1.

39. Ellery Queen, *The Roman Hat Mystery* (New York: Stokes, 1929).

40. Francis M. Nevins, Jr., *Royal Bloodline: Ellery Queen, Author and Detective* (Bowling Green, Ohio: Popular Press, 1974).

41. John McAleer, *Rex Stout: A Biography* (Boston: Little, Brown, 1977).

42. Rex Stout (Anonymous), *The President Vanishes* (New York: Farrar and Rinehart, 1934).

43. *Rex Stout: A Biography*, p. 255.

44. Rex Stout, *Fer-de-Lance* (New York: Farrar and Rinehart, 1934).

45. William S. Baring-Gould, *Nero Wolfe of West Thirty-Fifth Street: The Life and Times of America's Largest Private Detective* (New York: The Viking Press, 1969).

46. William S. Baring-Gould, *Sherlock Holmes of Baker Street. A Life of the World's First Consulting Detective* (New York: Clarkson N. Porter, Inc., 1962).

47. Bantam paperback edition, 1970, p. 105.

48. A.A. Fair, *The Bigger They Come* (New York: William Morrow, 1939). As *Lam to the Slaughter* (London: Hamish Hamilton, 1939).

49. Irwin Porges, *Edgar Rice Burroughs: The Man Who Created Tarzan* (Provo, Utah: Brigham Young University, 1976).

50. Gabe Essoe, *Tarzan of the Movies: A Pictorial History of More Than Fifty Years of Edgar Rice Burroughs' Legendary Hero* (Secaucus, New Jersey: The Citadel Press, 1968).

51. *Ibid.* p. 115.

52. *All Hell Broke Loose*, p. 675.

53. Bernard F. Dick, *The Star-Spangled Screen. The American World War II Film* (Lexington: The University Press of Kentucky, 1996).

54. Brian W. Aldiss (with David Wingrove), *Trillion Year Spree: The History of Science Fiction* (London: Victor Gollancz, 1986).

55. Christy Campbell, *Target London. Under Attack from the V-Weapons During WWII* (London: Little, Brown, 2012).

56. Robert Jungk, *Brighter Than a Thousand Suns: A Personal History of the Atomic Scientists* (Berlin: Alfred Scherz Verlay, 1956, as *Heller als tausent Sonnen*). American edition: Harcourt, Brace & Co., 1958, translated by James Cleagh.

57. George Orwell, *Nineteen Eighty-Four* (London: Secker and Warburg, 1949).

58. May 8, 1884, to December 26, 1972. Biography: *Truman* (William Collins, London, 1986), by Roy Jenkins.

59. Jeremy Isaacs and Taylor Downing, *Cold War* (London and New York: Bantam Press, 1998).

60. W.H. Auden, *The Age of Anxiety* (New York: Random House, 1947).

61. Graham Greene, *Our Man in Havana* (London: William Heinemann, 1958).
62. *Secret Intelligence in the Twentieth Century* (Panther paperback edition, London, 1978, p. 324).
63. Victor Marchetti and John D. Marks, *The CIA and the Cult of Intelligence* (New York: Alfred A. Knopf, 1974; revised edition: Dell Books, 1980).
64. Winston Churchill, *The Second World War* (Boston: Houghton-Mifflin, 1948–1953, in six volumes). Definitive edition: Cassell, London, ditto).
65. *The Great Spy Films*, p. 169.
66. *The Great Movie Serials*, pp; 160–1.
67. William Rotsler, *Blackhawk* (New York: Warner Books, 1982).
68. William B. Todd and Ann Bowden, *Tauchnitz International Editions in English 1841–1955: A Bibliographical History* (New York: Bibliographical Society of America, 1988).
69. *UnderCover*, p. 51.
70. Richard A. Lupoff, *The Great American Paperback* (Portland, Oregon: Collectors Press, 2001).
71. Ron Goulart, *The Dime Detectives* (New York: The Mysterious Press, 1988).
72. *Ibid*. p. 233.

Chapter Seven

1. September 11, 1916, to June 16, 1975.
2. Edward S. Aaronns, *Death in a Lighthouse* (New York: Phoenix Press, 1938). As *The Cowl of Doom* (Hangmann's House, New York, 1946).
3. Lee Server, *Encyclopedia of Pulp Fiction Writers* (New York: Checkmark Books, 2002).
4. *Ibid*. p. 1.
5. Edward Ronns, *No Place to Live* (Philadelphia: David McKay, 1947). As *Lady, the Guy Is Dead* (Avon paperback edition, New York, 1950).
6. Edward Ronns, *Gift of Death* (Philadelphia: David McKay, 1948).
7. Paul Ayres, *Dead Heat* (Drexel Hill, Pennsylvania: Bell, 1950).
8. Edward S. Aarons, *Nightmare* (Philadelphia: David McKay, 1948).
9. Edward S. Aarons, *Assignment to Disaster* (New York: Gold Medal, 1955).
10. *Ibid*. pp. 19–20.
11. *Ibid*. p. 22.
12. *Ibid*. p. 19.
13. Edward S. Aarons, *Assignment—Angelina* (New York: Gold Medal, 1958).
14. *Ibid*. pp. 18–19.
15. *Ibid*. p. 19.
16. *Ibid*. p. 130.
17. *Ibid*. p. 160.
18. *Ibid*. p. 65.
19. *Assignment—Disaster*, p. 62.
20. *Ibid*. p. 9.
21. *Assignment—Mara Tirana*, p. 175.
22. *Assignment—Manchurian Doll*, p. 66.
23. *Ibid*. pp. 67–68.
24. *Ibid*. p. 57.
25. *Ibid*. p. 148.
26. *Assignment—Cong Hai Kill*, p. 13.
27. *Ibid*. p. 26.
28. *Assignment—Black Viking*, pp. 90–92.
29. *Assignment—Unicorn*, p. 150.
30. *Ibid*. pp. 15–16.
31. *Assignment—Zoraya*, p. 40.
32. Donald McCormack and Katy Fletcher, in *Spy Fiction. A Connoisseur's Guide*.
33. www.mysteryfile.com/Aarons/Durell.
34. Edward Ronns, *The Black Orchid* (New York: Pyramid, 1959).
35. Edward Ronns, *But Not for Me* (New York, Pyramid, 1959).
36. Edward S. Aarons, *Hell to Eternity* (New York: Gold Medal, 1960).
37. Edward S. Aarons, *The Defenders* (New York: Gold Medal, 1961).

Chapter Eight

1. March 24, 1916, to November 20, 2006.
2. Donald Hamilton, *Date with Darkness* (New York: Rinehart, 1947).
3. Donald Hamilton, *The Steel Mirror* (New York: Rinehart, 1948).
4. Donald Hamilton, *Murder Twice Told* (New York: Rinehart, 1950).
5. Donald Hamilton, *Death of a Citizen* (New York: Gold Medal, 1960).
6. *Ibid*. p. 8.
7. *Ibid*. p. 136.
8. *The Silencers*, p. 8.
9. *Murderers' Row*, p. 24 (Coronet paperback edition, London, 1966, p. 24: with a slight title change to *Murderer's Row*).
10. *Ibid*. pp. 24–5.
11. *The Ambushers*, p. 90.
12. *Ibid*. pp. 5–6.
13. *Ibid*. p. 6.
14. *The Shadowers*, p. 6.
15. *The Devastators*. Coronet paperback edition, London, 1967, p. 80.
16. Donald Hamilton, *The Mona Intercept* (New York: Gold Medal, 1980).
17. *The Annihilators*, p. 2.
18. *The Damagers*, pp. 29–30.
19. June 7, 1917, to December 25, 1995. Né Dino Paul Crocetti. Films include *The Young Lions* (1958); *Rio Bravo* (1959); *Ocean's Eleven* (1960).
20. Born 1913 or 1914. Birth name: Stephen Coulter. Other "Charles Hood" novels: *Let Sleeping Girls Lie* (1965); *Shamelady* (1966); *Once in a Lifetime*/aka *Sergeant Death* (1966); *The Man above Suspicion* (1969); *Asking for It* (1971).
21. Cited in *Dino: Living High in the Dirty Business of Dreams* (Doubleday, New York, 1992), by Nick Tosches.
22. Richard Meyers, *TV Detectives* (La Jolla, California: A.S. Barnes; and London: The Tantivy Press, 1981).

23. *Ibid.* p. 223.

24. Bruce Scivally, *Booze, Bullets and Broads: The Story of Matt Helm* (Wilmette, Illinois: Henry Gray, 2013).

25. August 23, 1928, to November 18, 2004. Films include *The Magnificent Seven* (1960); *Charade* (1963); *Cross of Iron* (1977).

26. Jack Pearl, *Our Man Flint* (New York: Pocket Books, 1965).

27. Bradford Street, *In Like Flint* (New York: Dell, 1967).

28. Henry Reymons, *Deadlier Than the Male* (Hodder paperback original, London, 1967) and *Some Girls Do* (ditto, 1969).

29. *The Rough Guide to James Bond*, p. 93.

30. Donald Hamilton, *Night Walker* (New York: Dell, 1954). UK title: *Rough Company* (Allan Wingate, London, 1954).

31. Donald Hamilton, *Cruises with Kathleen* (New York: David McKay, 1980).

32. © 2015 by Interjet AB and Keith Wease.

33. Keith Wease, CreateSpace Independent Publishing Platform, USA, 2013.

Chapter Nine

1. May 12, 1915, to August 10, 1986.

2. John Jakes, *On Secret Service* (New York: E.P. Dutton, 2000).

3. McGoohan was born in Astoria, Queens, New York City, and spent his early life in Ireland. He held dual Irish-American citizenship. Films include *Hell Drivers* (1957); *Ice Station Zebra* (1968); *Braveheart* (1995).

4. Richard Telfair, *Target for Tonight* (New York: Dell First Edition, 1962).

5. Robert Sellers, *Cult TV: The Golden Age of ITC* (London: Plexus, 2006).

6. *Ibid.* pp. 43–44.

7. October 27, 1924, to February 26, 1999.

8. Michael Avallone, *The Tall Dolores* (New York: Holt Rinehart, 1953).

9. Michael Avallone, *The Case of the Violent Virgin* (New York: Ace Double paperback, 1957: *The Case of the Bouncing Betty*).

10. Bill Pronzini, *Gun in Cheek: A Study of "Alternative" Crime Fiction* (New York: Coward, McCann & Geoghegan, 1982), p. 63.

11. *Istanbul*, p. 109.

12. Nicholas Browne, *Seven Against Greece*. pp. 8–9.

13. Lew Louderback, *Danger Key*, p. 68.

14. William L. Rohde, *The Judas Spy*, pp. 84–5.

15. Willis T. Ballard, *The Kremlin File*, pp. 10–11.

16. Jon Messmann, *The Death Strain*, Star paperback edition, London, 1972, pp. 84–6.

17. John Messmann, *Operation Ché Guevara*, Tandem paperback edition, London, 1970, p. 27.

18. January 15, 1924, to August 9, 2005.

19. *Shadow—Go Mad!* pp. 20–21.

20. *Ibid.* p. 52.

21. *Ibid.* pp. 55–57.

22. *Destination: Moon*, pp. 145–6.

23. October 19, 1928, to March 7, 2004.

24. *Dr. Nyet*, pp. 13–16.

25. *Ibid.* pp. 18–19.

26. Ted Mark, *The Man from Charisma* (New York: Dell, 1971).

27. Troy Conway, *The Coxeman Comes* (New York: Paperback Library, 1967). Aka *The Berlin Wall Affair* (1969) and *Don't Bite Off More Than You Can Chew* (1972).

28. May 20, 1911, to December 24, 1986. Novels include *The Borgia Blade* (1953); *The Hunter Out of Time* (1965); *Carty* (1977).

29. Jennifer DeRoss, *Forgotten All-Star: A Biography of Gardner F. Fox* (2019), www.pulpheropress.com.

30. *I'd Rather Fight Than Swish*, p. 11.

31. *The Wham! Bam! Thank You, Ma'am Affair*, pp. 31–32.

32. Rod Gray, *The Lady from L.U.S.T.* (New York: Belmont/Tower, 1967). Later retitled *Lust, Be a Lady Tonight*.

33. K & G paperback edition, London, 1968, p. 15.

34. *Ibid.* p. 31.

35. Glen Chase, *The Italian Connection* (New York: Leisure Books, 1973).

36. Paul Kenyon, *The Ecstasy Connection* (New York: Pocket Books, 1974).

37. *Diamonds Are for Dying*, pp. 44–5.

38. Clyde Allison, *Our Man from Sadisto* (New York: Ember Library, 1965).

39. *Operation T*, pp. 11–12.

40. *The Orgy at Madame Dracula's*, p. 7.

41. Michael Avallone, *The Man from Avon* (New York: Avon, 1967).

Chapter Ten

1. Adam Diment, *The Dolly Spy* (London: Michael Joseph, 1967).

2. *The Kiwi Contract*, pp. 16–17.

3. *The Irish Beauty Contract*, p. 25.

4. *Ibid.* pp. 7–8.

5. Charles Messenger, *Northern Ireland: The Troubles* (London: Hamlyn/Bison Books, 1985).

6. *The Death Bird Contract*, pp. 135–6.

7. July 10, 1914, to July 22, 1986.

8. Charles Kelly, *Gunshots in Another Room: The Forgotten Life of Dan J. Marlowe* (New York: Asclepian Imprints, Ltd., 2012).

9. Dan Marlowe, *Backfire* (New York: Berkley, 1961).

10. *Operation Hammerlock*, pp. 87–8.

11. *Operation Deathmaker* (Coronet paperback edition, London, 1975), pp. 172–3.

12. As *You Could Call It Murder* (New York: Foul Play Press, 1987).

13. *The Thief Who Couldn't Sleep* (No Exit Press, London, 1996), p. 194.

14. *The Canceled Czech*, p. 20.

15. *Ibid.* p. 33.
16. *Tanner on Ice*, p. 19.
17. *Ibid.* p. 56.
18. *Pattern for Panic* (Gold Medal revised edition, 1961, p. 16).
19. *Darling, It's Death*, p. 50.
20. *The Trojan Hearse*, p. 130.
21. *The Second Longest Night*, p. 11.
22. October 9, 1918, to January 23, 2007.
23. E. Howard Hunt, *The Berlin Ending* (New York: G.P. Putnam's Sons, 1973).
24. David St. John, *On Hazardous Duty* (New York: Signet, 1965). Retitled *Hazardous Duty* (Frederick Muller, London, 1966).
25. Ian Fleming, *Octopussy, and The Living Daylights* (London: Jonathan Cape; and New York: New American Library, 1966).
26. E. Howard Hunt, *Cozumel* (New York: Stein and Day, 1985).
27. March 13, 1912, to March 23, 1980.
28. Bill S. Ballinger, *The Body in the Bed* (New York: Harper, 1948).
29. *The Spy in the Jungle*, pp. 12–13.
30. *Ibid.* p. 52.
31. *Ibid.* p. 15.
32. *The Chinese Mask*, p. 7.
33. Graeme Flanagan, *The Australian Vintage Paperback Guide* (New York: Gryphon Books, 1994).
34. *Come Die with Me*, pp. 23–4.
35. *Ibid.* p. 30.
36. *Ibid.* p. 29.
37. *Ibid.* pp. 127–8.
38. *Ibid.* p. 56.
39. March 9, 1918, to July 17, 2006.
40. Mickey Spillane, *Primal Spillane. The Early Stories: 1941-1942*, edited and with an Introduction by Max Allan Collins and Lynn F. Myers, Jr. (New York: Gryphon Books, 2003).
41. Mickey Spillane, *I, the Jury* (New York: E.P. Dutton, 1947).
42. *One Lonely Knight*, p. 6.
43. *The Snake* (Corgi paperback edition, 1965, p. 9).
44. *One Lonely Knight*, p. 105.
45. Mickey Spillane, *Day of the Guns* (New York: E.P. Dutton, 1964).
46. *The By-Pass Control* (Signet paperback edition, p. 18).
47. *One Lonely Knight*, p. 114.
48. *TV Detectives*, p. 91.
49. Martin Sands, *Maroc-7* (London: Pan, 1967).
50. Mickey Spillane, *The Delta Factor* (New York: E.P. Dutton, 1967).
51. Mickey Spillane and Max Allan Collins, *Complex 90* (New York: Titan Books, 2013).
52. David Wise and Thomas B. Ross, *The Espionage Establishment* (New York: Random House, 1967).
53. *The Living Bomb* (Digit paperback edition, London, 1965, p. 7).
54. *Ibid.* p. 80.
55. *The Doomsday Bag*, p. 23.

Chapter Eleven

1. July 17, 1928, to December 9, 2005.
2. Gregory Stephenson, *Comic Inferno: The Satirical World of Robert Sheckley* (San Bernardino, California: The Borgo Press, 1997).
3. http://www.bignewsmag.com/archives/bignews/november2001/dain.html.
4. *Calibre.50*, p. 24.
5. *Ibid.* p. 70.
6. *Dead Run*, pp. 69–70.
7. *Live Gold*, p. 15.
8. *Ibid.* p. 16.
9. *Ibid.* p. 18.
10. *Ibid.* p. 152.
11. *Comic Inferno*, p. 114.
12. *White Death*, p. 2.
13. *Time Limit*, p. 38.
14. *Ibid.* p. 137.
15. *Comic Inferno*, p. 118.
16. Robert Sheckley, *The Game of X* (New York: Delacorte Press, 1965).
17. Jonathan Cape edition, London, 1967, p. 10.
18. Joe Claro, *Condorman* (New York: Scholastic Book Services, 1981); Heather Simon, ditto (London: New English Library, 1981).
19. June 3, 1922, to February 3, 2012.
20. *The Spy Who Loved America*, pp. 5–7.
21. *Ibid.* p. 10.
22. *Ibid.* p. 8.
23. *Ibid.* p. 108.
24. *Ibid.* pp. 139–140.
25. *A Silent Kind of War*, p. 17.
26. Jack Laflin, *The Reluctant Spy* (New York: Belmont, 1966).
27. Peter Rabe, *From Here to Maternity* (New York: Vanguard Press, 1955).
28. Peter Rabe, *Blood on the Desert* (New York: Gold Medal, 1958).
29. Peter Rabe, *Girl in a Big Brass Bed* (Greenwich, Connecticut: Gold Medal, 1965).
30. *The Spy Who Was 3 Feet Tall*, pp. 12–13.
31. *Ibid.* p. 61.
32. Peter Rabe, *Tobruk* (New York: Bantam, 1967).

Chapter Twelve

1. *The Great Radio Heroes*, p. 253.
2. *Ibid.* p. 252.
3. Paul Donovan, *The Radio Companion* (London: HarperCollins, 1991).
4. Dave Rogers, *Danger Man and The Prisoner* (London: Boxtree, 1989).
5. *Ibid.* p. 57.
6. Dave Rogers, *The Complete Avengers* (London: Boxtree, 1989).
7. February 6, 1922, to June 25, 2015. Films include *The Small Back Room* (1949); *The Battle of the River Plate* (1956); *Rehearsal for Murder* (1982).
8. July 20, 1938, to September 10, 2020. Films include *A Midsummer Night's Dream* (1968); *The Assassination Bureau* (1969); *The Hospital* (1971).

9. Cited in *The Los Angeles Times* for April 11, 1998 (obituary by Dennis Mclellan).

10. *TV Detectives*, p. 107.

11. April 11, 1920, to May 3, 2010.

12. *Book and Magazine Collector* (No. 122, May 1994).

13. Peter O'Donnell, *Modesty Blaise* (London: Souvenir Press, 1965).

14. Crest edition, pp. 13–14.

15. Larry Forrester, *A Girl Called Fathom* (New York: Gold Medal, 1967). Other books include *Battle of the April Storm* (1969) and *Diamond Beach* (1974).

16. Cited in Andrew Lycett's *Ian Fleming*, p. 420.

17. Jon Heitland, *The Man from U.N.C.L.E. Book: The Behind-the-Scenes Story of a Television Classic* (New York: St. Martin's Press, 1987).

18. November 22, 1932, to November 11, 2016. Other films include *Bullitt* (1968); *Demon Seed* (1977: voice, uncredited); *Brass Target* (1978).

19. September 23, 1933– . Born in Glasgow. Other films include *Billy Budd* (1962); *The Greatest Story Ever Told* (1965); *Hear My Song* (1990).

20. *TV Detectives*, p. 100.

21. October 25, 1886, to October 16, 1972. Born in Weedon Bec, Northamptonshire, England. Films include *Rebecca* (1940); *Spellbound* (1945); *The Desert Fox* (1951).

22. Robert Vaughn, *A Fortunate Life* (New York: Thomas Dunne Books/St. Martin's Press, 2008).

23. *Ibid.* pp. 147–8.

24. Kurt Peer, *TV Tie-Ins: A Bibliography of American Tie-In Paperbacks* (Tucson, Arizona: Neptune Publishing, 1997).

25. *Ibid.* p. 121.

26. Don D'Ammassa, *Masters of Adventure: James Bond and His Rivals* (Managansett Press, 216).

27. *Ibid.* p. 335.

28. Souvenir Press/Four Square edition, p. 88.

29. *Leo Margulies: Giant of the Pulps*, pp. 160–162.

30. Walter B. Gibson, *The Coin of Diablo Affair* (New York: Wonder Press, 1965).

31. November 2, 1942– . Née Stefania Zolya Paul Federkiewicz. Born in Hollywood, California. Films include *Experiment in Terror* (1962); *The Boatniks* (1970); *Escape to Athena* (1978).

32. Helen MacInnes, *The Venetian Affair* (New York: Harcourt Brace, 1963).

33. Robert Miall, *The Protectors* (London: Pan, 1973).

34. *Cult TV*, p. 226.

35. Roger Fulton, *The Encyclopedia of TV Science Fiction* (London: Boxtree, 1995).

36. August 16, 1930, to March 24, 2010. Films include *PT109* (1963); *Bob & Carol & Ted & Alice* (1969); *Hannie Caulder* (1971).

37. July 12, 1937– . Films include *Man and Boy* (1971); *California Suite* (1978); *The Meteor Man* (1993).

38. *Cult TV*, pp. 80–81.

39. *TV Tie-Ins*, p. 97.

40. *Masterstroke*, pp. 6–7.

41. *Ibid.* pp. 9–10.

42. *Ibid.* pp. 52–53.

43. Patrick J. White, *The Complete Mission Impossible Dossier* (New York: Avon Books, 1991).

44. *TV Detectives*, pp. 123–4.

45. *Dossier*, p. 22.

46. *Ibid.* pp. 49–50.

47. *Ibid.* p. 14.

48. *Ibid.* p. 63.

49. *Ibid.* p. 40.

50. *Ibid.* p. 44.

51. March 18, 1926, to March 14, 2010. Films include *War Paint* (1953); *Wolf Larsen* (1958); *A Rage to Live* (1965).

52. *TV Detectives*, p. 124.

53. James Arness and James E. Wise, Jr., *James Arness: An Autobiography* (Jefferson, North Carolina: McFarland, 2001).

54. *Dossier*, p. 116.

55. *Ibid.* pp. 38–39.

56. *Dossier*, p. 244.

57. *TV Tie-Ins*, p. 129.

58. *Dossier*, p. 276.

59. *Ibid.* p. 433.

60. *Ibid.* p. 437.

61. *Ibid.* p. 438.

62. *Cult TV*, p. 251.

63. Don Adams and Bill Dana, *Get Smart: Would You Believe?* (New York: Bantam, 1982).

64. *TV Detectives*, p. 114.

65. Richard Wormser, *The Wild West* (New York: Signet, 1966).

66. *Cult TV*, p. 33.

67. *Ibid.* p. 143.

68. September 14, 1927, to March 24, 1997.

69. Martin Caidin, *Marooned* (New York: E.P. Dutton, 1964).

70. Martin Caidin, *Cyborg* (New York: Arbor House, 1972).

71. Mayflower paperback edition London, 1974, pp. 46–47.

72. *TV Detectives*, pp. 177–178.

73. Ray Galton and Alan Simpson, *The Spy with a Cold Nose* (London: Arrow, 1966).

Chapter Thirteen

1. Andy Lane and Paul Simpson, *The Bond Files: An Unofficial Guide to the World's Greatest Secret Agent* (London: Virgin Books, 1998).

2. *Licence to Thrill*, pp. 76–7.

3. Robert Sellers, *The Battle for Bond: The Genesis of Cinema's Greatest Hero* (London: Tomahawk Press, 2007).

4. Christopher Bray, *Sean Connery: The Measure of a Man* (London: Faber and Faber, 2010).

5. *Ibid.* p. 134.

6. *Ibid.* pp. 136–7.

7. Roger Moore (with Gareth Owen), *Bond on Bond: The Ultimate Book on 50 Years of Bond Movies* (London: Michael O'Mara Books, 2012).

8. October 19, 1931, to December 12, 2020.

9. John le Carré, *The Spy Who Came in from the Cold* (London: Victor Gollancz, 1963).

10. John le Carré, *Tinker, Tailor, Soldier, Spy* (London: Hodder & Stoughton, 1974).

11. David Monaghan, *Smiley's Circus: A Guide to the Secret Service of John le Carré* (London: Orbis, 1986).

12. Adam Sisman, *John le Carré: The Biography* (London: Bloomsbury, 2015).

13. *Ibid.* p. 233.

14. February 18, 1929– .

15. *Spy Fiction*, p. 72.

16. Len Deighton, *The Ipcress File* (London: Hodder & Stoughton, 1962).

17. *Spy Fiction*, p. 73.

18. March 14, 1933– . Né Maurice Joseph Micklewhite. Born in Rotherhithe, London. Other films include *Zulu* (1964); *Educating Rita* (1983); *The Cider House Rules* (1999).

19. Mike Ripley, *Kiss, Bang: The Boom in British Thrillers from CASINO ROYALE to THE EAGLE HAS LANDED* (London: HarperCollins, 2017).

20. March 18, 1915, to April 9, 1999. Other novels include *Winter Kills* (1964) and *The Whisper of the Axe* (1976).

21. Colin Cross, *The British Empire* (London: Hamlyn, 1972).

22. Jeremy Black, *The Politics of James Bond: From Fleming's Novels to the Big Screen* (Westport, Connecticut, and London: Praeger, 2001).

23. *Ibid.* pp. 61–62.

24. Andy Lane and Paul Simpson, *The Bond Files: An Unofficial Guide to the World's Greatest Secret Agent* (London: Virgin Books, 1998, plus revised editions).

25. *The Politics of James Bond*, p. 78.

26. I*N FL*MNG, *Alligator* (Boston: Vanitas, 1962).

27. Kingsley Amis (as Robert Markham), *Colonel Sun* (New York: Harper, 1968).

28. John Gardner, *Licence Renewed* (London: Jonathan Cape, 1981).

29. Trevanian, *The Eiger Sanction* (New York: Crown, 1972).

30. Trevanion, *The Loo Sanction* (New York: Crown, 1973).

31. June 12, 1931, to December 14, 2005.

32. *The Eiger Sanction* (Panther paperback edition, 1975, p. 11).

33. *Ibid.* p. 17.

34. William F. Buckley, Jr. *Saving the Queen* (New York: Doubleday, 1976).

35. William F. Buckley, Jr. *Last Call for Blackwood Oakes* (New York: Harcourt, 2005).

36. William F. Buckley, Jr. *Who's on First* (New York: Doubleday, 1980).

37. July 15, 1931– .

38. Clive Cussler, *The Mediterranean Caper* (New York: Pyramid, 1973).

39. Clive Cussler, *Pacific Vortex!* (New York: Bantam, 1983).

40. Clive Cussler, *Iceberg* (New York: Dood, Mead, 1975).

41. Clive Cussler, *Raise the Titanic!* (New York: The Viking Press, 1976).

42. Clive Cussler (and Craig Dirgo), *Clive Cussler and Dirk Pitt Revealed* (New York: Pocket Books, 1998).

43. April 12, 1947, to October 1, 2013.

44. Tom Clancy, *Patriot Games* (New York: G.P. Putnam's, 1986).

45. Martin H. Greenberg (editor), *The Tom Clancy Companion* (New York: Berkley, 1992).

46. Stuart Woods, *Deep Lie* (New York: W.W. Norton, 1986).

47. May 25, 1927, to March 12, 2001.

48. Robert Ludlum, *The Scarlatti Inheritance* (Cleveland: World, 1971).

49. Robert Ludlum, *The Osterman Weekend* (Cleveland: World, 1972).

50. Robert Ludlum, *The Bourne Identity* (New York: Marek, 1980).

51. James Grady, *Six Days of the Condor* (New York: Norton, 1973).

52. Fletcher Knebel and Charles W. Bailey II, *Seven Days in May* (New York: Harper & Row, 1962).

53. Philip Wylie, *The Spy Who Spoke Porpoise* (New York: Doubleday, 1969).

54. March 2, 1968– . Other films include *Sylvia* (2003); *Munich* (2005); *The Girl with the Dragon Tattoo* (2011).

55. December 12, 1927, to October 3, 1995. Books include *The Guns of Terra 10* (1970); *Copp for Hire* (1987); *The Metaphysics of the Novel* (2003), with Linda Pendleton.

56. Andrew Nette and Iain McIntyre (editors), *Sticking It to the Man: Revolution and Counterculture in Pulp and Popular Fiction* (Oakland, CA: PM Press, 2020).

Epilogue

1. Stephen Grey, *The New Spymasters: Inside Espionage from the Cold War to Global Terror* (London: Viking, 2015).

2. Gordon Corera, *Intercept: The Secret History of Computers and Spies* (London: Weidenfeld & Nicolson, 2015).

3. Duncan White, *Cold Warriors: Writers Who Waged the Literary Cold War* (London: Little, Brown, 2019).

Bibliography

Amis, Kingsley. *The James Bond Dossier* (1966).

Black, Jeremy. *The Politics of James Bond: From Fleming's Novels to the Big Screen* (2001).

Bonn, Thomas L. *UnderCover: An Illustrated History of American Mass Market Paperbacks* (1982).

Chapman, James. *Licence to Thrill: A Cultural History of the James Bond Films* (1999).

Crowdy, Terry. *The Enemy Within: A History of Espionage* (2006).

D'Ammassa, Don. *Masters of Adventure: James Bond and His Rivals* (2016).

Everson, William K. *The Detective in Film* (1972).

Goulart, Ron. *Great History of Comic Books* (1986).

Harmon, Jim. *The Great Radio Heroes* (1967).

Harmon, Jim, and Donald F. Glut. *The Great Movie Serials: Their Sound and Fury* (1972).

Hutchinson, Don. *The Great Pulp Heroes* (1996).

Masters, Anthony. *Literary Agents* (1987).

McCormack, Donald, and Katy Fletcher. *Spy Fiction: A Connoisseur's Guide* (1990).

Meyers, Richard. *TV Detectives* (1981).

Pearson, John. *The Life of Ian Fleming* (1966).

Rubenstein, Leonard. *The Great Spy Films* (1979).

Usborne, Richard. *Clubland Heroes* (1953; revised edition, 1974).

Index

9 781476 673639